Paul Curran
14th August 1995

SOFTWARE ENGINEERING METRICS

I: Measures and Validations

THE McGRAW-HILL
INTERNATIONAL SERIES IN SOFTWARE ENGINEERING

Consulting Editor

Professor D. Ince
The Open University

Titles in this Series

Portable Modula-2 Programming – Woodman, Griffiths, Souter and Davies
SSADM: A Practical Approach – Ashworth and Goodland
Software Engineering: Analysis and Design – Easteal and Davies
Introduction to Compiling Techniques: A First Course Using ANSI C, LEX and
YACC – Bennett
An Introduction to Program Design – Sargent
Object-Oriented Databases: Applications in Software Engineering – Brown
Object-Oriented Software Engineering with C^{++} – Ince
Expert Database Systems: A Gentle Introduction – Beynon-Davies
Practical Formal Methods with VDM – Andrews and Ince
SSADM Version 4: A User's Guide – Eva
A Structured Approach to Systems Development – Heap, Stanway and Windsor
Rapid Information Systems Development – Bell and Wood-Harper
Software Engineering Environments: Automated Support for Software
Engineering – Brown, Earl and McDermid
Systems Construction and Analysis: A Mathematical and Logical Framework –
Fenton and Hill
SSADM V4 Project Manager's Handbook – Hammer
Knowledge Engineering for Information Systems – Beynon-Davies
Introduction to Software Project Management and Quality Assurance – Ince,
Sharp and Woodman
Software System Development: A Gentle Introduction – Britton and Doake
Introduction to VDM – Woodman and Heal
An Introduction to SSADM Version 4 – Ashworth and Slater
Discrete Event Simulation in C – Watkins
Objects and Databases – Kroha
Object-Oriented Specification and Design with C++ – Henderson
Software Engineering Metrics Volume I: Measures and Validations – Shepperd
Software Tools and Techniques for Electronic Engineers – Jobes
Reverse Engineering and Software Maintenance: A Practical Approach –
Lano and Haughton
Coding in Turbo Pascal – Sargent
A Primer on Formal Specification – Turner and McCluskey
Design of Concurrent Systems – Mett, Crowe and Strain-Clarke
An Introduction to Software Engineering Using Z – Ratcliff

SOFTWARE ENGINEERING METRICS
I: Measures and Validations

Edited by
Martin Shepperd
Bournemouth University

McGRAW-HILL BOOK COMPANY

London · New York · St Louis · San Francisco · Auckland
Bogotá · Caracas · Lisbon · Madrid · Mexico
Milan · Montreal · New Delhi · Panama · Paris · San Juan
São Paulo · Singapore · Sydney · Tokyo · Toronto

Published by
McGRAW-HILL Book Company Europe
Shoppenhangers Road, Maidenhead, Berkshire, SL6 2QL, England
Telephone 0628 23432
Fax 0628 770224

British Library Cataloguing in Publication Data
Shepperd, Martin
   Software Engineering Metrics. – Vol. 1:
   Measures and Validations. – (McGraw-Hill
   International Series in Software Engineering)
   I. Title II. Series
   005.1

   ISBN 0-07-707410-6

Library of Congress Cataloging-in-Publication Data
Shepperd, Martin
   Software engineering metrics / Martin Shepperd.
      p. cm. – – (McGraw-Hill international series in software
  engineering)
   Includes bibliographical references and index.
   Contents: Contents: 1. Measures and validations.
   ISBN 0-07-707410-6
   1. Computer software– –Quality control. 2. Computer software–
  –Validation.   I. Title. II. Series.
  QA76.76.Q35S54 1993
  005.1'4 – – dc20   93-35431
                                                                  CIP

12345 CUP 97654
Typeset by Alden Multimedia Ltd
and printed and bound in Great Britain at the University Press, Cambridge

To Linda

CONTENTS

PREFACE

This book argues that software metrics, or software measurement, is potentially one of the most important aspects of the discipline known as software engineering. Without measurement, we cannot compare the effectiveness of differing methods, tools, techniques and designs. Without measurement, we cannot understand the complex processes that make up a software project. Without measurement, we cannot make any objective statement concerning the quality of the software products that we claim to engineer. And without measurement, we do not know where a project or organization is, let alone where it is heading. That is the potential for metrics, but all too frequently software engineers have failed to fully realize this potential. This is despite the comparatively long history of metrics; early code metrics were first proposed as long ago as 1972.

What are the reasons, then, for this failure to benefit fully from applying metrics to the software engineering process? The first reason is that software measurement is deceptively simple, and in some minimalist sense it is not difficult. There is no problem in collecting all manner of software measurements. Obtaining *useful* measurements is possibly less straightforward. Owing to the seeming simplicity of the task, much work has been conducted on an *ad hoc* and theoretically impoverished basis, leading to problems of interpretation and meaning. The second reason is that the majority of the metrics proposed in the literature never venture far beyond speculation and there exists a shortage of thorough and dispassionate metrics validation work; thus, many of the better-known metrics actually rest upon remarkably flimsy empirical foundations. The final reason is that the various products and processes that we attempt to model and characterize by metrics are extraordinarily complex and diverse. It is perhaps not entirely surprising that some of our work—based upon a single, or very small number of metrics—is insufficiently rich to fully capture all the aspects of interest.

This might seem a rather despondent position to adopt. But to return to the original proposition, metrics have a great deal of potential, indeed, I would argue that they are essential if we are successfully to put software development on to an engineering footing. This book charts the history of the subject, recording both the birth pains and the successes; it also describes research and its application in overcoming some of the above problems and considers the future of software engineering metrics as the subject reaches its majority.

Structure of the book

The book is organized into two volumes, each comprising three main parts. Volume One covers the important software metrics developed over the past twenty years and addresses the question of validity: what basis have we for believing that a metric adequately represents the product or process attribute claimed? This is an extremely important question, and one that needs to be answered before a metric can be applied in earnest. Volume Two deals with more specific topics relating to tool support, techniques and methods for formulating, collecting and most significantly analysing metrics. It also provides the some background in statistics, measurement theory and process modelling.

Although the sections of Volume One need not necessarily be read in sequential order, the reader unfamiliar with the subject would be advised to start with the first three parts. These provide a survey of software product metrics, commencing with some of the earliest and most influential work in software metrics in Part II. This provides a historical perspective. A review is given of more contemporary metrics work in Part III, with the emphasis upon products derived early in a project life cycle, notably design and specification. Part IV addresses the fundamental topic of validation, enabling us to proceed beyond mere speculation and to develop confidence in the utility of a metric. Finally, a detailed bibliography is given including majority of important software metric sources published over the past twenty years.

Acknowledgements

First and foremost, I would like to record my thanks to Jackie Harbor, Jenny Ertle and Andy Ware at McGraw-Hill for their help and encouragement during a task that at times appeared unending! I also wish to thank Darrel Ince for prompting me to edit this book in the first place, and all the contributing authors and publishers who have made this book possible by giving permission for their work to be included.
The individual credits are as follows:

A. J. Albrecht and J. R. Gaffney   'Software function, source lines of code and development effort prediction: a software science validation', reprinted with permission from *IEEE Trans. on Softw. Eng.*, 9(6): 639–48, 1983.

V. R. Basili and B. T. Perricone 'Software errors and complexity: an empirical investigation', *CACM*, 27(1): 42–52, 1984. Reproduced with permission of ACM.

B. W. Boehm   'Software Engineering Economics', reprinted with permission from *IEEE Trans. on Softw. Eng.*, 10(1): 7–19, 1984.

B. Curtis, S. Sheppard and P. Milliman   'Third time charm: stronger prediction of programmer performance by software complexity metrics', reprinted with permission from *Proc. 4th IEEE Intl. Conf. on Softw. Eng.*, pp. 356–60, 1979.

R. D. Gordon and M. H. Halstead   'An experiment comparing Fortran programming times with the Software Physics Hypothesis', *Proc. AFIPS*, pp. 935–7, 1976. Reproduced with permission of AFIPS Press.

P. G. Hamer and G. D. Frewin   'M. H. Halstead's software science: a critical examination', reprinted with permission from *Proc. IEEE 6th Int. Conf on Softw. Eng*, pp. 197–206, 1982.

S. Henry and D. Kafura   'The evaluation of software systems' structure using quantitative software metrics', *Softw. Pract. & Expr.*, 14(6): 561–73, 1984. Reproduced by permission of John Wiley and Sons Ltd.

D. H. Hutchens and V. R. Basili   'System structure analysis: clustering with data bindings', reprinted with permission from *IEEE Trans. on Softw. Eng.*, 11(8): 749–57, 1985.

D. C. Ince and M. J. Shepperd   'An empirical and theoretical analysis of an information flow based design metric', *Proc. European Software Eng. Conf.*, pp. 86–99. Reproduced by permission of Springer-Verlag, Heidelberg.

D. Kafura and J. T. Canning   'A validation of software metrics using many metrics and two resources', reprinted with permission from *Proc. 8th Int. Conf. Softw. Eng.* pp. 378–85, 1985.

C. F. Kemerer   'An empirical validation of software cost estimation models', *CACM* 30(5): 461–29, 1987. Reproduced with permission of ACM.

T. J. McCabe   'A complexity measure', reprinted with permission from *IEEE Trans. on Softw. Eng.*, 2(4): 308–20, 1976.

E. Oviedeo   'Control flow, data flow and program complexity', reprinted with permission from *Proc. COMPSAC 80*, pp. 146–52, 1980.

M. J. Shepperd   'A critique of cyclomatic complexity as a software metric', *Softw. Eng. J.*, 3(2): 1–8, 1988. Reproduced by permission of IEE Publishing Department.

D. A. Troy and S. H. Zweben   'Measuring the quality of structured designs', *J. of Syst. & Softw.*, 2(2): 113–20, 1981. Reprinted by permission of the publishers. Copyright 1981 by Elsevier Science Publishing Company Inc.

S. S. Yau, J. S. Collofello and T. M. MacGregor   'Ripple effect analysis of software maintenance', reprinted with permission from *Proc. COMPSAC '78*, pp. 60–5, 1978.

Martin Shepperd
Bournemouth

PART ONE

Software Measurement: Past, Present and Future

FIRST THINGS

The first issue that ought to be addressed is exactly what do we mean by a metric, leading to the next question of what do we mean by a software engineering metric? It will doubtless come as no surprise that there are a variety of definitions! In short, however, there are those who suggest that a metric is a measurement, no more and no less, and there are those who would argue that a metric implies not only a measurement but also an underlying theory or model into which that measurement enters. This distinction is an important one—and one to which we will return later—since measurement without some underlying theory degenerates to the aimless collection and storage of meaningless numbers. For example, we could collect the height of all the software engineers within an organization, but these measurements have no value because we have no theory concerning the relationship between software engineering and height. It is not evident whether tall engineers are a good, bad or indifferent thing from the point of view of software engineering.

The message is clear: measurements *ought* to have an associated theory or model, and in this respect software engineering measurements do not differ from any other form of measurement. Unfortunately, this message has not always been treated as an imperative by workers in the field of software engineering metrics. Consequently, this book uses the term 'metric' as meaning merely a measurement, and a software engineering metric is merely a software engineering measure. However, useful, or potentially useful, metrics inevitably will have defined underlying models explicitly.

Next we turn to software engineering metrics. It is often convenient to characterize metrics as falling into two classes: those associated with products such as specifications and program code, and those associated with processes such as design inspections and debugging. Clearly, both classes of metric are important, although to date work on product metrics is further advanced, and this is reflected by the emphases of the papers in this book.

WHY?

There have been two principal motivating forces for the current interest in software metrics. First, there has been the general dissatisfaction with the present state of software engineering, the frequent overruns of projects both in terms of costs and in delivery dates, quality problems with installed systems and failure to satisfy users. These problems are often collectively referred to as the 'software crisis'. From a management perspective, the root problem would seem to lie in the absence of quantitative feedback that results in projects getting out of control. This is summarized by DeMarco's aphorism, 'You can't control what you can't measure' (DeMarco 1982). The second motivation has been the need for a more analytical and empirically based approach to the still immature discipline of software engineering. For example, we need better to understand why software maintenance is difficult, how method A contrasts with method B, the costs associated with approach C, and for what application area technique D is unsuitable. These questions lend themselves to an overtly quantitative approach.

Evidently, there is an enormous range of potential applications for software engineering metrics. Three examples are given to illustrate the potential diversity of the area. First, a trend analysis of user-requested changes could be used when following rapid prototyping techniques to determine when to stop building prototypes (Mayhew 1990). Second, a system architecture metric could be used to analyse a software design in order to identify the potentially most problematic modules (Shepperd 1990c), which could then be assigned to the most experienced and able software engineers. Third, the size of a proposed system could be predicted from a requirements specification by means of function points, so as to estimate costs at a very early stage in the project (Albrecht 1984 and Chapter 8 below; IFPUG 1992).

THE PAST

Early work on software metrics tended to focus almost exclusively upon program code as the obvious output or produce of the development process. The simplest software complexity metric is lines of code (LOC). The basis of LOC is that program length can be used as a predictor of program characteristics such as reliability and ease of maintenance. Despite, or possibly even because of, the simplicity of this metric, it has been subjected to severe criticism (see McCabe, Chapter 2 below; deMarco 1982; Ejiogu 1985). Certainly there are serious difficulties with defining what actually constitutes a line of code; consequently, modifications such as the number of source statements or machine code instructions generated have been advanced. However, none of these modifications could exactly be described as being in vogue. It seems reasonable, therefore, to adopt the suggestion of Basili and Hutchens (1983) that the LOC metric be regarded as a baseline metric to which all other metrics be compared. We should expect an effective code metric to perform better than LOC, and so, as a minimum, LOC offers a 'null hypothesis' for empirical evaluations of software metrics.[1]

One of the earliest attempts to provide a code metric based on a coherent model of software complexity was provided by the late Maurice Halstead. His approach was highly eclectic, drawing from thermodynamics, information theory, cognitive psychology and reverse compilation (Halstead 1972). This led to the postulation of a set of laws that Halstead saw as being analogous to natural laws (Halstead 1972, 1977a) and which became known as software science. Initially he was concerned only with software algorithms, but the work was subsequently broadened to cover programs, software systems and, indeed, any field dealing with 'Man the Symbol Manipulator' (Halstead 1972).

Early empirical validations of software science seemed to produce very high correlations between predicted and actual results.[2] Studies related software science measures to development time (Gordon and Halstead, Chapter 1 below; Halstead

---

[1] In passing, it is also worth noting that much empirical work (e.g. Kitchenham 1981a; Henry and Kafura 1981a; Basili and Perricone, Chapter 10 below) has shown the metric to correlate strongly with other metrics, most notably McCabe's cyclomatic complexity (Chapter 2 below), as demonstrated by Shepperd (Chapter 12 below).

[2] Careful review of the methods and analytical techniques employed, for example by Hamer and Frewin (1982, and see Chapter 11 below), suggest that these correlations are less significant than was first believed—a point that will be returned to in Part IV on Validations.

1977a), incidence of software bugs (Funami and Halstead 1976), program recall (Love 1977) and program quality (Love and Bowman 1976; Elshoff 1976a; Fitzsimmons 1978). Ottenstein (1976a) even reported the successful application of software science counts to the problem of detecting student plagiarism. Unfortunately, subsequent work has been rather more equivocal. The first indication of problems with the software science came in the late 1970s, when researchers (Fitzsimmons and Love 1978) attempted to apply the metrics to two sets of independently published experimental data, due to Gould (1975) of program debugging and to Weissman (1974) of program comprehension. In both cases, correlations were weaker than previously reported or not statistically significant. Another study by Bowen (1978) found only a modest correlation between the metric and number of errors detected in 75 modules. Particularly disconcerting was the fact that it was out-performed by the much scorned LOC metric.

A pattern of confusion began to emerge as it became apparent that some researchers had been correlating errors with Halstead's effort metric (E) (Funami and Halstead 1976; Fitzsimmons and Love 1978) and others with his difficulty or level metric (Bowen 1978, Feuer and Fowlkes 1979; Smith 1980).

Another large study of over 400 modules by Basili and Phillips (1981) found that the effort metric did not predict development time significantly better than LOC. Yet another study of program comprehension (Woodfield et al. 1981b) found that, for small-scale software, there was a correlation between E and program recall. A more recent study still (Basili et al. 1983) reports that LOC out-performs E for effort and error prediction. However, to add to this already confused situation, many of the early studies have been subsequently questioned, both on statistical and experimental grounds (Lister 1982; Hamer and Frewin, Chapter 11 below).

What may be concluded from our review of these empirical investigations into Halstead's metric work? Disarray seems to be the most predominant feature. Nevertheless, certain patterns emerge: researchers have attempted to apply the software science model to a very large range of software products and processes; there seems to be little standardization, even in such fundamental areas as counting the basic inputs for his set of equations, and this alone must account for some of the variations in results (Elshoff 1978b; Fitsos 1980; Christensen et al. 1981; Salt 1982; Conte et al. 1982).

Software science has attracted much interest because it was the first attempt to provide a coherent framework within which software could be measured. It has the advantage that, since it deals with tokens, it is fairly language-independent. Moreover, the basic inputs may all be easily extracted automatically.[3] None the less, very serious objections have been levelled at software science, so it would appear that its present role is very limited, especially as a universal model of program complexity. Despite these difficulties and the absence of a clear pattern in the empirical analyses described above, there remains widespread and uncritical reference to it, even in the recent literature and textbooks. Possibly the most important legacy of software science is in the way that it attempts to provide a coherent and explicit

---

[3] *Vide* the 200-line Pascal program given by DeMarco (1982) to obtain the basic software science counts. The cynic might suggest that ease of collection could have been a contributory factor to the extraordinary level of interest in empirical investigations of software science.

model of program complexity, as a framework within which to measure and make interpretations.

An alternative but equally influential code metric was McCabe's cyclomatic complexity, $v(G)$ (see Chapter 2 below). His objectives were twofold: first, to predict the effort of testing the software and thereby to identify appropriate decompositions of the software into modules; second, to predict complexity-related characteristics of the resultant software.

The model that McCabe adopted was to view software as a directed graph with edges representing the flow of control and nodes as statements. In effect, this is a simplified flow chart. Complexity was hypothesized as being related to control flow complexity; that is, the more loops, jumps and selections the program contains, the more complex it is to understand. A suggested practical application of the metric was to provide an upper limit to module complexity, beyond which a module should be subdivided into simpler components. A value of $v(G) = 10$ was suggested, although it was accepted that in certain situations, notably large case structures, the limit might need to be relaxed.

As with the software science metrics, McCabe's ideas attracted a great deal of interest, and again, owing to the comparative simplicity of calculating the metric, many empirical validations have been performed. His original validation (see Chapter 2 below) was based upon conformance of the metric to intuitive judgements of program complexity, and in fact this approach was continued by many of the other early validations and extensions (e.g. Myers 1977; Hansen 1978).

Others adopted a more objective approach to empirical validation. Results ranged widely. Henry and Kafura, while studying the UNIX operating system, found a highly significant correlation in excess of 0.95 between $v(G)$ and reported changes.[4] This is in complete contrast to other studies that report correlations as insignificant as $r = -0.09$ between the metric and bug location (Bowen 1978). Studies adopted varying interpretations as to exactly what $v(G)$ was measuring or predicting. Basili and Perricone (Chapter 10 below) dealt with error density, whereas Kitchenham (1981) and Shen et al. (1985) examined absolute error counts. Basili, in yet another study (Basili et al. 1983), attempted to relate $v(G)$ to programming effort, as did Gaffney (1979b). Sylvia Sheppard (Sheppard et al. 1979a) correlated $v(G)$ to the ability to recall a program, and Sunohara et al. (1981) observed the relationship with design effort. Curiously, there do not seem to have been any attempts to investigate the links with testing effort or number of test cases used.

To summarize, there has been—and still is—much interest in capturing software complexity in terms of the complexity of control flow. There have been various approaches to measuring control flow complexity. These range from McCabe's simple model (see Chapter 2), which can be characterized by the number of simple decisions plus one, to more sophisticated models which account for nesting depth (e.g. Piowarski 1982) or are based upon considerations of entropy (Chen 1978). Of these metrics, cyclomatic complexity is the most thoroughly validated, with various empirical studies attempting to correlate the metric to error-proneness, maintainability,

---

[4]This result must be treated with some caution, as Henry and Kafura based their analysis upon procedures that were subject to one or more changes—for whatever reason—from a new release of UNIX.

understandability and development effort. These have produced erratic results. The most startling observations are the consistently high correlations with LOC and the out-performing of $v(G)$ by LOC in a significant number of cases (Basili and Hutchens; Curtis *et al.* 1979a; Kitchenham 1981; Paige 1980; Wang and Dunsmore 1984). Few of the other metrics described have been subjected to anything other than the most cursory empirical scrutiny, a point emphasised by the review of graph-theoretic metrics in (Shepperd, Chapter 12 below).

As a consequence of the shortcomings of the more straightforward code-based product metrics, effort has been directed towards combining the best aspects of existing metrics. Such metrics are frequently termed *hybrid metrics*.

Harrison and Magel (1981) attempt to combine Halstead's metric with an extension to McCabe's metric based on nesting level. They argue that neither metric is individually sufficient; however, when used in combination, a metric results that is 'more intuitively satisfying'. No further validation is offered. A similar approach was adopted by Oviedo (Chapter 3 below), who combined control flow and data flow into a single program complexity metric. The metric was validated by applying it to a number of 'good' and 'bad' programs published in the literature. Although a start, more serious work on empirical validation is required.

Hansen (1978) proposed a 2-tuple of cyclomatic complexity and operand count (defined to be arithmetical operators, function and subroutine calls, assignments, input and output statements and array subscription). However, the value of 2-tuples as useful metrics has been questioned (Baker and Zweben 1980; Conte *et al.* 1986). This is because comparisons are difficult to make between differing measurements, for example $<a,b>$ and $<c,d>$ where $a < c$ and $b > d$.[5]

Potier *et al.* (1982) describe an intriguing method of bypassing the problem of *n*-tuples by constructing a decision tree. In their study of error data, both software science and cyclomatic measures are combined, in order to identify error-prone modules. Using non-parametric discriminant analysis, they identified various threshold values for the different metrics, which were then entered into a decision tree. Curiously, the software science measure, program vocabulary or *n*, was found to be the metric most effective at discriminating between reliable and error-prone modules and thus was placed at the top of the tree.[6] Even when using decision trees to combine metrics into a composite approach, one metric tends to predominate; namely the one applied at the root node of the decision tree. Consequently, the approach will not always be very applicable.

Arguably, the most extreme variant of the hybrid approach is the one put forward by Munson and Koshgoftaar (1990) in the form of their relative complexity metric. They state that:

---

[5] More formally, we do not have closure of the $>$ relation, and thus we cannot generate even a weak order. These problems are addressed by some of the papers describing classical measurement theory in Volume Two of this anthology.

[6] It is not reported whether LOC was examined as a potential discriminant although, given the widely discovered association between LOC and the software science measures, one might suspect that it would perform well. This also highlights a problem of using statistically driven metrics in that extremely bizarre models may emerge—as in this case, where it is difficult to see the impact of *n* upon the number of errors other than as a proxy for module size.

'unlike other metrics, the relative complexity metric combines, simultaneously, *all* attribute dimensions of *all* complexity metrics'...[7]

The approach is entirely statistical in that it is based upon the factor analysis of an arbitrary set of code metrics, without regard for the meaning of the base-set metrics. Using this method, there is no limit to the number of metrics that can be combined. What the resultant relative complexity metric means is quite a different proposition.

In short, despite attracting a considerable level of attention in the research community, none of the code metrics described above can be regarded as particularly promising. The recurring pattern is one of researchers correlating metrics, obtained by applying different counting rules to differing software quality factors and obtaining divergent results. Strong associations with program size measures appear to be the only recurring result. Some metrics might be useful when tailored to specific environments and problems, but, as a general means of obtaining insights into, and as a method of combating, software complexity, they have little to commend them. This, coupled with their late availability in the life cycle, suggests that attention is better directed towards design and specification metrics.

THE PRESENT

If the past can be characterized by its emphasis upon code-level metrics, then it is reasonable to characterize present work as stressing those measures available early on in a software project—specifically, design and specification. This change in focus reflects a more general drift of software engineering concern over the past decade from code to the early products of a software project.

Unlike code metrics, design metrics can be obtained at a much earlier stage in the software development process while a significant proportion of project resources remain uncommitted. For example, a design can be reworked in order to avoid anticipated problems such as high maintenance costs for the final product, and this may be accomplished without the need to abandon code and thus waste a great deal of development effort. This type of early feedback has been a major motivator for work in the field of design metrics.

Most interest has centred around structural or architectural aspects of a design, sometimes termed *high-level design*. The architecture describes the way in which the system is divided into components, and how the components are interrelated. Some measures also require information extracted from low-level design—the internal logic of design components—often expressed in a program design language. It is perhaps surprising that there has been little consideration of database systems where there tends to be limited functionality and most of the design effort is directed towards the data model. Exceptions are work by Geritsen *et al.* (1977); DeMarco's Bang metric for 'data-strong' systems (DeMarco 1982), which is derived from an entity relationship diagram; and some early work on database design measurement (Gray *et al.* 1991). These metrics are more fully described later in this section.

There are two general problems that all design metrics encounter: the lack of

[7]The emphasis is mine.

sufficiently formal notations, and validation difficulties. Ideally, a metric should be extracted automatically; certainly, all the relevant information must be available. However, software engineers tend to use a wide variety of notations, many of them informal, where a high reliance is placed upon natural language descriptions. This makes it very difficult to extract meaningful measurements. To counter this, a number of special-purpose notations have been proposed (Bowles 1983; Bean *et al.* 1984; Ince 1984), or conformance to suitable existing ones such as module hierarchy charts suggested (Yin and Winchester 1978; Benyon-Tinker 1979; Chapin 1979). Another alternative has been to infer design or structural properties from the resultant code (Henry and Kafura 1981a). Such an approach must be considered a last resort since the advantages of early feedback are squandered.

Initial work (Haney 1972; Channon 1974; Myers 1978; Soong 1977), although of undoubted value, suffered from the disadvantage that it was not fully objective. Estimates of one kind or another are required. A crucial aspect of a metric is that the measurement is objective and repeatable. Since software systems are frequently very large, it is desirable that the metric can be obtained automatically by a software tool. None of the above are candidates for objective, automatable product metrics.

Other more recent approaches are potentially automatable. The almost universal model adopted is based upon the idea of system complexity formulated by the architect Alexander (1964). This was adapted for software development by the functional design methodology of Stevens *et al.* (1974), in particular their design evaluation criteria of maximizing module cohesion and minimizing module coupling. Cohesion may be regarded as the singleness of purpose or function of a module. A module that plays the national anthem and solves crosswords has a low cohesion because it performs two functions that are completely unrelated. This is generally considered to be an undesirable property of a module, since it will result in it being harder to understand and more difficult to modify. In an informal sense we can predict that, if a design comprises modules with low cohesion, this will result in various undesirable properties in the final product. Coupling is in many ways the corollary of cohesion. It is the degree of independence of one module from another. Minimising connections between modules makes them easier to understand and update.

Probably the most influential class of design metric is that known as information-flow-based measures. These view inter-module couplings as information flow channels. Module A is able to influence module B by means of information passed from module A to module B, which has the potential to cause B to modify its behaviour. Information flows occur either by parameter-passing or by shared global data structures. It is argued—with some empirical justification (for instance Shepperd and Ince 1991b)—that design decisions in terms of how systems are partitioned into modules, and how these modules interface with the systems into which they are embedded, will have far-reaching consequences upon error-proneness, maintainability, the scope for re-use and so forth. The classic example of such a metric is the Henry–Kafura information flow metric (Henry and Kafura 1981a, and Chapter 6 below).

An approach rather different from the previous class of design metrics is based upon an exploratory data analysis technique known as *cluster analysis*. This technique attempts to group objects together on the basis of similarity so that the most similar objects will be grouped together first. The output is usually a dendogram or cluster tree, which reveals the order of clustering. A number of researchers (Belady and Evangelisti 1981; Hutchens and Basili, Chapter 5 below; Selby and Basili 1988; Ince and Shepperd 1989b, 1990) have tried to harness this method for the generation of some idealised module hierarchy based upon the principle of grouping the most similar modules closest together within the module hierarchy. The usual indicator of similarity has been taken to be module couplings or shared information flows. Although this is an intriguing idea, there is a long way to go before this class of metric reaches maturity. Possibly the greatest stumbling block is that the shape of the idealised module hierarchy or dendogram is highly dependent upon the choice of clustering algorithm.

The validity of concentrating upon inter-modular measures and connections in particular has been considerably strengthened by the empirical work of Troy and Zweben (see Chapter 13 below). Their study of 73 designs and associated implementations indicated that those measures related to module coupling were most effective at predicting the incidence of errors. These measures included the number and type of module interconnections and the number of global data structure references, and in fact they form the basis of the majority of design metrics presently in use.

As suggested earlier, a relatively unexplored area is the application of metrics to the problems of database design. Geritsen *et al.* (1977) report on some speculative work, although, rather curiously, their main objective was the quantitative definition of what constituted a very large database. Until recently there has been little follow-up work. Gray *et al.* (1991) describe some attempts at British Telecom to find analogous metrics to the information flow metrics for database designs in terms of relational and entity-relationship models. However, the metrics have yet to be supported by independent empirical validation.

The benefits of design metrics, in that they provide early feedback about the developing software product, are even more evident for metrics derived from the product specifications. Correspondingly, the difficulties are greater and research in this field is still scarce.

Albrecht (1979 and Chapter 8 below) suggests a simple metric based upon a count of 'function points'. A specification is analysed to identify the different functions described, and these are given weightings according to the relative complexity of the function type. For example, interfacing with external systems is considered to be more complex than processing queries. Normally, the result is then adjusted to better reflect local environmental factors using 14 general system characteristics, such as processing complexity, performance and multiple sites.

The function point metric is usually used as a predictor of development effort, although it also has applications for productivity assessment. For useful predictions to be made, function points require calibration so that they are converted into units of interest, typically person-months. Since organizations and software development environments differ so widely, this may well be best done at a local level (see Chapter 16 below). Symons (1988, 1991) describes some modifications to Albrecht's approach for entity-relationship-based systems, and Jones (1987) among others, has suggested modifications to extend the approach to real-time software.

Function points do, however, have drawbacks. The weightings in the formula are fairly arbitrary and may need considerable modification according to the type of application, experience and ability of the software developers, the development environment and the programming language. Identifying functions from the specification can be a rather subjective process, particularly if working from an informal and unstructured specification where there is increased potential for both duplication and omission. Low and Jeffrey (1990a) report up to 30 per cent variation from the mean for counting points in an experiment based on 22 analysts working from the same specification. Notwithstanding these difficulties, the metric has been adopted by a considerable number of commercial organisations. This has tended to be most successful where projects are fairly homogeneous, and combined with the usage of structured specification techniques, such as data-flow diagramming.

An alternative approach to specification metrics is provided in the form of DeMarco's Bang metric (DeMarco 1982). The metric is derived from more structured specification notations (data-flow diagrams, data dictionaries, entity relationship diagrams and state transition diagrams), thereby simplifying the measurement process. DeMarco attempts to classify software as either 'function-strong', such as a robotics system, or 'data-strong', such as an information retrieval system. This is an important distinction, since it acknowledges that for many systems many of the key design decisions are embedded not in the functional structure, that is in modules and their interfaces, but in the data structure and the relationships between data objects. To date, most metrics research has concentrated on 'function-strong' systems.

In some ways, this review of current developments in software metrics has presented a rather bleak view of what is a potentially promising and important field of software engineering. There are several recurring themes.

First, the majority of metrics are presented in such a fashion that it is unclear exactly what is being measured. Terms such as 'complexity' and 'quality' abound. As a direct result, empirical evaluations have interpreted metrics in widely differing ways leading to conflicting validation results. Related are problems of ambiguously defined counting rules; however, until we employ more rigorous modelling techniques, these difficulties will be hard to overcome.

Second, most empirical studies have found that accurate prediction is not attainable at present from design and specification metrics—mainly as a result of calibration difficulties. However, in many instances more modest types of application have been shown to yield useful results. For example, design metrics can often highlight outlier or abnormal design units, and function points can help compare the performance of different project teams, methods and tools.

In conclusion, from our review of current practice we see that, although useful applications exist for code metrics, there is little doubt that design and specification metrics can offer additional benefits. There are three reasons for this. First, these metrics provide much earlier feedback about the nature of the software product. Second, the metric is measuring aspects of the software that are more abstract, namely function and structure. This is valuable, as it enables such metrics to be more widely applicable. The difficulty with code metrics is that they tend to be oriented towards specific languages or types of applications. Third, most of the design metrics, especially those based on measures that include inter-modular aspects of complexity, are founded on much more convincing models of software complexity. Certainly these models are more in line with the current thinking in software engineering.

THE FUTURE

If the present is not all that auspicious, what of the future? I shall now briefly review some emerging principles that may combine to result in measurement becoming an integral part of the software engineering process.

The first principle is that there is a need to treat the *validation* of software metrics more seriously. Empty speculation is too easy, and unless greater effort is devoted to the task of evaluation, the take-up of metrics will always be limited. It is therefore now appropriate to consider the desirable features of a metric. Although it is usual to speak of metric evaluation, strictly speaking, it is the model into which the metric enters that is validated. As has already been indicated, the model establishes the meaning of a metric. Without a model, no evaluation is possible.

There are two complementary approaches to model evaluation. The model may be analysed on a theoretical basis. In particular, one might search for the following characteristics:

1. The model must conform to widely accepted theories of software development and cognitive science. Admittedly, this is a rather subjective criterion. However, consider the following example. A metric that predicts that a monolithic piece of software will have a lower incidence of errors than one divided into a number of modules must be viewed with suspicion. In such circumstances the onus would certainly be on the proponent to demonstrate the adequacy of the underlying theory.
2. The model must be as formal as possible. In other words, the relationship between the input measurements and the output predictions must be precise in all situations. Further, the mapping from the real world onto the model must also be made as rigorous as possible.
3. The model must use measurable inputs rather than estimates or subjective judgements. Failure to do so leads to inconsistencies between different users of the metric and to potentially anomalous results.[8] Automation is not possible without satisfaction of this criterion.

These rather general model attributes can be refined in order to provide a good deal more precision by means of the axiomatic approach. Here the desired properties of the metric are specified mathematically as axioms which are then proved to be invariant to the model; see for example the work of Zuse (1991; Zuse and Bollmann 1989), which is chiefly concerned with measurement-theoretic properties such as scale, and (Shepperd and Ince 1991a), which is more concerned with user-defined model properties.

In addition, a model should be subjected to empirical evaluation. A model may have all the attributes listed above, might satisfy a large set of axioms, and yet might completely fail to describe the 'real world' that it purports to capture. Empirical

---

[8]This seems to be a potential shortcoming of function points; *vide* Low and Jeffery (1990a).

validations are an equally necessary and complementary validation technique. In order that these may be meaningful, they also require certain attributes. In brief, the desiderata are: large-scale empirical validations in a variety of different environments, particularly industrial ones; adequate controls, so that it is possible for a null hypothesis to stand; and different teams of workers.[9]

The ordering of model evaluations is intentional, since meaningful empirical work is of questionable significance when based upon meaningless models of software. Therefore, theoretical analysis of the properties of a model ought to precede empirical validation. Furthermore, theoretical evaluation is often much quicker, and is consequently a cheaper and easier method of exposing some of the potential weaknesses in a model than a full-blown empirical study.

The second principle or lesson to be learnt is the need for *methods* for the development, selection and tailoring of software metrics. Almost the only work on methods is the goal question metric (GQM) paradigm for software metrics (Basili and Rombach 1988; Rombach and Basili 1987; Rombach and Ulery 1989a). This is based on the idea that measurement ought to be carried out for a purpose, and that it is only within the context of a purpose or goal that a metric may be determined to be useful. The approach can be characterized as top-down, and is in marked contrast to the current practice of obtaining a metric and then hunting around for some meaning.

The third principle to be drawn from our review of progress in software engineering metrics is the need for a greater concern with the *application* of metrics and models once they have been satisfactorily evaluated. In other words, metrics researchers must also consider the issue of how these metrics are to be used by software engineers. One reason why this may become important is that, by focusing solely upon a product, say a system architecture, one loses sight of the fact that the same product may enter into a number of different processes, and therefore may take on a number of different meanings. For example, an engineer may be designing an architecture from scratch, doing some maintenance work, optimising the architecture to enhance performance, searching for reusable components or restructuring an ageing software system. In each case, the architecture takes on a different meaning, a point not captured by our product-oriented view of measurement and modelling. Again, it may be more fruitful to look for a general framework rather than focus too strongly upon individual metrics and applications. One possibility is to apply some of the concepts and formalisms from the area of software engineering research known as process modelling.[10] Shepperd (1992) describes some early work into quantitative process models which more precisely describe how metrics are to be integrated into software engineering projects.

In short, the field of software engineering metrics might be described as having great potential, but it is a potential that has yet to be fully exploited. The key to the future exploitation process lies in our ability to learn from the past.

---

[9]Of course, in an ideal world one would give full regard to all these factors. Unfortunately, in the world of limited resources that we happen to inhabit, compromises must often be made.

[10]For an example of the coverage of this type of work, the reader is referred to the *Proceedings* of ACM International Process Modelling Workshops; alternatively, Humphrey (1989) and Curtis *et al.* (1992) in Volume II give good reviews.

PART TWO

Beginnings: Code Complexity Measures

This section describes the very early work in software engineering measurement, all of it based on program code. Despite subsequent criticism, these early ideas have proved to be remarkably influential on the thinking of more recent researchers. Maurice Halstead can reasonably be regarded as the pioneer of software metrics. He originated the idea that software measurements might be employed to model and hence predict various software characteristics; for instance, the count of program tokens might be related to the time to write the code or its reliability. If such relationships could be demonstrated to hold in practice, then this work would revolutionise software development. It is hardly surprising, therefore, that this work has excited a great deal of interest, and it remains the most widely cited and referred-to metric, even in the recent literature (e.g. Prather 1988; Schneider 1988) and software engineering textbooks (e.g. Arthur 1985; Wiener and Sincovec 1984; Sommerville 1992).

Halstead drew from many sources to postulate a set of general laws that Halstead saw as being analogous to natural laws (1972, 1977a). Initially software algorithms were the object of interest, but this rapidly blossomed out to 'linguistics, psychology, or any field dealing with "Man the Symbol Manipulator" ' (Halstead 1972). Indeed, it was suggested that software science might usefully be employed for such diverse fields as semantic partitioning, child development psychology and Shakespearean analysis (Halstead 1979b)! Not to be outdone, a recent study has even attempted to apply software science to the problem of modelling compiler performance (Shaw *et al.* 1989).

Halstead originally described this work as *software physics* (Halstead 1972), but this was subsequently discarded in favour of the soubriquet, *software science* (Halstead 1977a), which is now the generally accepted term. The underlying concept is that software comprehension is a process of mental manipulation of program tokens. These tokens can be characterized as either operators (executable program verbs such as IF, DIV and READ) or operands (variables and constants). This enables a program to be conceived of as a continuous sequence of operators and their associated operands.

Halstead suggested that manipulation of each token requires its retrieval from a programmer's mental dictionary made up of the entire program vocabulary, and that this was by means of a binary search mechanism. Therefore, the number of mental comparisons, or dictionary accesses, required to understand the piece of software can easily be calculated from the size of the vocabulary and the total number tokens that are used.

Halstead's model assumes that programmers make a constant number of these dictionary comparisons, or *elementary mental discriminations* (EMDs), per second. By adapting work by the psychologist Stroud (1967), he suggested that the time required to generate the program could be calculated by using the Stroud number S, which is the number of EMDs the brain is able to make per second. Stroud estimated S to lie within the range 5–20. By using a value of $S = 18$, Halstead was able to predict values of T in seconds.

Software science has attracted much interest because it was the first attempt to provide a coherent framework within which software could be measured. It has the advantage that, since it deals with tokens, it is fairly language-independent.

Moreover, the basic inputs can all be easily extracted automatically. Chapter 1, by Gordon and Halstead, briefly outlines the software science model and then describes a simple empirical validation of the model and time taken to implement a number of small Fortran programs. The authors conclude that the evidence is supportive of their ideas.

Serious objections have subsequently been levelled at software science, which will be examined in more detail in Part IV on the evaluation of metrics. Possibly the most important legacy of software science is in the way that it attempts to provide a coherent and explicit model of program complexity, as a framework within which to measure and make interpretations, and in the way that Halstead was prepared to borrow from other disciplines.

The next major contribution to the software metrics arena was the graph-theoretic work by McCabe, on program control flow complexity. McCabe argued that decisions within programs increased the difficulty of testing, and that consequently this should be taken into account when dividing software into modules. In Chapter 2 he suggests that the cyclomatic number, v, of any program flow graph, G, is a useful measure of complexity. This may be computed in a variety of ways, although perhaps the easiest is merely by counting the number of decisions and adding 1. Like the Halstead work, McCabe's metric rapidly achieved the status of a classic, having been the subject of a number of empirical validations and minor modifications. Again like the Halstead work, more recently there has been some disquiet concerning the validity of the cyclomatic number as a software metric.[1] None the less, McCabe's work is of importance because it draws attention to the influence of program control flow on many software engineering activities—most notably testing—and because McCabe foresaw the need for a more quantitative approach if programming was ever to be regarded as an engineering practice. It is also noteworthy that, even in the early days, McCabe recognized the need for software tools to facilitate the process of metric collection.

The final paper in this part of the book is again based upon code metrics, but represents something of a maturing of the earlier metrics work. Oviedo asserted that program complexity was the outcome of more than one factor and therefore should be modelled by more than one metric,[2] in this case a combination of program control flow—in a manner not dissimilar to McCabe—and data flow. However, as he recognized in his paper, there is a need for more empirical support for this metric. Thus, his work is more remarkable for highlighting the need for further sophistication in the development of models to underly software measurement than for the actual metrics proposed.

In many ways, these three papers may be regarded as embodying much of the thinking of the decade of the 1970s. All three proposed radically new ideas that have subsequently been adopted and adapted. All three appreciated the potential benefits for software engineers of a more quantitative approach. All three recognized the need for empirical support. Unfortunately, all three also viewed code as being the

---

[1]This disquiet concerning McCabe's work is reviewed at length in Part IV.
[2]Approaches based on more than one metric are sometimes known as *hybrid metrics*.

most important software engineering artefact, and all had rather ill defined notions of what exactly was being measured, preferring to use terms such as 'complexity' and 'quality'. Notwithstanding the last two concerns, it is hard to overestimate the contribution of these pioneers to the subsequent progress and development of software metrics.

1

AN EXPERIMENT COMPARING FORTRAN PROGRAMMING TIMES WITH THE SOFTWARE PHYSICS HYPOTHESIS

R. D. Gordon and M. H. Halstead

Purdue University

ABSTRACT

Recent discoveries in the area of algorithm structure or software physics[1] have produced a number of hypotheses.[2] One of these relates the number of elementary mental discriminations required to implement an algorithm to measurable properties of that algorithm, and the results of one set of experiments confirming this relationship have been published (Halstead 1975). That publication, while significant, made no claim to finality, suggesting instead that further experiments were warranted. This paper will present the results of a second set of experiments, having the advantage of being conducted in a single implementation language, Fortran, from problem specifications readily available in computer textbooks.

The first section of this paper presents the timing hypothesis, and the elementary equations upon which it rests. The second section presents the details of the experiment and the results that were obtained, and the third section contains an analysis of the data.

---

[1] [Software physics is now more generally referred to as Software Science. M. J. S.]

[2] See Bohrer (1975); Bulut and Halstead (1974); Bulut *et al.* (1974); Halstead (1972; 1973a, b, 1975); Halstead and Bayer 1973); Kulm (1974); Ostapko (1974a, b); Zislis (1975); Zweben and Fung (1979). [Purdue University technical reports have been omitted from this list of references. M. J. S.]

1.1 TIMING HYPOTHESIS

Measurable properties of any implementation of any algorithm include:

$$\eta_1 = \text{the count of distinct operators}$$

$$\eta_2 = \text{the count of distinct operands}$$
$$\text{(variables or constants)}$$

$$N_1 = \text{total uses of operators}$$

$$N_2 = \text{total uses of operands}$$

The vocabulary, η, is given by:

$$\eta = \eta_1 + \eta_2 \qquad (1.1)$$

and the length, N, is:

$$N = N_1 + N_2 \qquad (1.2)$$

From these properties, it is possible to obtain the volume, V, in bits, as:

$$V = N \; \log_2 \eta \qquad (1.3)$$

and the implementation level, L, where $L \leq 1$, as:

$$L = \frac{\eta_1^{\;*}}{\eta_1} \; \frac{\eta_2}{N_2} \qquad (1.4)$$

where $\eta_1^{\;*}$, the minimum possible number of operators, will equal 2 for most algorithms (1 for the name of a function, plus 1 for a grouping symbol operator). It has been shown that the product $L \times V$ is invariant under translation from one language to another, and that, for programs without impurities (see Bohrer 1975; Bulut *et al.* 1974; Halstead 1972):

$$N = \eta_1 \; \log_2 \; \eta_1 + \eta_2 \; \log_2 \eta_2 \qquad (1.5)$$

From this point, the following nine steps yield the timing equation:

1. A program consists of N selections from η elements.
2. A binary search of η elements requires $\log_2 \eta$ comparisons.
3. A program is generated by making $N \log_2 \eta$ comparisons.
4. Therefore, the volume, V, is a count of the number of comparisons required.
5. The number of elementary mental discriminations required to complete one comparison measures the difficulty of the task.
6. The level, L, is the reciprocal of the difficulty.
7. Therefore E, the count of elementary mental discriminations required to generate a program, is given by:

$$E = \frac{V}{L} \qquad (1.6)$$

8. S, the speed with which the brain makes elementary mental discriminations can be obtained from psychology (Stroud 1967) as:

$$5 \leq S \leq 20 \text{ discriminations per second.}$$

9. Therefore, the time to generate a *preconceived* program, by a *concentrating* programmer, *fluent* in a language, is:

$$\hat{T} = \frac{V}{SL} \tag{1.7}$$

Equation (1.7) may be expressed in more basic terms by substituting for V from (1.3), and for L from (1.4), with $\eta_1^* = 2$, giving:

$$\hat{T} = \frac{\eta_1 N_2 N \log_2 \eta}{2S\eta_2} \tag{1.8}$$

The effect of possible impurities (Bulut and Halstead 1974) may be eliminated from (1.8) by substituting for N from (1.5). Letting $S = 60 \times 18 = 1080$ will then give, for time (in minutes),

$$\hat{T} = \frac{\eta_1 N_2 (\eta_1 \log_2 \eta_1 + \eta_2 \log_2 \eta_2) \log_2 \eta}{2160 \eta_2} \tag{1.9}$$

Each of the variables on the right-hand side of (1.9) can be readily measured (or counted) in any computer program, and the experiment described in the next section was designed to compare results from that equation with observed programming times.

1.2 EXPERIMENTAL PROCEDURE

Eleven problems were arbitrarily selected from two published sources. In selecting candidates for the experiment, problems were sought which were stated in a non-procedural form. Further, the problem statement had to be complete. That is, in the course of solving a particular problem, specific laws of physics, mathematics, etc., would not have to be derived. The problems finally selected were taken from Knuth (1969) and from Maurer and Williams (1972) and cover a wide range of topics including character manipulation, list processing, simulation experiments and mathematical analysis. The source of each problem statement is cited in Table 1.1.

On each of 11 days, one of these problems was implemented by the senior author. In order to maintain a consistent level of performance, all work was conducted in a quiet room, free from distractions, during the same period of each day. The time required to implement the problem fully was obtained. This total time included the number of minutes spent reading the statement of the problem, preparing flow charts

Table 1.1 Experimental data

Program specifications				Software parameters				Implementation
No.	Ref.*	Page	Problem	η_1	η_2	N_1	N_2	Time (min)
G1	K	158	21	15	11	59	51	19
G2	K	159	23	20	24	231	197	92
G3	K	196	7	16	12	64	49	16
G4	K	377	17	19	21	131	113	39
G5	K	158	22	7	10	38	35	21
G6	K	154	10	9	14	69	62	30
G7	M	32	3.2.21	12	8	30	23	5
G8	M	32	3.2.23	19	15	73	55	24
G9	M	88	8.3.2	22	32	124	104	43
G10	M	89	8.3.4	25	34	261	222	91
G11	M	27	3.2.4	14	10	29	21	5

* K = Knuth (1969); M = Maurer and Williams (1972).

and writing preliminary versions of the code, writing the final version of the code, desk checking, and the time spent working to correct errors in the program. Time to keypunch was not included.

For a number of reasons, including availability and fluency, all of the algorithms were implemented in Fortran. In the course of solving a problem, the correctness of the implementation was checked by executing a sufficiently complex test case for which a correct answer was known. In some cases the solution to a problem was written as a subroutine and testing required that a main routine be written. In such a case only the preparation of the subroutine was considered for the experiment. In addition, several implementations made use of subroutines previously written. Such routines were also not included.

After each program was completed, a careful count was made to determine values of η_1, η_2, N_1 and N_2. In obtaining these values all read, write, declarative statements and comments were ignored. The results are shown in Table 1.1

1.3 ANALYSIS OF THE DATA

The programming time predicted by theory was obtained for each program by applying equation (1.9) to the data in Table 1.1. This result, T, can be compared with the observed value, T in Table 1.2. In addition, a count of the number of statements in each program was obtained, and the programs were ordered according to these values.

The average of the calculated values, 34 minutes, is fortuitously close to the observed value, 35 minutes. The coefficient of correlation is 0.934, only slightly smaller than the value of 0.952 reported in an earlier experiment (Halstead 1975). In further agreement with that experiment, the correlation between length and observed times, 0.887, is lower than between observed and calculated times.

Table 1.2 Experimental results

Program No.	Statement count	Programming time (min)	
		T observed	T (1.9)
G7	7	5	4.6
G11	8	5	5.4
G5	11	21	2.5
G6	15	30	6.8
G3	18	16	15.6
G1	18	19	14.6
G8	18	24	22.9
G4	32	39	43.6
G2	36	92	81.5
G9	38	43	49.2
G10	59	91	128.5
Means		35.0	34.1

In conclusion, it may again be observed that one more set of experimental data does not contradict the simple hypothesis. As a result, further carefully controlled experiments by others would appear to be warranted.

2

A COMPLEXITY MEASURE

Thomas J. McCabe

US Department of Defense, National Security Agency

ABSTRACT

This paper describes a graph-theoretic complexity measure and illustrates how it can be used to manage and control program complexity. The paper first explains how the graph-theory concepts apply and gives an intuitive explanation of the graph concepts in programming terms. The control graphs of several actual Fortran programs are then presented to illustrate the correlation between intuitive complexity and the graph-theoretic complexity. Several properties of the graph-theoretic complexity are then proved which show, for example, that complexity is independent of physical size (adding or subtracting functional statements leaves complexity unchanged) and that complexity depends only on the decision structure of a program.

The issue of using nonstructured control flow is also discussed. A characterization of nonstructured control graphs is given and a method of measuring the 'structuredness' of a program is developed. The relationship between structure and reducibility is illustrated with several examples.

The last section of this paper deals with a testing methodology used in conjunction with the complexity measure; a testing strategy is defined that dictates that a program can either admit of a certain minimal testing level or can be structurally reduced.

2.1 INTRODUCTION

There is a critical question facing software engineering today: how can we modularize a software system so that the resulting modules are both testable and maintainable? That the issues of testability and maintainability are important is borne out by the

22

fact that we often spend half of the development time in testing (Boehm 1973) and can spend most of our dollars in maintaining systems (Commack and Rogers 1973). What is needed is a mathematical technique that will provide a quantitative basis for modularization and allow us to identify software modules that will be difficult to test or maintain. This paper reports on an effort to develop such a mathematical technique which is based on program control flow.

One currently used practice that attempts to ensure a reasonable modularization is to limit programs by physical size (e.g., IBM—50 lines, TRW—2 pages). This technique is not adequate, which can be demonstrated by imagining a 50-line program consisting of 25 consecutive 'IF–THEN' constructs. Such a program could have as many as 33.5 million distinct control paths, only a small percentage of which would probably ever be tested. Many such examples of live Fortran programs that are physically small but untestable have been identified and analysed by the tools described in this paper.

2.2 A COMPLEXITY MEASURE

In this section a mathematical technique for program modularization will be developed. A few definitions and theorems from graph theory will be needed, but several examples will be presented in order to illustrate the applications of the technique.

The complexity measure approach we will take is to measure and control the number of paths through a program. This approach, however, immediately raises the following nasty problem: 'Any program with a backward branch potentially has an infinite number of paths.' Although it is possible to define a set of algebraic expressions that give the total number of possible paths through a (structured) program, using the total number of paths has been found to be impractical. Because of this, the complexity measure developed here is defined in terms of basic paths which, when taken in combination, will generate every possible path.

The following mathematical preliminaries will be needed, all of which can be found in Berge (1973).

Definition 1   The cyclomatic number $v(G)$ of a graph G with n vertices, e edges, and p connected components is[1]

$$v(G) = e - n + p$$

Theorem 1   In a strongly connected graph G, the cyclomatic number is equal to the maximum number of linearly independent circuits.

The applications of the above theorem will be made as follows. Given a program, we will associate with it a directed graph that has unique entry and exit nodes. Each

---

[1] The role of the variable p will be explained in Section 2.4. For these examples assume $p = 1$.

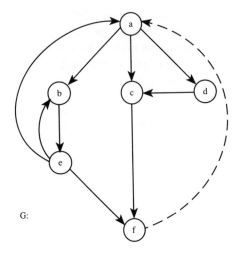

G:

Figure 2.1

node in the graph corresponds to a block of code in the program where the flow is sequential and the arcs correspond to branches taken in the program. This graph is classically known as the program control graph (see Ledgard and Marcotty (1975), and it is assumed that each node can be reached by the entry node and that each node can reach the exit node. For example, Fig. 2.1 depicts a program control graph with entry node a and exit node f.

Theorem 1 is applied to G in the following way. Imagine that the exit node (f) branches back to the entry node (a). The control graph G is now strongly connected (there is a path joining any pair of arbitrary distinct vertices), so Theorem 1 applies. Therefore, the maximum number of linearly independent circuits in G is $9 - 6 + 2$. For example, one could choose the following five independent circuits in G:

$$B1: (abefa), (beb), (abea), (acfa), (adcfa)$$

It follows that B1 forms a basis for the set of all circuits in G and that any path through G can be expressed as a linear combination of circuits from B1. For instance, the path (abeabebebef) is expressable as $(abea) + 2(beb) + (abefa)$. To see how this works, it is necessary to number the edges on G as in Fig. 2.2. Now for each member of the basis B1, associate a vector as follows:

	1	2	3	4	5	6	7	8	9	10
(abefa)	1	0	0	1	0	0	0	1	0	1
(beb)	0	0	0	1	1	0	0	0	0	0
(abea)	1	0	0	1	0	0	0	0	0	0
(acfa)	0	1	0	0	0	1	0	0	0	1
(adcfa)	0	0	1	0	0	1	1	0	0	1

The path $(abea(be)^3fa)$ corresponds to the vector 2004200111, and the vector addition of (abefa), 2(beb) and (abea) yields the desired result.

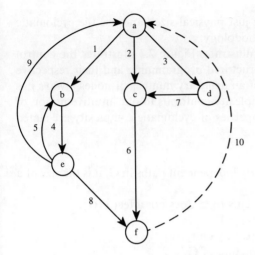

Figure 2.2

In using Theorem 1, one can choose a basic set of circuits that correspond to paths through the program. The set B2 is a basis of program paths.

B2: (abef), (abeabef), (abebef), (acf), (adcf)

Linear combination of paths in B2 will also generate any path. For example,

$$(abea(be)^3f) = 2(abebef) - (abef)$$

and

$$(a(be)^2abef) = (a(be)^2f) + (abeabef) - (abef)$$

The overall strategy will be to measure the complexity of a program by computing the number of linearly independent paths $v(G)$, control the 'size' of programs by setting

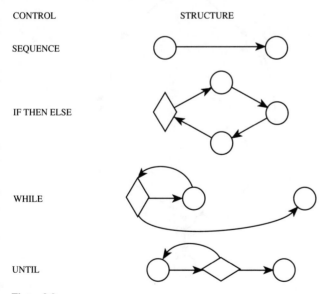

Figure 2.3

an upper limit to $v(G)$ (instead of using just physical size), and use the cyclomatic complexity as the basis for a testing methodology.

A few simple examples may help to illustrate. Figure 2.3 illustrates the control graphs of the usual constructs used in structured programming and their respective complexities. Notice that the sequence of an arbitrary number of nodes always has unit complexity and that cyclomatic complexity conforms to our intuitive notion of 'minimum number of paths'. Several properties of cyclomatic complexity are stated below:

1. $v(G) \geqslant 1$.
2. $v(G)$ is the maximum number of linearly independent paths in G; it is the size of a basis set.
3. Inserting or deleting functional statements to G does not affect $v(G)$.
4. G has only one path if and only if $v(G) = 1$.
5. Inserting a new edge in G increases $v(G)$ by unity.
6. $v(G)$ depends only on the decision structure of G.

2.3 WORKING EXPERIENCE WITH THE COMPLEXITY MEASURE

In this section a system that automates the complexity measure will be described. The control structures of several PDP-10 Fortran programs and their corresponding complexity measures will be illustrated.

To aid my research into control structure complexity, a tool was built to run on

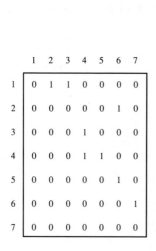

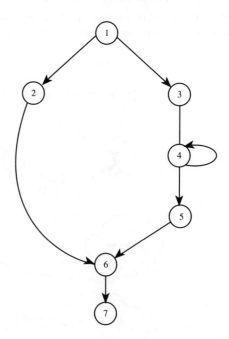

Figure 2.4 Connectivity matrix.

PDP-10 that analyses the structure of Fortran programs. The tool, FLOW, was written in APL to input the source code from Fortran files on disk. FLOW would then break a Fortran job into distinct subroutines and analyse the control structure of each subroutine. It does this by breaking the Fortran subroutines into blocks that are delimited by statements that affect control flow: IF, GOTO, referenced LABELS, DO, etc. The flow between the blocks is then represented in an $n \times n$ matrix (where n is the number of blocks), having a 1 in the i–jth position if block i can branch to block j in 1 step. FLOW also produces the 'blocked' listing of the original program, computes the cyclomatic complexity, and produces a reachability matrix (there is a 1 in the i–jth position if block i can branch to block j in any number of steps). An example of FLOW's output, where the matrices in Figs 2.4 and 2.5 are derived from the following code, is shown below:

```
        IMPLICIT INTEGER(A-Z)
        COMMON / ALLOC / MEM(2048),LM,LU,LV,LW,LX,LY,LQ,LWEX,
            NCHARS,NWORDS
        DIMENSION MEMORY(2048),INHEAD(4),ITRANS(128)
        TYPE 1
1       FORMAT('DOMOLKI STRUCTURE FILE NAME?' $)
        NAMDML = 0
        ACCEPT 2,NAMDML
2       FORMAT(A5)
        CALL ALCHAN(ICHAN)
        CALL IFILE(ICHAN,'DSK',NAMDML,'DAT',0,0)
        CALL READB(ICHAN,INHEAD,132,NREAD,$990,$990)
        NCHARS = INHEAD(1)
        NWORDS=INHEAD(2)
        NTOT = (NCHARS + 7)*NWORDS
        LTOT = (NCHAR + 5)*NWORDS
****** BLOCK NO. 1 **************************
        IF(LTOT,GT,2048) GO TO 900
****** BLOCK NO. 2 **************************
```

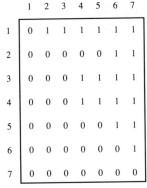

	1	2	3	4	5	6	7
1	0	1	1	1	1	1	1
2	0	0	0	0	0	1	1
3	0	0	0	1	1	1	1
4	0	0	0	1	1	1	1
5	0	0	0	0	0	1	1
6	0	0	0	0	0	0	1
7	0	0	0	0	0	0	0

END

Figure 2.5 Closure of connectivity matrix.

```
        CALL READB(ICHAN,MEMORY,LTOT,NREAD,$990,$990)
        LM = 0
        LU = NCHARS*NWORDS + LM
        LV = NWORDS + LU
        LW = NWORDS + LV
        LX = NWORDS + LW
        LY = NWORDS + LX
        LQ = NWORDS + LY
        LWEX = NWORDS + LQ
***** BLOCK NO. 3 **************************
        DO 700 I = 2,NWORDS
        MEMORY(LWEX + I) = (MEMORY(LW + I),OR,(MEMORY(LW + I)*2))
   700 CONTINUE
***** BLOCK NO. 4 **************************
        CALL EXTEXT(ITRANS)
        STOP
***** BLOCK NO. 5 **************************
   900 TYPE 3,LTOT
     3  FORMAT('STRUCTURE TOO LARGE FOR CORE; ',18,' WORDS' /
           ' SEE COOPER        ' / )
        STOP
***** BLOCK NO. 6 **************************
   990 TYPE $
     4  FORMAT(' READ ERROR, OR STRUCTURE FILE ERROR; ' /
            'SEE COOPER        ' / )
        STOP
        END
```

A few of the control graphs that were found in live programs are presented in Figs. 2.6–2.15. The actual control graphs from FLOW appear on a DATA DISK CRT, but they are hand-drawn here for purposes of illustration. The graphs are presented in increasing order of complexity in order to suggest the correlation between the complexity numbers and our intuitive notion of control flow complexity.

One of the more interesting aspects of the automatic approach is that, although FLOW could be implemented much more efficiently in a compiler level language, it is still possible to go through a year's worth of a programmer's Fortran

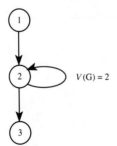

Figure 2.6

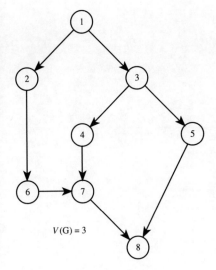

$V(G) = 3$

Figure 2.7

code in about 20 minutes. After seeing several of a programmer's control graphs on a CRT, one can often recognize 'style' by noting similar patterns in the graphs. For example, one programmer had an affinity for sequencing numerous simple loops as in Figs. 2.16 and 2.17. It was later revealed that these programs were

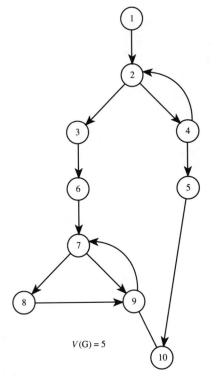

$V(G) = 5$

Figure 2.8

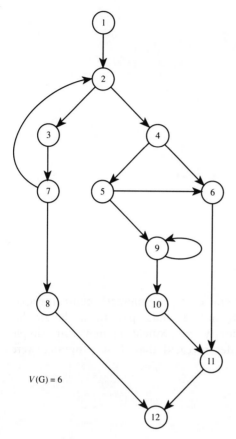

$V(G) = 6$

Figure 2.9

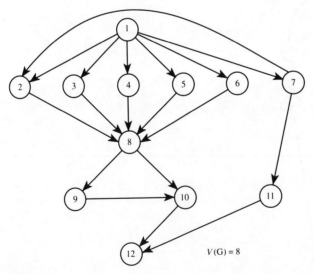

$V(G) = 8$

Figure 2.10

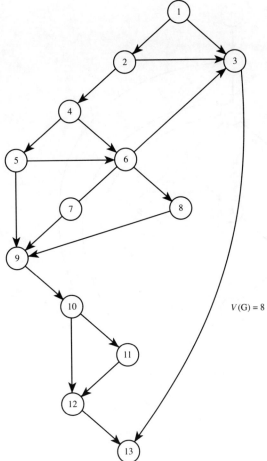

$V(G) = 8$

Figure 2.11

eventually to run on a CDC6600 and the 'tight' loops were designed to stay within the hardware stack.

These results have been used in an operational environment by advising project members to limit their software modules by cyclomatic complexity instead of physical size. The particular upper bound that has been used for cyclomatic complexity is 10, which seems like a reasonable, but not magical, upper limit. Programmers have been required to calculate complexity as they create software modules. When the complexity exceeded 10 they had to either recognize and modularize subfunctions or redo the software. The intention was to keep the 'size' of the modules manageable and allow for testing all the independent paths (which will be elaborated upon in Section 2.7). The only situation in which this limit has seemed unreasonable is when a large number of independent cases followed a selection function (a large case statement), which was allowed.

It has been interesting to note how the individual programmer's style relates to the complexity measure. I have been delighted to find several programmers who never

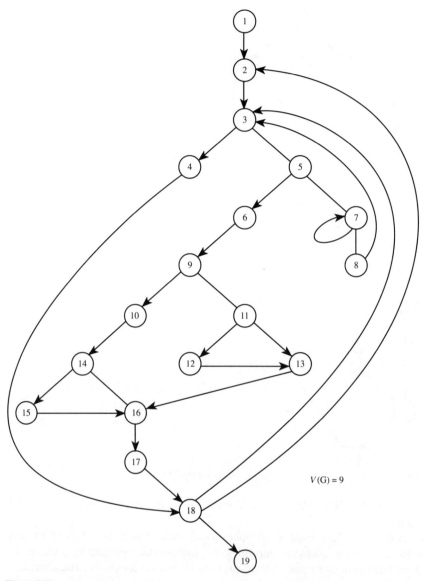

Figure 2.12

had formal training in structured programming but consistently write code in the 3–7 complexity range which is quite well structured. On the other hand, FLOW has found several programmers who frequently wrote code in the 40–50 complexity range (and who claimed there was no other way to do it). On one occasion I was given a DEC tape of 24 Fortran subroutines that were part of a large real-time graphics system. It was rather disquieting to find, in a system where reliability is critical, subroutines of the following complexity: 16, 17, 24, 24, 32, 34, 41, 54, 56, and 64. After confronting the project members with these results, I was told that

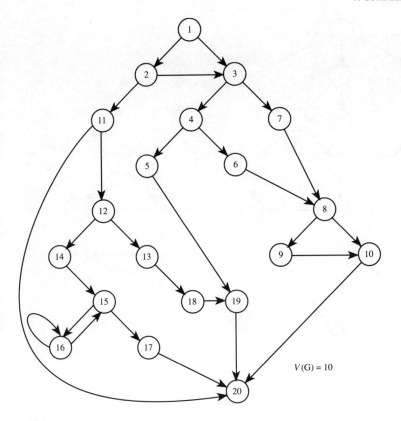

$V(G) = 10$

Figure 2.13

the subroutines on the DEC tape were chosen because they were troublesome, and indeed, a close correlation was found between the ranking of subroutines by complexity and a ranking by reliability (performed by the project members).

2.4 DECOMPOSITION

The role of p in the complexity calculation $v = e - n + 2p$ will now be explained. Recall in Definition 1 that p is the number of connected components. The way we defined a program control graph (unique entry and exit nodes, all nodes reachable from the entry, and the exit reachable from all nodes) would result in all control graphs having only one connected component. One could, however, imagine a main program M and two called subroutines A and B having a control structure shown in Fig. 2.18.

---

[2] A graph is connected if for every pair of vertices there is a chain going from one to the other. Given a vertex a, the set of vertices that can be connected to a, together with a itself, is a connected component. [Note that this is a weaker condition than strongly connected and does not require the additional edge linking the exit to entry node, shown in Fig. 2.1—M.J.S.]

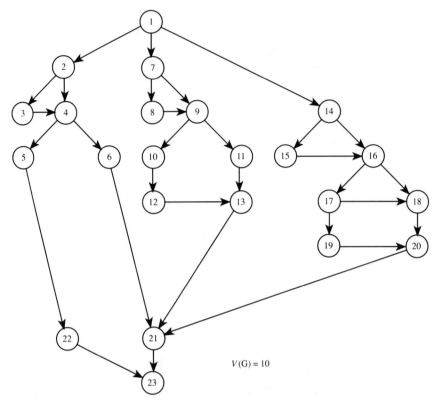

$V(G) = 10$

Figure 2.14

Let us denote this total graph with three connected components[2] as $M \cup A \cup B$. Now, since $p = 3$ we calculate complexity as

$$v(M \cup A \cup B) = e - n + 2p = 13 - 13 + 2 \times 3 = 6$$

This method with $p \neq 1$ can be used to calculate the complexity of a collection of programs, particularly a hierarchial nest of subroutines as shown in Fig. 2.18.

Notice that $v(M \cup A \cup B) = v(M) + v(A) + v(B) = 6$. In general, the complexity of a collection C of control graphs with k connected components is equal to the summation of their complexities. To see this let $C_i, 1 \leqslant i \leqslant k$, denote the k distinct connected components, and let e_i and n_i be the number of edges and nodes in the ith connected component. Then

$$v(C) = e - n + 2p = \sum_{1}^{k} e_i - \sum_{1}^{k} n_i + 2k$$

$$= \sum_{1}^{k}(e_i - n_i + 2) = \sum_{1}^{k} v(C_i)$$

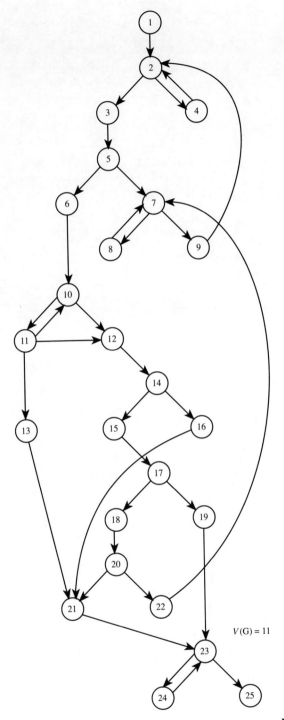

$V(G) = 11$

Figure 2.15

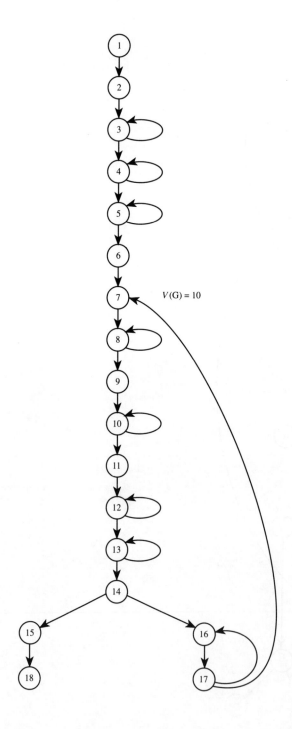

Figure 2.16

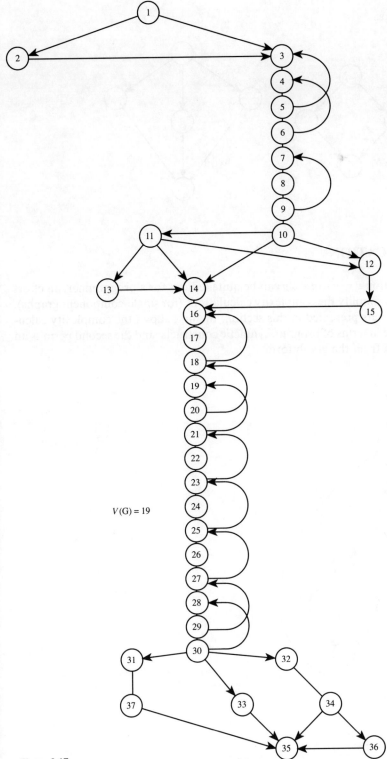

Figure 2.17

$V(G) = 19$

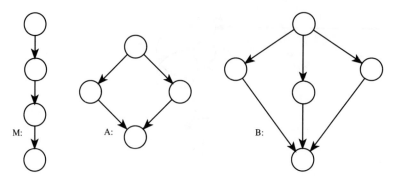

Figure 2.18

2.5 SIMPLIFICATION

Since the calculation $v = e - n + 2p$ can be quite tedious for a programmer, an effort has been made to simplify the complexity calculations (for single-component graphs). There are two results presented in this section: the first allows the complexity calculations to be done in terms of program syntactic constructs, and the second permits an easier calculation from the graph form.

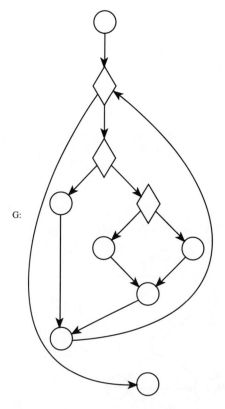

Figure 2.19

Mills (1972) proves the following: if the number of function, predicate, and collecting nodes in a structured program is θ, π and γ, respectively, and e is the number of edges, then

$$e = 1 + \theta + 3\pi$$

Since for every predicate node there is exactly one collecting node and there are unique entry and exit nodes, it follows that

$$n = \theta + 2\pi + 2$$

Assuming $p = 1$ and substituting in $v = e - n + 2$, we get

$$v = (1 + \theta + 3\pi) - (\theta + 2\pi + 2) + 2 = \pi + 1$$

This proves that the cyclomatic complexity of a structured program equals the number of predicates plus one, for example in Fig. 2.19, complexity $v(G) = \pi + 1 = 3 + 1 = 4$. Notice how in this case complexity can be computed by simply counting the number of predicates in the code and not having to deal with the control graph.

In practice, compound predicates such as IF, "C1 AND C2" THEN are treated as contributing 2 to complexity, since without the connective AND we would have

IF C1 THEN IF C2 THEN

which has two predicates. For this reason, and for testing purposes, it has been found to be more convenient to count conditions instead of predicates when calculating complexity.[3]

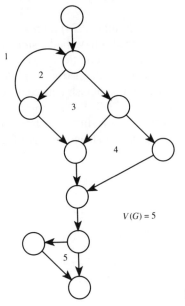

$V(G) = 5$

Figure 2.20

---

[3] For the CASE construct with N cases, use $N - 1$ for the number of conditions. Notice, once again, that a simulation of CASE with IF's will have $N - 1$ conditions.

It has been proved that in general the complexity of any (unstructured) program is $\pi + 1$.

The second simplification of the calculation of $e - n + 2p$ reduces the calculation of visual inspection of the control graph. We need Euler's formula, which is as follows. If G is a connected plane graph with n vertices, e edges and r regions, then

$$n - e + r = 2$$

Just changing the order of the terms, we get $r = e - n + 2$, so the number of regions is equal to the cyclomatic complexity. Given a program with a plane control graph, one can therefore calculate v by counting regions, as in Fig. 2.20.

2.6 NONSTRUCTURED PROGRAMMING

The main thrust in the recent popularization of structured programming is to make programmers aware of a few syntactic constructs[4] and tell them that a structured program is one written with only these constructs. One of the difficulties with this approach is it does not define for programmers what constructs they should not use; i.e., it does not tell them what a structured program is *not*. If the programming population had a notion of what constructs to avoid and they could see the inherent difficulty in these constructs, perhaps the notion of structuring programming would be more psychologically palatable. A clear definition of the constructs that structured programming excludes would also sensitize programmers to their use while programs are being created, which (if we believe in structured programming) would have a desirable effect.

One of the reasons why I think this is important is that, as Knuth (1974) points out, there is a time and a place when an unstructured GOTO is needed. I have had a similar experience structuring Fortran jobs—there are a few very specific conditions when an unstructured construct works best. If it is the case that unstructured constructs should be allowed only under special circumstance, one then needs to distinguish between the programmer who makes judicious use of a few unstructured GOTO's as compared with the programmer who is addicted to them. What would help is, first, a definition of the unstructured components and, second, a measure of the structureness of a program as well as the complexity of a program.

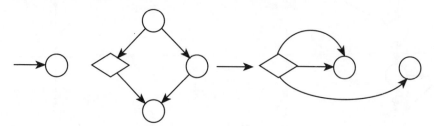

Figure 2.21

---

[4] The usual ones used (sometimes called D-structures) are shown in Fig. 2.21.

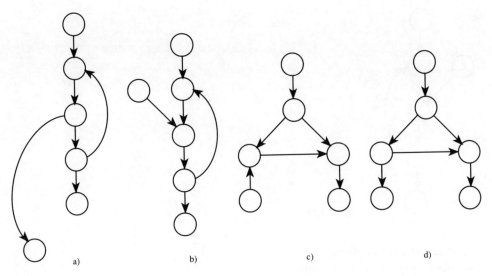

Figure 2.22

Rao Kasaraju (1974) has a result that is related: a flow graph is reducible[5] to a structured program if and only if it does not contain a loop with two or more exits. This is a deep result but not, however, what we need, since many programs that are reducible to structured programs are not structured programs. In order to have programmers explicitly identify and avoid unstructured code, we need a theorem that is analogous to, for example, Kuratowski's theorem in graph theory. Kuratowski's theorem states that any nonplanar graph must contain at least one of two specific non-planar graphs that he describes. The proof of nonplanarity of a graph is then reducible to locating two specific subgraphs, whereas showing nonplanarity without Kuratowski's result is, in general, much more difficult.

The four control structures shown in Fig. 2.22 were found to generate all non-structured programs.

A number of theorems and results will now be stated without proof.

Result 1   A necessary and sufficient condition that a program[6] is nonstructured (one that is not written with just D-structures) is that is contains as a subgraph either (a), (b) or (c) (as shown in Fig 2.22).

The reason why graph (d) was slighted in Result 1 is that any three of the four graphs will generate all the unstructured programs; this will be illustrated later. It is convenient to verbalize the graphs (a)–(d), respectively, as follows:

(a) Branching out of a loop
(b) Branching into a loop

---

[5] Reducibility here means that the same function is computed with the same actions and predicates although the control structure may differ.

[6] Assuming the program does not contain unconditional GOTOs.

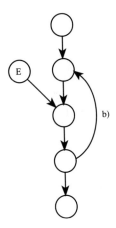

Figure 2.23

(c) Branching into a decision
(d) Branching out of a decision

The following version of Result 2 may seem more intuitively appealing.

A structured program can be written by not 'branching out of or into a loop, or out of or into a decision'.

The following result gives insight into why a nonstructured program's logic often becomes convoluted and entwined.

Result 2 A nonstructured program cannot be just a little nonstructured. That is, any nonstructured program must contain at least two of the graphs (a)–(d). Part of the proof of Result 2 will be shown here because it helps to illustrate how the control flow in a nonstructured program becomes entangled. We show, for an example, how graph (b) cannot occur alone. Assuming we have graph (b) (Fig. 2.23), the entry node E occurs either before, after, or from a node independent of the loop. Each of these three cases will be treated separately.

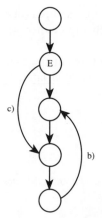

Figure 2.24

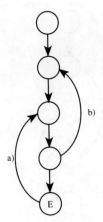

Figure 2.25

Case 1   E is 'before' the loop E is on a path from entry to the loop, so the program must have a graph like that in Fig. 2.24. Notice how E is a split node at the beginning of a decision that is branched into. So in this case we have a (c) graph along with the original (b) graph.

Case 2   E is 'after' the loop, the control graph would appear as shown in Fig. 2.25. Notice how a type (a) graph must appear.

Case 3   E is independent of the loop. The control graph would look like that shown in Fig. 2.26. The graph (c) must now be present with (b). If there is another path that can go to a node after the loop from E, then a type (d) graph is also generated. Things are often this bad, and in fact much worse.

Similar arguments can be made for each of the other nonstructured graphs to show that (a)–(d) cannot occur alone. If one generates all the possible pairs from (a)–(d), it is interesting to note that they all reduce to four basic types (see Fig. 2.27). This leads us to the following result.

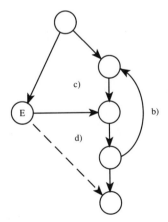

Figure 2.26

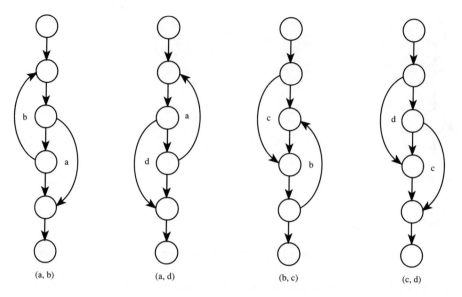

(a, b)   (a, d)   (b, c)   (c, d)

Figure 2.27

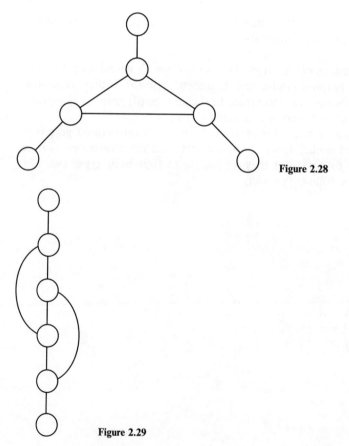

Figure 2.28

Figure 2.29

Result 3   A necessary and sufficient condition for a program to be nonstructured is that it contains at least one of: (a, b), (a, d), (b, c), (c, d). Result 4 is now obvious.

Result 4   The cyclomatic complexity of a nonstructured program is at least 3. It is interesting to notice that, when the orientation is taken off the edges, each of the four basic graphs (a)–(d) are isomorphic to the nondirected graph in Fig. 2.28. Also if the graphs (a, b)–(c, d) have their directions taken off, they are all isomorphic to the graph in Fig. 2.29.

By examining the graphs (a, b)–(c, d) one can formulate a more elegant nonstructured characterization.

Result 5   A structured program can be written by not branching out of loops or into decisions; (a) and (d) provide a basis.

Result 6   A structured program can be written by not branching into loops or out of decisions; (b) and (d) provide a basis.

A way to measure the lack of structure in a program or flow graph will be briefly commented upon. One of the difficulties with the nonstructured graphs mentioned above is that there is no way they can be broken down into subgraphs with one entry and one exit. This is a severe limitation, since one way in which program complexity can be controlled is to recognize when the cyclomatic complexity becomes too large—and then identify and remove subgraphs with unique entry and exit nodes.

Result 7   A structured program is reducible[7] to a program of unit complexity.

Figure 2.30 illustrates how a structured program can be reduced. In the nonstructured graphs in Fig. 2.31, however, such a reduction process is not possible. Let m be the number of proper subgraphs with unique entry and exit nodes. Notice in G1, G2 and G3 that m is equal to 0, 1 and 2, respectively. The following definition of essential complexity ev is used to reflect the lack of structure.

Definition $ev = v - n$

For the graphs of Fig. 2.31 we have $ev(G1) = 6$, $ev(G2) = 5$ and $e(G3) = 4$. Notice how the essential complexity indicates the extent to which a graph can be reduced. G1 cannot be reduced at all since its complexity is equal to its essential complexity. G2 and G3, however, can be reduced as shown in Fig. 2.32.

This last result is stated for completeness.

Result 8   The essential complexity of a structured program is one.

2.7 A TESTING METHODOLOGY

The complexity measure v is designed to conform to our intuitive notion of complexity and, since we often spend as much as 50 per cent of our time in test and debug

---

[7] Reduction is the process of removing subgraphs (subroutines) with unique entry and exit nodes.

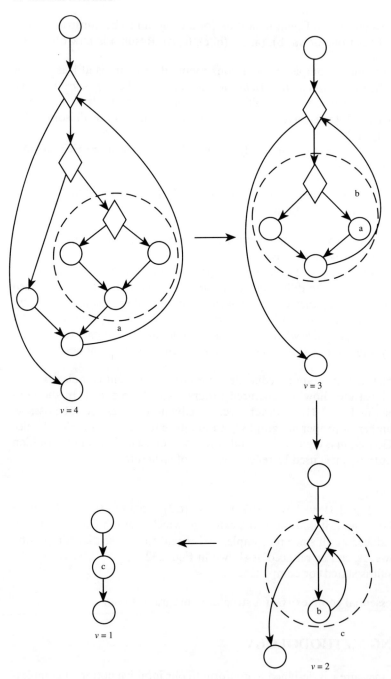

Figure 2.30

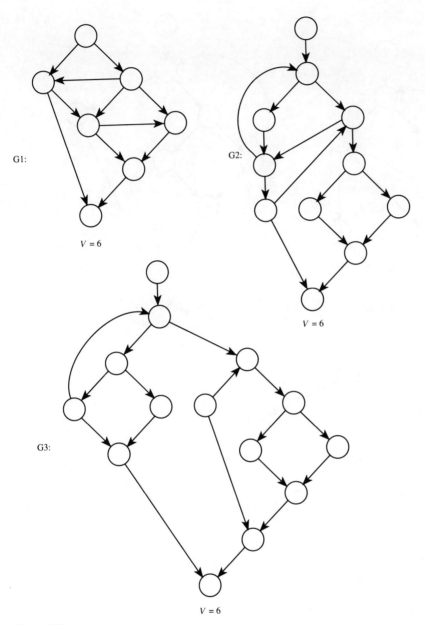

G1:

V = 6

G2:

V = 6

G3:

V = 6

Figure 2.31

mode, the measure should correlate closely with the amount of work required to test a program. In this section the relationship between testing and cyclomatic complexity will be defined and a testing methodology will be developed.

Let us assume that a program P has been written, its complexity v has been calculated, and the number of paths tested is ac (actual complexity). If ac is less than v, then

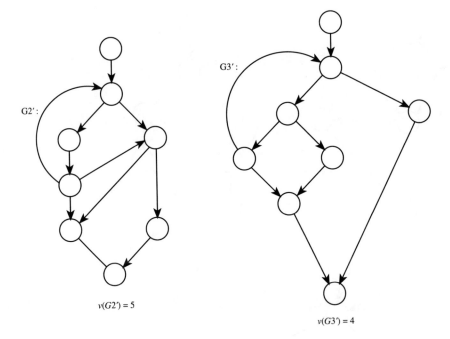

$v(G2') = 5$

$v(G3') = 4$

Figure 2.32

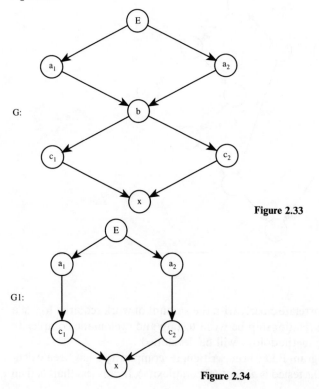

Figure 2.33

Figure 2.34

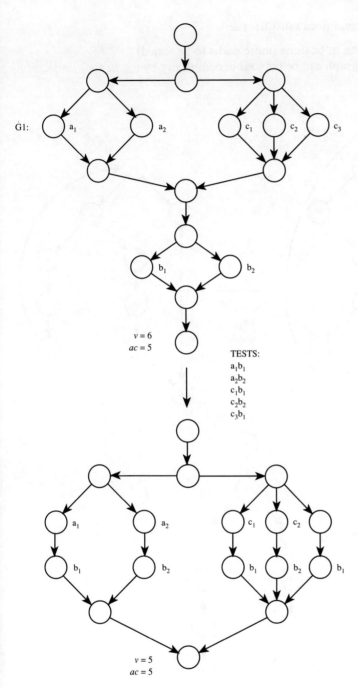

G1:

$v = 6$
$ac = 5$

TESTS:
a_1b_1
a_2b_2
c_1b_1
c_2b_2
c_3b_1

$v = 5$
$ac = 5$

Figure 2.35

one of the following conditions must be true:

1. There is more testing to be done (more paths to be tested).
2. The program flow graph can be reduced in complexity by $v - ac$ ($v - ac$ decisions can be taken out).

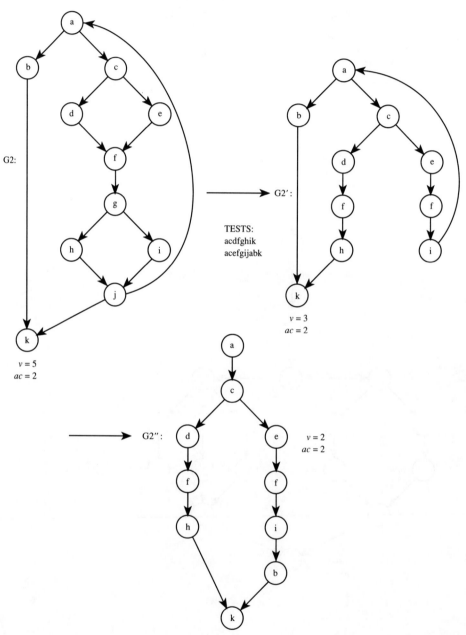

Figure 2.36

3. Portions of the program can be reduced to in line code (complexity has increased to conserve space).

Up to this point the complexity issue has been considered purely in terms of the structure of the control flow. This testing issue, however, is closely related to the data flow because it is the data behavior that either precludes or makes realizable the execution of any particular control path. A few simple examples may help to illustrate.

Assume we start with the flow graph shown in Fig. 2.33. Suppose that $ac = 2$ and the two tested paths are [E, a_1, b, c_2, x] and [E, a_2, b, c_1, x]. Then, given that paths [E, a_1, b, c_1, x] and [E, a_2, b, c_2, x] cannot be executed, we have $ac < v$ so case 2 holds and G can be reduced by removing decision b, as in Fig. 2.34. Notice how in G $v = ac$ and the complexity of G1 is less than the complexity of G.

In our experience, this approach is most helpful when programmers are required to document their flow graph and complexity and to show explicitly the different paths tested. It is often the case, when the actual number of paths tested is compared with the cyclomatic complexity, that several additional paths are discovered that would normally be overlooked. It should be noted that v is only the minimal number of independent paths that should be tested. There are often additional paths to test. It should also be noted that this procedure (like any other testing method) will by no means guarantee or prove the software—all it can do is surface more bugs and improve the quality of the software.

Two more examples are presented without comment in Figs. 2.35 and 2.36.

Appendix

[Not included]

3

CONTROL FLOW, DATA FLOW AND PROGRAM COMPLEXITY

Enrique I. Oviedo

State University of New York at Buffalo

ABSTRACT

This chapter reports on the initial stages of a study of program complexity in the context of high-level languages. The goal of the research has been the development of techniques to measure program attributes and the formulation of a model of program complexity against which the complexity of a program for a task may be measured or, at least, be compared with another program for the same task. We analyse, in particular, how the concepts of control flow and data flow can be used to define objective criteria to compare alternative implementations of an algorithm, and to develop useful programming guidelines.

3.1 INTRODUCTION

There can be no real software engineering or programming science without objective measures for the factors which contribute to the quality program (Gilb 1977). A recurring concept in the literature is the inverse relationship between program quality and program complexity. But there is no satisfactory definition of program complexity. In spite of the extensive research in software engineering, there are no commonly accepted standards and tests by means of which the complexity of programs can be measured, and there is no general agreement on the factors that affect the complexity of programs.

This paper reports on the initial stages of a study of program complexity in the context of high-level languages. The goal of the research has been the development of techniques to measure program attributes and the formulation of a model of program complexity against which the complexity of a program for a task may be measured or, at least, compared with another program for the same task.

The amount of knowledge about the language in which a program is written which is incorporated in different program complexity measures varies widely. For example, the program clarity measure of software science only requires distinguishing between operators and operands, whereas measures based on the control flow of the program or the execution profile of the program require extensive knowledge of the syntax and semantics of the programming language (see Halstead 1977a; McCabe, Chapter 2 above; Robinson and Torsun 1977). Obviously, the more linguistic knowledge used to analyse programs, the more information can be extracted about the contents of the program to improve the predictive power of program complexity measures. The availability of more information, however, may make it more difficult to formulate simple and well behaved measures. This trade-off between the amount of information to be extracted from programs and the difficulty of interpreting it is a basic problem in the area of program complexity and its measurement. The rest of the paper will analyse how the concepts of control flow and data flow and their measurement can help satisfy our efforts at understanding program complexity.

Control structures and data structures are fundamental and closely intertwined program components (as exemplified by the title of Wirth's (1976) book, *Algorithms + Data Structures = Programs*). It would be widely agreed that the appropriate choice of control and data structures can make programs more readable, easier to debug and more reliable. This general argument, and the results of studies that suggest that the control flow and data flow of programs play an important role in the ability of programmers to understand, trace and debug programs (Green 1977; Miller 1978; Shneiderman 1977), lead us to formulate a model of program complexity based on the control flow and data flow characteristics of programs.

3.2 DEFINITION OF A PROGRAM

In order to define precisely control flow and data flow complexity measures, we adopt the following rather abstract definition of a program:

Definition 1 A program consists of a finite sequence of statements. This sequence starts with a PROGRAM statement, designating input variables (e.g. PROGRAM(X1, X2, X3)), and ends with an END statement designating output variables (e.g. END(X1, X5)). The other statements may be of the following types:

(a) Assignment statements, X1 = expression
(b) Conditional statements, i.e.

IF b1 THEN S1, or IF b1 THEN S1 ELSE S2, ,

where b1 is a Boolean expression and S1 and S2 are statements (or compound statements; see (c) below)
(c) Compound statements, e.g. {S1; S2;. . . ;SN;}
(d) Unconditional GOTO statements, e.g. GOTO L1, or computed GOTO statements, e.g. GOTO(L1, L2,. . .,LN) a1, where L1, L2 and LN are labels and a1 is an INTEGER expression.
(e) Loop statements, e.g. WHILE b1 DO S1 ENDWHILE or REPEAT S1 UNTIL b1, where b1 is a Boolean expression and S1 is a (compound) statement

The following remarks can be made about this definition:

1. Variables are scalars (e.g. A,B,C) or scalars indexed by an integer expression (e.g. $A[1]$, $A[J]$, $A[I^*K]$).
2. Because we shall ignore the types of variables and expressions and the dimensions of indexed variables in our measures, they are also ignored in Definition 1.
3. The language defined in Definition 1 contains no input or output statements. Rather, we shall assume that all variables in the PROGRAM statement are implicitly read and assigned a value and that all variables in the END statement are implicitly output.
4. The computed GOTO statement (like the one in Fortran) is included to allow complex control flow programs where each statement could be followed by the execution of every other statement in the program.

It is my contention that this abstract definition contains both enough generality to encompass programs written in a variety of high-level languages and enough specificity to allow us to define meaningful complexity measures.

My approach in defining a model of program complexity is based on the assumption that, in order to understand, trace and debug a program, a programmer must, at least, be able to determine (a) the statements that precede and the statements that follow each statement in a program, and (b) the set of variable references affected by each variable assignment and the set of assignments by which each referenced variable could have been defined.

On this assumption, we proceed now to define control flow complexity and data flow complexity.

3.3 CONTROL FLOW COMPLEXITY

Our approach to control flow complexity will be to extract a flow graph from a program and then to study properties of this abstraction. In order to define control flow complexity, we first define the following concepts: flow graph, program block and program flow graph.

Definition 2 A flow graph is a finite directed graph containing a set of nodes N and a set of edges E which satisfy the following conditions:

1. There is a unique node $b \in N$ such that b has no predecessor and only one

successor and every node in N can be reached from b. Node b is called the entry or beginning node of the flow graph.
2. There is a unique node $f \in N$ such that, $f \neq b, f$ has no successors and f can be reached from every node in N. Node f is called the exit or final node of the flow graph.

Throughout this paper, flow graphs will be characterized by the 4-tuple $\{b, S, f, E\}$, where $S = N - \{f, b\}$. The *immediate successors* of a node n_i are all of the nodes n_j for which $\{n_i, n_j\}$ is an edge in E. The *immediate predecessors* of a node n_j are all of the nodes n_i for which (n_i, n_j) is an edge in E. The *successors* of a node n_i are all the nodes n_j for which there exists a path from n_i to n_j. The *predecessors* of a node n_j are all the nodes n_i for which there exists a path from n_i to n_j.

In order to obtain the flow graph corresponding to any program, we must be able to extract from the program a set of edges E representing program branches and a set of nodes N, each of which represents a sequence of statements without branches into it or out of it, except for the first and the last statements respectively. We call such a sequence of statements a program block, for which a formal definition is:

Definition 3 A *program block* is

(a) a PROGRAM statement, or
(b) an END statement, or
(c) a Boolean expression with its associated keywords (i.e. IF b1, WHILE b1 DO, UNTIL b1), or
(d) a group of sequentially executed statements defined as follows.

A statement A is a block entry if it is

1. the first statement after the PROGRAM statement, or
2. labelled by a label that appears in an unconditional or computed GOTO statement, or
3. a THEN statement, or
4. an ELSE statement, or
5. a REPEAT statement, or
6. the first statement after a conditional GOTO statement (e.g. statement S2 in Fig. 3.1(c), or
7. a statement that can be reached from two or more blocks (e.g. a statement following a conditional statement; see also statement S5 in Fig. 3.1(a), or
8. a statement that is executed immediately after a WHILE b1 DO block (e.g. statements S1 and S2 in Fig. 3.1(b), or
9. the first statement after an UNTIL b1 block.

The block belonging to a block entry A consists of A and all the statements following A up to and including

- an ENDWHILE statement, or
- a computed or unconditional GOTO statement, or
- a statement that is immediately followed by a block entry or program block.

(a) .

```
S1;
IF b1
THEN S2
ELSE {S3;S4;}
S5;
```

(b) .

```
WHILE b1 DO S1;
ENDWHILE:
S2;
```

(c) .

```
S1;
IF b1 THEN GOTO L1;
S2;
L1:S3;
```

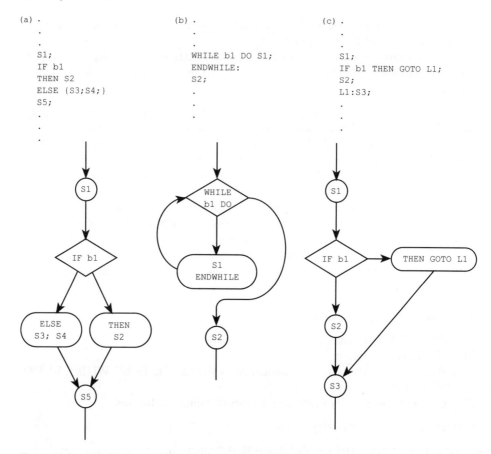

Figure 3.1 Program blocks and flow graphs according to Definitions 2 and 3.

Definition 4 A *program flow graph* is a flow graph in which

1. Each node in N corresponds to a block of the program.
2. The edges in E correspond to the program branches. If the nodes n_i and n_j of the flow graph correspond to the program blocks n_i and n_j, then an edge (n_i, n_j) exists if
   (a) the block n_j follows block n_i in the program, or
   (b) block n_i consists of a GOTO statement (e.g. GOTO L, GOTO$(\ldots, L, \ldots)$ a l) and L is the label of the first statement in block n_j.

Figure 3.1 contains three examples which illustrate Definitions 2 and 3 for simple programs.

Definition 5 The *control flow complexity* (CF) of a program with a program flow graph $\{b, S, f, E\}$ is

$$CF = ||E|| \tag{3.1}$$

where $|| \ ||$ stands for set cardinality.

Given that by definition node b has one successor and node f has no successor, and defining $SUCC(n_i)$ as the number of immediate successors of node n_i, the control flow complexity of a given flow graph can be calculated as

$$CF = 1 + \sum_{i=1}^{\|S\|} SUCC(n_i) \qquad (3.2)$$

With Definition 5, therefore, we state a belief that the control structure complexity of a program can be measured directly as the number of branches connecting program blocks in the program. Note that we have not made a distinction between the transfers of control within the program control structures (e.g. the branches to the THEN and ELSE parts of a conditional statement) and between the control structures (e.g. a GOTO from a loop into another loop), nor have we differentiated between forward and backward GOTOs. However, Definition 5 could easily be refined to weight more heavily the branches corresponding to unstructured constructs like jumps into loops or conditional statements.

3.3.1 Limits on the values of program control flow complexity

According to Definition 5, a program with a flow graph $\{b, S, f, E\}$ has maximum CF when each node in S is succeeded by f and by all other nodes in S, in which case

$$CF_{max} = 1 + \sum_{i=1}^{\|S\|} (\|S\| + 1) - \|S\|^2 + \|S\| + 1 \qquad (3.3)$$

We call this program a *fully connected* program. Conversely, a program has minimum

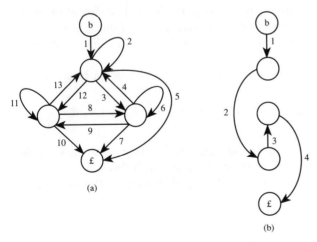

(a)

(b)

Figure 3.2 (a) A flow graph of a fully connected program, $\|S\| = 3$ and $CF = 9 + 3 + 1 = 13$; (b) a flow graph of a sequentially connected program, $\|S\| = 3$ and $CF = 4$.

CF when each node in S has at most one successor; then

$$CF_{\min} = 1 + \sum_{i=1}^{\|S\|} 1 = \|S\| + 1 \tag{3.4}$$

We call this program a *sequentially connected* program. Representations of programs with maximum and minimum CF when $S = 3$ are shown in Fig. 3.2.

3.4 DATA FLOW COMPLEXITY

Several studies (Chapin 1979; Dunsmore and Gannon 1979) indicate that the size of the set of variable references affected by each variable assignment and the set of assignments where each referenced variable could have been defined have a significant effect on the ability of a programmer to understand, trace and debug a program. We can surmise that the difficulty in understanding the definition–reference relationships in a program can be quantified by counting the number of variable definitions (references) associated with each variable reference (definition) in that program. In order to define precisely these definition–reference (def–ref) relationships in a program, and from these to define a measure of the data flow complexity of a program, we need a number of definitions.

Definition 6 As implied in Definition 1, a *variable definition* takes place in a PROGRAM statement or in an assignment statement. On the other hand, a *variable reference* takes place when the variable is used in an expression or an END statement. Two types of def–ref relationships are distinguished:

1. Those in which both definition and reference are in the same block
2. Those in which the definition and reference are in different blocks

A *locally available* variable definition for a program block is a definition of the variable in the block. A *locally exposed* variable reference in a block is a reference to a variable that is not preceded in the block by a definition of that variable (see Allen and Cooke 1976).

We proceed now to define when a variable definition can reach a block.

Definition 7 A variable definition in block n_i is said to *reach* block n_k if

1. The definition is locally available in block n_i.
2. There is a path from n_i to n_k (i.e., n_k is a successor of n_i) along which the variable is not locally available in any block on the path. In line with this definition, we say that a variable definition in a block *kills* all other definitions of this variable that might otherwise reach the block.

Now we define the following sets:

D_i the set of locally available definitions in block n_i
P_i the set of variable definitions that reach n_i and are not killed in n_i

A_i the set of variable definitions available (i.e. those that can possibly reach successors of n_i) upon exit from n_i

R_i the set of variable definitions that reach n_i

then

$$R_i = \bigcup_j A_j \qquad (3.5)$$

for all blocks n_j that are immediate predecessors of n_i, and

$$A_i = P_i \cup D_i \qquad (3.6)$$

In order to arrive at a plausible definition of *data flow complexity* (DF), it seems reasonable to assume that

1. A programmer can determine the def–ref relationships within blocks more easily than the def-ref relationships between blocks.
2. The number of different variables that are locally exposed in each block is more important than the total number of locally exposed variable references in each block (since in the case of multiple references to the same variable (e.g. $J = I + (i - 5)**I$) then the programmer would need to find the associated definition(s) only once).

Using these assumptions, we adopt the following definition of block data flow complexity:

Definition 8   Let V_i be the set of variables whose references are locally exposed in block n_i. Then block n_i's *data flow complexity* is

$$DF_j = \sum_{j=1}^{\|V_i\|} DEF(v_j) \qquad (3.7)$$

where $DEF(v_j)$ represents the number of available definitions of variable v_j in the set R_i.

Thus, DF_i counts all prior definitions of locally exposed variables in n_i that reach n_i. For example, if block n_i consists of the statements $X = Y$; $A = B * Y * (C - B)$; $Z = 2 + A$; and the set of variable definitions that can reach block n_i is $R_i = \{C_j, B_j, Y_k, B_k\}$ (i.e., if the definitions of C and B in block n_j and the definitions of Y and B in block n_k can reach block n_j), then, according to Definition 8, we have $V_i = \{C, B, Y\}$ and

$$DF_i = \sum_{j=1}^{3} DEF(v_j) = 4$$

(See Figs. 3.4 and 3.5 for additional examples.) Using Definition 8, we give next a definition of data flow complexity.

Definition 9   Given a program with a flow graph $\{b, S, f, E\}$, the *data flow complexity* is

$$DF = \sum_{i=1}^{\|S\|} DF_i + DF_f \qquad (3.8)$$

This definition merely says that *data flow complexity* of a program is defined as the sum of the data flow complexities of each block of the program.

3.4.1 Data flow complexity and structured variables

Thus far, we have restricted ourselves to scalar variables. As it stands, Definition 9 is not usable for indexed or other structured variables because it is not possible to determine, without program execution or interpretation, which elements of an array Z are defined and referenced in a statement like $Z[J] = Z[K]^*Z[3^*W]$. For this reason, we adopt the following conventions for determining the sets R_i, A_i and V_i or a block n_i with respect to arrays:

1. One or more references to elements of an array in block n_i are considered as a single reference to the array.
2. One or more assignments to elements of an array in block n_i are considered as a single definition to the array.
3. An array definition in block n_i does not kill the definitions of this array which are available from predecessors of block n_i.

According to these conventions, in the following program, two definitions of array Z can reach blocks 3 and 4 (one from block b and one from block 1), and four definitions of array Z can reach block f:

```
block b:   PROGRAM(Z,J,K,L)
block 1:   Z[L] = L; Z[L+1] = L+1;
block 2:   IF J = K
block 3:      THEN {Z[J] = J + 1; Z[J + 1] = J + 2}
block 4:      ELSE {Z[J] = J - 1; Z[J + 1] = J - 2}
block f:   END(Z)
```

3.4.2 Limits on the values of data flow complexity

A program with a flow graph $\{b, S, f, E\}$ and a set V of distinct variables, has the minimum possible data flow complexity if:

1. Each variable in V is defined once either in the PROGRAM statement or in an assignment statement in one of the program blocks.
2. Each variable in V is referenced only once either in the END statement or in one of the program blocks. (We assume here that, if a variable is defined but not referenced, then the definition can be eliminated from the program.) Therefore,

$$DF_{\min} = \sum_{i=1}^{\|S\|} DF_i + DF_f = \|V\| \tag{3.9}$$

The condition that each variable in V must be defined at most once leads to programs where

1. Assignment statements are used to initialize variables only and, therefore, variables keep that initial value throughout the program.

2. Looping constructs cannot be used because they would either loop for ever or would not loop at all since the initial value of the Boolean conditions controlling their execution could not change.

Such programs are particularly interesting because they are of the type that has been proposed by the advocates of applicative or functional programming (e.g. Bauer 1976), who argue that assignment statements lead to remote and complex connections of data analogous to the effect of GOTOs on control structures. Therefore, it is claimed, assignment statements should not be used and programs should be written using function calls, value parameters and conditional statements. A program where each variable in V may be defined at most once (i.e. an applicative style program) has maximum data flow complexity when all the variables in V are referenced in all the program blocks. Thus,

$$DF_{\text{applicative max}} = \sum_{i=1}^{\|S\|} (\|V\|) + \|V\| = \|V\| (\|S\| + 1) \qquad (3.10)$$

Thus, applicative programs have data flow complexity in the range given by equations (3.9) and (3.10).

A program with a flow graph $\{b, S, f, E\}$ and a set V of distinct variables has maximum possible data flow complexity when all the variables in V:

1. Are initialized in the PROGRAM statement and defined in all the program blocks
2. Are references in all the program blocks and the END statement
3. Can reach all the program blocks

Therefore,

$$DF_{\text{max}} = \sum_{i=1}^{\|S\|} \|V\| * (\|S\| + 1) + \|V\| (\|S\| + 1)$$

$$= \|V\| (\|S\|^2 + 2\|S\| + 1) \qquad (3.11)$$

3.5 A PROGRAM COMPLEXITY MODEL

In addition to the control flow and data flow characteristics of a program, there are other factors which may affect the ability of a reader to understand it such as indentation, comments, mnemonic variable names, variable types, etc. I believe, however, that as a first approximation, the following definition encompasses a significant part of our intuitive notion of program complexity.

Definition 10   Given a program with CF and DF complexities, the *program complexity* is

$$C = CF + DF \qquad (3.12)$$

More generally, we would prefer $C = \alpha CF + \beta DF$ for suitable weights α and β.

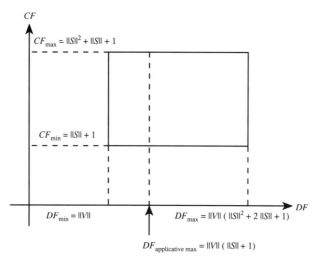

Figure 3.3

But for this initial, simple model there seems to be no valid reason to choose anything but $\alpha = \beta = 1$. From the foregoing, then, the complexities of all programs with $\|S\|$ program blocks and $\|V\|$ variables lie in the area shown in Fig. 3.3.

In order to test the model, I have gathered from the literature numerous pairs of equivalent programs which were published as examples, in the authors' opinions, of good and bad programming styles. For the majority of these program comparisons, it was found that the 'better' programs had smaller CF and DF than the 'worse' programs (see Figs. 3.4 and 3.5). These exemplary programs, however, were small (20 to 30 lines), and experiments in a more realistic setting must be carried out to analyse the model's predictive power, and also to determine if the assumption that $\alpha = \beta = 1$ needs to be modified as a function of the language, the problem or the algorithm. Obviously, before we can analyse large programs, the definitions of CF and DF have to be generalized to take into account procedure and function calls, and the different types of parameter passing techniques.

3.6 CONCLUSIONS AND FURTHER RESEARCH

The model of program complexity proposed here represents the beginnings of a research effort to formalize the concept of program complexity. The model is intuitively appealing, and the measures CF and DF can be obtained by computer analysis of programs. We are currently involved in developing a system that will do just this for various high-level languages. With this system we shall be able to determine how useful our model is in measuring the complexity of actual programs.

As mentioned above, there are well known algorithms to obtain CF and DF as defined in this paper. These algorithms require only a static analysis of the program text and have been used extensively for code optimization and for the detection of control flow and data flow anomalies (Allen and Cooke 1976; Fosdick and Osterweil 1976).

```
PROGRAM(X, Y, Z)
(*FINDS THE SMALLEST OF
      THREE NUMBERS*)
SMALL = X;
IF(Y.LT.SMALL) THEN SMALL = Y;
IF(Z.LT.SMALL) THEN SMALL = Z;
END(SMALL);
```

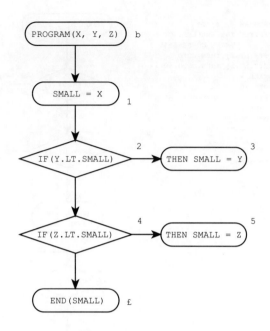

Block	V_i	R_i				DF_i
1	{X}	{X_b, Y_b, Z_b}				1
2	{Y, SMALL}	{X_b, Y_b, Z_b, $SMALL_1$}				2
3	{Y}	{X_b, Y_b, Z_b, $SMALL_1$}				1
4	{Z, SMALL}	{X_b, Y_b, Z_b, $SMALL_1$, $SMALL_3$}				3
5	{Z}	{X_b, Y_b, Z_b, $SMALL_1$, $SMALL_3$}				1
F	{SMALL}	{X_b, Y_b, Z_b, $SMALL_1$, $SMALL_3$, $SMALL_5$}				3

$CF = \|E\| = 8$

$DF = \Sigma DF_i = 11$

Figure 3.4

In addition to the transfers of control and the def–ref relationships, there are other program attributes that affect the complexity of programs and that can be quantified. In particular, we note that it would be interesting to develop measures for data structure properties and module interfaces.

The importance attached to the influence of the properties of data structures on the complexity and quality of programs is borne out by the extensive research activity in abstract data types. The sets of legal operators that may be applied with each variable and/or the units associated with each variable, for example, can be used to define a measure of the extent to which a compiler or an interpreter could automatically detect the illegal use of operators (e.g. addition of Boolean variables) or the inconsistent use of variables (e.g. addition of variables with incompatible units) (Gannon 1977). Similarly, data type declarations and assertions (e.g. subranges, loop invariants, etc.) provide additional information to the programmer and the compiler about the values that may be assigned to the variables in the

```
PROGRAM(X, Y, Z)
(*FINDS THE SMALLEST OF
    THREE NUMBERS*)
IF(X.LT.Y) THEN GOTO 30
IF(Y.LT.Z) THEN GOTO 50
SMALL = Z
GOTO 70
30 IF(X.LT.Z) THEN GOTO 60
SMALL = Z
GOTO 70
50 SMALL = Y
GOTO 70
60 SMALL = X
70 END(SMALL)
```

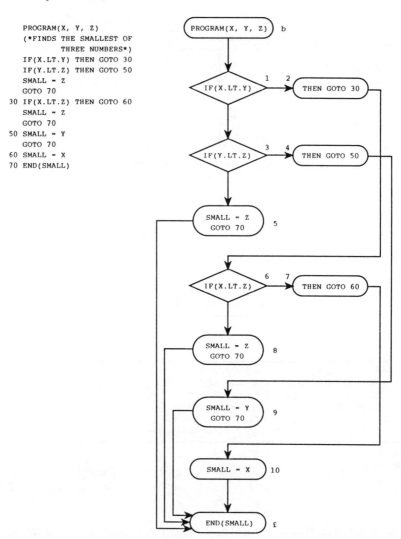

Block	V_i	R_i	DF_i
1	$\{X, Y\}$	$\{X_b, Y_b, Z_b\}$	2
2	$\{\}$	$\{X_b, Y_b, Z_b\}$	0
3	$\{Y, Z\}$	$\{X_b, Y_b, Z_b\}$	2
4	$\{\}$	$\{X_b, Y_b, Z_b\}$	0
5	$\{Z\}$	$\{X_b, Y_b, Z_b\}$	1
6	$\{X, Z\}$	$\{X_b, Y_b, Z_b\}$	2
7	$\{\}$	$\{X_b, Y_b, Z_b\}$	0
8	$\{Z\}$	$\{X_b, Y_b, Z_b\}$	1
9	$\{Y\}$	$\{X_b, Y_b, Z_b\}$	1
10	$\{X\}$	$\{X_b, Y_b, Z_b\}$	1
f	$\{SMALL\}$	$\{X_b, Y_b, Z_b, SMALL_5, SMALL_8, SMALL_9, SMALL_{10}\}$	4

$CF = ||E|| = 14$
$DF = \Sigma DF_i = 14$

Figure 3.5

program. We need to define measures of the effect of this information on the complexity, reliability and quality of programs.

Programming languages provides a variety of mechanisms (e.g. parameters, scope of variables, etc.) to control and limit the number of variables that are accessible or known in each subroutine or function of a program. Based on these mechanisms, we can define measures of variable accessibility for program modules. Variable accessibility, for example, would range from completely unrestricted, in the case that all the program variables were global, to strictly limited, in the case where, by means of parameters and local variables, the number of variables accessible in each module is reduced to the minimum necessary (Chapin 1978; Wulf and Shaw 1973). The objective definition of program attributes, such as complexity, reliability, accessibility, etc., and the development of techniques to measure them, together with the methods to prove the correctness and to measure the run time behaviour of programs, will form the basis for the development of a programming science. We have attempted here to formalize the notion of program complexity by defining it in terms of the control flow and data flow characteristics of programs. It remains to be shown if functionally equivalent programs are non-trivially different from the control flow and data flow points of view, and if the model presented here is more accurate and reliable than models of program complexity that are based only on the program control flow or on the program operators and operands.

PART THREE

Early Life Cycle Metrics: Design and Specification

By the end of the 1970s, researchers were beginning to appreciate the importance of the earlier stages of a software project, for example such activities as specification and design. This shift in software engineering thinking is reflected in much of the metrics work of the 1980s and the early 1990s. The potential benefits from moving back up the software life cycle are considerable, since poor specification and design decisions are frequently the most costly, and have the most devastating impact upon a project. Furthermore, early information enables more strategic decision-making; by the time code metrics are available, most project resources will have been committed. Part III covers a number of design and specification metrics.

One of the earliest design metrics is the *ripple metric* proposed by Yau, Collofello and McGregor in 1978 and reprinted here as Chapter 4.[1] This represents a departure from the earlier code metrics in two respects. First, it has as its level of concern the architecture or structure of the software system, as opposed to lower-level details of the code implementation. And second, it is concerned with how the functional parts of the system—frequently termed 'modules'—interact. The interaction is important, as it is the means whereby errors propagate from one module to another during maintenance activities. Clearly, it is desirable to minimise these propagation paths between modules, and so a maintainable design may be regarded as one with few paths, thus containing the impact of a maintenance change within a few modules. The ripple metric is intended to aid the software designer in identifying and reducing these connections. This is potentially very significant, since typically up to 80 per cent of a project's costs are expended upon software maintenance. Unfortunately, as Kafura and Reddy (1987) subsequently report, the metric does not appear to be very reliable unless one has access to the completed code, because it is not otherwise possible to compute all ripple paths through a module. Notwithstanding this difficulty, the metric is important because it focuses attention on module couplings and enables the designer to consider the broader architectural features of a system.

Another approach to module couplings is provided by the paper on cluster analysis by Hutchens and Basili (Chapter 5). The idea that underlies their approach is that a mathematical technique of classifying objects may be applied to analyse, and minimise, the couplings within a system.[2] A cluster analysis algorithm groups together the most similar objects, thereby minimising inter-object connections. For software design the objects are modules and the index of similarity is data bindings resulting from shared data structures. The output from this analysis is a hierarchical clustering so that it is possible to determine the order in which modules cluster; those with strongest couplings cluster first. The paper then goes on to report on practical experiences of applying cluster analysis to industrial software in the form of a number of Fortran systems used by NASA.

This work has a range of potential applications, none of which have yet been fully exploited. First, the analysis may be used to help the software designer partition a design so as to minimise couplings between modules as promoted by Stevens *et al.* (1974) among others. Second, the shape of the cluster hierarchy, the so-called 'fingerprint', may be utilised to provide information regarding a design, for instance the

---

[1] Other early pioneers of design metrics include Yin and Winchester (1978) and McClure (1978).

[2] For a readable introduction to cluster analysis techniques, see Dubes and Jain (1980).

degree of information hiding (Parnas, 1972). Finally, there exists the possibility, as Hutchens and Basili suggest, of treating the cluster analysis as a method of evaluating automatically generated designs.[3] Perhaps the major unsolved difficulty with this work lies in the choice of clustering algorithm. There are numerous algorithms, and each of them can have a major impact on the way in which components cluster; yet there is, at present, little guidance for deciding which algorithm to use, so it remains a rather arbitrary aspect of this approach.

The *information flow metric* due to Henry and Kafura (Chapter 6) represents a third approach to measuring software designs, and in many respects has proved to be the most influential. As with the previous design metrics, the primary focus here is with couplings between modules; however, these are defined in terms of information flow mechanisms that can potentially couple two modules together, so that one module may influence the behaviour of the other. The information flows may either occur via parameterized communication or via shared global data structures. In addition, they suggest that module size should be taken into consideration and advocate lines of code (LOC) as a reasonable indicator of module size. Whatever the merits or demerits of LOC, it suffers from the serious disadvantage of being unavailable at design time.[4] A strength of the information flow approach is that the metric provides a module-by-module analysis of a design and therefore may be employed to identify outliers or 'rogue' modules—those with particular problems, for instance as a result of inadequate refinement, lack of data isolation or whatever. Henry and Kafura use the UNIX operating system to demonstrate this type of metric application. In addition, they illustrate how it is possible to compare alternative designs, so that, theoretically, one could produce a range of candidate solutions and then use the metric to identify the 'best' design.

The second group of papers have as their concern the requirements analysis and specification stages of a software project. One reason for the considerable level of interest in this area is the need to obtain accurate cost and size predictions very early on in a project. For software projects at least, this has proved notoriously difficult, with dramatic cost and delivery date over-runs being not infrequent. The excerpt from Boehm's paper (Chapter 7) summarizes work on cost estimation models including his own COCOMO model, the Wolverton model and Putnam's SLIM. (For more detailed accounts, readers should refer to Boehm's (1981) encyclopaedic book *Software Engineering Economics*.) He also considers the empirical support for these models, noting for instance that, for a sample of 63 projects at TRW, the model was able to predict within a 20 per cent accuracy level for 68 per cent of the projects. Boehm concludes by arguing that, until there is both a measure of agreement concerning data definitions and a commitment by organizations to data collection on a large scale so as to calibrate cost models,[5] there will be only limited progress in this arena.

---

[3] An alternative means of evaluating automatically created software designs is given by Ince and Hekmatpour (1988) in Volume Two of this work.

[4] This unavailability of LOC may be less of a problem than it appears, since a number of empirical studies have suggested that its contribution to the performance of the metric is at best marginal; consequently many researchers have excluded it from their analysis. See Ince (Chapter 15 below) for a more detailed discussion.

[5] The need to calibrate cost estimation models between different environments has been borne out by others, for example Kitchenham and Taylor (1984) and Kemerer (Chapter 16 below).

The models described by Boehm all assume that it is possible to estimate the size of the system to be delivered externally to the model, usually in terms of LOC. Albrecht and Gaffney (Chapter 8), on the other hand, adopt a rather different position to the cost estimation models described above, by attempting to provide a basis for estimating the size of a specification in terms of the amount of functionality that is to be delivered. This is known as *function point analysis*. It is based on analysing a specification document and deriving a weighted count of all the individual requirements, the weight depending upon the type of requirement with, for example, interface requirements receiving a different weight to an enquiry-type requirement. In many ways this approach is complementary to the algorithmic models, since it is possible to use the function points metric as an alternative size input to estimated LOC.[6] Function points are being widely adopted by the software industry and a number of derivatives have emerged, for example Mark II function points (Symons, 1988) and, for real-time applications, feature points (Jones, 1987).

To summarize, these more recent developments of metrics which can be collected from earlier stages of the software project appear to offer considerable promise, most notably in their ability to provide much needed information at a time when it is still possible for a project to react comparatively cheaply. But much work remains to be done before these metrics receive widespread acceptance, particularly in the domains of validation, tool support and their incorporation into software engineering environments and processes. These issues will be addressed in subsequent parts of this book and Volume Two of this work.

---

[6] Of course, there is the danger of over-adjusting for environmental factors by applying the technical complexity factors for the function points and then repeating the effect with the algorithmic model cost drivers. The simplest remedy is to use unadjusted function points.

4

RIPPLE EFFECT ANALYSIS OF SOFTWARE MAINTENANCE

S. S. Yau, J. S. Collofello and T. M. MacGregor

Northwestern University

ABSTRACT

Maintenance of large-scale software systems is a complex and expensive process. Large-scale software systems often possess a set of both functional and performance requirements. Thus, it is important for maintenance personnel to consider the ramifications of a proposed program modification from both a functional and a performance perspective. In this chapter the ripple effect that results as a consequence of program modification will be analysed. A technique is developed to analyse this ripple effect from both functional and performance perspectives. A figure-of-merit is then proposed to estimate the complexity of program modification. This figure can be used as a basis upon which various modifications can be evaluated.

4.1 INTRODUCTION

It is well known that the maintenance cost of large-scale software systems has been continuously increasing and has become the single dominant cost item during a large-scale software system's life cycle. Although maintenance activities have not been clearly defined—one may consider maintenance activities to include the processes of correcting software errors, improving performance and accommodating

71

new capabilities after the system is operational (Rammoorthy and Ho 1975, Belady and Lehman 1976; Mills 1976)—estimates of maintenance cost have ranged from 40% (Boehm 1973) to 67% (Zelkowitz 1978)[1] of the total cost during a large-scale software systems life cycle. It is obvious that, in order to reduce the high cost of software, the most effective way is to understand the nature of software maintenance and to develop more efficient maintenance techniques.

Although very little research has been done in this area, a significant result developed by Belady and Lehman (1976) is the two models for understanding the nature of software maintenance. The first model aids in understanding the internal distribution and propagation of errors in the program. In this model, errors are eliminated from the program through efforts of the programming team; the only purpose of the team is to eliminate errors in the program. The second model expands the role of the team to make decisions as to what actions (e.g. communications, administration, error correction, documentation, etc.) should be performed. Model 1 is a measure of complexity due to ageing. Model 2 shows a relationship between the budget, which bounds the total activity of error elimination and documentation plus other miscellaneous actions, and program complexity. These models are admittedly incomplete, but they do represent a significant starting-point in trying to understand the nature of software maintenance.

One of the important conclusions made by Belady and Lehman is that program complexity will always remain a monotonically increasing function of time, primarily because of maintenance activity. Thus, the primary thrust in performing software maintenance research should be to develop better maintenance techniques so that unexpected side-effects that usually greatly increase the complexity of the modified program will not be introduced.

In this paper, we shall present a software maintenance technique for helping the maintenance programmer to deal with the ripple effect, from the location of the modification to the other parts of the system that are affected by the modification. Ripple effect is the phenomenon by which changes to one program area have tendencies to be felt in other program areas (Haney 1972). One aspect of this ripple effect is logical in nature. It involves identifying program areas that require additional maintenance activity to ensure their consistency with the initial change. Another aspect of this ripple effect concerns the performance of the system. It involves analysing changes to one program area which may affect the performance of other program areas. The maintenance technique presented in this paper analyses this ripple effect from both the logical and the performance perspectives. This is required since a large-scale program usually has both functional and performance requirements which must be preserved by the maintenance activity.

The maintenance technique based on ripple effect analysis can be a powerful tool for maintenance practitioners. It can help them understand the scope of effect of their changes on the program. It also aids them in determining what parts of the program must be checked for consistency. The net results of applying our technique are:

---

[1] [More recent data suggests that maintenance costs are increasing yet further as a proportion of total costs—M.J.S.]

- Smoother implementation of changes is made.
- Fewer faults are injected into the program during the changes.
- Less degradation (through increased understanding) of program structure occurs.
- The growth rate of complexity decreases.
- The overall program's operating life is extended.

Another significant product of our analysis of ripple effect is the computation of the complexity of a proposed program modification. The complexity proposed in this paper provides a measure that reflects the amount of work involved in performing maintenance and, thus, provides a standard on which comparisons of modifications can be made.

It should be noted that the maintenance technique presented in this paper is independent of the language used in the program and applicable to existing programs as well as newly implemented programs incorporating state-of-the-art design techniques. The technique does not provide maintenance personnel with proposals for modifying the program. Instead, the technique is applied after the maintenance personnel have generated a number of possible maintenance proposals. The complexity of modification can then be computed for each of the proposed program modifications, and the maintenance personnel can then select the best modification from both a logical and a performance perspective. The changes felt in other program areas as a result of the modification can then be made consistent by analysis of the ripple effect.

4.2 LOGICAL RIPPLE EFFECT

Maintenance involves changes of a program to correct errors, improve efficiency and extend the program's capability. When making a program modification, the maintenance practitioner tries to choose a solution that is compatible with the rest of the program. A change of this sort would try to use existing program variables when realizing the modification. Unfortunately, the practitioner cannot always choose a solution that is compatible. Instead of using program variables to realize a solution, the practitioner might be forced to redefine several program variables in order to introduce an acceptable solution. Solutions of this type tend to spawn errors in other program areas, because the maintenance practitioner fails to check all portions of the program affected by the initial change to ensure their consistency. Program areas that are inconsistent with an initial change contain potential errors.

To illustrate this concept, let us assume that a modification is made to the program shown in Fig. 4.1. Let the result of this modification re-define the variable definition CSID to X1*X1. To complete the modification, the practitioner must examine all other program areas for inconsistency caused by CSID. A scan of the program reveals that control definition (CSID.GE.O) in module IROOTS can be inconsistent with the new definition of CSID. The maintenance practitioner must examine (CSID.GE.O) to ensure that it is compatible with the initial modification. Failure to supply this additional maintenance effort results in (CSID.GE.O) being spawned as a potential error.

```
C
C MODULE MAIN
C SOLUTION OF THE QUADRATIC EQUATION
C A*X*X + B*X + C = 0
      COMMON XR1,XR2,XI
      READ 100  (A,B,C)
100 FORMAT (3F10.4)
      X1 = -B/(2.*A)
      XR = X1*X1
      DISC = XR - C/A
      CSID = X1*X1 - C/A
      CALL RROOTS (CSID,DISC,X1)
      WRITE 100  XR1,XR2,XI
      END

C
C MODULE RROOTS
      SUBROUTINE RROOTS (CSID,DISC,X1)
      COMMON XR1,XR2,XI
      IF (DISC.LT.0) GOTO 10
      X2 = SQRT(DISC)
      XR1 = X1 = X2
      XR2 = X1 - X2
      XI = 0.
 10 CONTINUE
      CALL IROOTS (CSID,DISC,X1)
      RETURN

C
C MODULE IROOTS
      SUBROUTINE IROOTS (CSID,DISC,X1)
      COMMON XR1,XR2,XI
      IF (CSID.GE.0) GOTO 10
      X2 = SQRT (-DISC)
      XR1 = X1
      XR2 = X1
      XI = X2
 10 CONTINUE
      RETURN
```

Figure 4.1. An example for illustrating logical ripple effect.

The phenomena by which a change to CSID in the module affects control definition (CSID.GE.O) in IROOTS is defined as *logical ripple effect*. For small programs, such as that shown in Fig. 4.1, logical ripple effect can be completely accounted for by manually scanning the program to identify all potential errors that require additional maintenance activity to ensure their compatibility with the initial modification. For large-scale programs composed of many modules, manually scanning of the program is slow, time-consuming, costly, and may result in some potential errors being undetected. Identification of program areas containing potential errors can be automated using error flow analysis, where all program variable definitions involved in the initial modification represent primary error sources from which inconsistency propagates to other program areas. In essence, those program variable definitions are the sources from which potential errors flow. By knowing the primary error sources involved in a program modification and the program's error characteristics, program areas affected by logical ripple effect can be identified. These areas require additional maintenance activity.

Identification of affected program areas is made by internally tracking each primary error source and its respective secondary error sources within the respective module to a point of exit. A secondary error source is a variable or control definition implicated through the usage of a primary error source. Secondary error sources must be examined to ensure that they are not inconsistent with the variables involved in the initial change. A point of exit in a module exists at a place in the module where another module is invoked or at its normal termination point. At each point of exit, a determination is made as to which primary and secondary error sources propagate across module boundaries. Those error sources that propagate across module boundaries become primary error sources within those modules whose effects must be traced. Tracing and propagation continue until no new secondary error sources are created.

To illustrate these concepts, let us re-examine the program shown in Fig. 4.1. Variable definition CSID is a primary error source which can be traced through module MAIN without creating any new secondary error sources. At the exit point of MAIN, which is the invocation call to RROOTS, a determination is made by examining RROOTS invocation call that primary error source CSID propagates to RROOTS. CSID becomes a primary error source associated with RROOTS whose effect must be traced. Tracing CSID through RROOTS does not cause any secondary error sources to be created. At an exit point of RROOTS, a determination is made that CSID propagates to IROOTS. CSID becomes a primary error source associated with IROOTS. Tracing the flow of CSID reveals that CSID creates secondary error source (CSID.GE.$\emptyset$). Tracing and propogation halt because no new secondary error sources can be created. CSID is a primary error source. (CSID.GE.$\emptyset$) is a secondary error source which must be examined to ensure that it is not inconsistent with the initial modification.

Computation of logical ripple effect for a modular program is a complex process which requires the completion of two functional stages of processing before logical ripple can be computed. Stage 1, lexical analysis, produces the basis which is used by the second stage for computing logical ripple effect. For each module in a precedence order defined from the program's invocation graph, the module's text is statically scanned to produce a control flow graph based on program blocks (Aho and Ullman 1977). A program block is a maximal set of ordered statements such that it is always executed from the first statement to the last statement and all the statements are executed if one of them is executed. Lexical analysis characterizes each program block v_i in terms of its source capable set C_i, its potential propagator set P_i and a flow mapping $C_i \leftarrow f(P_i)$. C_i is the set of definitions in block v_i which cause potential errors to exist within and flow from v_i. P_i is the set of all usages in v_i which can cause elements in the source capable set to flow from v_i. To illustrate this characterization, consider the block of statements in module IROOTS shown in Fig. 4.1 composed of $X2 = SQRT(-DISC)$, $XR1 = X1$, $XR2 = X1$, and $XI = X2$. Lexical analysis produces the following characterization sets: $C_i = \{X2, XR1, XR2, XI\}$, $P_i = \{DISC, X1\}$, and flow mapping $[\{X2, XI\} \leftarrow f(DISC); \{XR1, XR2\} \leftarrow f(XI)]$. The source capable set, potential propagator set and flow mapping define the error flow properties of the block. The error flow properties of various blocks in the module in conjunction with control flow graph of the module form a characterization used by stage 2 to compute ripple effect.

Stage 2 of the functional processing applies an algorithm to compute ripple effect. The algorithm operates upon each module characterization to trace error sources from their points of definition to their exit points. The algorithm is initialized with a set of modules and their primary error sources involved in the initial change. These are supplied by the maintenance practitioner. For each module M_j initially involved in the modification, the algorithm traces the intra-module flow of potential errors from the primary error sources through the various program blocks. When the flow of error sources stabilizes, the algorithm applies a block identification criterion to determine which blocks within the module must be examined to ensure that they are not inconsistent with the initial change. After block identification is complete, a propagation criterion is applied to module M_j to define those error sources that flow from M_j to other modules that M_j invokes, and to modules that invoke M_j. Error flow across module boundaries constitutes inter-module error flow. For each module affected by inter-module error flow, the algorithm traces intra-module error flow in the same manner as for M_j to determine the net effect that the propagated error sources have on their respective modules. The algorithm executes in this manner until inter-module error flow stabilizes. An intermediate result that exists at this point is the set of modules in the program that are affected by the inter-module flow of error sources created by the primary error sources involved in the change. The algorithm completes its execution by applying a ripple effect criterion to each module affected by inter-module error flow to determine if the module requires additional maintenance activity to ensure that the module is not inconsistent with the initial change. In this example, both modules RROOTS and IROOTS are affected by the inter-module error flow; however, only IROOTS is affected by ripple effect.

4.3 PERFORMANCE RIPPLE EFFECT

Analysis of performance ripple effect requires the identification of modules whose performance may change as a consequence of software modifications. This is a complex task. The identification is complicated by the fact that performance dependencies often exist among modules that are otherwise functionally and logically independent. A *performance dependency relationship* is defined to exist from module A to module B if and only if a change in module A can have an effect on the performance of module B.

It is obvious that, when a logical or functional error is discovered in the software, this error can affect other modules. Analogously, when a performance change is made, the scope of effect of the change can be determined by examining the mechanisms by which this change can affect other modules. We have identified the following eight mechanisms which may exist in large-scale programs by which changes in performance as a consequence of a software modification are propagated throughout the program:

1. *Parallel execution*   In the maintenance phase it is possible to introduce software modifications to a module which can destroy its ability to be executed with other modules in parallel. Major changes in performance may result because of execution delays and contention for resources previously alleviated through the parallel execution.
2. *Shared resources*   When modules are forced to share resources, the times when each module requests and releases common resources are important performance parameters. In a multi-programming environment, performance degradation may be experienced by modules whose execution is being affected by the denial of requested resources which are currently dedicated to other modules.
3. *Interprocess communication*   When one module must send a message to another module, the performance of the module receiving the message is dependent upon when the message is sent. Thus, modifications to the module sending the message that alter the time when the message is sent can affect the performance of the module designated to receive the message.
4. *Called modules*   Modifications to modules in the maintenance phase can be divided into two types. A bounded modification to a module is a modification that does not alter the performance of the module. An unbounded modification to a module is a modification that does alter the performance of the module. An unbounded modification to a called module will affect the performance of all modules calling it.
5. *Shared data structures*   Changes in the contents of shared data structures can affect the performance of other modules utilizing the shared data structure. The basic dynamic attributes contributing to performance in this area are module's storage and retrieval times for entries in the data structures.
6. *Sensitivity to the rate of input*   Changes in input rates to a process can have major repercussions in terms of its functional and performance requirements. For example, it can lead to saturation and possibly overflow of data structures involved with the processing of the input. The increased frequency of input arrivals may also lead to interruptions in processing which can lead to both functional and performance requirement violations.
7. *Execution priorities*   During the maintenance phase, it is important for the maintenance practitioner to recognize the effect of a proposed modification with respect to the existing priorities in the system. Modification of existing priorities can create conflicts in the system such as resource contention, which can lead to performance degradation.
8. *Abstractions*   The use of abstractions is a popular design tool and adds to the maintainability of the system by hiding design decisions. From the performance

perspective of maintainability, however, abstractions are 'Trojan horses'. This is because a change in the implementation of the abstraction will very likely affect the performance of the abstraction, and, thus, the performance of all modules utilizing the abstraction. This is a classic example of a case where a modification to the software during maintenance does not produce any functional or logical changes, but does result in performance changes.

Performance attributes of a program are defined as attributes corresponding to measurements of key aspects of the execution of the program. There is a distinct relationship between performance attributes and the eight mechanisms for the propagation of performance changes. These eight mechanisms operate as links between the performance attributes of modules; in other words, a change in a performance attribute of one module can affect a performance attribute in another module via one of the eight mechanisms.

We have identified the following 13 performance attributes linked with the eight mechanisms discussed above:

1. The ability of the module to execute in parallel with another module
2. For each resource in contention, the relative time that the module seizes the resource
3. For each resource in contention, the relative time that the module releases the resource
4. The relative time that the module begins execution
5. The relative time that the module transmits a message to another module
6. The execution time of the module
7. For each resource utilized in the module, the resource utilization by the module
8. For each dependent iterative structure in the module, the number of iterations
9. For each data structure, the storage and retrieval times for entries in the data structure
10. For each data structure, the number of entries in the data structure
11. For each data structure, the service time of an entry in the data structure, i.e. the relative time that an entry remains in the data structure before being serviced
12. For each dependent iterative structure in the module containing overhead incurring references, the number of iterations
13. The rate of input to the module

There is also a relationship between the performance attributes and the performance requirements of the program. The performance requirements can be decomposed qualitatively into performance attributes that contribute to either the preservation or the violation of the performance requirements. Thus, we can associate a set of performance attributes with each performance requirement such that, if a performance attribute in the set is affected by a modification, then the performance requirement associated with this set is also affected.

Since the performance attributes of a program correspond to measurements of key aspects of the execution of the program, they can be affected during the maintenance process by modifications to the program. A *critical section* of a program can be associated with each performance attribute such that, if this critical section

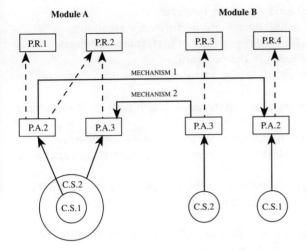

Figure 4.2. Relationship of performance requirements (P.R.), performance attributes (P.A.), critical sections (C.S.), and the mechanisms for propagation of performance changes in a program.

is modified, the corresponding performance attribute may be affected. For example, if the performance attribute under consideration is the execution time between when a module begins execution and when it transmits a message, the corresponding critical section is that section of code between module invocation and transmission of the message.

The relationship of performance attributes, performance requirements, critical sections and the mechanisms for the propagation of performance changes in a program forms the basis for the concept of a performance-change ripple effect as a consequence of software modification. When a critical section is modified, it may affect the corresponding performance attributes. A change in these performance attributes may then ripple, i.e. may affect other performance attributes via any applicable mechanisms.

This performance-change ripple effect is illustrated in Fig. 4.2. In this example, assume we are attempting to identify the performance ripple effect as a consequence of modifying C.S.1 of module A. In this example, P.A.2 and P.A.3 of module A would be affected. Thus, performance requirements P.R.1 and P.R.2 would have to be retested to ensure that they have not been violated. In addition, P.A.2 of module B would be affected via mechanism 1. Thus, P.R.4 would have to be retested to ensure that it too has not been violated.

4.4 MAINTENANCE TECHNIQUE

In this section, we outline our maintenance technique which analyses both logical and performance ripple. The maintenance technique analyses the program with respect to the proposed modification in order to identify the program blocks that may be affected by the modification and must be analysed for consistency, as well as the performance requirements that may be affected by the modification. The maintenance technique consists of the following steps:

1. Perform lexical analysis on all modules in the program.
2. Decompose the performance requirements into performance attributes.
3. Identify all of the mechanisms for the propagation of performance changes, critical sections and performance attributes in the program.
4. For each module initially involved in the maintenance change, determine its primary error sources.
5. Apply the ripple effect algorithm to compute the set of blocks in each module affected by ripple.
6. Identify the critical sections initially involved in the maintenance change.
7. For each of the critical sections, identify the corresponding performance attributes affected.
8. Utilizing the performance dependency relationships in existence in the program, construct a ripple list of modules and their performance attributes which are affected by the modification.
9. Identify the performance requirements that are affected by modification of the performance attributes identified in the previous step.

The maintenance technique can be automated for large-scale software. At present, we are refining the algorithms involved in this technique. The results will be presented in subsequent papers.[2]

4.5 COMPLEXITY OF PROGRAM MODIFICATION

In this section, we propose an estimate of the complexity of program modification, which should reflect the amount of programmer's effort require to incorporate a particular program modification and to take care of all its ripple effect. This figure can be used as a basis upon which various program modifications can be evaluated in terms of programmer's effort.

Let us consider that a modification η_p is to be made on a module M_j that will require the changes of the set B_{jp} of blocks in M_j without any ripple effect consideration. Let ψ_{jp} be the set of modules that have to be examined and possibly changed due to η_p or its ripple effect, and let it include M_j. Let E_{ip} be the set of blocks in module $M_i \in \psi_{jp}$ that have to be examined and possibly changed because of η_p and its ripple effect from both logical and performance points of view. Then, the programmer's effort required to perform the modification η_p on M_j and take care of all its ripple effect can be estimated by the following expression:

$$G(Q_j, B_{jp}) + \sum_{M_i \in \psi_{jp}} \{D(Q_i) + F(Q_i, E_{ip}) + G(Q_i, E_{ip})\},$$

where Q_i is the complexity of module M_i; $D(Q_i)$ is the amount of programmer's effort to understand M_i, which is a function of Q_i; $G(Q_i, B_{jp})$ is the programmer's effort for making the modification η_p; and $F(Q_i, E_{ip})$ and $G(Q_i, E_{jp})$ are the programmer's effort for examining E_{ip} and making the necessary changes due to η_p's ripple effect in M_i.

---

[2] [See e.g. Yau and Collofello (1985). M.J.S.]

If the original modification η_p involves t modules, $M_j^k, k = 1, 2, \ldots, t$, then the programmer's effort required to perform the modification η_p and take care of all its ripple effect will depend upon the way the programmer is doing the changes, such as whether the programmer will perform the changes in M_j^k in a particular sequence and this ripple effect for one module before starting the changes in the next module in the particular sequence, or will perform the changes in M_j^k and their ripple effect in some fashion involving more than one module at a time. For large-scale programs, in order to have a better chance to avoid introducing errors, it is a good practice for the programmer to perform the changes in M_j^k and their ripple effect in the former way. In this case, the programmer's effort required to perform the modification η_p on $M_j^k, k = 1, 2, \ldots, t$, and take care of all its ripple effect in a particular sequence of M_j^k can be estimated by the following expression:

$$\sum_{k=1}^{t} G(Q_j^k, B_{jp}^k) + \sum_{M_i \in \bigcup_{k=1}^{} \psi_{jp}^k} D(Q_i) + \sum_{k=1}^{t} \sum_{M_i \in \psi_{jp}^k} \{F(Q_i, E_{ip}) + G(Q_i, E_{ip})\}$$

where ψ_{jp}^k is the set of modules that have to be examined and possibly changed as a result of the changes of η_p in M_j^k and its ripple effect; $G(Q_j^k, E_{ip}^k)$ is the programmer's effort for performing the changes of η_p in M_j^k in the particular sequence after all the changes in preceding modules and their ripple effect have been taken care of; and $F(Q_i, E_{ip})$ and $G(Q_i, E_{ip})$ are the programmer's effort for examining E_{ip} and making the necessary changes arising from the ripple effect in M_i for the original changes in M_j^k in the particular sequence.

It is noted that in these estimates the complexity Q_i of the modules M_i involved plays an important role in the required programmer's effort. The complexity of the program structure above the module level is not explicitly included in any particular term of these estimates, but it is implicitly considered when we identify the ripple effect of program modification.

It is also noted that, among the terms in these estimates, $\Sigma D(Q_i)$ and $\Sigma F(Q_i, E_{ip})$ constitute most of the programmer's total effort. In other words, the amount of programmer's effort $\Sigma G(Q_i, E_{ip})$ required to make the changes of the code is only a small portion of the total effort, and in some cases it may be neglected in evaluating various proposed program modifications. Future work is required to establish quantitative measures of these terms.

4.6 CONCLUSION

In this paper we have presented the framework of a maintenance technique for ana-lysing the ripple effect of program modifications from both logical and performance perspective. This technique can be automated and serves as a valuable tool for both maintenance programmers and managers. The details of the algorithms in this technique will be presented in subsequent papers. We are also in the process of demonstrating the automation of this technique.

Much work still needs to be done in this area. In addition to developing quantitative measures of the programmer's effort described in the last section, we also need to develop techniques for generating various modifications to satisfy specification changes.

ACKNOWLEDGEMENTS

This work was supported by Rome Air Development Center, US Air Force, under Contract no. F30602-76-C-0397.

5

SYSTEM STRUCTURE ANALYSIS: CLUSTERING WITH DATA BINDINGS

David H. Hutchens and Victor R. Basili

Clemson University and University of Maryland

ABSTRACT

This chapter examines the use of cluster analysis as a tool for system modularization. Several clustering techniques are discussed and used on two medium-size systems and a group of small projects. The small projects are presented because they provide examples (that will fit into a paper) of certain types of phenomenon. Data bindings between the routines of the system provide the basis for the bindings. It appears that the clustering of data bindings provide a meaningful view of system modularization.

5.1 INTRODUCTION

An aspect of complexity that has long been recognized, but seldom measured, is the complexity associated with system modularization, i.e. the grouping of procedures into modules within the system. It has been argued by many (Myers 1978; Yourdon and Constantine 1979) that system modules should have small interfaces (parameters and shared data) and that the internal components of the modules should be strongly connected. It has also been suggested that modules should be developed so that a fault is contained within a small module. Faults might be used as a means of determining if modularization techniques have placed together those procedures that are often sharing faults.

The analysis of the interface between the small components of the system can be used to determine the modularization that those interfaces define. This analysis is called *clustering*, and the modules so defined will be referred to as clusters. Armed with this knowledge, one might ask questions about how closely the current modularization (as described in the documentation) corresponds with the modularization defined by the clustering. One might also consider the strength and coupling of the modularization of the system defined by the clustering. The information gained from this work should be of interest to designers and maintainers. It may also be used to obtain a modularization of a system that has no (or little) existing high-level documentation, giving maintainers a handle on the structure of the system.

The more closely the objectively defined modules correspond to the modules defined by the developer, the better one should feel about the design. However, it is unlikely that the two views of the system will correspond exactly. Something can be learned about a system from the differences. It may also be possible to derive some basic measurements of the quality of the modularity from the results of this analysis. These measures may provide a means of comparing various design proposals and monitoring systems during maintenance.

Each of these possibilities will be considered in the following sections. Having stated the research goals, it is now appropriate to consider the work that has been done by others and provide the foundations of this work.

5.2 BACKGROUND

Data organization metrics are measures of data use and visibility. Several types of data organization metrics appear in the literature. Some of these are briefly mentioned here. *Data binding* (Basili and Turner 1975) is an example of a module interaction metric. *Span* (Elshoff 1976b) measures the proximity of references to each data item. As such, it qualifies as a data organization metric. *Slicing* (Weiser 1981) can also be considered a data organization metric. A slice is that (not necessarily consecutive) portion of code that is necessary to produce some prescribed partial output from the program. *Fan-in* (Henry et al. 1981) measures the number of procedures that pass data, through parameters or globals, into a given procedure. *Fan-out* is the number of procedures receiving data from the given procedure. Yao and Collofello (1980) use detailed data flow analysis to determine a measure they call *stability*.

5.2.1 Data bindings

Data bindings will be used in this paper to measure the interface between the components of a system. In order to compare this work with other work that has used data bindings, several levels of data bindings will be defined.

A *potential data binding* is defined as an ordered triple (p, x, q) where p and q are procedures and x is a variable within the static scope of both p and q. Potential data bindings reflect the possibility of a data interaction between two components, based upon the locations of p, q and x. That is, there is a possibility that p and q can communicate via the variable x without changing or moving the definition of x.

Whether or not x is mentioned inside of p or q is irrelevant in the computation of potential data bindings.

A *used data binding* is a potential data binding where p and q use x for either reference or assignment. The used data binding requires more work to calculate than the potential data binding as it is necessary to look inside the components p and q. It reflects a similarity between p and q (they both use the variable x).

An *actual data binding* is defined as a used data binding where p assigns a value of x and q references x. The actual data binding is slightly more difficult to calculate, as a distinction between reference and assignment must be maintained. Thus, more memory is required but there is little difference in computation time. The actual data binding counts only those used data bindings where there may be a flow of information from p and q via the variable x. The possible orders of execution for p and q are not considered.

A *control flow data binding* is defined as an actual data binding where there is a 'possibility' of control passing to q after p has had control. The possibility is based on a fairly simple control flow analysis of the program. To be more precise, a possibility is said to exist whenever either (a) there exists a chain of calls from p to q or vice versa, or (b) there exists a procedure r such that there are chains of calls from r to p and from r to q and there exists a path in the directed control flow graph of r connecting the call chain p with the call chain to q. The solution to the general problem of allowable control flow sequences (where allowable means there exists data that will cause the sequence to be followed) is known to be uncomputable. However, one might improve on this measure by using techniques of data flow analysis to prove more paths impossible and thereby to remove more data bindings. It seems unlikely that this added effort will yield enough improvement to justify the effort. This binding requires considerably more computation effort than actual data bindings because static data flow analysis must be performed. Note that a control flow data binding of the form (p, x, q) may exist even though q can never execute after p (because of the dynamic properties of the program).

As an example, consider the following portions of code. The parameter of the call is assumed to be call by value.

```
INT a, b, c, d
PROC p1
  /*uses a, b */
  /*assigns a */
  . . .
  CALL p2
  . . .
PROC p2
  /* uses a, b */
  /* assigns b */
  . . .
  CALL p3 (x)
  . . .
  CALL p4
```

```
    ...
PROC p3 (int e)
    /* uses c, d, e */
    /* assigns c */
    ...
PROC p4
    /* uses c, d */
    /* assigns d */
    ...
START p1
```

In this example, the potential data bindings are

$$(p1, a, p2), (p1, a, p3), (p1, a, p4),$$
$$(p2, a, p1), (p2, a, p3), (p2, a, p4),$$
$$(p3, a, p1), (p3, a, p2), (p3, a, p4),$$
$$(p4, a, p1), (p4, a, p2), (p4, a, p3),$$
$$(p1, b, p2), (p1, b, p3), (p1, b, p4),$$
$$(p2, b, p1), (p2, b, p3), (p2, b, p4),$$
$$(p3, b, p1), (p3, b, p2), (p3, b, p4),$$
$$(p4, b, p1), (p4, b, p2), (p4, b, p3),$$
$$(p1, c, p2), (p1, c, p3), (p1, c, p4),$$
$$(p2, c, p1), (p2, c, p3), (p2, c, p4),$$
$$(p3, c, p1), (p3, c, p2), (p3, c, p4),$$
$$(p4, c, p1), (p4, c, p2), (p4, c, p3),$$
$$(p1, d, p2), (p1, d, p3), (p1, d, p4),$$
$$(p2, d, p1), (p2, d, p3), (p2, d, p4),$$
$$(p3, d, p1), (p3, d, p2), (p3, d, p4),$$
$$(p4, d, p1), (p4, d, p2), (p4, d, p3),$$
$$(p1, e, p3), (p2, e, p3), (p4, e, p3).$$

However, the used data bindings are only

$$(p1, a, p2), (p2, a, p1), (p1, b, p2), (p2, b, p1),$$
$$(p3, c, p4), (p4, c, p3), (p3, d, p4), (p4, d, p3),$$
$$(p2, e, p3).$$

Actual data bindings are

$$(p1, a, p2), (p2, b, p1), (p3, c, p4), (p4, d, p3), (p2, e, p3)$$

and control flow data bindings restrict the set to just

$$(p1, a, p2), (p2, b, p1), (p3, c, p4), (p2, e, p3).$$

Using data bindings The Belady and Evangelisti (1981) study applied used data bindings in determining modules for a system. Based on the study of an IBM operating system, the authors concluded that certain metrics of modularity could be derived from clustering. They used a technique that gave a flat (non-hierarchic) partitioning of the components of the system into modules.

The use of data bindings to determine the appropriate modularization has its drawbacks. A module that hides a data structure is easily found by a data bindings modularization technique. However, a module that defines an abstract data type and has no local data that is shared among the operations on the type will not be located using this method. The reason is that there is no *direct* data bindings between the operations of the module. All of the interactions are indirect through the procedures that use the abstraction. Hence, there are relatively few data bindings between them, and they do not tend to cluster.

It would seem that the abstract data type modules need a different measure of connectivity. However, only explicit syntax such as the package of Ada (TM) (DoD 1982) or the module of MODULA (Wirth 1977) allow abstract data types to be automatically recognized as utility functions and removed from the analysis. Except as noted for specific utility routines, this issue will be ignored in the rest of this paper.

5.2.2 Definition of clustering

Since the components will be grouped based on the strength of their relationships with each other, a reasonable starting point is *mathematical taxonomy*, often referred to as clustering. The idea has been used (see Belady and Evangelisti 1981) to partition a large system into subsystems.

Because there are so many clustering methods and algorithms that have been published (e.g. Anderberg 1973; Duran and Odell 1974; Van Amden 1975; Everitt 1974), the choice of techniques to use is not easy. Owing to our belief that systems and programs are best viewed as hierarchy of modules and our hope that the levels of the hierarchy will provide fertile ground for the definition of measures, this paper will concentrate on clustering methods that exhibit their results in this fashion. This section will give a formal definition of a hierarchic clustering method based on the one presented in Jardin and Sibson (1971).

A *dissimilarity matrix d* for an ordered set P of n elements is defined to be an $n \times n$ matrix such that

1. $d(a, b) \geqslant 0$
2. $d(a, b) = d(b, a)$
3. $d(a, a) = 0$

for all a, b $1 \leqslant a \leqslant n, 1 \leqslant b \leqslant n$. That is, d is a non-negative, real, symmetric matrix with zeros on the main diagonal.

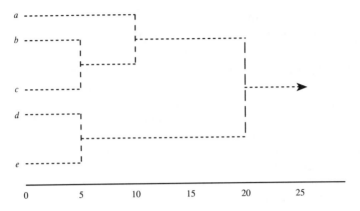

Figure 5.1.

D is defined to be a *dendrogram* over P if

1. D: $[0, \text{infinity}) \rightarrow E(P)$.
2. $0 \leqslant x \leqslant y \Rightarrow D(x) \leqslant D(y)$.
3. There exists $x > 0$ such that $D(x) = P \times P$.
4. Given $x \geqslant 0$, there exists $y > 0$ such that $D(x + y) = D(x)$.

where $E(P)$ is the set of equivalence relations on P. That is, (1) given any non-negative real number x (a level), D yields an equivalence relation. The clusters defined for level x are the equivalence partitions of P defined by $D(x)$. Furthermore, (2) given level $y > x$, each cluster at level x is contained in some cluster at level y. Also, (3) there exists some level at which all of P is in a single cluster. Lastly, (4) is just a uniqueness technicality to handle the ambiguity at those levels where D is discontinuous. Hence a dendrogram might be pictured as drawn in Fig. 5.1. This dendrogram shows (a), (b, c) and (d, e) forming clusters at level 5, (a, b, c) and (d, e) at level 10, and all collapsing together at level 20.

A dendrogram may be represented as a tree where the branches of the tree are the clusters with associated levels and the leaves are the elements of P. The tree for the dendrogram in Fig. 5.1 might be given in Lisp-like notation as

$$(20\,(10a(5bc))(5de)).$$

A *hierarchic cluster method* is a function from the set of dissimilarity matrices to the set of dendrograms over an ordered set P. The basic algorithms that will be used to implement the cluster methods are *agglomerative*, or bottom-up. They iteratively create larger and larger groups, until the elements have coalesced into a single cluster. The elements chosen for grouping are the ones with the smallest dissimilarity. Given an algorithm, a cluster method is determined, although the converse is not true. Algorithms are introduced here because they provide a reasonable way of specifying the cluster methods.

The character of the individual algorithms is determined by the method used to compute the new dissimilarity matrix at each iteration. The dissimilarity between two elements should not change during an iteration. However, at each iteration some elements are replaced by a single element representing a newly formed cluster. It is the dissimilarity between the newly formed clusters and the other elements (including other newly formed clusters) that must be specified.

The classical algorithms include 'single-link', which takes the smallest dissimilarity between the elements of each pair of newly formed clusters as the new dissimilarity coefficient between them. This gives clusters whose elements are connected at the given level. Another algorithm uses the largest dissimilarity between the elements as the new coefficient and gives clusters that are completely connected at the given level. (Strictly speaking, the clusters are completely connected only if all of the elements that combine into a single cluster during one iteration are pairwise related by the same dissimilarity.) Other well-known algorithms use the average dissimilarity or the weighted average dissimilarity as the new coefficient.

5.2.3 Data sources

The Software Engineering Laboratory (SEL) (NASA 1982) data were collected during the development of production software for the NASA Goddard Space Flight Center. The systems used in this work are ground-support systems for satellites and were written in Fortran by Computer Sciences Corporation. The developers have a large amount of experience in building this type of system. Both the users and the developers feel that the overall system designs are fairly good.

Data concerning effort, errors, methods, reused code and other relevant information have been collected for several projects. Most of the data are supplied by the developer on forms prepared for use by the SEL. These forms are normally filled out by the programmer or manager most closely involved with the subject of the form as the knowledge required becomes available. The data have been used to investigate many aspects of system development.

5.3 A MODULARITY STUDY

A technique will be presented that automatically produces a hierarchic module decomposition for a system. The technique is based on data bindings and clustering algorithms. There are several choices to be made in determining the best technique for this application. Some reasonable choices are presented and analysed. The techniques are then used on some sample systems and the results are given.

5.3.1 Specialized clustering techniques

The use of data bindings to determine dissimilarity requires that we abstract the data to give a symmetric matrix. Let $b(i, j)$ be the number of control flow data bindings of the form (i, x, j) or (j, x, i) for some program variable x. A dissimilarity matrix may be computed from the binding matrix b in several ways.

Recomputed bindings   One way was chosen that captures the intuitive notion that, if a component of the system is entirely connected to just one other component, that connection should be computed as a lower dissimilarity than any connection that is not complete. It is based on the percentage of the bindings that connect to either of the two components and are shared by the two components. That is, let p be the dissimilarity matrix defined by

$$p(i, j) = \frac{(\text{sum}\, i + \text{sum}\, j - 2b(i, j))}{(\text{sum}\, i + \text{sum}\, j - b(i, j))}$$

where sum i is the number of data bindings in which i occurs and sum j is the number of data bindings in which j occurs. Since

$$\text{sum}\, i + \text{sum}\, j - b(i, j)$$

is the number of data bindings in which either i or j occur and

$$\text{sum}\, i + \text{sum}\, j - 2b(i, j)$$

is the number of data bindings in which either i or j occur but not both, $p(i, j)$ is the probability that a random data binding chosen from the union of all bindings associated with i or j is not in the intersection of all bindings associated with i and j. Note that, if components i and j have no external connections, then

$$\text{sum}\, i = \text{sum}\, j = b(i, j)$$

and $p(i, j) = 0$. Note also that, if i and j share no common data, then $b(i, j) = 0$ and $p(i, j) = 1$.

For an example, consider the program in Section 5.2.1 with the actual bindings

$$(p1, a, p2), (p2, b, p1), (p3, c, p4), (p4, d, p3), (p2, e, p3).$$

A binding matrix can be computed such that the (i, j)th entry is the number of data bindings between the ith and the jth procedures, giving

	p1	p2	p3	p4
p1	0	2	0	0
p2	2	0	1	0
p3	0	1	0	2
p4	0	0	2	0

Then the dissimilarity matrix computed as outlined above is

	p1	p2	p3	p4
p1	0	1/3	1	1
p2	1/3	0	4/5	1
p3	1	4/5	0	1/3
p4	1	1	1/3	0

Another degree of freedom in clustering is the choice of the algorithm. While any of the previously presented algorithms might be used, they do not correspond to the intuitive notion that the dissimilarity between two clusters should be directly related to the number of data bindings that cross the boundary. To achieve this property, a new dissimilarity matrix is computed from the bindings matrix at each iteration in the clustering process. This, however, introduces another problem. Each of the algorithms stated earlier has the property that, if the elements with least dissimilarity are merged (into perhaps several clusters) at one iteration, then the next dissimilarity matrix will have entries that are all greater than the least non-diagonal entry of the last matrix. If the dissimilarity matrix is recomputed at each iteration based on the bindings matrix, it is possible that the new matrix will contain values that are smaller than any that existed in the last matrix. The resulting tree from this new approach is not a dendrogram.

As an example, start with the following binding matrix for the elements (A, B, C):

$$0 \quad 1 \quad 2$$
$$1 \quad 0 \quad 3$$
$$2 \quad 3 \quad 0$$

That is, there are three procedures, A, B, and C, with 1 data binding between A and B, 2 between A and C, and 3 between B and C. This produces the dissimilarity matrix

$$0 \quad 5/6 \quad 4/6$$
$$5/6 \quad 0 \quad 3/6$$
$$4/6 \quad 3/6 \quad 0$$

Joining B and C into a cluster produces a new binding matrix:

$$0 \quad 3$$
$$3 \quad 0$$

The new dissimilarity matrix is

$$0 \quad 0$$
$$0 \quad 0$$

causing (BC) to be united with (A) at level 0 to get the tree

$$(0 \ A(1/2 \ B \ C))$$

which is clearly not a dendrogram (since the level of a node must be greater than the level of a son and $0 \leqslant 1/2$).

The tree can be converted to a dendrogram in a natural way. If it is assumed that any cluster that was created with a lower value than its son was really included in the same cluster (at the same level) as its son, the tree can be collapsed into a dendrogram.

The above example would thus give the simple dendrogram described by

$$(1/2 \ A \ B \ C)$$

The dendrogram obtained from the latter approach has many good properties. Each cluster is based on the bindings to the other clusters, regardless of how late in the clustering process it was formed. This method will be called *recomputed binding clustering*.

Expected bindings A problem with the proposed clustering method is that the levels are somewhat incomparable. That is, at a point in the algorithm where there are a large number of elements (e.g. 50), there is less likelihood that two components will have a very large percentage of their total bindings occuring between them than when there are a few elements (e.g. 3). It seems reasonable to attempt to weight the binding levels relative to the total number of elements under consideration in a given iteration. In particular, if there are n elements under consideration and there are k bindings involving either element i or element j, one would expect $k/(n-1)$ of the bindings to be between i and j were the bindings to be distributed in a uniformly random way. Hence those with exactly $k/(n-1)$ interconnections should have a similar level whether $n = 5$ or $n = 250$. One might therefore compute the new dissimilarity as

$$d(i, j) = (k/(n-1))/\text{bind}\,(i, j)$$

for each i not equal to j at each iteration. This method will be referred to as *expected binding clustering*.

Consider the example of the four procedures $p1, p2, p3$ and $p4$ from Section 5.2.1. If we take the used data bindings, the binding matrix is

	$p1$	$p2$	$p3$	$p4$
$p1$	0	2	0	0
$p2$	2	0	1	0
$p3$	0	1	0	2
$p4$	0	0	2	0

This gives the dissimilarity matrix of

	$p1$	$p2$	$p3$	$p4$
$p1$	0	1/2	I	I
$p2$	1/2	0	5/3	I
$p3$	I	5/3	0	1/2
$p4$	I	I	1/2	0

where I is infinity. The first iteration combines $(p1, p2)$ and $(p3, p4)$ at level 1/2, giving the new binding matrix

$$\begin{array}{cc} 0 & 1 \\ 1 & 0 \end{array}$$

The new dissimilarity matrix happens to be the same as the binding matrix, and we get the expected binding dendrogram

$$(1\ (1/2\ p1\ p2)\ (1/2\ p3\ p4))$$

This dendrogram is intuitively satisfying, as $p1$ and $p2$ seem to be closely bound and $p3$ and $p4$ seem to be closely bound. Note that, if we use the control flow data bindings, $p3$ and $p4$ no longer seem so closely bound. Computing the expected binding dendrogram for these bindings yields

$$(1\ p3\ p4(1/2\ p1\ p2))$$

reflecting the reduced cohesion between $p3$ and $p4$.

5.3.2 System fingerprints

The clusters that are derived from a system are analogous to a star system. That is, there may be several small subsystems that revolve around the main subsystems. This analogy leads to the naming of some various types of system fingerprints.

Each of these fingerprints will be illustrated by a program chosen from the group of class projects used by the Basili and Reiter (1981) study. These programs implement a small language on a stack-based machine, simulated for the students by the three procedures POP, PUSH, and INTERP. Not surprisingly, these three procedures tend to cluster quickly. Control-flow data bindings were computed for these projects and form the basis for the analysis.

Indentation will take the place of parentheses in the examples. That is, the dendrogram

$$(8 \ A \ (5 \ B \ C))$$

will be given as

$$8 \ A$$

$$5 \ B \ C$$

Planetary systems are those that have several subsystems that are connected to form the whole system. These systems may (although not necessarily) have a larger subsystem that acts as the core of the system.

As an example, the following is an expected binding cluster of one of the 19 compiler projects. For example binding clusters in the following example, all level numbers were multiplied by 100 and hence are expressed as percentages.

```
66   COMMENT ASIMPID BACKUP
     54   HASH ALLOCATERETURN DUMPSYMBOLS FINDIT
          LOOKUP ALLOCATESEGMENT ALLOCATEARG
          ADDRESS
          27   ACONST
               24   AARRID AID
                    19   AFUNCID ASCAN ARPAREN
                         AEVALEXP EXPRESSION ALPAREN
                         AFLUSH APRODCODE ASTACKOR
                         ADOIFLUSH
          45
               42   DCL CODEGEN SEGMENT
                7   POP INTERP PUSH
               41   PROGRAM
                    32   STMT CONSTGEN
          13   NEXTCHAR SCAN NEXTSYMB
               SPECIALCHAR IDENTIFIER CONSTANT
```

Notice how the clusters tend to form distinct parts of the compiler. The group at the bottom (at level 13) is the scanner. The group a few lines above it (at level 7) is the interpreter. An interesting group is the large cluster close to the top (at level 27). This cluster was written by one of the members of the programming team (his name began with an A). Also notice how all of the routines fall together when the symbol table routines are added (at level 54).

Black hole systems have no visible planets. The clustering process finds one key subsystem that then absorbs the rest of the system. This may be a natural phenomenon associated with the way the system is built, or it may be a bias of the clustering scheme. Since the bindings are recomputed at each iteration in the process, a cluster that has already been formed may contain more bindings with other elements than do small elements. Hence the strongest connection that exists may be with the already formed and growing black hole. If this happens, the black hole may tend to absorb procedures before their relationships with other parts of the system are discovered.

The following example is also an expected binding cluster of one of the 19 compiler projects:

```
100  STMTLIST DCLLIST
     87  HEADING ACTUALLIST
         86  CODEDUMP INPUTCHAR ASSIGN IFSTMT
             WHILESTMT RETURNSTMT READSTMT
             WRITESTMT EXP LOGICALPROD RELATION
             ADDEXP MULTIEXP FACTOR
         24  POP
             16  INTERP PUSH
         71  CALLSTMT
             65  SCANNER
                 55  PROGRAM
                     53  ACTUAL VARIABLE
                         PRIMARY
                         46  SEGMENTLIST
                             FORMALPARM
                             41  SEARCHSYMTAB
                                 SYMTABDUMP
                                 36  ARRAYDCLLIST IDLIST
```

The symbol table routines, SEARCHSYMTAB, SYMTABDUMP, ARRAYDCLLIST and IDLIST, seem to dominate this program in a different way from the previous one. Here they are the quickest to cluster and then they form a nucleus about which everything else revolves. It would seem that this group was less effective in isolating the symbol table from the other routines. One might guess, just from the appearance of the clusters, that many of the routines in this program have intimate knowledge of the structure of the symbol table. This is most clearly true of ARRAYDCLLIST and IDLIST, which build entries directly in the table.

Gas cloud systems are those that show no tendency to cluster. These systems are possibly poorly designed as there is no strength to the modules and a large degree of coupling between them. None of the compilers provides a clear example of this type of system. However, the following dendrogram has some of the properties:

```
87  MAIN ASSIGNMENT SEGRETURN STATEMENT IO
    EXPRESSION PROGRAM WHILESTMT IFSTMT LOAD
    JUMP PARSE INITIALIZE DECLARATION SEGMENT
    SEARCH SEGCALL PRIMARY
    76  POP
```

```
73  INTERP PUSH
83  SCAN NUMBER IDENTIFIER GETNEXTNONBLANK
```

This dendrogram is a recomputed binding clustering of one of the compiler projects. Note that the majority of the procedures fall together at one level. While this system does show modularity with the scanner and interpreter, the rest of the system does not display much modularity.

5.3.3 Using weighted clustering

If the black hole syndrome is caused by the clustering method, a reasonable approach to correct its bias is to change the weighting of the bindings when producing the dissimilarity matrix for the next iteration. The weighting would cause bindings to large clusters to be discounted slightly to allow the planets to form. This could be done by replacing each occurrence of $b(i, j)$ in the equation that computes the dissimilarity matrix with $b(i, j) * w(i, j)$ where $w(i, j)$ depends on the size of element i and element j.

5.3.4 Measurements

Several measurements can be taken on the clustered system. The more obvious ones include the number and sizes of the clusters. Other interesting measurements that may be taken from the dendrogram are the strength and coupling levels of the clusters. These are available from the levels at which the clusters form. If several clusters form at level 76 and then collapse into a single cluster at level 87, then it may be said that they have a strength of 76 and a coupling of 87. For example, note how the preceding compiler examples have a module of the interpreter (containing POP, PUSH and INTERP) that has a low degree of coupling and a high degree of strength. The numbers just given are from the last example. Note also that, even though the interpreter module is essentially the same in all the projects, the measurements are quite different. This type of analysis appears to be sensitive to the environment of the module. The values of these measures may have more meaning if they are viewed for a single system as it changes over time.

The stability of the system with respect to data interactions can be examined by evaluating the changes in the dendrograms as data bindings are added or removed from the binding matrix. In fact, whole procedures could be removed from the analysis to see what the system structure is without them. This may be particularly useful if parts of the system are built as virtual machines, utility functions or data abstractions. A particular layer of the system could then be examined while assuming that all of the lower layers act as primitives. This approach is best taken by removing the lower layers of the system and treating calls to them as references and definitions of the global variables that they use.

5.3.5 Case studies

The clustering techniques presented have been applied to two medium-size systems that are part of the SEL (NASA 1982) data collection effort. The systems consist of approximately 100 000 and 64 000 lines of Fortran source code, including comments. The larger one was designed as two distinct load modules, one of which has two distinct functions which are not used together in a single execution. Thus there are essentially three programs to analyse. The three programs were not independent, however, as they contained several common subsystems. The actual data bindings were used because they are much cheaper to calculate than control flow data bindings.

Several routines that were designated as utility routines were removed from the analysis as described in the preceding section. This removal was helpful in determining the true relationships among the remaining routines. Without the removal of the utility routines, they provided a second-order relationship between the routines that called them. For example, there was a user-written utility routine that converted one form of date to another. When two very different routines both called this date routine, a two-step path was created between them (for example, (p, x, date) and (q, x, date) are data bindings where p and q each call date with parameter x). Even though there was no actual data relationship between them, they were pulled together in the clustering algorithm. After removal of the utility routine, their direct relationship emerged. The location and removal of utility routines is not automatable. However, these routines tend to be ones that do all of their communication via parameters and return values and are called by more than one other routine. Hence it is possible to automate part of the search for these routines.

The second project, while smaller than the first, is not broken into independent portions so it actually provides a larger example. The second project also has more errors that involve multiple modules, so it is better suited for some of the analysis that follows.

Finding functional clusters   One of the goals of the study was to determine if any of the methods were able to pick out logical modules in the software. The system was designed as several subsystems, and these subsystems were further refined with the major emphasis of design placed on functionality. If the clustering approach is to be useful, the modularization given by the clustering techniques should be similar to the developers' subsystems. There was a close correspondence between the two views of the system.

An interesting note can be made about the places where the cluster and the subsystem designation differ. In a talk with one of the developers, it became clear that these differences occurred with routines that operated on data that were different from those used by the rest of the routines in the subsystem. From this it may be concluded that there is, in this environment, a strong relationship between the functionality of routines and the data usage of the routines. But at the same time, something can be gained by looking at the system from another viewpoint. That is, functionality is not the only view of the system. The maintainer should also be aware of the data usage that actually exists. This information is not necessarily contained in the calling chart documentation even if the documentation is current.

Error analysis   The study of errors involving changes to more than one routine can

Table 5.1[a]

	SL	RB	EB	WB
Large-1	780	571	653	605
Large-2	827	571	629	727
Large-3	6 014	4 635	5 172	6 462
Small	13 571	14 765	14 175	25 321

[a] SL = single link; RB = recomputed binding; EB = expected binding; WB = weighted binding.

yield insights into the effectiveness of the clustering techniques. The NASA–SEL database contains error histories for the systems being studied. For a given clustering, the errors that involved more than one routine were attached to the smallest cluster that contained all of the routines involved (that is, it is attached to the smallest cluster that covers the error). The number of errors attached to each cluster was multiplied by the number of routines in the cluster and the products summed over the clusters. The resultant number is an indication of how well a given technique places all of the routines that were involved in a given error into a single cluster at a low level. A low number indicates that many errors were contained in small clusters.

The results of the error study were inconclusive because the NASA–SEL environment tends to generate a small number of interface errors and because only two projects have been examined. The majority of such errors were confined to the developers' subsystems so they tended to be somewhat localized by the clustering techniques as well.

Clustering technique comparison   Another goal of this study was to determine if there was a difference between clusters that are generated by the various clustering techniques presented earlier. Based on these two case studies, it appears that the expected binding cluster and the recomputed binding cluster are similar to each other and better than the other methods tested. Better here refers to (1) locality of errors and (2) clusters that capture the developers' subsystems and place the individual routines with reasonable siblings at the lower clustering levels.

Table 5.1 illustrates the differences among the clustering techniques as measured by error*module_size count. Smaller values indicate that errors were contained in smaller modules. The weighted binding did not perform well according to this test. For the large system recomputed binding seems to have been superior, but for the small system single link did better. It must be remembered that Large-1, Large-2 and Large-3 contain portions of common code, so that there are not four independent observations in these results.

5.6 CONCLUSIONS

Several clustering methods have been presented and analysed on some small and medium-sized programs. It appears that clustering by data bindings can select the logical modules of a system.

This study has not produced sufficient evidence to determine which module-generated techniques are best at reducing the scope (i.e. the size of an encompassing module) of development errors. All three subsystems of the larger case study favour the recomputed bindings technique. However, the other case study favours the standard shortest link method. Further work in this area should focus on the selection of the algorithm. In particular, the algorithms should be tried on some very large systems to see if they still work well. One should be wary of the application of random cluster methods to this (or any) domain.

The dendrograms resulting from the data bindings counts can provide fingerprints of some basic design decisions. In particular, examples were shown which distinguish between the use of data hiding versus the global use of data structures.

The case studies show a large degree of correspondence between the automatically generated module structures and those defined by the developers. The places where these differ are instructive in the explanation of procedure connectivity.

The value of clustering may be greatest when it is used on a single system as it evolves over time. Such a use would allow the maintenance personnel to be aware of the changing relationships among the components of the system. Clustering may also be used to test the hypothesis that system modularity tends to deteriorate over time. Once the modules have been determined, it is possible to use clustering to determine measures of the strength and coupling of the modules. The dendrogram gives a fingerprint or classification of the system.

Several measures have been proposed for evaluating the automatically derived module hierarchy. These measures have not been adequately evaluated owing to the lack of a proper set of data.

There were some inconclusive tests conducted with respect to modularization. Among these is the question of which technique provides the best description of the system modularity. Perhaps the choice should depend on whether the goal is to localize errors, mimic the designer, or compute measures of strength and coupling. Indeed, the question of how to compute measures of strength and coupling is still unresolved. The use of clustering analysis and data binding holds promise of providing meaningful pictures of high-level system interactions. One might readily ask if these pictures are useful to the designer or maintainer of the software. The answer lies in further research and experimentation.

Appendix

[Not included]

Acknowledgements

This work was supported in part by the Air Force Office of Scientific Research under Contract AFOSR-F49620-80-C-001 to the University of Maryland. Computer support was provided in part by the Computer Science Center at the University of Maryland.

6

THE EVALUATION OF SOFTWARE SYSTEMS' STRUCTURE USING QUANTITATIVE SOFTWARE METRICS

Sallie Henry and Dennis Kafura

Virginia Polytechnic Institute

ABSTRACT

The design and analysis of the structure of software systems has typically been based on purely qualitative grounds. In this paper we report on our positive experience with a set of quantitative measures of software structure. These metrics, based on the number of possible paths of information flow through a given component, were used to evaluate the design and implementation of a software system (the UNIX operating system kernel) which exhibits the interconnectivity of components typical of large-scale software systems. Several examples are presented which show the power of this technique in locating a variety of both design and implementation defects. Suggested repairs. which agree with the commonly accepted principles of structured design and programming, are presented. The effect of these alterations on the structure of the system and the quantitative measurements of that structure lead to a convincing validation of the utility of information flow metrics.

6.1 INTRODUCTION

Much of the work in software system structuring has explicitly recognized the fundamental relationship between the complexity of a system, its structure, and its quality and reliability (Myers 1976). For example, the use of structured design methodologies

99

allows the controlled introduction of complexity via levels of abstractions, virtual machines or layered hierarchies (Dijkstra 1968b; Liskov 1972; Haberman *et al.* 1976). By establishing an ordered discipline during the design phase these techniques have had notable success in producing higher-quality, lower-cost software systems. The common principle shared by these design methodologies is the careful structuring of the connections among the components of the system. There are, however, numerous ways to determine when components are 'connected'. Several of the proposed relations defining a connection are: control flow (calling hierarchy) (Dijkstra 1968b); 'uses' (Parnas 1976); memory allocation (Parnas 1974); dependency (Janson 1977); and shared assumptions (Channon 1974). Our approach defines a connection between two components to exist if there is a possible flow of information from one to the other. This view of structure led to the definition and validation of a set of quantitative measures of software structure (Henry 1979). This approach, based on the structure created by the flow of information within a system, is inherently and significantly different from the approach used in Halstead's 'software science' (Halstead 1977a). The principal difference is that Halstead's technique embodies no notion of the structure of the object being measured, whereas the information flow view is entirely founded on a concept of structure.

The information flow complexity metric has been shown to be highly correlated with the occurrence of errors and has also been found to be statistically independent of other measures (Kafura and Henry 1981). In this paper we will show how this complexity measurement can be used to identify and repair structural defects in large-scale systems. This technique is illustrated by an analysis of the UNIX operating system kernel.

The decision to analyse an operating system, although dictated by our background and interest in operating systems, is defensible on its own merits. Among large-scale systems, operating systems are important objects of study because they form the interface between the hardware and the applications programs. The operating system also creates the virtual machine environment which is critical to the success of the applications which it supports. In addition, operating systems consist of more lines of code than most application programs and tend to be more complex, both in design and in the interrelationships of its parts. Thus, an operating system is a sound basis for the measurement and validation of software structure metrics.

The UNIX operating system was chosen as the vehicle for the information flow analysis for several reasons. First, UNIX is written in a high-level language and its internal mechanisms are well documented (Lions 1977; Ritchie and Thompson 1974). Second, UNIX is a large enough operating system to use as a reasonable experimental basis yet is small enough for a manageable research project with limited resources. The third reason for selecting UNIX is the fact that UNIX software is used in production environments. UNIX is not a toy or experimental system, nor was it written to illustrate or defend a favoured design methodology. Fourthly, UNIX is universal in that it is installed in many environments and on several different machines. Thus, we expect our results to be understood, and perhaps criticized, in detail by a larger audience. The fifth reason is the functionality of UNIX. UNIX, containing a powerful I/O system, a simple virtual memory structure, dynamic task creation and deletion, simple interprocess communication and some protection features, possesses the typical spectrum of operating system functions.

In Section 6.2 we briefly define the types of information flow and show how the information flow paths can be used to define a measure of structural complexity. Section 6.3 contains a study of the UNIX kernel and illustrates the way in which the complexity metric is used to identify, analyse and rectify defects in the system structure. Finally, in Section 6.4 we indicate the current work in progress to refine and develop the techniques described in this paper.

6.2 INFORMATION FLOW CONCEPTS AND DEFINITIONS

In this section various types of flows of information are informally presented by example. The mechanisms of deriving these flows are bypassed here but are given in Henry (1979). Following the example, formal definitions related to the flow of information are given.

Figure 6.1 shows a simple system consisting of six modules (A, B, C, D, E and F), a data structure (DS), and the connections among these components. Figure 6.2 shows possible skeleton code for this system. As indicated in the skeleton code, module A retrieves information from DS and then calls B passing a parameter; module B then updates DS. C calls D, passing a parameter. Module D calls E with a parameter, and E returns a value to D which D then uses and passes to F. The function of F is to update DS.

The various types of information flow that may be observed in the example system are summarized in Fig. 6.3. The direct local flows are simply the ones created by parameter passing. There are also two indirect local flows. The first of these, from E to D, results when E returns a value which D uses in its computation. The second indirect flow, from E to F, results when other information that D receives from E is passed unchanged to F. This latter flow is an example of a 'side-effect' relationship between E and F. There also exist two flows of information through the global data structure which are termed *global flows*.

An important property of the information flows illustrated in Fig. 6.3 is that they are easily computable from a straightforward procedure-by-procedure analysis using established compile-time techniques of data flow analysis (Hecht 1978; Allen 1974).

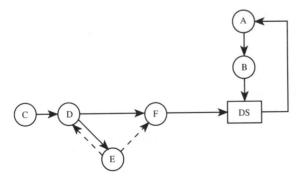

Figure 6.1 An example of information flow

```
Procedure A()              Procedure D(P)
    .                          .
    .                          .
    .                          .
X = DS × 1                 Q:= E(P);
B(X);                      F(P, C);
    .                          .
    .                          .
    .                          .
End A;                     End D;
Procedure B(X);            Procedure E(P);
    .                          .
    .                          .
DS;= X;                    E:= P+3;
    .                          .
    .                          .
    .                          .
End B                      End E;
Procedure C(P);            Procedure F(PQ);
    .                          .
    .                          .
D (P);                     DS; = P+Q;
    .                          .
    .                          .
End C;                     End F;
```

Figure 6.2 Possible skeleton code for example in Fig. 6.1

Direct local flows:	A → B
	C → D
	D → E
	D → F
Indirect local flows:	E → D
	E → F
Global flows:	B → A
	F → A

Figure 6.3 Types of information flow for example in Fig. 6.1

It is also important to note that the information flow analysis may be performed immediately after the design phase when the external specifications have been completed but before the implementation has begun. As indicated below, the measurements taken at this point rely only on: (1) sufficient information to determine the inter-procedure data flows, and (2) estimates of the code length. Based on these measures, the design can be evaluated for possible flaws before the investment in implementation has begun.

The local flows illustrated earlier in this section can be used to formulate a measure of procedure complexity. The terms fan-in, fan-out, complexity and module are specifically defined in terms of information flows in order to present this measure.

Definition 1 The *fan-in* (*fan-out*) of a procedure is the number of local flows terminating at (emanating from) that procedure.

The complexity of a procedure depends on two factors: the complexity of the procedure code, and the complexity of the procedure's connections to its environment. Obeying the general principle of parsimony, we elected to use the simplest possible measures for each of these two components and to assume that these components are independent and, hence, their effect multiplicative. A very simple length measure was used as an index of procedure code complexity. The length of a procedure was defined as the number of lines of text in the source code for the procedure. This measure includes embedded comments but does not include comments preceding the procedure statement. Because of the sparse use of embedded comments and the typical occurrence of only one statement per line in the UNIX source code, this length measure is essentially equivalent to counting the number of statements in the procedure. Simple length measures, such as the number of source statements, are known to have positive correlations, albeit not the strongest correlations, with the occurrence of errors (Bowen 1978; Basili and Phillips 1981). The connections of a procedure to its environment are determined by the fan-in and the fan-out. This leads to the following definition of procedure complexity.

Definition 2 The *complexity* of a given procedure is

$$\text{length} * (\text{fan-in} * \text{fan-out}) ** 2.$$

The term (fan-in * fan-out) represents the total possible number of combinations of an input source to an output destination. This term is squared to reflect the common experience that the difficulty in understanding, testing or modifying an operating system stemmed less from the action of a single component than from the inter-relationships among the components. In weighting this connectivity factor, we used the simplest non-linear function—a quadratic. The power of 2 used in this weighting is the same as Brook's law of programmer interaction (Brooks 1975), Belady's formula for system partitioning (Belady and Evangelisti 1981) and Brown's square law for communications problems (Brown 1980).

A previous paper (Henry and Kafura 1981b) reported that this definition of procedure complexity was highly correlated with the errors in the UNIX operating system, with a correlation coefficient of 0.95. Another significant result, reported in Kafura, Henry and Harris (1981) showed that the information flow complexity metric was significantly different from two other software metrics: McCabe's cyclomatic complexity (see Chapter 2 above) and Halstead's software science measures (Halstead 1977a). The relationships among these three metrics are shown in Fig. 6.4. As can be seen in this figure, the Halstead measures (N, the length; $NHAT$, the length approximator; V, volume and E, effort) are highly correlated with McCabe's cyclomatic complexity. However, it can also be seen that the information flow complexity is only weakly correlated with any of the other measures. This result is sensible because both the Halstead and the McCabe measurements are formed from

	N	$NHAT$	V	F	$McCabe$	$Information\ flow$
N	1.0	0.94	0.99	0.92	0.91	0.32
$NHAT$		1.0	0.94	0.81	0.84	0.20
V			1.0	0.94	0.91	0.31
E				1.0	0.84	0.38
McCabe					1.0	0.34
Information flow						1.0

Figure 6.4 Relationships among matrices

Module	Description
buf	Buffer information for the block I/O system
file	File information for each open file
filesys	Super block information for resource allocation
inode	General information for active files
kl11	Character device information for each terminal
lp11	Device information for the line printer
mount	Super block information for mounted files
proc	Process information for each active process
text	Text segment information for unaltered code
u	All process information not needed for swapping

Figure 6.5 UNIX module descriptions

counts of simple lexical tokens in the code, whereas the information flow measure concentrates on the patterns of communication between components in the system.

The procedure complexities are used to establish module complexities. The global flow information was used to form an operational definition of a module. This definition, reflecting Parnas's information-hiding principle (Parnas 1977), is as follows.

Definition 3 A *module* with respect to a data structure, D, consists of those procedures which either directly update D or directly retrieve information from D.

Using this operational definition, the complexity of a module is taken as the sum of the complexities of the module's constituent procedures.

The information flow analysis was performed for each data structure in the UNIX operating system. Only a subset of the UNIX modules is presented in this paper. Figure 6.5 displays the modules discussed in this paper and their corresponding descriptions.

It is interesting to note that a high percentage of a module's complexity is due to a few very complex procedures. The data in Table 6.1 show that, in all but one case, the three most complex procedures constituted more than 85 per cent of the total module complexity.

Table 6.1 Percentage of module complexity for largest procedures

Module	Complexity	Number of procedures in module	Complexity of three largest procedures	%
buf	3 541 083	23	3 468 024	98
file	33 062	10	29 425	89
filesys	268 807	11	254 080	95
inode	13 462 921	28	12 984 995	96
kl11	3 262	17	2 120	65
lp11	855	5	829	97
mount	135 503	6	135 084	99
proc	436 151	30	379 693	87
text	24 886	6	24 831	99

6.3 ANALYSIS OF UNIX LEVEL HIERARCHY

Given hierarchical ordering of the modules of a system into levels, the cumulative level complexity may be computed by summing the module complexities for each level and accumulating this sum across successively higher levels. A hierarchy for the UNIX modules listed in the previous section is given in Table 6.2. These modules and levels form the core of the UNIX system and include the handling of character devices, block devices, the file system and process management.

Graph 1 in Fig. 6.6 shows the cumulative level for the UNIX hierarchy defined above. Level 0, which has a complexity of only 4117, is taken as the base line of this graph. Note the dramatic increase in complexity between levels 0 and 1, and levels 1 and 2 compared with the more modest increases for the other levels. As explained below, such a steep slope in the complexity curve may be caused by several factors, one of which is a missing level of abstraction.

The intuition behind this interpretation of the slope of the cumulative complexity curve is illustrated in Fig. 6.7. In part (a) each of the procedures at level 1 calls the two procedures at level 0, combining their returned values to form a needed result. All of the level 1 procedures use the level 0 procedures in the same way. In effect, each level 1 procedure is fabricating for itself a local version of a common, though missing abstraction. The substance of the missing abstraction consists of the operations performed by each of the level 1 procedures on the level 0 procedures.

It is easy to see that the structure in Fig. 6.7(a) implies a large number of information flow paths and that these paths are indicative of: (1) an inherent complexity in the design of the relationships between the components, and (2) lurking reliability and maintenance problems if alterations to one or both of the level 0 procedures is attempted. Compare this situation with the one diagrammed in Fig. 6.7(b), where the level of abstraction has been identified and established as a separate element in the design. The number of information flow paths has been reduced and the structure of these paths has been regularized. The operation of each of the level 1 procedures is simplified and the immediate effects of changes to the level 0 procedures are more localized.

The beneficial effects of inserting the missing level of abstraction is not surprising. What is interesting is that the density of the information flow paths, which leads to the accelerated increase in complexity across the adjacent levels, appears to be a natural, automatic and quantitative indicator of where such desirable abstractions are absent. We will next show how this insight was applied to the UNIX system.

The large increase in complexity between level 1 and level 2, illustrated in graph 1

Table 6.2 Hierarchy for UNIX modules

Level 5	proc, text
Level 4	mount
Level 3	file, filesys
Level 2	inode
Level 1	buf
Level 0	kl11, lp11

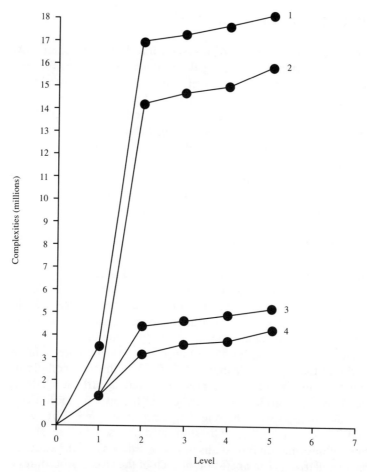

Figure 6.6 Accumulated complexities for UNIX hierarchies

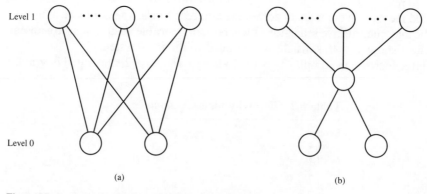

Figure 6.7 A missing level of abstraction in a simple structure

of Fig. 6.6, led us to analyse the fan-in and fan-out relationships between these two levels. This analysis showed that two procedures in the level 1 buf module, GETBLK and BREAD, accounted for approximately 70 per cent of the complexity of the entire buf module. Thus, our attention focused on possible missing abstractions involving these two procedures.

The buf data structure contains buffer information for the block I/O system. Examination of the buf module reveals that the buf data structure is used for several logically distinct functions. Buffers are allocated for five separate functions:

1. Swapping space
2. User file space and pipes
3. The super block (this contains information used in allocating resources)
4. The i-list (used by the inode module)
5. Temporary storage.

The first four of these functions correspond to distinct areas of the physical disk, whereas the last function does not correspond to any use of physical disk space. These separate spaces are manipulated in distinct ways. The operations provided by the buf structure, however, fail to differentiate among these five distinct logical functions. This failure is the root cause of the complexity of the buf module because it leads to an exaggerated fan-in and fan-out for some buf procedures. To remedy this situation, an additional level of abstraction, distinguishing the five functions noted above, was added. It will be shown that the addition of this structural abstraction, desirable from an aesthetic standpoint, also leads to a reduction in the complexity measurements for the buf module.

To add the level of abstraction to the buf module, it is necessary to divide the local flow for GETBLK and BREAD into the functions mentioned above. The procedures outside the buf module, which previously called GETBLK or BREAD directly, will now call one of the five new procedures, each implementing one of the five specific functions. These new procedures will in turn call GETBLK or BREAD. In adding these five procedures, the logical structure of buf is changed. These procedures represent a level of abstraction which logically changes the interface to buf from the other modules. The addition of the new level will reduce the fan-in and fan-out for GETBLK and BREAD, thus reducing their complexities. In the original system the fan-in for GETBLK is 19 and the fan-out is 11. For BREAD the fan-in and fan-out are 19 and 14, respectively. Figure 6.8 displays the fan-in and fan-out for GETBLK and BREAD with the addition of the procedures A, B, C, D and E. These new procedures correspond to the five functions of the buf structure listed above and constitute the new level of abstraction. The numbers at the bottom of the figure indicate the fan-in and fan-out for GETBLK and BREAD from procedures within the buf module; i.e., five procedures inside the buf structure contribute to the fan-in for GETBLK. The new fan-in for GETBLK is 9 and the fan-out is 11. The new complexity for GETBLK is 806 400 as compared with the previous complexity of 2 446 136, or a 67 per cent reduction. The new fan-in for BREAD is 7 and the fan-out is 9. Its new complexity is 83 200 as compared with the previous 919 828, representing a reduction of 91 per cent.

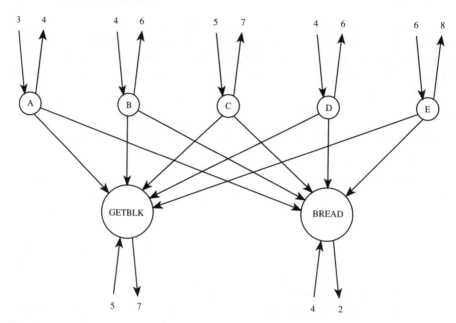

Figure 6.8 Fan-in and fan-out for GETBLK and BREAD with additional level of abstraction

Since each of the new procedures is relatively simple, it will be assumed that each of the procedures A, B, C, D and E has 10 lines of code. The complexities of these procedures are:

A: 9 000
B: 23 040
C: 39 690
D: 23 040
E: 64 000

The complexity of this new level is 158 770, and the new complexity for the buf module is 962 335. The previous complexity for buf was 3 541 083, resulting in a 73 per cent reduction.

Graph 2 in Fig. 6.6 represents the cumulative complexity curve for the modified system (i.e. the system with procedures A–E added at level 1). It is interesting to note that the addition of code to implement the missing abstraction has actually reduced the total system complexity. This fact is quite appealing to our sense that complexity depends on proper structure rather than mere size. Such a phenomenon—reducing complexity by adding to the size—does not seem to arise in any of the other measures of software complexity.

Even though the complexity of GETBLK was substantially reduced, the fan-in and fan-out remained large. The procedures within the buf module are the cause of this factor. The next iteration of the redesign process would be to investigate the code for those procedures that interact with GETBLK in the buf module. It may be necessary to add another level of refinement to the buf module. This possible redesign is not pursued further in this paper.

Table 6.3 Complexities for the revised NAMEI procedure

	Fan-in	Fan-out	Length	Complexity
NAMEI	17	13	31	1 514 071
NAMEI'	2	6	79	11 376
NAMEI''	2	5	63	6 300

There is still a large increase in complexity between level 1 and level 2 as shown by graph 2 of Fig. 6.6. Examination of the inode module at level 2 reveals that its high module complexity is due primarily to the NAMEI procedure, which accounts for 86 per cent of the module complexity. There are two reasons for this high complexity. First, NAMEI consists of 155 lines of code. For the UNIX system this is a very long procedure, and its length indicates a possible implementation problem. This is referred to as an 'implementation' problem because the inherent cause of the code length is not due to the functional specifications for NAMEI but to the way in which these specifications are coded. Secondly, NAMEI has a fan-in and a fan-out of 13 and 21, respectively. This indicates a possible design problem. This type of problem is classified as a 'design' problem because it stems from the basic way in which NAMEI is connected to its environment. No amount of re-implementation that preserves the original specifications, and hence the original connections to other components, can remedy this problem. These two possible problems of NAMEI are investigated further. The implementation problem is considered first and the design problem second.

The NAMEI procedure contains an initialization section and a large loop with a nested inner loop. Each of these three pieces performs an identifiable, separable and complete function. This understanding of the code suggests that NAMEI could have been further refined into three procedures, called NAMEI, NAMEI' and NAMEI'' in the following text, in such a way as to reduce its complexity value. Our changes to NAMEI removed the large loop to NAMEI' and the inner loop to NAMEI''. This implementation change reflects accepted standards of good programming practice. The fan-in, fan-out, length and complexity of NAMEI, NAMEI' and NAMEI'' are given in Table 6.3. The complexity of the new NAMEI is now 1 531 747. This change in the implementation of NAMEI represents an 87 per cent reduction in complexity and a 74 per cent reduction for the inode module. The complexity of the inode module is now 3 442 673. Graph 3 of Fig. 6.6 shows the cumulative complexity for the UNIX hierarchy with this implementation change to NAMEI.

The second problem with NAMEI, indicated by a high fan-in and fan-out in the initial measurements, was a design problem. In general, NAMEI accesses a file directory and returns a pointer to an inode structure. NAMEI is called for three distinct types of directory access:

1. Seek a named directory entry.
2. Create a new directory entry.
3. Delete an existing directory entry.

These three types of access are logically distinct and are related only by their common

Table 6.4 Complexities for modifications to the inode module

	Fan-in	Fan-out	Complexity
SEEK	8	10	64 000
CREATE	4	3	1 440
DELETE	1	3	90
NAMEI	4	6	3 100
NAMEI'	2	6	11 376
NAMEI"	2	5	6 300

use of the directory. Since the type of access is passed as one of the parameters to NAMEI, Myers (1976) would classify it as 'logical strength'. A logical strength procedure with high complexity indicates a possible missing functional abstraction in the design. We refer to such a design flaw as a missing functional abstraction because the problem results from an inadequate separation of functions in formulating the external specifications of the procedure. The needed separation is a functional, as opposed to data, abstraction because no new logical entities are created, as with the changes to the buf module earlier, but the functions applied to existing structures are specialized.

The missing functional abstraction is realized by adding three procedures which interface with the NAMEI procedure, thus changing the logical structure of the inode module. Table 6.4 shows the fan-in, fan-out and complexity for these three procedures and for NAMEI. Again, it is assumed that each of these procedures is 10 lines of code in length. Note that the fan-in and fan-out for NAMEI' and NAMEI" do not change. By adding this level of refinement, the complexity of NAMEI is reduced by 98 per cent to 20 776. The complexity of the new level is 65 490, and the new complexity of the inode module is 1 931 702, an additional 44 per cent reduction.

With both the implementation and the design enhancements to NAMEI, the inode module complexity has been reduced by 86 per cent. Graph 4 in Fig. 6.6 displays the resulting cumulative complexity.

It should be emphasized again that the system designer or maintainer may compute these complexities prior to the implementation of, or modification to, the code. The difficulties in accomplishing a design or implementation change may then be compared with the resulting reduction in complexity. For example, the designer may evaluate the graphs of accumulated complexities for various changes, as in Fig. 6.6. Because of manpower, time or budget constraints, it may be possible only to implement either the changes to buf or inode, but not both. Since the change to inode results in a much lower complexity, that change would have priority over the change to buf. Similar analysis would then show that the design change to inode should have a higher priority than the implementation change to inode.

6.4 CONCLUSIONS

In summary, the complexity measurements presented in the previous sections indicate areas for redesign and reimplementation as demonstrated in the reworked buf and inode modules. In both of these examples, several procedures were added which increased the number of lines of code in the system. The logical structures created by this extra code succeeded in reducing the number of connections among the system components, thus reducing the complexity. It must be recognized that the additional code will cause an increase in the execution time of the affected operations. However, the added code is quite small, perhaps 30 lines in all, and should not adversely affect the system performance If, in other cases, such structure-enhancing modifications do cause noticeable increases in the execution time, this should be recognized as merely the natural balancing between factors which may be traded off against each other. Rather than decrying what may be an immutable relationship between structure and efficiency, we should be pleased to have at hand a method for quantitatively assessing the balance between these two factors. One other interesting feature of the restructing is that the addition of new code actually resulted in a decrease in the system complexity as measured by the information flow complexity. This is in stark contrast to all other software metrics, which will usually cause an increase in the measurements of complexity when the system size is increased. Again, by concentrating on structure rather than size, the information flow approach has captured the intuition that a large but well-structured system may be less complex than a smaller, but poorly structured system.

Three types of design and implementation difficulties were specified by the buf and inode examples. First, a data abstraction was illustrated by adding procedures to interface with the buf module. This change allows the logically distinct areas on the disk to be structurally separated. Second, the implementation change to NAMEI demonstrated inadequate refinement of the original code for NAMEI. Third, a functional abstraction was added to NAMEI which allowed the seek, create and delete functions of NAMEI to be separated. The analysis of these problem areas led to improvement in both the design and the implementation by reducing the number of connections among components and, thus, reducing the complexity.

An automated set of metrics is a necessary requirement for the designers and implementors of complicated software systems in order to allow the rapid, quantitative and objective evaluation of the system's structure. Since the set of metrics presented in this paper is based on information flow, all information connections between systems components are observed. The measurement also indicates areas of implementation or design difficulties as demonstrated by the buf and inode modules.

7

SOFTWARE ENGINEERING ECONOMICS

Barry W. Boehm

TRW Defense Systems Group

ABSTRACT

This chapter summarizes the current state of the art and recent trends in software engineering economics. It provides an overview of economic analysis techniques and their applicability to software engineering and management. It surveys the field of software cost estimation, including the major estimation techniques available, the state of the art in algorithm cost models and the outstanding research issues in software cost estimation.

[N.B. The first two sections of the original paper by Boehm are not reproduced here.]

7.3 SOFTWARE COST ESTIMATION

7.3.1 Introduction

All of the software engineering economics decision analysis techniques are only as good as the input data we can provide for them. For software decisions, the most critical and difficult of these inputs to provide are estimates of the cost of a proposed software project. In this section, we will summarize:

1. The major software cost estimation techniques available, and their relative strengths and difficulties

2. Algorithmic models for software cost estimation
3. Outstanding research issues in software cost estimation

7.3.2 Major software cost estimation techniques

Table 7.1 summarizes the relative strengths and difficulties of the major software cost estimation methods in use today.

1. *Algorithmic models* These methods provide one or more algorithms which produce a software cost estimate as a function of a number of variables that are considered to be the major cost drivers.
2. *Expert judgement* This method involves consulting one or more experts, perhaps with the aid of an expert-consensus mechanism such as the Delphi technique.
3. *Analogy* This method involves reasoning by analogy with one or more completed projects to relate their actual costs to an estimate of the cost of a similar new project.
4. *Parkinson* A Parkinson principle ('work expands to fill the available volume') is invoked to equate the cost estimate to the available resources.
5. *Price-to-win* Here, the cost estimate is equated to the price believed necessary to win the job (or the schedule believed necessary to be first in the market with a new product, etc.).
6. *Top-down* An overall cost estimate for the project is derived from global properties of the software product. The total cost is then split up among the various components.
7. *Bottom-up* Each component of the software job is separately estimated, and the results aggregated to produce an estimate for the overall job.

Table 7.1 Strengths and weaknesses of software cost estimation methods

Method	Strengths	Weaknesses
Algorithmic model	Objective, repeatable, analysable formula Efficient, good for sensitivity analysis Objectively calibrated to experience	Subjective inputs Assessment of exceptional circumstances Calibrated to past, not future
Expert judgement	Assessment of representativeness, interactions, exceptional circumstances	No better than participants Biases, incomplete recall
Analogy	Based on representative experience	Representativeness of experience
Parkinson Price-to-win	Correlates with some experience Often gets the contract	Reinforces poor practice Generally produces large overruns
Top-down	System-level focus Efficient	Less detailed basis Less stable
Bottom-up	More detailed basis More stable Fosters individual commitment	May overlook system-level costs Requires more effort

The main conclusions that we can draw from Table 7.1 are as follows:

- None of the alternatives is better than the others from all aspects.
- The Parkinson and price-to-win methods are unacceptable and do not produce satisfactory cost estimates.
- The strengths and weaknesses of the other techniques are complementary (particularly the algorithmic models versus expert judgement and top-down versus bottom-up).
- Thus, in practice, we shall use combinations of the above techniques, compare their results, and iterate on them where they differ.

Fundamental limitations of software cost estimation techniques Whatever the strengths of a software cost estimation techniques, there is really no way we can expect the technique to compensate for our lack of definition or understanding of the software job to be done. Until a software specification is fully defined, it actually represents a range of software products, and a corresponding range of software development costs.

This fundamental limitation of software cost estimation technology is illustrated in Fig. 7.1, which shows the accuracy within which software cost estimates can be made, as a function of the software life-cycle phase (the horizontal axis), or of the

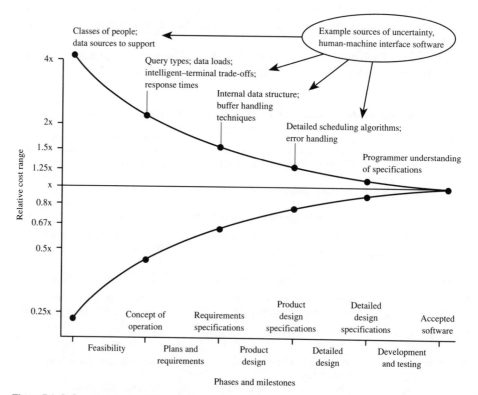

Figure 7.1 Software cost estimation accuracy versus phase.

level of knowledge we have of what the software is intended to do. This level of uncertainty is illustrated in the figure with respect to a human–machine interface component of the software.

When we first begin to evaluate alternative concepts for a new software application, the relative range of our software cost estimates is roughly a factor of 4 on either the high or the low side.[1] This range stems from the wide range of uncertainty we have at this time about the actual nature of the product. For the human–machine interface component, for example, we do not know at this time what classes of people (clerks, computer specialists, middle managers, etc.) or what classes of data (raw or pre-edited, numerical or text, digital or analog) the system will have to support. Until we pin down such uncertainties, a factor of 4 in either direction is not surprising as a range of estimates.

The above uncertainties are indeed pinned down once we complete the feasibility phase and settle on a particular concept of operation. At this stage, the range of our estimates diminishes to a factor of 2 in either direction. This range is reasonable because we still have not pinned down such issues as the specific types of user query to be supported, or the specific functions to be performed within the microprocessor in the intelligent terminal. These issues will be resolved by the time we have developed a software requirements specification, at which point we will be able to estimate the software costs within a factor of 1.5 in either direction.

By the time we complete and validate a product design specification, we will have resolved such issues as the internal data structure of the software product and the specific techniques for handling the buffers between the terminal microprocessor and the central processors on one side, and between the microprocessor and the display driver on the other. At this point, our software estimate should be accurate to within a factor of 1.25, the discrepancies being caused by some remaining sources of uncertainty such as the specific algorithms to be used for task scheduling, error handling, abort processing and the like. These will be resolved by the end of the detailed design phase, but there will still be a residual uncertainty of about 10 per cent based on how well the programmers really understand the specifications to which they are to code. (This factor also includes such consideration as personnel turnover uncertainties during the development and test phases.)

7.3.3 Algorithmic models for software cost estimation

Early development Since the earliest days of the software field, people have been trying to develop algorithmic models to estimate software costs. The earliest attempts were simple rules of thumb, such as:

● On a large project, each software performer will provide an average of one checked-out instruction per man-hour (or roughly 150 instructions per man-month).

---

[1] These ranges have been determined subjectively, and are intended to represent 80 per cent confidence limits, that is, 'within a factor of 4 on either side, 80 per cent of the time'.

- Each software maintenance person can maintain four boxes of cards (a box of cards held 2000 cards, or roughly 2000 instructions in those days of few comment cards).

Somewhat later, some projects began collecting quantitative data on the effort involved in developing a software product, and its distribution across the software life cycle. One of the earliest of these analyses was documented in Benington (1956). It indicated that, for very large operational software products on the order of 100 000 delivered source instructions (100 KDSI), the overall productivity was more like 64 DSI/man-month; that another 100 KDSI of support-software would be required; that about 15 000 pages of documentation would be produced and 3000 hours of computer time consumed; and that the distribution of effort would be as follows:

Program specs	10%
Coding specs	30%
Coding	10%
Parameter testing	20%
Assembly testing	30%

with an additional 30 per cent required to produce operational specs for the system. Unfortunately, such data did not become well known, and many subsequent software projects went through a painful process of rediscovering them.

During the last 1950s and early 1960s, relatively little progress was made in software cost estimation, while the frequency and magnitude of software cost overruns was becoming critical to many large systems employing computers. In 1964 the US Air Force contracted with System Development Corporation (SDC) for a landmark project in the software cost estimation field. This project collected 104 attributes of 169 software projects and treated them to extensive statistical analysis. One result was the 1965 SDC cost model (Nelson 1966), which was the best possible statistical 13-parameter linear estimation model for the sample data:

$$MM = -33.63$$

$$+ 9.15 \text{ (lack of requirements) (0-2)}$$

$$+ 10.73 \text{ (stability of design) (0-3)}$$

$$+ 0.51 \text{ (per cent math instructions)}$$

$$+ 0.46 \text{ (per cent storage/retrieval instructions)}$$

$$+ 0.40 \text{ (number of subprograms)}$$

$$+ 7.28 \text{ (programming language) (0-1)}$$

$$- 21.45 \text{ (business application) (0-1)}$$

$$+ 13.53 \text{ (stand-alone program) (0-1)}$$

$$+ 12.35 \text{ (first program on computer) (0-1)}$$

+ 58.82 (concurrent hardware development) (0-1)

+ 30.61 (random access device used) (0-1)

+ 29.55 (difference host, target hardware) (0-1)

+ 0.54 (number of personnel trips)

− 25.20 (developed by military organization) (0-1).

The numbers in parentheses refer to ratings to be made by the estimator.

When applied to its database of 169 projects, this model produced a mean estimate of 40 man-months (MM) and a standard deviation of 62 MM; not a very accurate predictor. Further, the application of the model is counterintuitive; a project with all zero ratings is estimated at minus 33 MM; changing language from a higher-order language to assembly language adds 7 MM, independent of project size. The most conclusive result from the SDC study was that there were too many nonlinear aspects of software development for a linear cost estimation model to work very well.

Still, the SDC effort provided a valuable base of information and insight for cost estimation and future models. Its cumulative distribution of productivity for 169 projects was a valuable aid for producing or checking cost estimates. The estimation rules of thumb for various phases and activities have been very helpful, and the data have been a major foundation for some subsequent cost models.

In the late 1960s and early 1970s, a number of cost models were developed which worked reasonably well for a certain restricted range of projects to which they were calibrated. Some of the more notable examples of such models are those described in Aron (1969), Weinwurm (1970) and Wolverton (1974).

The essence of the TRW Wolverton model (Wolverton 1974) is shown in Fig. 7.2 (page 120), which shows a number of curves of software cost per object instruction as a function of relative degree of difficulty (0 to 100), novelty of the application (new or old), and type of project. The best use of the model involves breaking the software into components and estimating their costs individually. Thus, a 1000 object-instruction module of new data management software of medium (50 per cent) difficulty would be costed at $46/instruction, or $46 000.

This model is well calibrated to a class of near-real-time government command and control projects, but is less accurate for some other classes of projects. In addition, the model provides a good breakdown of project effort by phase and activity.

In the late 1970s, several software cost estimation models were developed which established a significant advance in the state of the art. These included the Putnam SLIM Model (Putnam 1978), the Doty Model (Herd *et al*. 1977), the RCA PRICE s model (Freiman and Park 1979), the COCOMO model (Boehm 1981), the IBM−FSD model (Walston and Felix 1977), the Boeing model (Black *et al*. 1977), and a series of models developed by GRC (Carriere and Thibodeau 1979). A summary of these models, and of the earlier SDC and Wolverton models, is shown in Table 7.2 in terms of the size, program, computer, personnel and project attributes used

Table 7.2 Factors used in various cost models

Group	Factor	SDC, 1965	TRW, 1972	PUTNAM, SLIM	Doty	RCA, PRICE S	IBM	Boeing, 1977	GRC, 1979	COCOMO	SOFCOST	DSN	Jensen
Size attributes	Source instructions	×		×	×		×	×		×	×	×	×
	Object instructions	×	×	×	×	×					×		
	Number of routines					×				×	×		
	Number of data items						×				×	×	
	Number of output formats				×				×				×
	Documentation						×				×		×
	Number of personnel	×		×			×	×			×		×
Program attributes	Type	×	×	×	×	×	×	×		×	×		×
	Complexity	×	×	×		×	×				×		
	Language	×		×						×	×	×	×
	Reuse			×		×		×	×	×	×	×	×
	Required reliability			×		×		×	×	×	×	×	×
	Display requirements				×						×		
Computer attributes	Time constraint		×	×	×	×	×	×	×	×	×	×	×
	Storage constraint			×	×	×	×		×	×	×	×	×
	Hardware configuration	×				×							
	Concurrent hardware	×			×		×						
	Development	×				×				×	×	×	×
	Interfacing equipment, S/W										×	×	
Personnel attributes	Personnel capability			×		×	×			×	×	×	×
	Personnel continuity						×					×	×
	Hardware experience	×	×	×	×	×	×	×	×	×	×	×	×
	Applications experience			×		×	×		×	×	×	×	×
	Language experience			×		×	×		×	×	×	×	×

Project attributes							
Tools and techniques		×		×	×	×	×
Customer interface	×			×	×	×	×
Requirements definition	×	×		×	×	×	× ×
Requirements volatility	×	×	×	×	×	× ×	×
Schedule		×			×	×	
Security		×		×	×	×	
Computer access	×	×		× ×	×	× ×	× ×
Travel/rehosting/multi-site	×	×	×		×	×	
Support software maturity		×			×		
Calibration factor		×	×		×		
Effort equation $MM_{NOM} = C(DSI)^X$, $X =$	1.0	1.047	0.91	1.0	1.05–1.2	1.0	1.2
Schedule equation $t_D = C(MM)^X$, $X =$		0.35	0.35		0.32–0.38	0.356	0.333

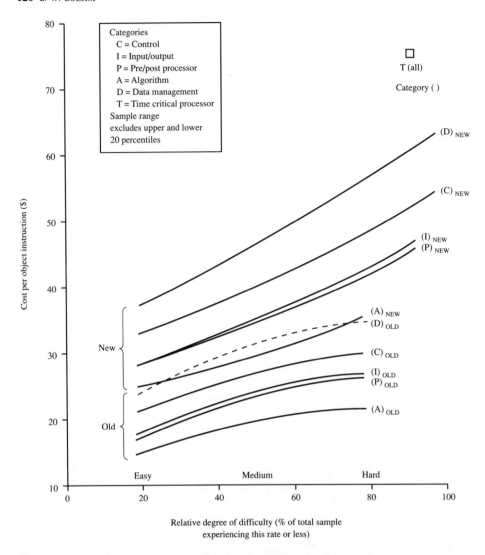

Figure 7.2 TRW Wolverton model. Cost per object instruction versus relative degree of difficulty.

by each model to determine software costs. The first four of these models are discussed below.

The Putnam SLIM model The Putnam SLIM model (Putnam 1978; Putnam and Fitzsimmons 1979) is a commercially available (from Quantitative Software Management, Inc.) software product based on Putnam's analysis of the software life cycle in terms of the Rayleigh distribution of project personnel level versus time. The basic effort macro-estimation model used in SLIM is

$$S_s = C_k K^{1/3} t_d^{4/3}$$

where

S_s = number of delivered source instructions
K = life-cycle effort in man-years
t_d = development time in years
C_k = a 'technology constant'

Values of C_k typically range between 610 and 57 314. The current version of SLIM allows one to calibrate C_k to past projects or to estimate it as a function of a project's use of modern programming practices, hardware constraints, personnel experience, interactive development and other factors. The required development effort (DE) is estimated as roughly 40 per cent of the life-cycle effort for large systems. For smaller systems, the percentage varies as a function of system size.

The SLIM model includes a number of useful extensions to estimate such quantities as manpower distribution, cash flow, major-milestone schedules, reliability levels, computer time and documentation costs.

The most controversial aspect of the SLIM model is its trade-off relationship between development effort K and development time t_d. For a software product of a given size, the SLIM software equation above gives

$$K = \frac{\text{constant}}{t_d^4}$$

For example, this relationship says that one can cut the cost of a software project in half simply by increasing its development time by 19 per cent (e.g. from 10 to 12 months). Figure 7.3 shows how the SLIM trade-off relationship compares with those of other models. (See Boehm (1981: Chapter 27) for further discussion of this issue.)

On balance, the SLIM approach has provided a number of useful insights into software cost estimation, such as the Rayleigh-curve distribution for one-shot software efforts, the explicit treatment of estimation risk and uncertainty, and the cube-root relationship defining the minimum development time achievable for a project requiring a given amount of effort.

The Doty model   This model (Herd *et al.* 1977) is the result of an extensive data analysis activity, including many of the data points from the SDC sample. A number of models of similar form were developed for different application areas. As an example, the model for general application is

$$MM = 5.288 \, (\text{KDSI})^{1.047} \qquad \qquad \text{for KDSI} \geqslant 10$$

$$MM = 2.060 \, (\text{KDSI})^{1.047} \left(\prod_{j=1}^{14} f_j \right) \qquad \text{for KDSI} < 10$$

The effort multipliers f_i are shown in Table 7.3. This model has a much more appropriate functional form than the SDC model, but it has some problems with stability, as it exhibits a discontinuity at $\text{KDSI} = 10$, and produces widely varying estimates via the f factors. (Answering 'yes' to 'first software developed on CPU' adds 92 per cent to the estimated cost.)

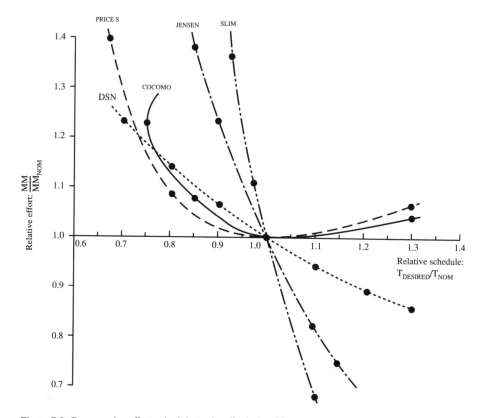

Figure 7.3 Comparative effort-schedule trade-off relationships.

The RCA PRICE S model PRICE S (Herd *et al.* 1977) is a commercially available (from RCA, Inc.) macro cost-estimation model developed primarily for embedded system applications. It has improved steadily with experience; earlier versions with a wide varying subjective complexity factor have been replaced by versions in which a number of computer, personnel and project attributes are used to modulate the complexity rating.

PRICE S has extended a number of cost-estimating relationships developed in the early 1970s such as the hardware constraint function shown in Fig. 7.4 (Boehm 1973). It was primarily developed to handle military software projects, but now also includes rating levels to cover business applications.

PRICE S also provides a wide range of useful outputs on gross phase and activity distributions analyses, and on monthly project cost–schedule-expected progress forecasts. PRICE S uses a two-parameter beta distribution rather than a Rayleigh curve to calculate development effort distribution versus calendar time.

PRICE S has recently added a software life-cycle support cost estimation capability called PRICE SL (Kuhn 1982). It involves the definition of three categories of support activities:

- *Growth* The estimator specifies the amount of code to be added to the product.

Table 7.3 Doty model for small programs*

$$MM = 2.060I^{1.047} \prod_{f=1}^{f=14} f_j$$

Factor	f_j	Yes	No
Special display	f_1	1.11	1.00
Detailed definition of operational requirements	f_2	1.00	1.11
Change to operational requirements	f_3	1.05	1.00
Real-time operation	f_4	1.33	1.00
CPU memory constraint	f_5	1.43	1.00
CPU time constraint	f_6	1.33	1.00
First software development on CPU	f_7	1.92	1.00
Concurrent development of ADP hardware	f_8	1.82	1.00
Timeshare versus batch processing in development	f_9	0.83	1.00
Developer using computer at another facility	f_{10}	1.43	1.00
Development at operational site	f_{11}	1.39	1.00
Development computer different from target computer	f_{12}	1.25	1.00
Development at more than one site	f_{13}	1.25	1.00
Programmer access to computer	f_{14}	{Limited	1.00
		{Unlimited	0.90

*Less than 10 000 source instructions.

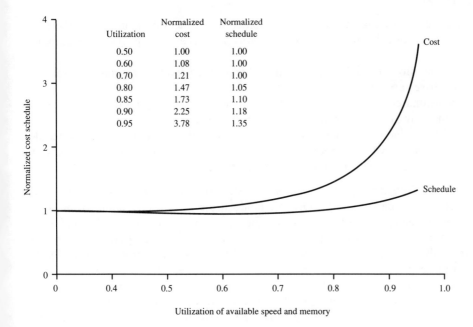

	Normalized	Normalized
Utilization	cost	schedule
0.50	1.00	1.00
0.60	1.08	1.00
0.70	1.21	1.00
0.80	1.47	1.05
0.85	1.73	1.10
0.90	2.25	1.18
0.95	3.78	1.35

Utilization of available speed and memory

Figure 7.4 RCA PRICE s model: Effect of hardware constraints.

PRICE SL then uses its standard techniques to estimate the resulting life-cycle-effort distribution.

- *Enhancement* PRICE SL estimates the fraction of the existing product that will be modified (the estimator may provide his own fraction), and uses its standard techniques to estimate the resulting life-cycle effort distribution.
- *Maintenance* The estimator provides a parameter indicating the quality level of the developed code. PRICE SL uses this to estimate the effort required to eliminate remaining errors.

The COnstructive COst MOdel (COCOMO) The primary motivation for the COCOMO model (Boehm 1981) has been to help people understand the cost consequences of the decisions they will make in commissioning, developing and supporting a software product. Besides providing a software cost estimation capability, COCOMO therefore provides a great deal of material which explains exactly what costs the model is estimating, and why it comes up with the estimates it does. Further, it provides capabilities for sensitivity analysis and trade-off analysis of many of the common software engineering decision issues.

COCOMO is actually a hierarchy of three increasingly detailed models which range from a single macro estimation scaling model as a function of product size to a micro estimation model with a three-level work breakdown structure and a set of phase-sensitive multipliers for each cost driver attribute. To provide a reasonably concise example of a current state of the art cost estimation model, the intermediate level of COCOMO is described below.

Intermediate COCOMO estimates the cost of a proposed software product in the following way:

1. A nominal development effort is estimated as a function of the product's size in thousands of delivered source instructions (KDSI) and the project's development mode.
2. A set of effort multipliers is determined from the product's ratings on a set of 15 cost driver attributes.
3. The estimated development effort is obtained by multiplying the nominal effort estimate by all of the product's effort multipliers.
4. Additional factors can be used to determine dollar costs, development schedules, phase and activity distributions, computer costs, annual maintenance costs and other elements from the development effort estimate.

Step 1: Nominal effort estimation First, Table 7.4 is used to determine the project's development mode. Organic-mode projects typically come from stable, familiar, forgiving, relatively unconstrained environments, and were found in the COCOMO data analysis of 63 projects to have a different scaling equation from the more ambitious, unfamiliar, unforgiving, tightly constrained embedded mode. The resulting scaling equations for each mode are given in Table 7.5; these are used to determine the nominal development effort for the project in man-months as a function of the project's size in KDSI and the project's development mode.

For example, suppose we are estimating the cost to develop the microprocessor-based communications processing software for a highly ambitious new electronic

Table 7.4 COCOMO **software development modes**

Feature	Mode		
	Organic	Semidetached	Embedded
Organizational understanding of product objectives	Thorough	Considerable	General
Experience in working with related software systems	Extensive	Considerable	Moderate
Need for software conformance with pre-established requirements	Basic	Considerable	Full
Need for software conformance with external interface specifications	Basic	Considerable	Full
Concurrent development of associated new hardware and operational procedures	Some	Moderate	Extensive
Need for innovative data processing architectures, algorithms	Minimal	Some	Considerable
Premium on early completion	Low	Medium	High
Product size range	< 50 KDSI	< 300 KDSI	All sizes
Examples	Batch data reduction	Most transaction processing	Large, complex transaction
	Scientific models	systems	processing
	Business models	New OS, DBMS	systems
	Familiar OS, compiler	Ambitious inventory, production control	Ambitious, very large OS
	Simple inventory, production control	Simple command-control	Avionics Ambitious command-control

funds transfer network with high reliability, performance, development schedule and interface requirements. From Table 7.4 we determine that these characteristic best fit the profile of an embedded-mode project.

We next estimate the size of the product as 10 000 delivered source instructions, or 10 KDSI. From Table 7.5 we then determine that the nominal development effort for this embedded-mode project is

$$2.8(10)^{1.20} = 44 \text{ MM}.$$

Step 2: Determine effort multipliers Each of the 15 cost driver attributes in COCOMO has a rating scale and a set of effort multipliers which indicate by how

Table 7.5 COCOMO **nominal effort and schedule equations**

Development mode	Nominal effort*	Schedule
Organic	$(MM)_{NOM} = 3.2(KDSI)^{1.05}$	$T_{DEV} = 2.5(MM_{DEV})^{0.38}$
Semidetached	$(MM)_{NOM} = 3.0(KDSI)^{1.12}$	$T_{DEV} = 2.5(MM_{DEV})^{0.35}$
Embedded	$(MM)_{NOM} = 2.8(KDSI)^{1.20}$	$T_{DEV} = 2.5(MM_{DEV})^{0.32}$

*KDSI = thousands of delivered source instructions.

Table 7.6 Intermediate COCOMO **software development effort multipliers**

	Ratings					
Cost drivers	Very low	Low	Nominal	High	Very high	Extra high
Product attributes						
RELY: required software reliability	0.75	0.88	1.00	1.15	1.40	
DATA: data base size		0.94	1.00	1.08	1.16	
CPLX: product complexity	0.70	0.85	1.00	1.15	1.30	1.65
Computer attributes						
TIME: execution time constraint			1.00	1.11	1.30	1.66
STOR: main storage constraint			1.00	1.06	1.21	1.56
VIRT: virtual machine volatility*		0.87	1.00	1.15	1.30	
TURN: computer turnaround time		0.87	1.00	1.07	1.15	
Personnel attributes						
ACAP: analyst capability	1.46	1.19	1.00	0.86	0.71	
AEXP: applications experience	1.29	1.13	1.00	0.91	0.82	
PCAP: programmer capability	1.42	1.17	1.00	0.86	0.70	
VEXP: virtual machine experience*	1.21	1.10	1.00	0.90		
LEXP: programming language experience	1.14	1.07	1.00	0.95		
Project attributes						
MODP: use of modern programming practices	1.24	1.10	1.00	0.91	0.82	
TOOL: use of software tools	1.24	1.10	1.00	0.91	0.83	
SCED: required development schedule	1.23	1.08	1.00	1.04	1.10	

*For a given software product the underlying virtual machine is the complex of hardware and software (OS, DBMS, etc.) it calls on to accomplish its tasks.

much the nominal effort estimate must be multiplied to account for the project's having to work at its rating level for the attribute.

These cost driver attributes and their corresponding effort multipliers are shown in Table 7.6. The summary rating scales for each cost driver attribute are shown in Table 7.7, except for the complexity rating scale, which is shown in Table 7.8. (Expanded rating scales for the other attributes are provided in Boehm (1981).)

The results of applying these tables to our microprocessor communications software example are shown in Table 7.9. The effect of a software fault in the electronic fund transfer system could be a serious financial loss; therefore, the project's RELY rating from Table 7.7 is High. Then, from Table 7.6, the effort multiplier for achieving a High level of required reliability is 1.15, or 15 per cent more effort than it would take to develop the software to a nominal level of required reliability.

The effort multipliers for the other cost driver attributes are obtained similarly, except for the Complexity attribute, which is obtained via Table 7.8. Here, we first determine that communications processing is best classified under device-dependent operations (column 3 in Table 7.8). From this column, we determine that communication line handling typically has a complexity rating of Very High; from Table 7.6, then, we determine that its corresponding effort multiplier is 1.30.

Step 3: Estimate development effort We then compute the estimated development effort for the microprocessor communications software as the nominal development

Table 7.7 COCOMO software cost driver ratings

	Ratings					
Cost driver	Very low	Low	Nominal	High	Very high	Extra high
Product attributes						
RELY	Effect: slight inconvenience	Low, easily recoverable losses	Moderate, recoverable losses	High financial loss	Risk to human life	
DATA		$\dfrac{\text{DB bytes}}{\text{Prog DSI}} < 10$	$10 \leqslant \dfrac{D}{P} < 100$	$100 \leqslant \dfrac{D}{P} < 1000$	$\dfrac{D}{P} \geqslant 1000$	
CPLX	See Table 8					
Computer attributes						
TIME			≤ 50% use of available execution time	70%	85%	95%
STOR			≤ 50% use of available storage	70%	85%	95%
VIRT		Major change every 12 months Minor: 1 month	Major: 6 months Minor: 2 weeks	Major: 2 months Minor: 1 week	Major: 2 weeks Minor: 2 days	
TURN		Interactive	Averaged turnaround < 4 hours	4–12 hours	> 12 hours	
Personnel attributes						
ACAP	15th percentile*	35th percentile	55th percentile	75th percentile	90th percentile	
AEXP	≤ 4 months experience	1 year	3 years	6 years	12 years	
PCAP	15th percentile	35th percentile	55th percentile	75th percentile	90th percentile	
VEXP	≤ 1 month experience	4 months	1 year	3 years		
LEXP	≤ 1 month experience	4 months	1 year	3 years		
Project attributes						
MODP	No use	Beginning use	Some use	General use	Routine use	
TOOL	Basic microprocessor tools	Basic mini tools	Basic midi/maxi tools	Strong maxi programming test tools	Add requirements, design, management documentation tools	
SCED	75% of normal	85%	100%	130%	160%	

* Team rating criteria analyses (programming) ability, efficiency, ability to communicate and cooperate.

Table 7.8 COCOMO **module complexity ratings versus type of module**

Rating	Control operations	Computational operations	Device-dependent operations	Data management operations
Very low	Straightline code with a few non-nested SP[†] operators: DOs, CASEs, IFTHENELSEs. Simple predicates	Evaluation of simple expressions; e.g., $A = B + C* (D - E)$	Simple read, write statements with simple formats	Simple arrays in main memory
Low	Straightforward nesting of SP operators. Mostly simple predicates	Evaluation of moderate-level expressions; e.g., $D = SQRT (B**2 - 4.*A*C)$	No cognizance needed of particular processor or I/O device characteristics done at GET/PUT level. No cognizance of overlap	Single-file subsetting with no data structure changes, no edits, no intermediate files
Normal	Mostly simple nesting. Some intermodule control. Decision tables	Use of standard math and statistical routines. Basic matrix/vector operations	I/O processing includes device selection, status checking and error processing	Multi-file input and single file output. Simple structural changes, simple edits
High	Highly nested SP operators with many compound predicates. Queue and stack control. Considerable intermodule control	Basic numerical analysis: multivariate interpolation ordinary differential equations. Basic truncation, roundoff concerns	Operations at physical I/O level (physical storage address translations, seeks, reads, etc.). Optimized I/O overlap	Special-purpose subroutines activated by data stream contents. Complex data restructuring at record level
Very high	Re-entrant and recursive coding. Fixed-priority interrupt handling	Difficult but structured NA near-singular matrix equations, partial differential equations	Routines for interrupt diagnosis, servicing, masking. Communication line handling	A generalized parameter-driven file structuring routine. File building, command processing, search optimization
Extra high	Multiple resource scheduling with dynamically changing priorities. Micro-code-level control	Difficult and unstructured NA. Highly accurate analysis of noisy, stochastic data	Device timing-dependent coding. Micro-programmed operations	Highly coupled dynamic relational structures. Natural language data management

† SP = structured programming.

Table 7.9 COCOMO **cost driver ratings: microprocessor communications software**

Cost driver	Situation	Rating	Effort multiplier
RELY	Serious financial consequences of software faults	High	1.15
DATA	20 000 bytes	Low	0.94
CPLX	Communications processing	Very high	1.30
TIME	Will use 70% of available time	High	1.11
STOR	45K of 64K store (70%)	High	1.06
VIRT	Based on commercial microprocessor hardware	Nominal	1.00
TURN	Two hour average turnaround time	Nominal	1.00
ACAP	Good senior analysts	High	0.86
AEXP	Three years	Nominal	1.00
PCAP	Good senior programmers	High	0.86
VEXP	Six months	Low	1.10
LEXP	Twelve months	Nominal	1.00
MODP	Most techniques in use over one year	High	0.91
TOOL	At basic minicomputer tool level	Low	1.10
SCED	Nine months	Nominal	1.00
	Effort adjustment factor (product of effort multipliers)		1.35

effort (44 MM) times the product of the effort multipliers for the 15 cost driver attributes in Table 7.9 (1.35). The resulting estimated effort for the project is then

$$(44 \text{ MM}) (1.35) = 59 \text{ MM}.$$

Step 4: Estimate related project factors   COCOMO has additional cost estimating relationships for computing the resulting dollar cost of the project and for the break-down of cost and effort by life-cycle phase (requirements, design, etc.) and by type of project activity (programming, test planning, management, etc.). Further relationships support the estimation of the project's schedule and its phase distri-bution. For example, the recommended development schedule can be obtained from the estimated development man-months via the embedded-mode schedule equation in Table 7.5:

$$T_{\text{DEV}} = 2.5(59)^{0.32} = 9 \text{ months.}$$

As mentioned above, COCOMO also supports the most common types of sensitivity analysis and trade-off analysis involved in scoping a software project. For example, from Tables 7.6 and 7.7, we can see that providing the software developers with an inter-active computer access capability (low turn-around time) reduces the TURN effort mul-tiplier from 1.00 to 0.87, and thus reduces the estimated project effort from 59 MM to

$$(59 \text{ MM}) (0.87) = 51 \text{ MM}.$$

The COCOMO model has been validated with respect to a sample of 63 projects representing a wide variety of business, scientific, systems, real-time and support soft-ware projects. For this sample, Intermediate COCOMO estimates come within 20 per cent of the actuals about 68 per cent of the time (see Fig. 7.5). Since the residuals roughly follow a normal distribution, this is equivalent to a standard deviation of roughly 20 per cent of the project actuals. This level of accuracy is representative of the current state of the art in software cost models. One can do somewhat better

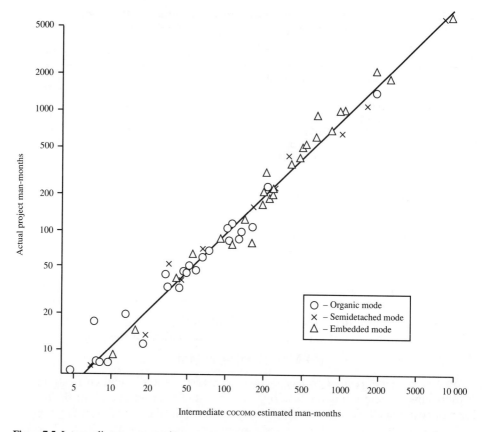

Figure 7.5 Intermediate COCOMO estimates versus project actuals.

with the aid of a calibration coefficient (also a COCOMO option), or within a limited applications context, but it is difficult to improve significantly on this level of accuracy while the accuracy of software data collection remains in the '±20 per cent' range.

A Pascal version of COCOMO is available for a nominal distribution charge from the Wang Institute, under the name WICOMO (Demshki *et al.* 1982).

Recent software cost estimation models   Most of the recent software cost estimation models tend to follow the Doty and COCOMO models in having a nominal scaling equation of the form $MM_{NOM} = c[KDSI]^x$ and a set of multiplicative effort adjustment factors determined by a number of cost driver attribute ratings. Some of them use the Rayleigh curve approach to estimate distribution across the software life cycle, but most use a more conservative effort–schedule trade-off relation than the SLIM model. These aspects have been summarized for the various models in Table 7.2 and Fig. 7.5.

The Bailey–Basili meta-model (Bailey and Basili 1981) derived the scaling equation

$$MM_{NOM} = 3.5 + 0.73[KDSI]^{1.16}$$

and used two additional cost driver attributes (methodology level and complexity) to model the development effort of 18 projects in the NASA–Goddard Software Engineering Laboratory to within a standard deviation of 15 per cent. Its accuracy for other project situations has not been determined.

The Grumman SOFCOST model (Dircks 1981) uses a similar but unpublished nominal effort scaling equation, modified by 30 multiplicative cost driver variables rated on a scale of 0–10. Table 7.2 includes a summary of these variables.

The Tausworthe Deep Space Network (DSN) model (Tausworthe 1981) uses a linear scaling equation ($MM_{NOM} = a[KDSI]^{1.0}$) and a similar set of cost driver attributes, also summarized in Table 7.2. It also has a well-considered approach for determining the equivalent KDSI involved in adapting existing software within a new product. It uses the Rayleigh curve to determine the phase distribution of effort, but uses a considerably more conservative version of the SLIM effort–schedule trade-off relationship (see Fig. 7.5).

The Jensen model (Jensen 1983a, b; Jensen and Lucas 1983) is a commercially available model with a similar nominal scaling equation and a set of cost driver attributes very similar to the Doty and COCOMO models (but with different effort multiplier ranges): see Table 7.2. Some of the multiplier ranges in the Jensen model vary as functions of other factors; e.g., increasing access to computer resources widens the multiplier ranges on such cost drivers as personnel capability and use of software tools. It uses the Rayleigh curve for effort distribution, and a somewhat more conservative effort–schedule trade-off relation than SLIM (see Fig. 7.5). As with the other commercial models, the Jensen model produces a number of useful outputs on resource expenditure rates, probability distributions on costs and schedules, etc.

7.3.4 Outstanding research issues in software cost estimation

Although a good deal of progress has been made in software cost estimation, a great deal remains to be done. This section updates the state-of-the-art review published in Boehm (1981), and summarizes the outstanding issues needing further research:

1. Software size estimation
2. Software size and complexity metrics
3. Software cost driver attributes and their effects
4. Software cost model analysis and refinement
5. Quantitative models of software project dynamics
6. Quantitative models of software life-cycle evolution
7. Software data collection

Software size estimation The biggest difficulty in using today's algorithmic software cost models is the problem of providing sound sizing estimates. Virtually every model requires an estimate of the number of source or object instructions to be developed, and this is an extremely difficult quantity to determine in advance. It would be most useful to have some formula for determining the size of a software product in terms of quantities known early in the software life cycle, such as the number and/or size of the

Table 7.10 Size ranges of software products performing same function

Experiment	Product	No. of teams	Size range (source-instr.)
Weinberg and Schulman	Simultaneous linear equations	6	33–165
Boehm *et al.*	Interactive cost model	7	1514–4606

files, input formats, reports, displays, requirements specification elements or design specification elements.

Some useful steps in this direction are the function-point approach in Albrecht (1979) and the sizing estimation model of Itakura and Takayanagi (1982), both of which have given reasonably good results for small to medium-sized business programs within a single data processing organization. Another more general approach is given by DeMarco (1982). This has the advantage of basing its sizing estimates on the properties of specifications developed in conformance with DeMarco's paradigm models for software specifications and designs: number of functional primitives, data elements, input elements, output elements, states, transitions between states, relations, modules, data tokens, control tokens, etc. To date, however, there has been relatively little calibration of the formulas to project data. A recent IBM study (Britcher and Gaffney 1982) shows some correlation between the number of variables defined in a state–machine design representation and the product size in source instructions.

Although some useful results can be obtained on the software sizing problem, one should not expect too much. A wide range of functionality can be implemented beneath any given specification element or I/O element, leading to a wide range of sizes. (Recall the uncertainty ranges of this nature in Fig. 7.3.) For example, two experiments, involving the use of several teams developing a software program to the same overall functional specification, yielded size ranges of factors of 3–5 between programs (see Table 7.10).

The primary implication of this situation for practical software sizing and cost estimation is that *there is no royal road to software sizing*. This is no magic formula that will provide an easy and accurate substitute for the process of thinking through and fully understanding the nature of the software product to be developed. There are still a number of useful things that one can do to improve the situation, including the following:

- Use techniques that explicitly recognize the ranges of variability in software sizing. The PERT estimation technique (Wiest and Levy 1977) is a good example.
- Understand the primary sources of bias in software sizing estimates; see Boehm (1981: Chapter 21).
- Develop and use a corporate memory on the nature and size of previous software products.

Software size and complexity metrics Delivered source instructions (DSI) can be faulted for being too low-level a metric for use in early sizing estimation. On the other hand, they can also be faulted for being too high-level a metric for precise software cost estimation. Various complexity metrics have been formulated to capture more accurately the relative information content of a program's instructions, such as the Halstead software science metrics (Halstead 1977a), or the relative control complexity of a program, such as the metrics formulated by McCabe in Chapter 2 above. A number of variations of these metrics have been developed: a good recent survey of them is given in Harrison et al. (1982).

However, these metrics have yet to exhibit any practical superiority to DSI as a predictor of the relative effort required to develop software. Most recent studies (Sunohara et al. 1981; Kitchenham 1981a) show a reasonable correlation between these complexity metrics and development effort, but no better a correlation than that between DSI and development effort.

Further, the recent analysis of the software science results indicates that many of the published software science 'successes' were not as successful as they were previously considered. It indicates that much of the apparent agreement between software science formulas and project data was due to factors overlooked in the data analysis: inconsistent definitions and interpretations of software science quantities, unrealistic or inconsistent assumptions about the nature of the projects analysed, overinterpretation of the significance of statistical measures such as the correlation coefficient, and lack of investigation of alternative explanations for the data. The software science use of psychological concepts such as the Stroud number have also been seriously questioned in Coulter (1983).

The overall strengths and difficulties of software science are summarized in Shen et al. (1983). Despite the difficulties, some of the software science metrics have been useful in such areas as identifying error-prone modules. In general, there is a strong intuitive argument that more definitive complexity metrics will eventually serve as better bases for definitive software cost estimation than will DSI. Thus, the area continues to be an attractive one for further research.

Software cost driver attributes and their effects   Most of the software cost models discussed above contain a selection of cost driver attributes and a set of coefficients, functions or tables representing the effect of the attribute on software cost (see Table 7.2). Chapters 24–28 of Boehm (1981) contain summaries of the research to date on about 20 of the most significant cost driver attributes, plus statements of nearly 100 outstanding research issues in the area.

Since the publication of Boehm (1981), a few new results have appeared. Lawrence (1981) provides an analysis of 278 business data processing programs which indicate a fairly uniform development rate in procedure lines of code per hour, some significant effects on programming rate arising from batch turnaround time and level of experience, and relatively little effect due to use of interactive operation and modern programming practices (owing, perhaps, to the relatively repetitive nature of the software jobs sampled). Okada and Azuma (1982) analysed 30 CAD/CAM programs and found some significant effects due to type of software, complexity, personnel skill level and requirements volatility.

Software cost model analysis and refinement   The most useful comparative analysis of software cost models to date is the Thibodeau (1981) study performed for the US Air

Force. This study compared the results of several models (the Wolverton, Doty, PRICE s and SLIM models discussed earlier, plus models from the Boeing, SDC, Tecolote and Aerospace Corporations) with respect to 45 project data points from three sources.

Some generally useful comparative results were obtained, but the results were not definitive, as models were evaluated with respect to larger and smaller subsets of the data. Not too surprisingly, the best results were generally obtained using models with calibration coefficients against data sets with few points. In general, the study concluded that the models with calibration coefficients achieved better results, but that none of the models evaluated was sufficiently accurate to be used as a definitive Air Force software cost estimation model.

Some further comparative analyses are currently being conducted by various organizations, using the database of 63 software projects in Boehm (1981), but to date none of these has been published.

In general, such evaluations play a useful role in model refinement. As certain models are found to be inaccurate in certain situations, efforts are made to determine the causes, and to refine the model to eliminate the sources of inaccuracy.

Relatively less activity has been devoted to the formulation, evaluation and refinement of models to cover the effects of more advanced methods of software development (prototyping, incremental development, use of application generators, etc.) or to estimate other software-related life-cycle costs (conversion, maintenance, installation, training, etc.). An exception is the excellent work on software conversion cost estimation performed by the Federal Conversion Support Center (Houtz and Buschbach 1981). An extensive model to estimate avionics software support costs using a weighted-multiplier technique has recently been developed (SYSCON Corporation 1983). Also, some initial experimental results have been obtained on the quantitative impact of prototyping in Boehm *et al.* (1984) and on the impact of very high-level non-procedural languages in Harel and McLean (1982). In both studies, projects using prototyping and VHLLs were completed with significantly less effort.

Quantitative models of software project dynamics   Current software cost estimation models are limited in their ability to represent the internal dynamics of a software project, and to estimate how the project's phase distribution of effort and schedule will be affected by environmental or project management factors. For example, it would be valuable to have a model that would accurately predict the effort and schedule distribution effects of investing in more thorough design verification, or pursuing an incremental development strategy, or varying the staffing rate or experience mix, of reducing module size, etc.

Some current models assume a universal effort distribution, such as the Rayleigh curve (Putnam 1978) or the activity distributions in Wolverton (1974), which are assumed to hold for any type of project situation. Somewhat more realistic, but still limited, are models with phase-sensitive effort multipliers such as PRICE s (Freiman and Park 1979) and Detailed COCOMO (Boehm 1981).

Recently, some more realistic models of software project dynamics have begun to appear, although to date none of them have been calibrated to software project data.

The Phister phase-by-phase model (Phister 1981) estimates the effort and schedule required to design, code and test a software product as a function of such variables as the staffing level during each phase, the size of the average module to be developed, and such factors as interpersonal communications overhead rates and error detection rates. The Abdel-Hamid–Madnick model (Abdel-Hamid and Madnick 1982), based on Forrester's system dynamics world-view, estimates the time distribution of effort, schedule and residual defects as a function of such factors as staffing rates, experience mix, training rates, personnel turnover, defect introduction rates and initial estimation errors. Tausworthe (1982) derives and calibrates alternative versions of the SLIM effort–schedule trade-off relationship, using an intercommunication-overhead model of project dynamics. Some other recent models of software project dynamics are the Mitre SWAP model and the Duclos (1982) total software life-cycle model.

Quantitative models of software life-cycle evolution   Although most of the software effort is devoted to the software maintenance (or life-cycle support) phase, only a few significant results have been obtained to date in formulating quantitative models of the software life-cycle evolution process. Some basic studies by Belady and Lehman analysed data on several projects and derived a set of fairly general 'laws of program evolution' (Belady and Lehman 1979; Lehman 1980). For example, the first of these laws states:

> A program that is used, and that as an implementation of its specification reflects some other reality, undergoes continual change or becomes progressively less useful. The change or decay process continues until it is judged more cost-effective to replace the system with a re-created version.

Some general quantitative support for these laws was obtained in several studies during the 1970s, and in more recent studies such as Kitchenham (1982). However, efforts to refine these general laws into a set of testable hypotheses have met with mixed results. For example, the Lawrence (1982) statistical analysis of the Belady–Lehman data showed that the data supported an even stronger form of the first law ('systems grow in size over their useful life'); that one of the laws could not be formulated precisely enough to be tested by the data; and that the other three laws did not lead to hypotheses that were supported by the data.

Software data collection   A fundamental limitation to significant progress in software cost estimation is the lack of unambiguous, widely used standard definitions for software data. For example, if an organization reports its 'software development man-months', do these include the effort devoted to requirements analysis, to training, to secretaries, to quality assurance, to technical writers, to uncompensated overtime? Depending on one's interpretations, one can easily cause variations of over 20 per cent (and often over a factor of 2) in the meaning of reported 'software development man-months' between organizations (and similarly for 'delivered instructions', 'complexity', 'storage constraint', etc.). Given such uncertainties in the ground data, it is not surprising that software cost estimation models cannot do much better than 'within 20 per cent of the actuals, 70 per cent of the time'.

Some progress towards clear software data definitions has been made. The IBM FSD database used in Walston and Felix (1977) was carefully collected using thorough data definitions, but the detailed data and definitions are not generally available. The NASA–Goddard Software Engineering Laboratory database (Basili 1980; Basili and Weiss 1982a; McGarry 1982) and the COCOMO database (Boehm 1981) provide both clear data definitions and an associated project database which are available for general use (and are reasonably compatible). The recent Mitre SARE report (Dumas 1983) provides a good set of data definitions.

But there is still no commitment across organizations to establish and use a set of clear and uniform software data definitions. Until this happens, our progress in developing more precise software cost estimation methods will be severely limited.

[Section 7.4 is not reproduced here.]

8

SOFTWARE FUNCTION, SOURCE LINES OF CODE AND DEVELOPMENT EFFORT PREDICTION: A SOFTWARE SCIENCE VALIDATION

Alan J. Albrecht and John E. Gaffney, Jr

IBM Corporate Information Systems and Administration and IBM Federal Systems Division

ABSTRACT

One of the most important problems faced by software developers and users is the prediction of the size of a programming system and its development effort. As an alternative to size, one might deal with a measure of the function that the software is to perform. Albrecht (1979) has developed a methodology to estimate the amount of the function the software is to perform in terms of the data it is to use (absorb) and to generate (produce). The function is quantified as 'function points', essentially, a weighted sum of the numbers of inputs, outputs, master files and inquiries provided to, or generated by, the software. This chapter demonstrates the equivalence between Albrecht's external input/output data flow representative of a program (the function points metric) and Halstead's 'software science' or 'software linguistics' model of a program as well as the 'soft content' variation of Halstead's model suggested by Gaffney (1979b).

Further, the high degree of correlation between function points and the eventual source lines of code (SLOC) of the program, and between function points and the work effort required to develop the code, is demonstrated. The function point measure is thought to be more useful than SLOC as a prediction of work effort because function points are relatively easily estimated from a statement of basic requirements for a program early in the development cycle.

The strong degree of equivalency between function points and SLOC shown in the paper suggests a two-step work-effort validation procedure, first using function points to estimate SLOC, and then using SLOC to estimate the work effort. This approach would provide validation of application development work plans and work effort estimates early in the development cycle. The approach would also more effectively use the existing base of knowledge on producing SLOC until a similar base is developed for function points.

The paper assumes that the reader is familiar with the fundamental theory of software science measurements and the practice of validating estimates of work effort to design and implement software applications (programs). If not, a review of Albrecht (1979), Halstead (1977a) and Gaffney (1981) is suggested.

8.1. FUNCTION POINTS BACKGROUND

Albrecht (1979) has employed a methodology for validating estimates of the amount of work effort (which he calls 'work-hours') needed to design and develop custom application software. The approach taken is 'to list and count the number of external user inputs, inquiries, outputs and master files to be delivered by the development project'. As pointed out by Albrecht (1979), 'these factors are the outward manifestations of any application. They cover all the functions in an application'. Each of these categories of input and output are counted individually and then weighted by numbers reflecting the relative value of the function to the user/customer. The weighted sum of the inputs and outputs is called 'function points'. Albrecht (1979) states that the weights used were 'determined by debate and trial'. They are given in Section 8.4.

The thesis of this work is that the amount of function to be provided by the application (program) can be estimated from an itemization of the major components of data to be used or provided by it. Furthermore, this estimate of function should be correlated to both the amount of SLOC to be developed and the development effort needed.

A major reason for using function points as a measure is that the point counts can be developed relatively easily in discussions with the user/customer at an *early* stage of the development process. They relate directly to user/customer requirements in a way that is more easily understood by the user/customer than SLOC.

Another major reason is the availability of needed information. Since it is reasonable to expect that a statement of basic requirements includes an itemization of the inputs and outputs to be used and provided by the application (program) from the user's external view, an estimate may be validated early in the development cycle with this approach.

A third reason is that function points can be used to develop a general measure of development productivity (e.g. 'function points per work-month' or 'work-hours per function point'), which may be used to demonstrate productivity trends. Such a measure can give credit for productivity relative to the amount of user function delivered to the user/customer per unit of development effort, with less concern for effects of technology, language level or unusual code expansion occasioned by macros, calls and code reuse.

It is important to distinguish between two types of work-effort estimates: a primary or 'task-analysis' estimate, and a 'formula' estimate. The primary work-effort estimate should always be based on an analysis of the tasks to be done, thus providing the project team with an estimate *and a work plan*. This paper discusses formula estimates, which are based solely on counts of inputs and outputs of the program to be developed, and not on a detailed analysis of the development tasks to be performed. It is recommended that such 'formula' estimates be used only to validate and provide perspective on primary estimates.

8.2 'SOFTWARE SCIENCE' BACKGROUND

Halstead (1977a) states that the number of tokens or symbols N constituting a program is a function of η_1 the 'operator' vocabulary size, and η_2 the 'operand' vocabulary size. His software length equation is

$$N = \eta_1 \log_2 \eta_1 + \eta_2 \log_2 \eta_2.$$

This formula was orginally derived to apply to a small program (or to one procedure of a large program) or function, that is, to apply to the program expression of an algorithm. Thus, the number of tokens in a program consisting of a multiplicity of functions or procedures is best found by applying the size equation to each function or procedure individually and summing the results.

Gaffney (1981) has applied the software length equation to a single-address machine in the following way. A program consists of data plus instructions. A sequence of instructions can be thought of as a string of 'tokens'. At the machine code level, for a single address machine, 'op. code' tokens generally alternate with 'data label' tokens. Exceptions do occur as a result of instructions that require no data labels. The op. codes may be referred to as 'operators' and the data labels as 'operands'. Thus, in an instruction of the form 'LA X', meaning, load accumulator with the content of location X, LA is the operator, and X is the operand. For single-address machine-level code, the case Gaffney (1981) analyses, one would expect to have approximately twice as many tokens (N) as instructions (I); that is, $I = 0.5N$. Gaffney (1981) applied the Halstead software length equation to object code for the AN/UYK-7 military computer (used in the Trident missile submarine's sonar system, as well as other applications). He determined a value for the coefficient b in the equation $I = bN$. It was $b = 0.478$, and the correlation between the estimate $I = 0.478N$ (where the estimate $\hat{N} = \eta_1 \log_2 \eta_1 + \eta_2 \log_2 \eta_2$) and the actual instruction count I was 0.916. Thus, the data correlated closely with the estimate from the software length equation.

Gaffney's work presumed that the number of unique instruction types (η_1) or operator vocabulary size employed, as well as the number of unique data labels (η_2) or operand vocabulary size used, was known. However, η_1 need not be known in order for one to estimate the number of tokens N or the number of instructions I. An 'average' figure for η_1 (and thus for $\eta_1 \log_2 \eta_1$) can be employed, or the factor $\eta_1 \log_2 \eta_1$ can be omitted, inducing some degree of error, of course. Indeed, Christiansen *et al.* (1981) have observed that 'program size is determined by the data that must be processed by the program'. Thus, one could take several different approaches to estimating software (code) size. The data label vocabulary size (η_2)

Table 8.1 DP service project data

Custom application number	Language	Input/output element counts[*]				Function points	Source lines of code (SLOC)	Work-hours
		IN	OUT	FILE	INQ			
1	Cobol	25	150	60	75	1750	130K	102.4K
2	Cobol	193	98	36	70	1902	318K	105.2K
3	Cobol	70	27	12	—	428	20K	11.1K
4	PL/1	40	60	12	20	759	54K	21.1k
5	Cobol	10	69	9	1	431	62K	28.8K
6	Cobol	13	19	23	—	283	28K	10.0K
7	Cobol	34	14	5	—	205	35K	8.0K
8	Cobol	17	17	5	15	289	30K	4.9K
9	Cobol	45	64	16	14	680	48K	12.9K
10	Cobol	40	60	15	20	794	93K	19.0K
11	Cobol	41	27	5	29	512	57K	10.8K
12	Cobol	33	17	5	8	224	22K	2.9K
13	Cobol	28	41	11	16	417	24K	7.5K
14	PL/1	43	40	35	20	682	42K	12.0K
15	Cobol	7	12	8	13	209	40K	4.1K
16	Cobol	28	38	9	24	512	96K	15.8K
17	PL/1	42	57	5	12	606	40K	18.3K
18	Cobol	27	20	6	24	400	52K	8.9K
19	Cobol	48	66	50	13	1235	94K	38.1K
20	PL/1	69	112	39	21	1572	110K	61.2K
21	Cobol	25	28	22	4	500	15K	3.6K
22	DMS	61	68	11	—	694	24K	11.8K
23	DMS	15	15	3	6	199	3K	0.5K
24	Cobol	12	15	15	—	260	29K	6.1K

[*] IN = no. of inputs; OUT = no. of outputs; FILE = no. of master files; INQ = no. of inquiries

could be estimated. Alternatively, it is suggested that (η_2^*), the number of conceptually unique inputs and outputs, can be used as a surrogate for (η_2). The estimate for (η_2^*) should be relatively easy to determine early in the design cycle, from the itemization of external inputs and outputs found in a complete requirements definition or external system design.

Some data by Dekerf (1981) suports the idea that I (and N) can be estimated as multiples of the variates $\eta_2 \log_2 \eta_2$ and $\eta_2^* \log_2 \eta_2^*$ (for example, $I = A\eta_2 \log_2 \eta_2$ where (A) is some constant). Dekerf counted tokens (N), operands (η_2) and conceptually unique inputs and outputs (η_2^*) in 29 APL programs found in a book by Allen (1978) of the IBM System Science Institute in Los Angeles. Using Dekerf's data, we have found that the sample correlation between N and $\eta_2^* \log_2 \eta_2^*$ is 0.918, and between N and $\eta_2, \log_2 \eta_2$ is 0.988.

In the following sections we demonstrate that these (and other) software science formulas, originally developed for (small) algorithms only, can be applied to large applications (programs), where (η_2^*) is then interpreted to mean the sum of overall external inputs and outputs to the application (program).

Function points (Albrecht 1979) can be interpreted as a weighted sum of the top-level input/output items (e.g. screens, reports, files) that are equivalent to (η_2^*). Also, as is shown subsequently, a number of variates based on function points can be used as the measure of the function that the application (program) is to provide.

8.3 DP SERVICES DATA

Table 8.1 provides data on 24 applications developed by the IBM DP Services organization. The language used in each application is cited. The counts of four types of external input/output elements for the application as a whole are given. The number of function points for each program is identified. The number of SLOC, including comments (all the SLOC were new) that implemented the function required, is identified. Finally, the number of work-hours required to design, develop and test the application is given.

8.4 SELECTION OF ESTIMATING FORMULAS

Using the DP Services data shown in Table 8.1, 13 estimating formulas were explored as functions of the 9 variates listed in Table 8.2. A basis for their selection is now provided.

Function points counts (F) is the variable determined using Albrecht's methodology (Albrecht 1979). Albrecht uses the following average weights to determine function points: number of inputs $\times 4$; number of outputs $\times 5$; number of inquiries $\times 4$; number of master files $\times 10$. Interfaces are considered to be master files. As stated in Albrecht (1979), the weighted sum of inputs, outputs, inquiries and master files can be adjusted within a range of ± 25 per cent, depending upon the estimator's assessment of the complexity of the program. As an example of the calculation of the number of function points, consider the data for custom application

Table 8.2 Estimating variates explored

Independent variate	Fomula basis	Dependent variable explored source lines of code		
		PL/1	Cobol	Work-hours
1. Function points	F	×	×	×
2. Function sort content	$(F/2)\log_2(F/2)$	×		×
3. Function potential volume	$(F+2)\log_2(F+2)$	×		
4. Function information content	$F\log_2 F$	×		×
5. I/0 count	V			×
5. Sort count	$(V/2)\log_2(V/2)$			×
7. Count information content	$V\log_2 V$			×
8. Source lines of Cobol	SLOC			×
9. Source lines of PL/1	SLOC			×

1 in Table 8.1. The number of function points is equal to

$$F = (25 \times 4) + (150 \times 5) + (75 \times 4) + (60 \times 10) = 1750.$$

The current 'Function Points Index Worksheet' being used in the IBM I/S organization is shown in the Appendix (Fig. 8.2). The major changes from Albrecht (1979) are
as follows:

1. Interfaces are separately identified and counted.
2. Provision is made for above-average and below-average complexities of the
   elements counted.
3. A more objective measure of processing complexity is provided.

The I/O count (V) is the total program input/output count without the weights
and processing complexity adjustment applied in function points. Both function
points and I/O count are treated as equivalent to Halstead's η_2^*, the unique input/out-
put (data element) count. The potential volume formula, $(F + 2) \log_2 (F + 2)$, was
developed by Halstead (1977a). The information content formula, $(F \log_2 F)$, also
used as a variate here, corresponds to $\eta_2^* \log_2 \eta_2^*$, an approximation to the factor
$\eta_2 \log_2 \eta_2$ in Halstead's software length equation.

The origin of the sort count variate, $(F/2) \log_2 (F/2)$, is as follows. Gaffney
(1979b) estimated the number of conditional jumps in a program to be

$$J = (\eta_2^*/2) \log_2 (\eta_2^*/2)$$

if it is assumed that the η_2^* (total number of conceptually unique inputs and
outputs) are equally divided between inputs and outputs. This is in keeping with
the following observations. If $\eta_2^*/2$ were to symbolize the number of items to be
sorted (by a data processing program), then the number of comparisons (and hence
conditional jumps) required would be on the order of J, as just defined (Stanat
and McAllister 1977). This form is used subsequently as the sort content where
either the variable F (function point) or V (I/O count) is employed in the place
of η_2^*.

8.5 DEVELOPMENT AND APPLICATION OF ESTIMATING FORMULAS

This section provides a number of formulas for estimating work hours and SLOC as
functions of function points (F), input/output count (V) and several of the variates
cited in Table 8.2, which themselves are functions of F and V, as described in the
previous section.

To demonstrate the equivalence of the various measures and also to show their
effectiveness as estimators, correlations were performed on the combinations of variates checked in Table 8.2. Table 8.3 summarizes the results of using the variates
checked to estimate SLOC in the Cobol and PL/1 applications (see Table 8.1), as indicated. The estimating model relating function points to PL/1 SLOC was found to be

Table 8.3 Summary comparison of the SLOC estimation approaches

Estimators of SLOC variables used	Relative error		Sample correlation between the variables and actual SLOC
	Avg.[†]	St. dev.	
1. Function points (Cobol)	0.229	0.736	0.854
2. Function points (PL/1)	0.003	0.058	0.997
3. Function sort content (PL/1)	0.007	0.057	0.997
4. Function potential volume (PL/1)	−0.002	0.057	0.997
5. Function information content (PL/1)	−0.002	0.057	0.997

   [*] The formulas used were:
    1. $\hat{S} = 118.7\,(F) - 6490$
    2. $\hat{S} = 73.1\,(F) - 4600$
    3. $\hat{S} = 13.9\,(F/2)\log_2{(F/2)} + 5360$
    4. $\hat{S} = 6.3\,(F+2)\log_2{(F+2)} + 4370$
    5. $\hat{S} = 6.3\,(F\log_2{F}) + 4500$
   [†] $(\hat{S} - S)/S$, where $\hat{S}$ = estimate and S = actual SLOC

quite different from the model for Cobol. Significantly more Cobol SLOC are required to deliver the same amount of function points than are required with PL/1 SLOC. The PL/1 data in particular closely approximate a straight line for all the measures. Any of the measures shown should be a good estimator for PL/1 SLOC. In the next section, these measures are further validated using additional data from three other application development sites.

Table 8.4 summarizes the results of using the variables checked in Table 8.2 and SLOC to estimate work effort. The correlations and standard deviations of the data for the estimating formulas, using the I/O count (V) and function point count (F) shown, suggest that any of them would be an effective 'formula' estimate. The measures based on I/O count show slightly, but not significantly, better statistics than those based on function points. The last two rows of Table 8.4 summarize the results of using SLOC to estimate work effort. It is shown that the estimating model based on the Cobol data is quite different from the model based on PL/1 data. Almost twice as much work effort is required to produce a SLOC of PL/1 as is required to produce a SLOC of Cobol. However, Table 8.3 shows that almost twice as much function is estimated to be delivered by a SLOC of PL/1 as is estimated to be delivered by a SLOC of Cobol. Therefore, it is advisable to keep these languages separated in estimating models based on SLOC.

Figure 8.1 is a scatter plot of actual function points and work-hours data, and estimation formula 1 from Table 8.4 plotted on the same graph.

The correlations and standard deviations of linear models of function points, function sort content, function information content, I/O count, I/O count sort content, I/O count information content and SLOC are given in Table 8.4. Each model could be an effective tool for validating estimates. The early availability of elements that comprise function points and I/O count for an application suggest that this validation could be done earlier in the development schedule than validations based on estimated SLOC.

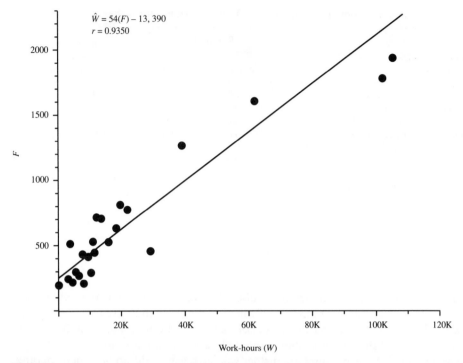

Figure 8.1

Table 8.4 Summary comparison of the work-hours estimation approaches

Estimators of work-hours variables used*	Relative error[†]		Sample correlation between the variables and actual work-hours
	Avg.	St. dev.	
1. Function points	0.242	0.848	0.935
2. Function sort content	0.192	0.759	0.945
3. Function information content	0.194	0.763	0.944
4. I/O count	0.206	0.703	0.945
5. I/O count sort content	0.195	0.630	0.954
6. I/O count information content	0.195	0.637	0.954
7. Source lines of code (PL/1)	0.023	0.213	0.988
8. Source lines of code (Cobol)	0.323	0.669	0.864

* The formulas used were:

1. $\hat{W} = 54(F) - 13\,390$
2. $\hat{W} = 10.75(F/2) \log_2 (F/2) - 8300$
3. $\hat{W} = 4.89(F \log_2 F) - 8762$
4. $\hat{W} = 309(V) - 15\,780$
5. $\hat{W} = 79(V/2) \log_2 (V/2) - 8000$
6. $\hat{W} = 35(V \log_2 V) - 8900$
7. $\hat{W} = 0.6713(S) - 13\,137$ (PL/1)
8. $\hat{W} = 0.3793(S) - 2913$ (Cobol)

[†] $(\hat{W} - W)/S$, where $\hat{W}$ = estimated and W = actual work-hours

Table 8.5. Some validation statistics

SLOC estimating formula[†]	Relative error[‡]		Sample correlation between $\hat{S}$ and S
	Avg.	St. dev.	
$\hat{S}_1$	−0.0753	0.5438	0.9367
$\hat{S}_2$	0.2406	0.5174	0.9367
$\hat{S}_3$	−0.0182	0.4151	0.9374
$\hat{S}_4$	0.0629	0.3983	0.9289

* For 'validation sites' 2, 3 and 4, see detailed data in Table 8.6.

[†] $\hat{S}_1 = 73.1F - 4600$ (based on the PL/1 cases)

$\hat{S}_2 = 53.2F + 12\,773$ (based on all 24 cases)

$\hat{S}_3 = 66F$ (a simplified model)

$\hat{S} = 6.3F\log F + 4500$ (based on the PL/1 cases)

derived from the DPS data

[‡] $(\hat{S} - S)/S$, where $S =$ actual SLOC and $\hat{S} =$ estimated SLOC.

8.6 VALIDATION

The previous section, and the related figure and tables, developed several estimating formulas and explored their consistency within the DP Services data used to develop the formulas. This section validates several SLOC estimation formulas developed from the DP Services data presented in Table 8.1 against three different development sites. While it is *interesting* to note relations between function points and SLOC, it is *significant* to know that these relations hold also on a different set of data from that employed to develop them originally. The excellent degree of fit obtained would tend to support the view that these (and the other) formulas not validated here have some degree of universality. Table 8.5 presents four formulas developed from the DP Services data, and the statistics of their validation on the data from the other three sites. Table 8.6 provides the data from the three sites from which the statistics in Table 8.5 are derived. The very high values of sample correlation between the estimated and actual SLOC for the 17 validation sites listed in Table 8.5 (i.e. > 0.92) are most encouraging.

8.7 CONCLUSION

The function point software estimation procedure appears to have a strong theoretical support based on Halstead's software science formulas. Apparently, some of Halstead's formulas are extremely robust and can be applied to the major inputs and outputs of a software product at the top level. At least for the applications analysed, both the development work-hours and application size in SLOC are strong functions of function points and input/output data item count. Further, it appears that basing applications development effort estimates on the amount of function to be provided by an application rather than on an estimate of SLOC may be superior.

Table 8.6 Validation of some SLOC estimating equations

Application number		Function points F	PL/1 SLOC S	$\hat{S}_1$ (KSLOC)	$\hat{S}_2$ (KSLOC)	$\hat{S}_3$ (KSLOC)	$\hat{S}_4$ (KSLOC)
1. DPS –	4	759	54K	50.9	53.2	50.1	50.2
2.	14	682	42K	45.2	49.1	45.0	44.9
3.	17	606	40K	39.7	45.0	40.0	39.8
4.	20	1572	110K	110.3	96.4	103.8	109.7
5. Site 2–	1	803	31.0K	54.1	55.5	53.0	53.3
6.	2	335	31.4K	19.9	30.6	22.1	22.2
7.	3	685	23.3K	45.5	49.2	45.2	45.2
8.	4	1119	126.6K	77.2	72.3	73.9	75.9
9.	5	712	40.9K	47.4	50.7	47.0	47.0
10.	6	261	19.9K	14.5	26.7	17.2	17.7
11. Site 3–	1	1387	120K	96.8	86.6	91.5	95.7
12.	2	1728	120K	121.7	104.7	114.0	121.6
13.	3	2878	150K	205.8	165.9	190.0	212.8
14. Site 4–	1	2165	123.2K	153.7	128.0	142.9	155.6
15.	2	236	16.3K	12.7	25.3	15.6	16.2
16.	3	3694	195.0K	265.4	209.3	243.8	280.3
17.	4	224	41.0K	11.8	24.7	14.8	15.5
18.	5	42	6.5K	−1.5	15.0	2.8	5.9
19.	6	1629	102.0K	114.5	99.4	107.5	114.0
20.	7	105	9.8K	3.1	18.4	6.9	8.9
21.	8	581	45.9K	37.9	43.7	38.3	38.1
Av. relative error				−0.060	0.186	−0.024	0.051
St. dev. of relative error				0.488	0.480	0.372	0.358
Correlation with S				0.938	0.938	0.938	0.997

The observations suggest a two-step estimate validation process, which uses function points or I/O count to estimate, early in the development cycle, the SLOC to be produced. The work effort would then be estimated from the estimated SLOC. This approach can provide an early bridge between function points, software science and SLOC, until function points and software science have a broader supporting base of productivity data.

APPENDIX: FUNCTION POINTS DEFINITIONS

This section provides the basic definitions supporting the measurement, recording and analysis of function points, work effort and attributes.

General

The following considerations are generally applicable to the specific definitions of function points, work effort and attributes in the paragraphs that follow.

Development work-product versus support work-product Development productivity should be measured by counting the function points added or changed by the development or enhancement project. Therefore, we have the following.

Development work-product This refers to the absolute value sum of all function points added or changed by the development or enhancement project. (Deleted function points are considered to be changed function points.)

Support productivity should be measured by counting the total function points supported by the support project during the support period. Therefore, we have the following.

Support work-product This encompasses the original function points of the application, adjusted for any changes in complexity introduced, plus any function points added, minus any function points deleted by subsequent enhancement projects.

Measurement timing To provide the work-product, work-effort and attributes measures needed for each development project, enhancement project and support project to be measured, the indicated measures should be determined at the following times in the application life cycle:

- The development work-product and attributes measures should be determined at the completion of the *external design phase* for each development and enhancement project (when the user external view of the application has been documented).
- The development work-product, work-effort and attributes measures should be determined at the completion of the *installation phase* for each development and enhancement project (when the application is ready for use).
- The support work-product, work-effort and attributes measures should be determined at the end of *each year* of support and use for each support project.

Application boundaries Normally, a single continuous external boundary is considered when counting function points. However, there are two general situations where counting function points for an application in parts is necessary.

1. The application is planned to be developed in multiple stages, using more than one development project. This situation should be counted, estimated and measured as *separate projects*, including all inputs, outputs, interfaces and inquiries crossing *all* boundaries.
2. The application is planned to be developed as a single application using one development project, but it is so large that it will be necessary to divide it into sub-applications for counting function points. The internal boundaries are arbitrary and are for counting purposes only. The sub-applications should be counted separately, but *none* of the inputs, outputs, interfaces or inquiries crossing the *arbitrary internal* boundaries should be counted. The function points of the sub-applications should then be summed to give the total function points of the application for estimation and measurement.

Brought-in application code   Count the function points provided by brought-in application code (reused code), such as: an IBM, IUP, PP or FDP; an internal shared application; or a purchased application if that code was selected, modified, integrated, tested or installed by the project team. However, do *not* count the function points provided by the brought-in code that provided user functions beyond that stated in the approved requirements.

Some examples follow.

1. Do count the function points provided by an application picked up from another IBM site, or project, and installed by the project team.
2. Do *not* count the function points provided by software, such as IMS or a screen compiler, if that software had been made available by another project team.
3. Do *not* count ADF updates of *all* files if the user only required updates of *three* files, even though the capability may be automatically provided.

Consider all users   Consider all users of the application, since each application may have provision for many specified user functions, such as:

- End user functions (enter data, inquire, etc.)
- Conversion and installation user functions (file scan, file compare discrepancy list, etc.)
- Operations user functions (recovery, control totals, etc.)

Function points measure

After the general considerations described in the preceding paragraphs have been decided, the function points measure is accomplished in three general steps:

1. Classify and count the five user function types.
2. Adjust for processing complexity.
3. Make the function points calculation.

The paragraphs in this section define and describe each of these steps. The first step is accomplished as follows.

Classify, to three levels of complexity, the following user functions that were made available to the user through the design, development, testing or support efforts of the development, enhancement or support project team:

1. External input types
2. External output types
3. Logical internal file types
4. External interface file types
5. External inquiry types

Then *list* and *count* these user functions. The counts should be recorded for use in the function points calculation, on an appropriate work-sheet. Examples of the useful function points work-sheets are provided in Fig. 8.2, function points work-sheet.

The definitions of each of the user functions to be counted, and the levels of complexity, are provided in the following paragraphs.

External input type Count each unique user *data* or user *control* input type that enters the external boundary of the application being measured, and *adds* or *changes* data in a logical internal file type. An external input type should be considered unique if it has a different *format*, or if the external design requires a *processing logic* different from other external input types of the same format. Do include external input types that enter directly as transactions from the user, and those that enter as transactions from other applications, such as, input files of transactions.

Each external input type should be classified within three levels of complexity, as follows.

- *Simple* Few data element types are included in the external input type, and few logical internal file types are referenced by the external input type. User human factors considerations are not significant in the design of the external input type.

- *Average* The external input type is not clearly either simple or complex.
- *Complex* Many data element types are included in the external input type, and many logical internal file types are referenced by the external input type. User human factors considerations significantly affect the design of the external input type.

Do *not* include external input types that are introduced into the application only because of the technology used.

Do *not* include input files of records as external input types, because these are counted as external interface file types.

Do *not* include the input part of the external inquiry types as external input types, because these are counted as external inquiry types.

External output type Count each unique user *data* or *control* output type that leaves the external boundary of the application being measured. An external output type should be considered unique if it has a different *format*, or if the external design requires a *processing logic* different from other external output types of the same format. Do include external output types that leave directly as reports and messages to the user, and those that leave as reports and messages to other applications, such as output files of reports and messages.

Each external output type should be classified within three levels of complexity, using definitions similar to those for the external input types. For reports, the following additional complexity definitions should be used.

- *Simple* One or two columns; simple data element transformations
- *Average* Multiple columns with subtotals; multiple data element transformations.
- *Complex* Intricate data element transformations; multiple and complex file references to be correlated; significant performance considerations.

Do *not* include external output types that are introduced into the application only because of the technology used.

Do *not* include output files of records as external output types, because these are counted as external interface file types.

Do *not* include the output response of external inquiry types as external output types, because these are counted as external inquiry types.

Logical internal file type   Count each major logical group of user *data* or *control* information in the application as a logical internal file type. Include each logical file, or within a data base, each logical group of data from the viewpoint of the user that is *generated, used* and *maintained* by the application. Count logical files as described in the external design, not physical files.

The logical internal file types should be classified within three levels of complexity as follows.

- *Simple*   Few record types; few data element types; no significant performance or recovery considerations
- *Average*   Not clearly either simple or complex
- *Complex*   Many record types; many data element types; performance and recovery are significant considerations

Do *not* include logical internal files that are *not* accessible to the user through external input, output, interface file or inquiry types.

External interface file type   Files *passed* or *shared* between applications should be counted as external interface file types within *each* application. Count each major logical group of users *data* or *control* information that enters or leaves the application, as an external interface file type. External interface file types should be classified within three levels of complexity, using definitions similar to those for logical internal file types.

Outgoing external interface file types should also be counted as logical internal file types for the application.

External inquiry type   Count each unique input/output combination, where an input caused and generates an immediate output, as an external inquiry type. An external inquiry type should be considered unique if it has a *format* different from other external inquiry types in either its input or output parts, or if the external design requires a *processing logic* different from other external inquiry types of the same format. Include external inquiry types that enter directly from the user, and those that enter from other applications.

The external inquiry types should be classified within three levels of complexity as follows.

1. Classify the input part of the external inquiry using definitions similar to the external input type.
2. Classify the output part of the external inquiry type using definitions similar to the external output type.
3. The complexity of the external inquiry type is the greater of the two classifications.

To help distinguish external inquiry types from external input types, consider that the input data of an external inquiry type is entered only to direct the search, and no update of logical internal file types should occur.

Do *not* confuse a query facility with an external inquiry type. An external inquiry type is a direct search for specific data, usually using only a single key. A query facility provides an organized structure of external input, output and inquiry types to compose many possible inquiries using many keys and operations. These external input, output and inquiry types should *all* be counted to measure a query facility.

Processing complexity The previous paragraphs define the external input, external output, internal file, external interface file and external inquiry types to be listed, classified and counted. The function points calculation describes how to use these counts to measure the standard processing associated with those user functions. This paragraph describes how to apply some general application characteristics to adjust the standard processing measure for processing complexity.

The adjustment for processing complexity should be accomplished in three steps, as follows.

1. The *degree of influence* of each of the 14 general characteristics, on the value of the application to the users, should be estimated.
2. The 14 degrees of influence(s) should be summed, and the total should be used to develop an *adjustment factor* ranging from 0.65 to 1.35. (This gives an adjustment of ±35 per cent.)
3. The *standard processing measure* should be multiplied by the adjustment factor to develop the work-product measure called function points.

The first step is accomplished as follows.

Estimate the degree of influence, on the application, of each of the 14 general characteristics that follow. Use the degree of influence measures in the following list, and record the estimates on a work-sheet similar to Fig. 8.2.

Degree of influence measures

- Not present, or no influence if present   = 0
- Insignificant influence   = 1
- Moderate influence   = 2
- Average influence   = 3
- Significant influence   = 4
- Strong influence, throughout   = 5

General application characteristics

1. The *data* and control information used in the application is sent or received over *communication* facilities. Terminals connected locally to the control unit are considered to use communication facilities.

CI/S & A Guideline (Draft)

4.1 FUNCTION POINTS CALCULATION

Application: _____ Appl ID: _____

Prepared by: _____ _/_/_ Reviewed by: _____ _/_/_

Notes:

● **Function count**

Type ID	Description	Simple	Average	Complex	Total
		Complexity			
IT	External input	____ × 3 = ____	____ × 4 = ____	____ × 6 = ____	____
OT	External output	____ × 4 = ____	____ × 5 = ____	____ × 7 = ____	____
FT	Logical internal file	____ × 7 = ____	____ × 10 = ____	____ × 15 = ____	____
EI	External interface file	____ × 5 = ____	____ × 7 = ____	____ × 10 = ____	____
QT	External inquiry	____ × 3 = ____	____ × 4 = ____	____ × 6 = ____	____
PC		Total unadjusted function points			____

● **Processing complexity**

ID	Characteristic	DI	ID	Characteristic	DI
C1	Data communications	____	C8	Online update	____
C2	Distributed functions	____	C9	Complex processing	____
C3	Performance	____	C10	Reusability	____
C4	Heavily used configuration	____	C11	Installation ease	____
C5	Transaction rate	____	C12	Operational ease	____
C6	Online data entry	____	C13	Multiple sites	____
C7	End user efficiency	____	C14	Facilitate change	____
PC				Total degree of influence	____

● **DI values**

— Not present, or no influence = 0   — Average influence = 3
— Insignificant influence = 1   — Significant influence = 4
— Moderate influence = 2   — Strong influence throughout = 5

PCA (processing complexity adjustment) = 0.65 + (0.01 × PC) = _____
FP (function points measure) = FC × FCA _____

Figure 8.2

2. *Distributed* data or processing *functions* are a characteristic of the application.
3. Application *performance* objectives, in either response or throughput, influenced the design, development, installation and support of the application.
4. A *heavily used* operational *configuration* is a characteristic of the application. The user wants to run the application on existing or committed equipment that will be heavily used.
5. The *transaction rate* is high, and it influenced the design, development, installation and support of the application.
6. *On-line data entry* and control functions are provided in the application.
7. The on-line functions provided emphasize *end-user efficiency*.
8. The application provides *on-line update* for the logical internal files.
9. *Complex processing* is a characteristic of the application. Examples are:

   - Many control interactions and decision points.
   - Extensive logical and mathematical equations.
   - Much exception processing resulting in incomplete transactions that must be processed again.

10. The application, and the code in the application, has been specifically designed, developed and supported for *reusability* in other applications, and at other sites.
11. Conversion and *installation ease* are characteristics of the application. A conversion and installation plan was provided and it was tested during the system test phase.
12. *Operational ease* is a characteristic of the application. Effective start-up, back-up and recovery procedures were provided, and they were tested during the system test phase. The application minimizes the need for manual activities, such as tape mounts, paper handling and direct on-location manual intervention.
13. The application has been specifically designed, developed and supported to be installed at *multiple sites* for multiple organizations.
14. The application has been specifically designed, developed and supported to *facilitate change*. Examples are:

    - Flexible query capability is provided.
    - Business information subject to change is grouped in tables maintainable by the user.

Function points calculation   The previous paragraphs described how the function types are listed, classified and counted, and how the processing complexity adjustment is determined. This paragraph describes how to make the calculations that develop the function points (FP) measures.

Using the definitions given at the beginning of this Appendix, two equations have been developed to define more specifically the *development work-product measure* and the *support work-product measure*:

$$\text{Development work-product FP measure } = (\text{Add} + \text{ChgA})$$

$$\text{PCA2} + (\text{DEL})\text{PCA1} = \underline{\quad}.$$

$$\text{Support work-product FP measure } = \text{Orig FP } + (\text{Add} + \text{ChgA})$$

$$\text{PCA2} - (\text{Del} + \text{ChgB})\text{PCA1} = \underline{\quad}.$$

Orig FP = adjusted FP of the application, evaluated as they were before the project started

Add = unadjusted FP added to the application, evaluated as they are expected to be at the completion of the project

ChgA = unadjusted FP changed in the application, evaluated as they are expected to be at the completion of the project

Del = unadjusted FP deleted from the application evaluated as they were before the project started

ChgB = unadjusted FP changed in the application, evaluated as they were before the project started

PCA1 = the processing complexity adjustment pertaining to the application before the project started

PCA2 = the processing complexity adjustment pertaining to the application after the project completion

PART FOUR
Validations

From the diversity and sheer number of different software metrics being proposed, it should be apparent that there exists a pressing need to be able to evaluate, discriminate and select. Hence it is no accident that this Part is the longest in the book; without some kind of validation process, it is hard to span the gulf between the 'speculators' and the 'doers' described by Belady and Lehman (1979). The first four papers focus upon code metrics as described in Part II above, while the remaining four have as their concern design and specification metrics, as described in Part III.

The empirical validations of the software science and cyclomatic complexity metrics by Curtis *et al.* (Chapter 9) and by Basili and Perricone (Chapter 10) were both significant in terms of the size of the software under investigation and the use of industrial programmers. They can also be viewed as a recognition of the need for external confirmation. In other words, prior to the widespread adoption of a metric, one would expect the findings of its progenitors to be repeated by other teams of researchers and investigators.

The validation by Curtis *et al.*—the third in a series of experiments—finds some support for both metrics, though it is noteworthy that the authors also reported a very high correlation between the count of program statements and the two metrics: software science effort, E, and cyclomatic complexity, $v(G)$. This is commented upon in Chapter 12. The study by Basili and Perricone is even more intriguing in its results. In this investigation the authors seek, among other objectives, to find a relationship between the incidence of software errors, the $v(G)$ metric and lines of code. Their counterintuitive finding was that error density *decreased* as cyclomatic complexity *increased*. Module length exhibited similar behaviour. This does not accord with conventional wisdom, and at the very least indicates that a certain degree of caution is required concerning the application of these code metrics.

In many senses, the critique by Hamer and Frewin of Halstead's software science (Chapter 11) represents something of a landmark paper in the evaluation of software metrics. Apart from their challenge to the then prevailing orthodoxy, they discuss some of the factors that permitted software science to be, in their words, 'both unsatisfactory *and* apparently accepted'. Reasons suggested for this state of affairs are the lack of available commercial data, the need for adequate modelling techniques and models, and the need for informed debate.

Shepperd's reappraisal in Chapter 12 of the cyclomatic complexity metric, like the Hamer–Frewin paper, questions a widely held assumption, namely the uncritical acceptance of McCabe's metric. A close inspection of the majority of published empirical validations reveals two unexpected results. First, the only consistent relationship is between the metric and lines of code. Second, for a significant number of validations, the metric is out-performed by lines of code in terms of predictive ability. Other more theoretical problems arise from the poorly articulated underlying model, such as the behaviour of the metric with respect to the structure of code and modularisation.

The next group of papers is concerned with the validation of early life-cycle metrics, notably design and specification metrics. Chapter 13, by Troy and Zweben, describes an empirical investigation into possible relationships between code modification data culled from a medium-sized, industrial software design and 21 different design measurements. The authors found that measurements related to module coupling were most strongly related to the change data; indeed, coupling measurements were able to account for 50–60 per cent of the variation in the code change data. Clearly, this is of some significance to those working with design metrics since it is supportive of those metrics that incorporate some notion of module coupling.

Kafura and Canning (Chapter 14) have conducted an empirical study of three large Fortran projects from NASA, again to validate a range of software metrics, principally design metrics. Their work is important because it introduces a number of new ideas concerning metric validation. They highlight the need to consider more than one dependent variable—in their case errors and coding time, because potential trade-offs exist between the two variables; for example, one could minimise coding time but at the expense of error rates. They also discuss the value of using more than one class of metric in order to improve the coverage of the model. Lastly, they stress the need to address alternative statistical techniques to the somewhat over-used—and much abused—correlation coefficient. Alternatives include outlier analysis[1] and a comparison of metric yields.

Chapter 15, by Ince and Shepperd, relates how theoretical deficiencies in the underlying model of a metric translate into poor practical performance. This is demonstrated in the context of the Henry–Kafura system design metric (see Chapter 6), where empirical analysis reveals that an alternative version of the metric, with the various theoretical deficiencies removed from its model, has far superior performance. The conclusion is drawn that the evaluation process should be concerned not merely with empirical validation, but also with the model upon which the metric rests.

Lastly in this Part is the paper by Kemerer (Chapter 16), which reports upon an empirical validation of four different models using specification metrics that are intended for software cost estimation. This validation is against 15 commercial projects from a consultancy company. Here Kemerer highlights many of the problems that attend empirical analysis. These include the impact of using *ex post*, as opposed to *ex ante*, model inputs. Estimates of lines of code or function points (Albrecht and Gaffney, Chapter 8 above) might be expected to be more accurate *after* a system has been delivered. On the other hand, cost estimates are more useful *before* a system has been delivered! Another intriguing problem is the impact of an estimate upon the project itself: is an estimate self-fulfilling? Notwithstanding these factors, the general conclusion is that all four models have difficulties with variations in software productivity and that, as a consequence, model calibration is an area requiring further attention.

The results from the evaluations described within this Part of the book do not make altogether comforting reading, as far as the current status of software metrics is concerned. It is important to realise, however, that evaluation is not a destructive process, but the precursor for improvement. The code metrics of Halstead and McCabe are now approaching 20 years in age. It would be surprising, therefore, if there were not scope for improvement. Such is the nature of modelling. Indeed, it is the very

---

[1] Outlier analysis and other statistical techniques are discussed in rather greater detail in Kitchenham and Pickard (1987), to be included in Volume Two of this work.

act of measuring that enables us to identify problems and possibilities for enhancement. We recognize the pioneering role of the early metrics workers, but we progress by learning from their mistakes as well as their successes.

Possibly the most important lessons to emerge from these evaluations are as follows:

- There is a need for clear and coherent models upon which to base metrics. These then greatly facilitate the process of empirical validation.
- The importance of using realistic sized systems for empirical analysis cannot be overstated.
- The meaningful use of statistics when interpreting empirical results is another point of great significance.
- The quest for general-purpose complexity metrics is an ambitious one, and resources might be better targeted upon more specific measurement goals.

9

THIRD-TIME CHARM: STRONGER PREDICTION OF PROGRAMMER PERFORMANCE BY SOFTWARE COMPLEXITY METRICS

Bill Curtis, Sylvia B. Sheppard and Phil Milliman

General Electric Company

ABSTRACT

This experiment is the third in a series investigating characteristics of software which are related to its psychological complexity. A major focus of this research has been to validate the use of software complexity metrics for predicting programmer performance. In this experiment we improved experimental procedures that produced only modest results in the previous two studies. The experimental task required 54 experienced Fortran programmers to locate a single bug in each of three programs. Performance was measured by the time taken to locate and successfully correct the bug. Much stronger results were obtained than in earlier studies. Halstead's E proved to be the best predictor of performance, followed by McCabe's $v(G)$ and the number of lines of code.

9.1 INTRODUCTION

Interest continues to grow in the use of quantitative metrics which assess the complexity of software. Such metrics are assumed to be valuable aids in determining the quality of software. Boehm *et al.* (1976) and McCall *et al.* (1977) proposed collections of such metrics which assess numerous factors that collectively constitute

159

this nebulous 'software quality'. Such factors include reliability, portability, maintainability, and myriad other abilities.

There are numerous potential uses for measures that assess these various quality factors. First, they can be used as feedback to programmers during development indicating potential problems with the code they have developed (Elshoff, 1978a). Use of metrics in this way would require guidelines for altering code so as to bring different metric values within acceptable limits.

A second use for metrics is in guiding software testing. McCabe (Chapter 2 above) proposed the cyclomatic number as a means of assessing the computational complexity of the software testing problem. Other metrics that index the quality or complexity of software may help identify modules or subroutines that are likely to be the most error-infested.

Another use for software metrics is in estimating maintenance requirements. If one or more metrics can be empirically related to the difficulty that programmers experience in working with software, then more accurate estimates can be made of the manpower that will be necessary during maintenance. However, empirical validity studies employing professional programmers will be necessary to validate the uses for software metrics described here.

In our recent article (Curtis *et al.*, 1979a), we reported two experiments relating the complexity metrics developed by Halstead and McCabe to the difficulty programmers experienced in understanding and modifying programs. The results we observed in these experiments were modest in that the correlations in the raw data were not large and lines of code usually predicted performance better than the complexity metrics.

These results were disappointing, since we believed that the complexity metrics captured constructs much more closely associated with factors that affect the psychological complexity of software than lines of code. That is, we believed that counts of operators, operands and elementary segments of the control flow would provide some insight to the difficulty that programmers experienced in working with software because they seem to be likely candidates for the 'chunks' or building blocks of information that programmers will use in mentally representing a program to themselves. A simple count of lines of code did not seem to possess this desirable characteristic. This assumption appeared to be true for less experienced programmers, but was not supported for more experienced programmers.

In our discussion of those results, we pointed out several limitations in the experimental procedures employed in obtaining the data which may have diluted the results we observed. First, all of the programs we studied were short (35–55 lines of code). The limited range of metric values calculated on programs of this length may not have been sufficient for an adequate test of the predictive worth of the metrics. Second, individual differences among programmers exerted significant effects on the results obtained. In order to control for these differences, the number of participants in the experiments would need to be increased. When the data from the first of our two experiments were transformed in an attempt to control for differences among programs and programmers, a correlation of -0.73 ($p \leqslant 0.001$) was obtained between program comprehension and Halstead's E. However, the question is not whether theories can be validated with mystical transformations of data, but whether the results of these heuristic transformations can be replicated in an experiment designed to overcome the limitations of previous research.

We performed a third experiment, hoping that an improvement in our experimental methods would lead to more encouraging results. This paper reports the results of this third experiment by testing the value of software complexity metrics in predicting the time required for a programmer to find a bug. Three different programs were developed, each with three different versions of control flow, and were presented to programmers in three different lengths varying from 25 to 225 lines of code. One of three different types of bugs was inserted in each program, for a total of 81 unique experimental programs.

9.2 METHOD

9.2.1 Participants

Fifty-four professional programmers from six different locations participated in this experiment. Thirty were civilian industrial employees; the others worked for the United States Armed Forces. The participants averaged 6.6 years of programming experience in Fortran, ranging from $\frac{1}{2}$ year to 25 years (s.d. $= 6.1$).

9.2.2 Experimental design

In order to control for individual differences in performance, a within-subject 3^4 factorial design was employed. Three types of control flow were defined for each of three programs, and each of these nine versions was presented in three lengths with three different bugs, for a total of 81 different experimental conditions. The first 27 participants each saw three of the programs, exhausting the 81 conditions. The second set of 27 participants replicated the conditions exactly except that the order of presentation of the tasks was different in each case.

Learning effects were expected on the basis of results obtained in previous experiments of this type (Sheppard and Love 1977). Therefore, the order of presentation was counterbalanced to assure that each level of independent variable appeared as the first, second or third task an equal number of times.

9.2.3 Procedure

A packet of materials for each participant included: (1) written instructions on the experimental tasks; (2) a short tutorial of commands used in Fortran 77; (3) a short preliminary task; (4) three experimental tasks; and (5) a questionnaire concerning previous experience.

All tasks included: input files, a Fortran program listing, a correct output, and the erroneous output produced by the program that contained the error. All differences between the correct output and the erroneous output were circled on the erroneous output. Also included were explanations of the purposes of any subroutines or functions not present but referenced by the program. Preliminary tasks were provided to reduce learning effects on the experimental tasks and to provide a basis for comparing the abilities of the participants to perform a task of this nature.

Following the initial exercise, participants were presented in turn with three separate programs comprising their experimental tasks. They were allowed to work at their own pace. When any of them thought they had found the program bug and could correct it, they raised their hands, and the experimenter verified the correction. If the line number or modification was not correct, participants were requested to try again until they could successfully complete the task. Maximums of 45 minutes for the preliminary task and 60 minutes for the experimental tasks were allowed; the time for each response was measured to the nearest minute.

9.2.4 Independent variables

Program Three programs were selected for the general applicability of their content and their comprehensibility to programmers. The first program sorted and categorized alphabetic response data to a questionnaire (Veldman 1967). Program 2, an accounting routine, produced income and balance statements (Nolen 1971). Program 3 kept track of students' test grades and calculated their semester averages (Brooks 1978). All programs were thoroughly tested prior to the experiment.

Length The inclusion of additional subroutines made it possible to present each program in three different lengths. The shorter programs had 25–75 statements, medium programs contained 100–150 statements and the longer programs contained approximately 175–225 statements.

Complexity of control flow Three control flow versions, performing identical tasks, were defined for each program. The naturally structured and graph-structured versions were implemented in Fortran IV, while a third version used Fortran 77 (Brainerd 1978), which includes the IF-THEN-ELSE, DO-WHILE, and DO-UNTIL constructs.

The Fortran 77 version of each program was implemented in a precisely structured manner. All flow proceeded from top to bottom, and only three basic control constructs were allowed: the linear sequence, structured selection, and structured iteration.

The graph-structured version of each program was implemented in Fortran IV from the Fortran 77 version, replacing the special constructs but producing code for which the control flow graphs of the two versions were identical. All nested relationships could be reduced through structured decomposition to a linear sequence of unit complexity. A full discussion of reducibility is presented by McCabe (1976; see Chapter 2 above).

Structured constructs are awkward to implement in Fortran IV (Tenny 1974). In order to test a more naturally structured flow, limited deviations were allowed in a third version of each program. These deviations included such practices as branching into or out of a loop or decision, and multiple returns.

Each program was indented following the nesting patterns presented in the code; that is, all DO loops and branching instructions were indented. For the naturally structured versions, decisions were arbitrarily made about the importance of various constructions and indenting was necessarily less standardized than for the graph-structured and Fortran 77 versions.

Type of bug   Program bugs are generally categorized as either syntactic or semantic. Syntax problems are easily detected during compilation and require less attention from programmers. For that reason, this experiment considered only semantic bugs. The categories of bugs selected were computational, logical and data bugs (Thayer 1976). Similar bugs in each category were defined for each of the three programs. The computational bugs involved a sign change in an arithmetic expression; the logic bugs were implemented by using the wrong operator in an IF condition; and the data bugs involved wrong index values for variables.

9.2.5 Complexity metrics

Halstead's E   Halstead's (1977a) effort metric (E) was computed precisely from a program (based on Ottenstein 1976a) whose input was the source code listings of 27 different programs used in this experiment: that is, the three distinct programs, each written in three versions of control flow and in three different lengths.
   The computational formula is:

$$E = \frac{\eta_1 N_2 (N_1 + N_2) \log_2 (\eta_1 + \eta_2)}{2 \eta_2}$$

where

η_1 = number of unique operators
η_2 = number of unique operands
N_1 = frequency of operators
N_2 = frequency of operands

McCabe's $v(G)$ McCabe's metric is the classical graph-theory cyclomatic number defined as:

$$v(G) = \sharp \text{ edges} - \sharp \text{ nodes} + 2(\sharp \text{ connected components}).$$

McCabe presents two simpler methods of calculating $v(G)$: the number of predicate nodes plus 1, or the number of regions computed from a planar graph of the control flow.

Total statements   The length of the program was the total number of Fortran statements.

9.2.6 Dependent variable

The dependent variable was the number of minutes necessary for the participant to locate the bug and correct it.

Table 9.1 Intercorrelations among complexity metrics

	Correlations	
Measures	E	$v(G)$
Subroutine		
$v(G)$	0.92***	
Length	0.89***	0.81***
Program		
$v(G)$	0.76***	
Length	0.56***	0.90***

Note: $n = 27$; ***$p < 0.001$.

9.3 RESULTS

Results of the experimental manipulations are described elsewhere (Sheppard et al. 1979a). Briefly, significant effects were observed for specific program and presentation order, but these differences were small. No significant effects were observed for types of bugs or control flow. The most significant effect was a program by bug interaction, which suggested the existence of context effects within which the bug was embedded.

The correlations reported here were computed on the 27 separate versions of the programs studied. These complexity measures were computed both on the total program and on the particular subroutine in which the bug was embedded. Performance scores on each of these 27 separate programs were computed as the average of six scores: two complete replications of the times to find three different bugs.

Intercorrelations among the measures of software complexity are reported in Table 9.1. Substantial intercorrelations were observed among Halstead's E, McCabe's $v(G)$ and length at the subroutine level, suggesting that within subroutines these metrics tended to measure a common construct of volume. When computed on the total program, however, the correlation between length and McCabe's $v(G)$ remained large, while the correlations for Halstead's E with these measures were substantially smaller, especially with lines of code.

Correlations between performance and complexity measures are presented in Table 9.2. At the subroutine level, all three measures predicted performance equally well, accounting for between 40 and 45 per cent of the variance in

Table 9.2 Correlations between performance and complexity measures

	Correlations	
Measures	Subroutine	Program
E	0.66***	0.75***
$v(G)$	0.63***	0.65***
Length	0.67***	0.52**

Note: $n = 27$; **$p \leqslant 0.01$; ***$p \leqslant 0.001$.

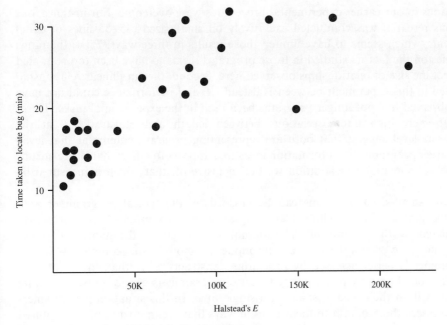

Figure 9.1 Scatterplot of Halstead's *E* with performance.

performance scores. (The percentage of the variance in performance accounted for is computed by squaring the correlation coefficient.) At the program level, however, strong differences were observed in the abilities of the complexity measures to predict performance. Correlations indicated that Halstead's *E* accounted for over twice as much variance in performance as length (56 *v* 27 per cent, respectively), while the variance accounted for by McCabe's $v(G)$ fell between these values (42 per cent). A stepwise multiple regression analysis indicated that length and McCabe's $v(G)$ added no increments to the prediction afforded by Halstead's *E*.

The scatterplot of performance with Halstead's *E* presented in Fig. 9.1 suggested the existence of a curvilinear trend in the data. The significance of this trend was tested using the second-degree polynomial regression approach suggested by Cohen and Cohen (1975) for investigating curvilinear relationships. A multiple correlation coefficient of 0.84 indicated that the curvilinear trend accounted for an additional 15 per cent ($p < 0.001$) of the variance beyond that accounted for by a linear relationship. However, with few data points in the right tail of this distribution for Halstead's *E*, it is difficult to extrapolate to the exact shape of the curvilinear trend. No curvilinear trend was detected with either the lines of code or McCabe's $v(G)$.

9.4 DISCUSSION

The results of this experiment not only replicated the results obtained in our previous research, but also demonstrated that far stronger results could be obtained when the limitations in our earlier experimental procedures were overcome. For instance, our previous research was conducted exclusively on small-sized (35–55 lines of code) programs, which seems to have limited those results in three ways. First, the range of values on the factors studied in those programs seems to have been too restricted to detect the size of relationships observed here. Second, the curvilinear relationship observed in this experiment between Halstead's E and performance could not have been observed had not longer programs been used in the experimental tasks. Third, the extremely high intercorrelations between length and Halstead's E at the subroutine level suggest that both are representing program volume at that level. With larger programs, the information measured appears to differ; that is, Halstead's E measures something in addition to, but inclusive of, that which is measured by length.

Many small-sized programs can be grasped by the typical programmer as a cognitive gestalt. The psychological complexity of such programs is adequately represented by the volume of the program as indexed by the number of lines. When the code grows beyond a subroutine or module, its complexity to the programmer is better assessed by measuring constructs other than the number of lines of code. This may result partly because programmers cannot grasp the entire program within their mental spans at a single time. In this situation programmers may represent the program to themselves in ways that are more accurately captured by counts of operators, operands and control paths. Thus, as the size of a program increases, Halstead's E seems to become a better measure of its psychological complexity.

A curvilinear relationship was detected between Halstead's E and performance. This curve suggests that as Halstead's E grows larger a program becomes more psychologically complex, but the increments in difficulty grow smaller and smaller. In the experimental task used in this debugging experiment, there seemed to be an amount of time that was typically required to locate a bug within a subroutine once the correct subroutine had been identified (approximately 16 minutes). The initial time required to identify the proper subroutine seemed to account for the curvilinear relationship observed.

The results of this experiment provide evidence that the software complexity metrics developed by Halstead and McCabe are related to the difficulty that programmers experience in locating errors in code. Thus, these metrics appear to be capable of satisfying the uses described earlier. They can be used in providing feedback to programmers about the complexity of the code they have developed, and to managers about the resources that will be necessary to maintain particular sections of code. Code that is more psychologically complex may also be more error-prone and difficult to test. Further evaluative research needs to assess the validity of these uses in ongoing software projects.

ACKNOWLEDGEMENTS

This study was supported by the Office of Naval Research, Engineering Psychology Programs (Contract No. N00014-77-C-0158). The views expressed in this paper, however, are not necessarily those of the Office of Naval Research or the US Department of Defense.

We are grateful to M. A. Borst and Judith McWilliams for helping implement this research; to Drs John O'Hare, Tom Love and Ben Shneiderman for their helpful comments; to Earl North, Col. Joan Shields and Capt. Webster for providing participants; to Beverly Day for manuscript preparation; and to Lou Oliver for his support of our efforts.

10

SOFTWARE ERRORS AND COMPLEXITY:
AN EMPIRICAL INVESTIGATION

Victor R. Basili and Barry T. Perricone

University of Maryland

ABSTRACT

An analysis of the distributions and relationships derived from the change data collected during development of a medium-scale software project produces some surprising insights into the factors influencing software development. Among these are the trade-offs between modifying an existing module and creating a new one, and the relationship between module size and error proneness.

10.1 INTRODUCTION

The identification of the various factors that have an effect on software development is of prime concern to software engineers. The specific focus of this paper is to analyse the relationships between the frequency and distribution of errors during software development, the maintenance of the developed software, and a variety of environmental factors. These factors include the complexity of the software, the

168

developer's experience with the application and the reuse of existing design and code. Such relationships can provide an insight into the characteristics of computer software and the effects that an environment can have on the software product. Such relationships can also improve the *reliability* and *quality* with respect to computer software. In an effort to acquire knowledge of these basic relationships, change data for a medium-scale software project were analysed. (Change data include any documentation that reports an alteration made to the software for a particular reason).

The overall objectives of this paper are threefold: first, to report the results of the analyses; second, to review the results in the context of those reported by other researchers (Basili and Weiss (1982a, b; Endres 1975; McCabe, see Chapter 2 above); and third, to draw some conclusions based on the first two objectives. The analyses presented in this paper encompass various types of distributions based on the collected change data. The most important are the error distributions observed within the software project.

10.1.1 Description of the environment

The software analysed in this paper is from a large set of projects being studied in the Software Engineering Laboratory (SEL). This particular project is a general-purpose program for satellite planning studies. These planning studies include mission manœuvre planning, mission lifetime, mission launch and mission control. The overall size of the software project was approximately 90 000 lines of code. The majority of the software project was coded in Fortran for execution on an IBM 360.

Although the system outlined here uses many algorithms similar to those of the original SEL projects, it still represents a new application for the development group.

The requirements for the system kept growing and changing, much more so than for the typical ground-support software. Owing to the commonality of algorithms from existing systems, the developers reused the design and code for many algorithms needed in the new system. Hence a large number of reused (modified) modules became part of the new system.

An approximation of the software's life cycle is displayed in Fig. 10.1. This figure illustrates only the approximate duration in time of the various phases of the software's life cycle. The information relating the amount of manpower involved with each of the phases was not specific enough to yield meaningful results, so it was not included.

10.1.2 Terms

This section defines the terms used in this paper. Please note that many of these terms often denote different concepts in the general literature.

Module A module is defined as a named subfunction, subroutine, or the main program of the software system. Only segments that contained executable code written in Fortran were used for the analyses. Change data from the segments that

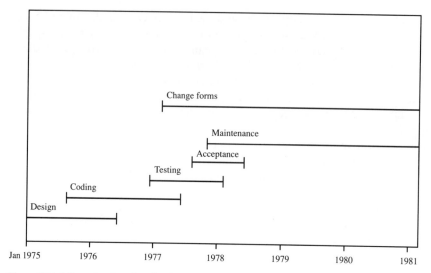

Figure 10.1 Life cycle of analysed software.

constituted the data blocks, assembly segments, common segments or utility routines were not included. However, a general overview of the data available on these segments is presented in Section 10.4.

There are two types of modules referred to in this paper. The first type is denoted as *modified*. These are modules that were developed for previous software projects and then modified to meet the requirements of the new project. The second type is referred to as *new*. These are modules that were developed specifically for the software project under analysis.

The entire software project contained 517 code segments, consisting of 36 assembly segments, 370 Fortran segments and 111 segments that were either common modules, block data or utility routines. Out of 517 code segments (72 per cent of the total modules), 370 met the adopted module definition and constituted the majority of the software project. Of the modules found to contain errors, 49 per cent were categorized as modified and 51 per cent as new modules.

Number of source and executable lines The number of source lines within a module refers to the number of lines of executable code and comment lines contained within it. The number of executable lines within a module refers to the number of executable statements: comment lines are not included.

Some of the relationships presented in this paper are based on a grouping of modules by module size in increments of 50 lines. This means that a module containing 50 lines of code or less was placed in the module size of 50, modules between 51 and 100 lines of code into the module size of 100, and so on. The number of modules contained in each module size category is given in Table 10.1 for all modules and for modules that contain errors (i.e. a subset of all modules) with respect to source and executable lines of code.

Table 10.1 Module size categories

No. of lines	All modules		Modules with errors	
	Source	Executable	Source	Executable
0–50	53	258	3	49
51–100	107	70	16	25
101–150	80	26	20	13
151–200	56	13	19	7
201–250	34	1	12	1
251–300	14	1	9	0
301–350	7	1	4	1
351–400	9	0	7	0
> 400	10	0	6	0
Total	370	370	96	96

Error   An error is something detected within the executable code that caused the module in which it occurred to perform incorrectly (i.e. contrary to its expected function).

Errors were quantified from two viewpoints, depending upon the goals of the error analysis. The first quantification was based on a textual rather than a conceptual viewpoint. This type of error quantification is best illustrated by an example. If a '*' is incorrectly used in place of a '+', then all occurrences of the '*' will be considered an error, even if the '*' appears on the same line of code or within multiple modules. The total number of errors detected in the 370 software modules was 215 contained within a total of 96 modules. This implies that 26 per cent of the modules analysed contained errors.

The second type of quantification measured the effect of an error across modules. Textual errors associated with the same conceptual problem were combined to yield one conceptual error. If a procedure was called with the same incorrect parameter list in multiple modules, this would constitute multiple textual errors but only one conceptual error. This is done only for the errors reported in Table 10.2. There is a total of 155 conceptual errors. All other studies in this paper are based upon the first type of error quantification.

Statistical terms and methods   All linear regressions of the data presented in this paper employ the least-squares principle as a criterion of goodness. (That is, 'choose as the "best-fitting" line the one that minimizes the sum of squares of the deviations of the observed values of y from those predicted' (Mendenhall and Ramey 1973).)

Pearson's product moment coefficient of correlation was used as an index of the strength of the linear relationship, regardless of the respective scales of measurement for y and x. This index is denoted by the symbol r. The measure for the amount of variability in y accounted for by linear regression on x is denoted as $r2$.

All of the equations and explanations for these statistics can be found in Mendenhall and Ramey (1973). It should be noted that other types of curve fits were conducted on the data. The results of these fits will be mentioned later in the paper.

10.2 BASIC DATA

The change data were collected over a period of 33 months (August 1977–May 1980). These dates correspond in time to the software phases of coding, testing, acceptance and maintenance (Fig. 10.1). The data collected for the analyses is not complete since changes were still being made to the analysed software. However, enough data was viewed in order to make the conclusions drawn from the data significant.

The change data was entered on detailed report sheets, which were completed by the programmer responsible for implementing the change. A sample of the change report form is given in the Appendix.[1] In general, the form required that several short questions be answered by the programmer implementing the change. These queries documented the cause of a change in addition to other characteristics and effects attributed to the change. The majority of this information was found useful in the analyses. The key information used from the form was:

- The date of the change or error discovery
- The description of the change or error
- The number of components changed
- The type of change or error
- The effort needed to correct the error.

It should be mentioned that the particular change report form shown in the Appendix is the most current form but was not uniformly used over the entire period of this study. In actuality, there were three different versions of the change report form; each form required slightly different information. Therefore, for the data that was not present on one form but could be inferred, the inferred value was used. An example of such an inference is that of determining the *error type*. Since the error description was given on all of the forms, the error type could be inferred with a reasonable degree of reliability. Data not incorporated into a particular data set used for an analysis was data for which inference was deemed unreliable. Therefore, the reader should be alert to the cardinality of the data set used as a basis for some of the relationships presented in this paper. A total of 231 change report forms were examined for the purpose of this paper.

The quality of the change and error data was checked in the following manner. First, the supervisor of the project looked over the change report forms and verified them (denoted by his or her signature and the date). Second, when the data was reduced for analysis, it was closely examined for contradictions. It should be noted that interviews with the individuals who filled out the change forms were not conducted. This was the major difference between this work and other error studies

---

[1] [This Appendix has not been reproduced here. M.J.S.]

performed by the SEL, where interviews were held with the programmers to help clarify questionable data (see Basili and Weiss 1982a).

The review of the change data yielded an interesting result. The errors due to previous correction attempts were shown to be three times as common after the form review process was performed; that is, before the review process they accounted for 2 per cent of the errors and after the review process they accounted for 6 per cent of the errors. These recording errors are probably attributed to the fact that the corrector of an error did not know that the error was due to a previous fix because the fix occurred several months earlier or was made by a different programmer.

10.3 RELATIONSHIPS DERIVED FROM DATA

This section presents and discusses the relationships derived from the change data.

10.3.1 Change distribution by type

Changes to the software can be categorized as error corrections or modifications (specification changes, planned enhancements, and clarity and optimization improvements). For this project, error corrections accounted for 62 per cent of the changes and modifications accounted for 38 per cent. In studies of other SEL projects, error corrections accounted for 40–64 per cent of the changes.

10.3.2 Error distribution by modules

Table 10.2 shows the number of modules that had to be changed because of an error. (Note that these errors are counted as conceptual errors.) It was found that 89 per cent of the errors could be corrected by changing only one module. This is a good argument for the modularity of the software. It also shows that there is not a large amount of interdependence among the modules with respect to an error.

Table 10.3 shows the number of errors found per module. The type of module is shown in addition to the total number of modules found to contain errors.

The largest number of errors found was 7 (located in a single new module) and 5 (located in 3 different modified modules and 1 new module). The remainder of the errors were distributed almost equally between the two types of module.

Table 10.2 Number of modules affected by an error (data set: 211 textual errors; 174 conceptual errors)

No. of errors	No. Modules affected
155 (89%)	1
9	2
3	3
6	4
1	5

Table 10.3 Numer of errors per module (data set: 215 errors)

No. of modules	New	Modified	Number of errors per module
36	17	19	1
26	13	13	2
16	10	6	3
13	7	6	4
4	1**	3*	5
1	1**		7

* Most error-prone modified modules.
** Most error-prone new modules.

The effort associated with correcting an error is specified on the form as (1) 1 hour or less, (2) 1 hour to 1 day (3) 1–3 days, or (4) more than 3 days. These categories were chosen because it is too difficult to collect effort data to a finer granularity. To estimate the effort from any particular error correction, an average time was used for each category; that is, assuming an eight-hour day, an error correction in category (1) was assumed to take 0.5 hour, in category (2) 4.5 hours, in category (3) 16 hours, and in category (4) 32 hours.

The types of errors found in the three most error-prone modified modules (* in Table 10.3) and the effort needed to correct them is shown in Table 10.4. If any type contained error corrections from more than one error correction category, the associated effort for them was averaged. The fact that the majority of the errors detected in a module is between one and three shows that the total number of errors that occurred per module is, on the average, very small.

The 12 errors contained in the two most error-prone new modules (** in Table 10.3) are shown in Table 10.5 along with the effort needed to correct them.

10.3.3 Error distribution by type

Figure 10.2 shows the distribution of errors by type. It can be seen that 48 per cent of the errors was attributed to incorrect or misinterpreted functional specifications or requirements.

Table 10.4 Effort to correct errors in the three most error-prone modified modules

	No. of errors (15 total)	Average effort to correct (hrs)
Misunderstood or incorrect specifications	8	24.0
Incorrect design or implementation of a module component	5	16.0
Clerical error	2	4.5

Table 10.5 Effort to correct errors in the two most error-prone new modules

	No. errors (12 total)	Average effort to correct (hrs)
Misunderstood or incorrect requirements	8	32.0
Incorect design or implementation of a module component	3	0.5
Clerical error	1	0.5

The error classification used throughout the Software Engineering Laboratory is given below. The person identifying the error indicates the class for each error.

A: Requirements incorrect or misinterpreted
B: Functional specification incorrect or misinterpreted
C: Design error involving several components
    1. Mistaken assumption about value or structure of data
    2. Mistake in control logic or computation of an expression
D: Error in design or implementation of single component
    1. Mistaken assumption about value or structure of data
    2. Mistake in control logic or computation of an expression
E: Misunderstanding of external environment
F: Error in the use of programming language/compiler
G: Clerical error
H: Error due to previous miscorrection of an error

The distribution of these errors by source is plotted in Fig. 10.2 with the appropriate subdistribution of new and modified errors displayed. This distribution shows that the majority of errors were the result of functional specification (incorrect or misinterpreted). Within this category, the majority of the errors (24 per cent) involved modified modules. This is most likely due to the fact that the

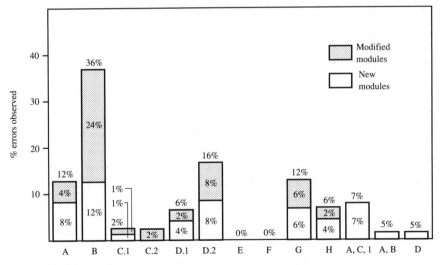

Figure 10.2 Sources of errors.

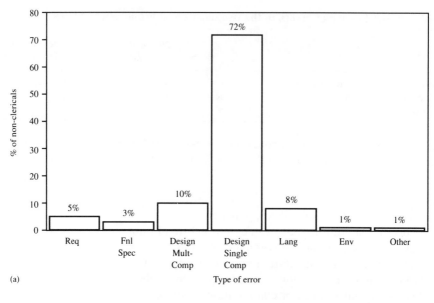

(a)

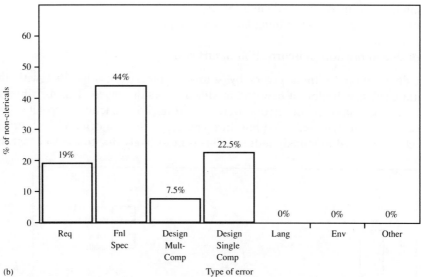

(b)

Figure 10.3. (a) Sources of errors on other nonclerical SEL projects. (b) Sources of nonclerical errors on this project.

reused modules were taken from another system with a different application. Thus, even though the basic algorithms were the same, the specification was not well enough defined or appropriately defined for the modules to be used under slightly different circumstances.

The distribution in Fig. 10.2 should be compared with the distribution of another system developed by the same organization, shown in Fig. 10.3(a) (Basili and Weiss 1982b). For a basis of comparison, the categories in Fig. 10.2 are mapped into a classification scheme (Fig. 10.3(b)) equivalent to those for Fig. 10.3(a) (eliminating the categories of G and H within Fig. 10.2). Figure 10.3 represents a typical ground-support software system and was rather typical of the error distributions for these systems. It is different from the distribution for the system we are discussing in that the majority of the errors were involved in the design of a single component. The reason for the difference is that in ground-support systems the design is well understood and the developers have had a reasonable amount of experience with the application. Any reused design or code comes from a similar system and the requirements tend to be more stable. An analysis of the two distributions makes the differences in the development environments clear in a quantitative way.

The percentage of requirements and specification errors is consistent with Endres's work (Endres 1975). Endres found that 46 per cent of the errors he viewed involved the misunderstanding of the functional specifications of a module. Our results are similar, even though Endres's analysis was based on data derived from a different software project and programming environment. The software project used in Endres's analysis contained considerably more lines of code per module, was written in assembly code, and was within the problem area of operating systems. However, both of the software systems Endres analysed did contain new and modified modules. In this study, of the errors due to the misunderstanding of a module's specifications or requirements (48 per cent), 20 per cent involved new modules while 28 per cent involved modified modules.

Although the existence of modified modules can shrink the cost of coding, the amount of effort needed to correct errors in modified modules might outweigh the savings. The effort graph (Fig. 10.4) supports this view: 50 per cent of the total effort required for error correction occurred in modified modules; errors requiring from one

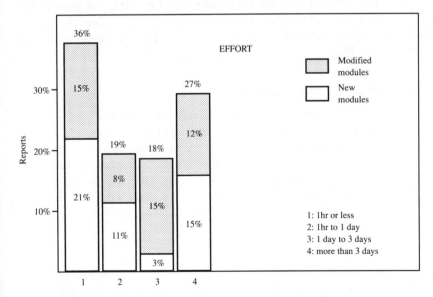

Figure 10.4 Effort graph.

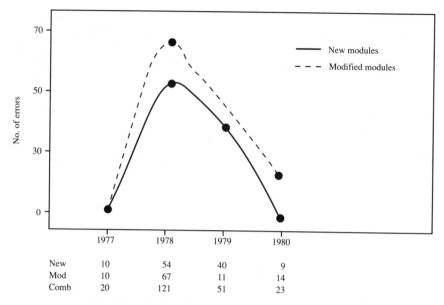

Figure 10.5 Number of errors occurring in modules.

day to more than three days to correct accounted for 45 per cent of the total effort, with 27 per cent of this effort attributable to modified modules within these greater effort classes. Thus, errors occurring in new modules required less effort to correct than those in modified modules.

The similarity between Endres's results and those reported here tend to support the statement that, independent of the environment and possibly the module size, the majority of errors detected within software are due to an inadequate form or misinterpretation of the specifications. This seems especially true when the software contains modified modules.

10.3.4 Overall number of errors observed

Figure 10.5 displays the number of errors observed in both new and modified modules. It can be seen that errors occurring in modified modules are detected earlier and at a slightly higher rate than those in new modules. One hypothesis for this is that the majority of the errors observed in modified modules are due to the misinterpretation of the functional specifications. Errors of this type would certainly be more obvious since they are more blatant than those of other types and, therefore, would be detected both earlier and more readily. (See next section).

10.3.5 Abstract error types

The authors adopted an abstract classification of errors into one of five categories with respect to a module: (1) initialization, (2) control structure, (3) interface, (4) data, and (5) computation. This was done in order to see if there existed recurring classes of errors in all modules, independent of size. These error classes are only roughly defined. It should be noted that, even though the authors were consistent with the categorization for this project, another error analyst may have interpreted the categories differently.

Failure to initialize or re-initialize a data structure properly upon a module's entry/exit is considered an *initialization error*. Errors that cause an 'incorrect path' in a module to be taken are considered *control errors*. Such a control error might be a conditional statement causing control to be passed to an incorrect path. *Interface errors* are those that were associated with structures existing outside the module's local environment but which the module used. For example, the incorrect declaration of a COMMON segment or an incorrect subroutine call is an interface error. An error in the declaration of the COMMON segment is considered an interface error and not an initialization error since the COMMON segment has been used by the module but is not part of its local environment. *Data errors* are those errors that are a result of the incorrect use of a data structure. Examples of data errors are the use of incorrect subscripts for an array, the use of the wrong variable in an equation, or the inclusion of an incorrect declaration of a variable local to the module. *Computation errors* are those that cause a computation to evaluate a variable's value erroneously. These errors could be equations that are incorrect not by virtue of the incorrect use of a data structure within the statement, but by miscalculations. An example of this error might be the statement $A = B + 1$ when the statement really needed was $A = B/C + 1$.

These five abstract categories basically represent all activities present in any module. They are further partitioned into errors of commission and omission. *Errors of commission* are those errors present as a result of an incorrect executable statement. For example, a commissioned computational error would be $A + B * C$ where the '$*$' should have been '$+$'. In other words, the operator was present but was incorrect. *Errors of omission* are those errors that are a result of forgetting to include some entity within a module. For example, a computational omission error might be $A = B$ when the statement should have read $A = B + C$. A parameter required for a subroutine call but not included in the actual call is an example of an interface omission error. In both of the above examples, some aspect needed for the correct execution of a module has been forgotten.

The results of this abstract classification scheme are given in Table 10.6. Since there was approximately an equal amount of new (49) and modified (47) modules viewed in the analysis, the results do not need to be normalized. Some errors and thereby modules were counted more than once, since it was not possible to associate some errors with a single abstract error type based on the error description given on the change report form.

According to Table 10.6, interfaces appear to be the major problem, regardless of the module type. Control is more of a problem in new modules than in modified modules. This is probably because the algorithms in the old modules had more test and debug time. On the other hand, initialization and data are more of a problem in modified modules. These facts, coupled with the small number of errors of omission in the modified modules, might imply that the basic algorithms for the modified modules were correct but needed some adjustment with respect to

Table 10.6 Abstract classification of errors

	Commission		Omission		Total	
	New	Modified	New	Modified	New	Modified
Initialization	2	9	5	9	7	18–25 (11%)
Control	12	2	16	6	28	8–36 (16%)
Interface	23	31	27	6	50	37–87 (39%)
Data	10	17	1	3	11	20–31 (14%)
Computation	16	21	3	3	19	24–43 (19%)
	28%	36%	23%	12%	115	107
	64%		35%			

data values and initialization for the application of that algorithm to the new environment.

10.3.6 Module size and error occurrence

Scatter plots for executable lines per module versus the number of errors found in the module were graphed. It was difficult to see any trend within these plots, so the number of errors per 1000 executable lines within a module size was calculated (Table 10.7). The number of errors was normalized over 1000 executable lines of code in order to determine if the number of detected errors within a module was dependent on module size. All modules within the software were included, even those with no detected errors. If the number of errors per 1000 executable lines was found to be constant over module size, this would show independence. An unexpected trend was observed: Table 10.7 implies that there is a higher error rate in smaller-sized modules. Since only the executable lines of code were considered, the larger modules were not COMMON data files. Also, the larger modules will be shown to be more complex than smaller modules in the next section. Then how could this type of result occur?

The most plausible explanation seems to be that the large number of interface errors spread equally across all modules is causing a larger number of errors per 1000 executable statements for smaller modules. Some tentative explanations for this behaviour are that: the majority of the modules examined were small (Table 10.1), causing a biased result; larger modules were coded with more care than smaller modules because of their size; and errors in smaller modules were more

Table 10.7 Errors per 1000 executable lines (including all modules)

Module size	Errors/1000 lines
50	16.0
100	12.6
150	12.4
200	7.6
> 200	6.4

Table 10.8 Average cyclomatic complexity for all modules

Module size	Average cyclomatic complexity
50	6.0
100	17.9
150	28.1
200	52.7
< 200	60.0

apparent. There may still be numerous undetected errors presented within the larger modules since all the 'paths' within the larger modules may not have been fully exercised.

10.3.7 Module complexity

Cyclomatic complexity (number of decisions +1) was correlated with module size (see McCabe, Chapter 2 above). This was done in order to determine whether or not larger modules were less dense or complex than smaller modules containing errors. Scatter plots for executable statements per module versus the cyclomatic complexity were graphed. Since it was difficult to see any trend in the plots, modules were grouped according to size. The complexity points were obtained by calculating an average complexity measure for each module size class. For example, all the modules that had 50 executable lines of code or less had an average complexity of 6.0. Table 10.8 gives the average cyclomatic complexity for all modules in each of the size categories. The complexity relationships for executable lines of code in a module are shown in Fig. 10.6. As can be seen from Table 10.8, the larger modules were more complex than the smaller ones.

Table 10.9 gives the number of errors per 1000 executable statements and the average cyclomatic complexity only for those modules containing errors. When these data are compared with Table 10.8, one can see that the average complexity of the error-prone modules was no greater than the average complexity of the full set of modules.

10.4 DATA NOT EXPLICITLY INCLUDED IN ANALYSES

The 147 modules not included in this study (i.e. assembly segments, common segments, utility routines) contained six errors. These six errors were detected within

Table 10.9 Complexity and error rate for erroded modules

Module size	Average cyclomatic complexity	Errors/1000 executable lines
50	6.2	65.0
100	19.6	33.3
150	27.5	24.6
200	56.7	13.4
> 200	77.5	9.7

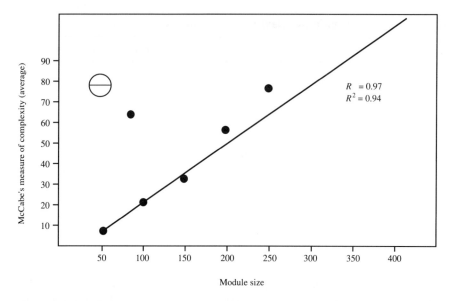

Figure 10.6 Complexity versus module size.

three different segments. One error occurred in a modified assembly module because of a misunderstanding or incorrect statement of the functional specifications for the module. The effort needed to correct this error was minimal (1 hour or less).

The other five errors occurred in two separate new data segments with the major cause of the errors also being related to their specifications. The effort needed to correct these errors was on the average from 1 hour to 1 day (1 day representing 8 hours).

10.5 CONCLUSIONS

The data contained in this paper helps explain and characterize the software developed. It is clear from the data that this was a new application for the developers, with changing requirements.

Modified and new modules were shown to behave similarly except for the types of errors prevalent in each and the amount of effort required to correct an error. Both had a high percentage of interface errors. However, new modules had an equal number of errors of omission and commission and a higher percentage of control errors. Modified modules had a high percentage of errors of commission and a small percentage of errors of omission with a higher percentage of data and initialization errors. Another difference was that modified modules appeared to be more susceptible to errors arising from the misunderstanding of the specifications. Misunderstanding of a module's specifications or requirements constituted the majority of detected errors. This duplicates Endres's earlier result, which implies that more work needs to be done on the form and content of the specifications and requirements in order for them to be used more effectively across applications.

There are some disadvantages to modifying an existing module for use instead of creating a new module. Modifying an existing module to meet a similar but different set of specifications reduces the development costs of that module. However, the disadvantage is that there are hidden costs. Errors contained in modified modules were found to require more effort to correct than those in new modules, although the two classes contained approximately the same number of errors. The majority of these errors were because of incorrect or misinterpreted specifications for a module. Therefore, there is a trade-off between minimizing development time and time spent to align a module to new specifications. However, if better specifications could be developed, it might reduce the more expensive errors contained within modified modules. In this case, the use of 'old' modules could be more beneficial in terms of cost and effort since the hidden costs would have been reduced.

One surprising result was that module size did not account for error-proneness. In fact, it was quite the contrary—the larger the module, the less error-prone it was. This was true even though the larger modules were more complex. Additionally, the error-prone modules were no more complex across size grouping than the error-free modules. This result implies that we are not yet ready to put artificial limits on module size and complexity.

In general, error analysis provides useful information. For this project, it shows that the developers were involved in a new application with changing requirements. It provides insight into the different ways of handling new and modified modules. It shows areas of potential problems with a new application. Ultimately, it allows us to identify the various factors that influence software development.

The results of this study are by no means conclusive. They pose more questions than they answer; they suggest that software development must be better understood. More data must be collected on different projects.

APPENDIX

[Not included].

ACKNOWLEDGEMENTS

The authors would like to thank F. McGarry, NASA Goddard Space Flight Center, for his cooperation in supplying the information needed for this study and his helpful suggestions on earlier drafts of this paper.

11

M. H. HALSTEAD'S SOFTWARE SCIENCE: A CRITICAL EXAMINATION

Peter G. Hamer and Gillian D. Frewin

Standard Telecommunication Laboratories Ltd

ABSTRACT

Karl Popper has described the scientific method as 'the method of bold conjectures and ingenious and severe attempts to refute them'. Software science has made 'bold conjectures' in postulating specific relationships between various 'metrics' of software code and in ascribing psychological interpretations to some of these metrics.

This chapter describes tests made on the validity of the relationships and interpretations that form the foundations of software science. The results indicate that the majority of them represent neither natural laws nor useful engineering approximations.

11.1 INTRODUCTION

During recent years there have been many attempts to define and measure the 'complexity' of a computer program. Maurice Halstead has developed a theory that gives objective measures of software complexity. Various studies and experiments have shown that the theory's predictions of the number of bugs in programs and of the time required to implement a program are amazingly accurate. It is a promising theory worthy of a much more probing scientific investigation.

(Fitzsimmons and Love 1978)

The only limiting factor to widespread application of the measures is the unavailability of the basic counts of operators and operands. When these become accepted as standard output from compilers we can look forward to the general use of the measures as a basic tool of analysts and programmers.

(Knijff 1978)

The above quotations from major reviews of 'software science' (as the field of study founded by the late Maurice Halstead had come to be known) fairly reflect the opinion of a significant section of the software engineering community. In recent years software science has been considered to be of sufficient importance and interest to be chosen as the topic of a special issue of the IEEE *Transitions on Software Engineering* (Yeh 1979) and as the subject of one of the ACM's occasional self-assessment procedures (ACM 1980). Software science has received comparatively little adverse comment in the literature, and the overwhelming impression is of a rapidly maturing discipline awaiting practical application.

We started to investigate software science with the intention of applying it to the quality management of the software development process. The promise of fundamental and invariant relationships, readily adjustable for alterations in the development environment, was extremely attractive for this purpose and for software management in general. It seemed prudent to verify the soundness of experimental confirmation, and of the basic theory, before building software-science-postulated relationships into our local tools and methods. This report covers the results of that verification. Although the work is concerned with the original Halstead papers and with early 'confirmations' rather than with more recent publications on relationships between operators and operands, it seems important that this report be published. Several current papers still quote the earlier work as if it provides good support for the basic postulations of software science.

While trying to gain a clear understanding of software science, we investigated in detail many of the published software science experiments, reworking them to be certain that we understood both the arguments and calculations. Two points became very clear. First, the essentially arithmetic relationships postulated within software science can, at best, capture only the central tendency of the true relationships. The failure to state the relationships statistically, which would permit description of the dispersion, seems to be a serious weakness both theoretically (only part of the relationship is captured and the range of statistical techniques available reduced) and practically (the significance of observed deviations from the mean is one of the most common questions that would arise). Second, the standard of experimental design is frequently very poor. In particular, many experiments designed to test whether particular hypotheses hold are virtually incapable of rejecting the hypotheses—they simply do not have the power to identify false hypotheses. In these circumstances experimental 'confirmation' of hypotheses may be illusory. Workers in this field seem to have received little or no help from their technical reviewers in developing adequate standards of experimental design.

11.2 THE BASIC SOFTWARE SCIENCE METRICS

Software science measures the complexity of a software module by calculations based on the incidence of references to operators and operands. There are four fundamental measurements:

- n_1: number of unique operators
- n_2: number of unique operands
- N_1: total number of operator occurrences
- N_2: total number of operand occurrences

From these four measurements, other simple metrics are derived:

- $n = n_1 + n_2$: the program *vocabulary*
- $N = N_1 + N_2$: the program *length*
- $V = N \log_2 n$: the program *volume*

The program length (N) is the closest software science equivalent to the more conventional count of executable statements; it probably reflects more accurately the differing 'complexities' of long and short statements. The program volume (V) represents the number of bits required to encode the program in an alphabet, with one 'character' per operand or operator.

11.3 MORE COMPLEX METRICS, AND SOFTWARE SCIENCE BELIEFS ABOUT THEM

Beyond the basic metrics, others have been defined such that, in the opinion of software science workers, simple psychological interpretations of the metrics are possible.

11.3.1 L: The level of abstraction

The level of abstraction at which a program is coded is believed to be the inverse of the difficulty experienced during the coding process. It is a function of both the power of the chosen programming language and the complexity of the algorithm being coded.

In Halstead (1972) L was defined as $(2/n_1)(n_2/N_2)$, and this has remained the *de facto* definition of L for software science workers ever since. In more recent articles the definition of L has been changed to V^*/V (see Halstead 1977a) for the definition of the potential volume V^*), and the original definition has been re-christened $\hat{L}$. The second definition is theoretically much more attractive at first sight; however, it is rarely used in practice (and for many programs the value of V^* is a matter of opinion rather than calculation; Lister (1982) describes this problem). In addition, Halstead believed that the values of L and $\hat{L}$ were virtually identical—which is questionable at best: see Johnson and Lister (1981), Oldehoeft (1979) and data in Halstead (1977a: Table 5.1).

This has resulted in a situation where most workers calculate $\hat{L}$ but conduct their algebraic arguments in terms of L, which is not measured. The relationships that have been investigated experimentally are those using $\hat{L}$, not those using L.

11.3.2 I: Intelligence content ($I = \hat{L}V$)

Obviously, the program volume V varies with both the algorithm coded and the language used. It is claimed that the product $\hat{L}V$ is *constant* for all implementations of an algorithm; that is, $I = \hat{L}V$ is independent of the language in which the algorithm is coded.

11.3.3 λ: Language level ($\lambda = LV^*$)

It is believed that the product LV^* is a function only of the language in which the program is written. This is the notional definition of the language level λ. In practice, V^* is replaced by $V\hat{L}$ and the value $\lambda = \hat{L}^2V$ calculated (ACM 1980), and this should be considered the *de facto* definition.

11.3.4 E: mental effort

E is notionally defined as V/L, although the *de facto* definition is $V/\hat{L}$. The latter value is sometimes also known as $\hat{E}$.

It is believed that E directly measures the number of 'elementary mental discriminations' required to code the program, i.e. the number of psychological 'moments' required for this activity. This concept is discussed in Section 11.5 below.

11.4 TESTING THE INVARIANTS: λ AND I

An experiment described in Halstead (1977a: Table 8.1) in which the same person coded 12 algorithms in each of three languages (PL/1, Fortran and APL) forms a good basis for determining the influences of the choice of algorithm and language on λ and I.

Use of analysis of variance, with its associated F-test, indicates clearly that both language and algorithm affect the values of $\lambda(F_{2,22} = 8.2; F_{11,22} = 5.9)$ and $I(F_{2,22} = 10.8; F_{11,22} = 10.6)$ at the 1% level of significance. Hence both metrics can be rejected as true invariants.

However it would be possible for these metrics to fail the above test and still be useful engineering approximations to invariants. Tests of this weaker criterion are, by their very nature, much less formal. We have chosen to assess the relative impacts of language and algorithm as follows. Language means are the mean values of the metric for implementations of different algorithms in the same language. The impact of the language is the (coefficient of) variation of language means, and the impact of algorithms is the variation of algorithm means. These values are shown below for the metrics λ, I and V:

Metric	Impact of language	Impact of algorithms
λ	0.33	0.56
I	0.17	0.33
V	0.06	0.87

These figures suggest that λ is influenced *less* by language than by algorithm, while I is a less satisfactory candidate for an algorithmic invariant than V (being influenced more by language and less by algorithm than V). Neither λ nor I seems to possess properties making their use as invariants reasonable.

As a footnote, figures in Halstead (1977a: Table 9.4) can be analysed to give figures for the influence of language and algorithm on λ. The values obtained (0.37 and 0.66) are comparable to those obtained above (0.33 and 0.56), which suggests that the data used for analysis here is not untypical.

11.5 PREDICTING CODING TIMES

11.5.1 The time equation

In Stroud (1967), the psychologist John Stroud restated his belief that the human brain processes information in discrete bursts, each burst of activity corresponding to a 'moment' of psychological time. Stroud believed that there are about 10 such moments of psychological time for every second of physical time, although this figure may vary between 5 and 20.

Halstead attempted to derive an estimate of the number of 'moments' required to code a program module (or a piece of technical prose). This estimate is the software science metric of effort (E), and its largely intuitive derivation is given in Halstead (1977a). E is stated to be the number of 'elementary mental discriminations' required to code the program, and, with the assumption that one such discrimination is made per psychological 'moment', this leads directly to the 'time equation':

$$T = E/S$$

where

$T =$ 'the time (in seconds) to generate a *preconceived* program, by a *concentrating* programmer *fluent* in [the] language [used]' (Gordon and Halstead 1976: see Chapter 1 above)

$E =$ the software science metric of effort

$S =$ the number of psychological 'moments' per second; typically, a figure of 18 is used in software science, which is close to Stroud's upper bound.

The derivation of the time equation is largely speculative, and before it can be considered in any way credible it requires experimental 'confirmation'. If the time equation does turn out to hold, then it represents an important link between software science and psychology.

Many experiments have been carried out to assess the validity of the time equation for technical prose, individual software modules and entire software projects, covering a truly amazing range of sizes from a few minutes to 11 758 man-months. So great was the apparent success of these experiments that it was claimed that

> it is apparent that we now have, quantitatively, a theoretical, experimentally verifiable, explanation for not just average programming times, but the decrease in hourly production rates accompanying increases in project size. When one remembers that ... [this equation] ... was originally tested, and actually derived, with programming tasks requiring from 5 to 90 *minutes*, its extension to real-world projects of this magnitude suggests that the most important variables have been identified, and their role, on the average or statistically speaking, is now understood. (Halstead 1978)

A re-examination of data from several experiments is shown below; it has not been found possible to agree with the conclusion reached by previous investigators, and the reasons for this are identified.

11.6 EXPERIMENTS INVOLVING INDIVIDUAL SOFTWARE MODULES

Typical of the software science experiments 'confirming' the time equation are those described in Halstead (1977a: Chapter 8). these experiments seem to rely on a presumption that if the (Pearson's) correlation coefficient between two sets of variables is nearly 1, then the variables are *proportional* to each other: such a presumption is unjustified.

Rather than trying to obtain a single figure of merit for the fit between the experimental data and the time equation, it is probably more informative to try to determine the relationship exhibited between the observed values of T and E and then see how closely this relationship corresponds to that predicted by the time equation. Observing that the relationship between T and E may well be curvilinear, but that null programs are very quick to write ($T = 0$ when $E = 0$), a power-law relationship between T and E would seem a sensible one to postulate. The traditional method of fitting data to a power curve (Yule and Kendall 1958) is to transform the data to $y = \ln(T)$ and $x = \ln(E)$ then find the straight line $y = A + Bx$ which is the least-squares best fit. Obviously, this corresponds to finding a power–law relationship between T and E of the form $T = e^A E^B$ with a criterion of best fit approximating to minimizing the *relative* error of the estimate of T.

While estimating the values of A and B, it is also possible to estimate the accuracy of these estimates (Topping 1958) and the relative accuracy of estimates of T. The relative accuracy is calculated as the standard deviation of log (actual value/estimated value), but for intelligibility is reported as a percentage error in the estimate of T. Table 11.1 contains the results of analysing some of Halstead's data in this way. If the time equation holds, then the values of A and B should be close to -2.89 and 1 (since $e^A = 1/S = 1/18$). This is evidently not the case. In the table the first two lines are for experimental programs and the third and fourth lines are for technical prose. As the figures all differ from those expected from the time

Table 11.1

Data source	No. of points	A	B	Relative accuracy (%)
Halstead (1977a: Table 8.1)	36	2.01 ± 0.46	0.51 ± 0.05	53
Halstead (1977a: Table 8.4)	11	1.45 ± 0.98	0.58 ± 0.10	58
Comer and Halstead (1979)	34	2.04 ± 0.56	0.51 ± 0.06	50
Comer and Halstead (1979)	11	1.11 ± 0.04	0.57 ± 0.04	28
Combination of above	92	1.69 ± 0.28	0.54 ± 0.03	51

equation, but do not differ substantially from each other, the data has also been pooled, with the results shown in the last line.

The figures seem to provide evidence that the time equation does not hold. Coding time is not proportional to E, and the evidence points more strongly to T being proportional to the square root of E if this analysis is to be believed. The relative accuracy of estimates of T obtained from even the best-fit power curve can only be described as poor, and there seems little practical value in pursuing a relationship between T and E from the data. Incidentally, the relationship between T and either length (N) or volume (V) is substantially more linear than that volume between T and E.

11.6.1 A medium-sized project

In an early software science paper (Funami and Halstead 1976), data published in Akiyama (1971) was analysed to test the time equation. Using $S = 18$, and an estimate of E for each module, a total time estimate of 84 man-months was obtained for the whole project represented by those modules. As the reported duration was 'about 100 man-months', this was taken to show that the time equation held. However, the calculations are based on two major assumptions: that coding represents 100 per cent of project effort, and that 100 per cent concentration was applied throughout the project. As both assumptions seem highly unrealistic, this experiment cannot be seen as confirming the time equation.

11.6.2 Experiments involving substantial software developments

In Halstead (1977b), a formula is developed to predict the total time required to develop a software system from knowledge of the number of delivered source statements. This formula corresponds very closely to the least-squares fit obtained between project duration and delivered lines of code observed for 60 IBM projects (Walston and Felix 1977a,b). As the work content of these projects varied between 3 and 11 758 man-months, this is, at first sight, strong evidence in support of the time equation.

However, there are two major flaws in Halstead's derivation of the relationship between project duration and lines of delivered code. The first is a repetition of that made in a previous section; it is assumed that 100% of project duration is spent coding. In fact, the figure is much lower and varies with both the size and type of project.

The second flaw is even more serious. Earlier, we followed the practice of estimating E for each software module and then summing the resultant time-estimates; the appropriateness of this method is confirmed by reference to Halstead (1977a: 47, 48). However, Halstead's formula is derived as if each software system contained a single module. As the metric of effort E is (approximately) proportional to the square of the lines of code in a module, this mistake results in substantial over-estimates of coding time. (The sum of the squares is less than the square of the sum.) For a project containing 100K statements (well within the range of projects considered), making the assumption that the modules within it are each 1K statements long reduces the estimate of coding time to 5% of Halstead's figure.

Hence Halstead's formula should relate the *coding time* of *single-module* (and inevitably *small*) projects to the number of delivered source lines. The fact that fortuitously it fits quite closely the least-squares fit observed between *project duration* and delivered source lines for *large, multi-module* projects cannot be construed as supportive evidence for the time equation.

11.6.3 Overall conclusions on predicting code time

It would seem virtually certain that the time equation does not hold on the evidence of small software modules and sections of technical prose. Attempts to apply the time equation to larger projects have shown a disturbing lack of understanding of the reality of large projects, and can only damage the credibility of software science.

11.7 PREDICTING THE BUG-RATES FROM E OR V

11.7.1 The initial theory

In Funami and Halstead (1976) it is argued that the number of 'bugs' coded should be proportional to the number of psychological 'moments' required to code the program. As software science holds that E is a direct measure of the number of such moments expended in coding, it follows that the number of bugs should be proportional to E.

In Funami and Halstead (1976) this simple theory was 'tested' by measuring the correlation coefficient between estimates of E and bug counts (B) for data published in Akiyama (1971). As the correlation coefficient was quite high (0.98), this was taken as evidence that E and B were linearly related.

Subsequently, in largely unreported work (mentioned in Ottenstein 1979) software science workers discovered that the rate of introducing bugs (measured by B/E) depended heavily on program size (as measured by E). This suggested that a nonlinear relationship existed between B and E notwithstanding the result of the Funami–Halstead experiment. Attempts to fit a power–law curve between B and E suggested that B was proportional to about the $\frac{2}{3}$ power of E.

At this point some software scientists realized that a fairly high correlation coefficient does *not* prove proportionality between the variables. Their failure to re-examine all previous software science experiments relying on such interpretations of the correlation coefficient is regrettable.

11.7.2 The second theory

This theory introduced a new psychological theory based on 'chunking', which is based in turn on a fusion between psychological and software science theories. It was postulated that the brain subdivided a large task into 'chunks', each chunk containing a number of psychological 'moments'. The chunk size was calculated by assuming the chunk to be an algorithm with a number of parameters equal to the length of short-term memory. The apparently arbitrary assumption was then made that, while processing a chunk, an average of L (the level of abstraction) bugs will be created. This results in the estimating equation:

$$B_V = E(L/3000) + (V/L)(L/3000) = V/3000.$$

The symbol B_V was defined as the number of *validation bugs*, that is the number of bugs identified during the validation and integration phase of a project.

We will reserve comment on the psychological aspects of this theory, but we feel obliged to point out that the claim to predict validation bugs is difficult to defend for at least two reasons:

1. The theory predicts only the number of bugs introduced during the mental activity of coding the preconceived algorithm; hence it cannot estimate errors introduced during other activities, which account for the majority of validation bugs (Boehm 1976).
2. The level of testing, and hence bugs removed, before the program is passed to the validation process is a function of the style, competence and organization of the development team. Hence the fraction of coding bugs reaching validation cannot be predicted from first principles.

11.7.3 Experiments using Akiyama's data

These experiments were based on a software project reported in Akiyama (1971) for which software science parameters were estimated in Funami and Halstead (1976). Unfortunately, there is strong evidence that Funami and Halstead's data contain significant errors. First, the number of bugs reported for module MC is mis-reported. Second, the techniques used to estimate the software science parameters n_1 and n_2 are unsound. The estimate of n_1 presumes that each subroutine call is to a different subroutine; the number of subroutine calls involved makes this view unrealistic. This fault causes n_1 to be substantially overestimated, which is reflected in an underestimate for n_2. The net effect of this is that the values of V (which depend on the term $n_1 + n_2$) are not substantially affected, but the values of E (which depend on a term n_1/n_2) *are* inflated. Values for both V and E are given in Akiyama (1971: Table 2); Funami and Halstead published values of E but not of V.

In Halstead (1977a), the values of V for Akiyama's modules were estimated *from the values of E* given by Funami and Halstead; while in Ottenstein (1979) V was calculated with the maximum accuracy possible, from values of N, n_1 and n_2 in Funami and Halstead. This resulted in the two workers making highly different estimates of B_V, as is shown:

Module	MA	MB	MC	MD	ME	MF
B_V (Halstead)	102	21	157	31	72	54
B_V (Ottenstein)	26	8	37	10	12	15

The reason for this discrepancy is, of course, the errors made in estimating n_1 and n_2 by Funami and Halstead, and the different impact they had on the estimates of V used by Halstead and by Ottenstein.

It would be pleasing to record that the wide discrepancy between these estimates was noticed by software science workers and traced back to its source. In fact, both Halstead and Ottenstein reported that these considerably different estimates were consistent with the figures reported by Funami and Halstead.

Halstead claimed, with some justification, that his estimate of *validation* bugs was reasonably close to the *total* bugs reported for the modules. Ottenstein estimated some figures off a rather limited graph to obtain the 'true' count of validation bugs, found that they did not agree very well with her estimates, and used instead an artificial figure of 'total bugs reported for the module' multiplied by the 'fraction of bugs in project reaching validation'.

Neither of these treatments gives the impression that software science workers have a clear definition of 'validation bug', and Ottenstein's use of a project-dependent constant is totally inconsistent with the derivation of the estimating equation from fundamental psychological and software science relationships.

11.7.4 An experiment using Lipow and Thayer's data

As was described earlier, the theory that B is proportional to V was developed in response to the experimental observation that the Funami–Halstead figures were consistent with a relationship of the form $B \propto E^{2/3}$.

Using the data from Akiyama (1971: Table 2), it can be calculated that $B \propto V^{0.85 \pm 0.17}$, which is not significantly nonlinear. This is to be expected, as the relationship $(B \propto V)$ was developed to be consistent with this data. Hence to have any confidence in the linearity of the relationship, it must be tested on at least one set of data not involved in its creation. Such a body of data was reported in Lipow and Thayer (1977). Fitting a power–law curve for this data results in the relationship $B \propto V^{1.29 \pm 0.11}$, which is significantly nonlinear and significantly different from the relationship observed for the data derived from Akiyama.

On analysing the relationship between bugs and V for the Lipow–Thayer data, software scientists (in this case, Ottenstein 1979) again fell into the trap of presuming that a high value of the correlation coefficient (in this case, 0.96) indicates proportionality. That this mistake can be made when testing a theory that was created to explain the nonlinearity of the relationship between B and E (which tests involving the correlation coefficient had failed to detect) is disturbing.

11.7.5 Conclusion on predicting bug-rates

Perhaps the most significant feature of the software science attempts to predict 'bugs' is the failure to develop a clear distinction between different types of bug, or to identify which type of bug their estimating equation predicts. Another criticism that can be levelled at this attempt to predict bugs from first principles is that no effort has been made to determine the origin of 'bugs' other than a simplistic assumption that they occur essentially at random and at an essentially unchangeable frequency. Apart from general experience, the work of people such as Jackson (1975) and Brinch Hansen (1977) is indicative that many 'bugs' originate in a mismatch between the 'structure' of the problem being solved and the structure of the program developed to solve it. In Berland (1978) an artificial problem is used to illustrate this; while Goodenough and Gerhart (1975) provide perhaps the classical illustration of just how error-prone highly competent people can be when they ignore the underlying structure of the problem—in this case glossing over a 'small' Jackson structure clash.

Since we were particularly interested in any proven relationships between the occurrence of 'bugs' and other characteristics of software, we continued by looking at data reported by Akiyama (1971: Table 2) and by Lipow and Thayer (1977). In both cases V/B was significantly different from the software science predicted 3000, and linearity was not found between counts of bugs and counts of other features of the code.

11.8 CONFIRMING PROGRAM LENGTH

One of the first relationships proposed was that $\hat{N} = n_1 \log_2(n_1) + n_2 \log_2(n_2)$ was an approximation for the metric N. Although it is difficult to see any practical application for this formula (which confirms rather than predicts length), it does represent a link between the counts of unique operators/operands and the count of their occurrence, and one that is of considerable theoretical interest.

11.8.1 Classical software science data

The mean and coefficient of variation of $\hat{N}/N$ for several groups of computer programs are shown in Table 11.2. Using the Kendall rank correlation coefficient to test if the ratio $\hat{N}/N$ was correlated with the value of $\hat{N}$ revealed no significant results, so it is reasonable to suppose that the relationship between $\hat{N}$ and N is substantially linear. As all six sets of data produce similar results, they have been pooled and the mean and variation of the entire collection has been calculated:

$$\hat{N}/N = 1.02 \pm 32\%$$

As the standard error of the mean is ±0.04, the closeness of the mean to unity should not be taken too literally. The fact remains that the mean is not significantly different from the prediction of unity. The high value for the variation of ±32 per cent implies that individual predictions are only of limited accuracy.

Table 11.2

Source in Halstead (1977a)	Mean and variation of $\hat{N}/N$ (%)
Table 5.1	1.04 ± 13
Table 8.1—PL/1	0.86 ± 49
Table 8.1—Fortran	1.15 ± 39
Table 8.1—APL	1.10 ± 37
Table 8.4	0.92 ± 37
Table 9.3	0.99 ± 16

11.8.2 Johnston and Lister's data

In Johnston and Lister (1981; also Lister 1981) doubt was cast on the validity of the relationship $\hat{N} = N$ for large Pascal programs. Analysis of their data gives the mean and variation of $\hat{N}/N$ as 0.63 ± 25 per cent. Again, use of the Kendall rank correlation coefficient gives no reason to suspect the $\hat{N}/N$ varies with $\hat{N}$.

As the standard error of the mean is ± 0.05, this mean value of $\hat{N}/N$ is unacceptably far from unity. Johnston and Lister ascribe the discrepancy to the fact that the Pascal control structures do not make any contribution to the count of unique operators n_1, while the use of labels to define control structure (as in Fortran) increases n_1. If each Pascal control structure is counted as a unique operator, then analysis yields $\hat{N}/N = 1.07 \pm 25$ per cent; again without any significant correlation between $\hat{N}/N$ and $\hat{N}$.

This is in far closer agreement with the results obtained in the previous section. As the standard error of the mean is ± 0.09, the mean is again sensibly equal to unity.

11.8.3 Data from technical prose

Halstead (1977a: Table 13.6) and Comer and Halstead (1979) contain data from three well-monitored experiments involving technical prose. Again, means and variations of $\hat{N}/N$ were calculated:

Source of data	Mean and variation of $\hat{N}/N$ (%)
Halstead (1977a)	0.99 ± 6
Comer and Halstead (1979)	0.79 ± 27
Comer and Halstead (1979)	0.92 ± 17

For the data from Cromer and Halstead (1979) the values of the Kendall rank correlation coefficient between $\hat{N}/N$ and $\hat{N}$ were significant, at 0.1 and 2 per cent levels respectively.

The data from Halstead (1977a) was used to demonstrate that $\hat{N} \simeq N$ for technical prose, and is consistent with that claim. Notice, however, that the accuracy for this data is far greater than that observed in the previous sections.

The well informed reader will be aware that the direct measurement of n_1 and n_2 is impractical for technical prose—see Halstead (1977a: Chapter 13). This problem is caused by the need to correct for the influences of synonyms—e.g. plurals of nouns and conjugations of verbs Halstead suggests that n_1' and n_2' should be measured without paying attention to such problems, and then $n_1 = 0.4n_1'$ and $n_2 = 0.4n_2'$ used. The results from Comer and Halstead suggest that either this practice is inadequate, or the relationship between $\hat{N}$ and N is (sometimes) nonlinear for prose.

11.8.4   Conclusions on confirming program length

It is remarkable that any simple relationship should exist between the counts of unique operators and operands and the counts of their total occurrences. However, the high variation of the prediction made from the proposed relationship (around 30 per cent) suggests that alternative formulations of equal or greater validity may well be found. The theoretical basis for Halstead's formula is certainly suspect; we have never been able to convince ourselves of its validity, and Johnson and Lister claim to have detected logical flaws in the arguments used.

The need to modify the counting technique for Pascal (and perhaps for technical prose) is indicative that software science has so far paid too little attention to identifying 'exceptions to the rule'—the traditional source of much scientific insight.

11.9 OVERALL CONCLUSION ON SOFTWARE SCIENCE

Software science could be examined on its theoretical basis, on its experimental basis, and on its general importance and practical value. This report has concentrated on experimental practice, and, we believe, has shown this to be inadequate to support the stated theory. Although not considered in any detail, the theoretical basis of the work also appears to be shaky, and not such as to justify much further effort along the lines started by Halstead. However, there is a great need, both academically and commercially, for a sound theoretical and practical understanding of the software development process. Although 'software science' (as displayed here) seems to have been interesting but abortive, the search for a sounder science of software must be continued.

Major objections to software science can be summarized as follows:

1. Non-probabilistic models are inherently unsuitable.
2. The counting rules for the basic metrics are ill-defined, arbitrary and not applicable to languages with structured and abstract data types.
3. In the interpretation of experimental results, undue weight has been given to the correlation coefficient.
4. There is a major division between software science theory and practice in the alternative families of metrics based on L and $\hat{L}$. The theory does not explain the existence of two such similar concepts, nor does it define them adequately.
5. The family of metrics based on L is almost certainly spurious since it depends on another ill-defined (and probably provably undefinable) metric, V^*.
6. As shown in this paper, *the claimed experimental support is largely illusory.*

In conclusion, the foundations of software science seems to be in a very weak state, both theoretically and experimentally. We would strongly advise against any attempt to use it in the practical evaluation and control of software development—unless and until convincing fresh support is produced. In order to be convincing, new work must avoid two traps: dependence on previous (unjustified) claims, and the use of experimental designs that have not been shown capable of rejecting false hypotheses. Although metrics based on counts of operators and operands are likely to play an important role, 'software science' (the relationships and interpretations postulated by Halstead) should be treated with the greatest caution.

11.10 BEYOND SOFTWARE SCIENCE

At the start of our examination of software science, we found very little in the published literature to suggest that there might be deficiencies in the theories, the experimental practice, the statistical methods or the supporting data. As soon as a close look was taken, however, this comfortable situation was found to be unjustified; and some of the details have been presented in this report. Other faults are now known to exist and have been reported (or will be reported elsewhere). Had we begun our investigation today, the general atmosphere would have been a little less favourable than it seemed in 1979/80.

However, in this final section we do not wish to dwell on software science, but on some of the influences that have led to its being both unsatisfactory *and* apparently accepted.

11.10.1 The lack of sufficient data

Some of the reasons for a lack of collected and published data on software development are as follows:

1. Commercial secrecy ('Will others learn things from our data which could be used to our commercial disadvantage?')
2. Commercial pressures ('Enough time and money goes into software development—record-keeping and analysis is an unprofitable extra'.)
3. Fear of comparisons (Within an organization both valid and mistaken interpretations may be equally unwelcome.)
4. Fear of provoking scorn ('Were our theory and interpretations from the data valid?')
5. Fear of meeting apathy ('Does anyone really want to see evidence from *our* experience?')
6. Unavailability of models and examples
7. Lack of knowledge of statistical theory and practice

11.10.2 The need for an adequate notation and a range of models

It is essential that models of predicted behaviour are expressed in terms suitable to allow representation and symbolic manipulation of the actual forces and interactions. The systems examined by software science appear to be essentially probabilistic and non-deterministic, but have been modelled in simple algebraic terms. As using a wrong or incomplete mode can obscure truth, it is essential that a range of more powerful models be developed and applied. Cross-fertilization with probability theory and statistics may be only the first stage in reaching a satisfactory notation for the statement of the laws of software science, while predictive models may have to wait for advances in the physics of individual and social behaviour. The attempt to include psychological theory within software science was praiseworthy, and it is almost certain that any advances *will* be cross-disciplinary. However, the acceptance of an idea from another discipline is not a guarantee that it is valid, either within its 'parent' discipline or in the one into which it has been transplanted; such contributions must be treated with additional care. Traditional academic respect for the practitioners of other disciplines must not be allowed to supplant the caution necessary to the experimenter.

Software scientists have generally adopted a very mechanistic view of the software development process. However, we feel that to ignore the social and environmental dimensions is to make a gross oversimplication: 'real-life' software is typically developed by cooperating, interactive groups of people; and these interactions are possibly the major distinction between the development of small programs and large systems. Elements of models of the processes may be found in management science, psychology, organization theory, communication science, linguistics, mathematics, economics, accountancy and political science, to list a few of the disciplines concerned with factors accepted as having been important to particular software developments. Theories that exclude—or ignore—them all, and data recorded without statements as to the environment in which they were obtained, do not add to the credibility of a science of software.

11.10.3 The need for informed debate

Software science workers seem to have been very poorly served both by their academic colleagues and by the software engineering community. Both seem to have passively accepted (or, perhaps, passively rejected) the software science conclusions, possibly without checking but certainly without public debate. It is partly to atone for their part in this conspiracy of apathy that we have decided to publish what must be a critical and contentious report, rather than quietly advising that software science is not ready for local application. We profoundly hope that we have identified more errors than we have made, and trust that any disputes will leave us all better informed and more capable of contributing to other investigations. It is our belief that the profession of software engineering cannot expect to be taken seriously unless a *substantial fraction* of its members engage in informed debate on a regular and serious basis.

Acknowledgements

We wish to acknowledge the helpful suggestions of a number of individuals, both within and outside of STL, who have read earlier drafts of this chapter: in particular, Professor C. A. R. Hoare, Professor M. M. Lehman and Dr G. Benyon-Tinker. Thanks are also due to Mr J. M. Farthing of STL for his help in checking the figures, and Mr F. W. Brice and other staff at STL for coping with the text.

12

A CRITIQUE OF CYCLOMATIC COMPLEXITY AS A SOFTWARE METRIC

Martin J. Shepperd

Wolverhampton Polytechnic

ABSTRACT

McCabe's cyclomatic complexity metric is widely cited as a useful predictor of various software attributes such as reliability and development effort. This critique demonstrates that it is based upon poor theoretical foundations and an inadequate model of software development. The argument that the metric provides the developer with a useful engineering approximation is not borne out by the empirical evidence. Furthermore, it would appear that for a large class of software it is no more than a proxy for, and in many cases is outperformed by, lines of code.

12.1 INTRODUCTION

The need for some objective measurement of software complexity has been long acknowledged. Two early contributions to this field are Halstead's 'software science' (Halstead 1977a) and the cyclomatic complexity approach of McCabe (1976; see Chapter 2 above). Both metrics are based upon the premiss that software complexity is strongly related to various measurable properties of program code.

Although initially well received by the software engineering community, software-science-based metrics have been increasingly subject to criticism.

Attacks have been made upon the underlying psychological model (Coulter 1983; Shen *et al.* 1983). The soundness of many empirical 'validations has been questioned (Hamer and Frewin 1982; see Chapter 11 above), and difficulties noted with counting rules (Lassez *et al.* 1981). The ability of software science metrics to capture program complexity in general would thus appear to be in great doubt.

It is thus rather surprising that the cyclomatic complexity metric has not been subjected to a similar degree of scrutiny to that given to software science. This is particularly the case given the high degree of acceptance of the metric within the software engineering community. It is widely cited,[1] subjected to a 'blizzard of refinements',[2] applied as a design metric (Hall and Preiser 1984) and described in best-selling textbooks on software engineering (Pressman 1992; Wiener and Sincovec 1984). Yet there have been comparatively few empirical studies; indeed, as a basic approach, the metric has been allowed to pass relatively unquestioned.

The hypothesis of a simple deterministic relationship between the number of decisions within a piece of software and its complexity is potentially of profound importance to the whole field of software engineering. This requires very careful evaluation.

The rest of the paper reviews the theories put forward by McCabe. Theoretical criticisms of the metric are outlined and the various empirical validations for the metric are reviewed, together with aspects of experimental design. It is concluded that cyclomatic complexity is questionable on both theoretical and empirical grounds. Therefore cyclomatic complexity is of very limited utility.

12.2 THE CYCLOMATIC COMPLEXITY METRIC

Given the increasing costs of software development, McCabe considered that a 'mathematical technique that will provide a quantitative basis for modularisation and allow us to identify software modules that will be difficult to test or maintain' was required. Use of a lines of code (LOC) metric was rejected since McCabe could see no obvious relationship between length and module complexity. Instead, he suggested that the number of control paths through a module would be a better indicator, particularly as this appeared to be strongly related to testing effort. Furthermore, much of the work on 'structured programming' in the early 1970s concentrated on program control flow structures (Dahl *et al.* 1972; Dijkstra 1968a).

Unfortunately, the number of paths through any software with a backward branch is potentially infinite. Fortunately, the problem can be resolved by the application of graph theory. The control flow of any procedural piece of software

---

[1] See Arthur 1985; Cobb 1978; DeMarco 1982; Dunsmore 1984; Harrison *et al.* 1982; Schneidewind 1979; Tanik 1980.

[2] See Curtis 1983; Hansen 1978; Harrison and Magel 1981; Iyengar *et al.*, 1982; Magel 1981; Myers 1978; Oviedo 1980 (see Chapter 3 above); Stetter 1984; Woodward *et al.* 1979.

```
BEGIN
   REPEAT
      writeln('Enter a number or zero to stop');
      readln(num);
   IF num > 0 THEN
      writeln(num, 'is positive')
   ELSE
      If num < 0 THEN
      writeln(num, 'is negative');
   UNTIL num = 0
END.
```

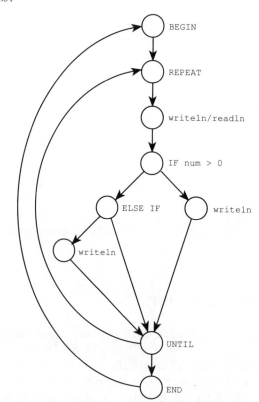

$$v(G) = 12-9+1$$
$$= 4$$

Figure 12.1 Derivation of $v(G)$ for an example program.

can be depicted as a directed graph, by representing each executable statement (or group of statements, where the flow of control is sequential) as a node, and the flow of control as the edges between them. The cyclomatic complexity of a graph is useful because, provided the graph is strongly connected, it indicates the number of basic paths (i.e. linearly independent circuits) contained within a graph, which, when used in combination, can generate all possible paths through the graph or program.

The cyclomatic complexity v of a program graph G is

$$v(G) = e - n + 1 \tag{12.1}$$

where e is the number of edges, and n is the number of nodes.

A strongly connected graph is one for which, given any two nodes *r* and *s*, there exist paths from *r* to *s* and *s* to *r*. Figure 12.1 shows an example derivation of cyclomatic complexity from a simple program and its related control graph. Note that the program graph is made strongly connected by the addition of an edge connecting the END node to the BEGIN node.

The process of adding an extra edge to the program graph can be bypassed by adding one to the cyclomatic complexity calculation. The calculation can be generalized for program graphs that contain one or more components,

```
PROCEDURE blankln(lines:integer);
BEGIN
   FOR ct: = 1 TO lines DO
     writeln
   END
END.

BEGIN{main program}
   writeln('Enter number of blank lines required');
   readln(num);
   IF num > 0 THEN
     blankln(num);
END.
```

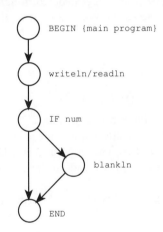

BEGIN {main program}

writeln/readln

IF num

blankln

END

$$v(S) = 9-9+(2*2)$$
$$= 4$$

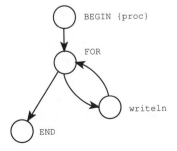

BEGIN {proc}

FOR

writeln

END

Figure 12.2. Derivation of $v(S)$ for a program with a subroutine.

subject to the restriction that each component contains a single entry and a single exit node. For a graph S with a set of connected components, the cyclomatic complexity is

$$v(S) = e - n + 2p \qquad (12.2)$$

where p is the number of connected components.

A multi-component program graph is derived if the software contains separate subroutines. This is illustrated in Fig. 12.2.

As McCabe observed, the calculation reduces to a simple count of conditions plus 1. He argued that, since a compound condition, for example

IF X < 1 AND Y < 2 THEN

was a thinly disguised nested IF, then each condition should contribute to module complexity, rather than merely counting predicates (see Fig. 12.3a and b). Likewise, a case state is viewed as a multiple IF statement (i.e., it contributes $n - 1$ to $v(G)$, where n is the number of cases).

McCabe saw a practical application of the metric in using it to provide an upper limit to module complexity, beyond which a module should be subdivided into simpler components. A value of $v(G) = 10$ was suggested, although he accepted that in certain situations, notably large case structures, the limit might be relaxed.

12.3 THEORETICAL CONSIDERATIONS

The counting rules for different control statements have been the subject of some controversy. Myers (1978) has argued that a complexity interval is a more effective measure of complexity than a simple cyclomatic number. The interval has a lower bound of decision statement count (i.e. predicate count) plus 1 and an upper bound of individual condition count plus 1.

Myers used the following three examples to support his modified form of the cyclomatic complexity metric:

<table>
<tr><td>IF X = 0 THEN...
        ELSE...;</td><td>$v(G) = 2$
Myers $= (2 : 2)$</td></tr>
<tr><td>IF X = 0 AND Y > 1 THEN...
             ELSE...</td><td>$v(G) = 3$
Myers $= (2 : 3)$</td></tr>
<tr><td>IF X = 0 THEN...
   IF Y > 1 THEN...
        ELSE...
   ELSE...;</td><td>

$v(G) = 3$
Myers $= (3 : 3)$</td></tr>
</table>

Myers's argument is that it is intuitively obvious that the third example is more complex than the second, a distinction not made by the cyclomatic

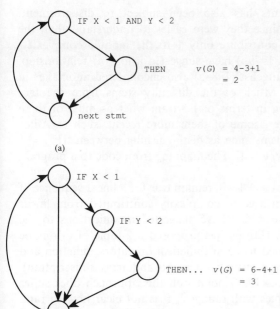

IF X < 1 AND Y < 2

THEN $v(G)$ = 4–3+1
                 = 2

next stmt

(a)

IF X < 1

IF Y < 2

THEN... $v(G)$ = 6–4+1
                  = 3

next stmt

(b)

Figure 12.3 Compound condition treated as a single decision and as separate decisions. (a) Treated as a single decision. (b) Treated as separate decisions.

number. The idea underlying his modification appears to be that there is more potential for inserting additional ELSE clauses into a program with a larger number of IF statements. They are not counted by the McCabe metric, as is demonstrated by the following two program fragments, both of which have cyclomatic complexities of 2:

IF X < 1 THEN

  ...; $v(G) = 2$

IF X < 1 THEN

  ...

ELSE

  ...; $v(G) = 2$

Since Myers's complexity interval does not directly count ELSE statements, it is arguable whether it represents much of an improvement over that of McCabe's metric. However, the criticism of cyclomatic complexity remains, in that it fails to distinguish between selections with and without ELSE branches. From the standpoint of psychological complexity, this is significant; however, since the number of basic paths remains unaltered, testing difficulty may not increase. Thus, the failure of cyclomatic complexity to count ELSE branches is a serious deficiency only if the metric is intended to capture complexity of comprehension.

The treatment of case statements has also been subject to disagreement. Hansen (1978) has suggested that, since they were easier to understand than the equivalent nested IFs, they should contribute only 1 to the module complexity. Other researchers (Basili and Reiter 1979b) have suggested a $\log_2(n)$ relationship, where n is the number of cases. Evangelist (1983a) also encountered anomalies in the application of counting rules. Much of the difficulty stems from the fact that McCabe was originally thinking in terms of Fortran, whereas most of these difficulties arise from other languages, some of them more recent, such as Ada.[3] Here one has to contend with problems such as distinguishing between 'IF $y = 1$ OR $y = 3$' and 'IF $y = 0$ OR ELSE $x/y > 1$'. The mapping from code to a program graph is ambiguous.

Another area of controversy is that $v = 1$ will remain true for a linear sequence of any length. Since the metric is insensitive to complexity contributed from linear sequences of statements, several researchers have suggested modifications to the simple use of cyclomatic complexity. Hansen has proposed a 2-tuple of cylomatic complexity and operand count (defined to be arithmetical operators, function and subroutine calls, assignments, input and output statements and array subscription). Unfortunately, as Baker and Zweben (1980) point out, this approach does suffer from the problem of 'comparing apples with oranges'. It is not clear how to rank in order of complexity the 2-tuples (i, j) and (l, k) where $i > l$ and $k > j$.

Stetter (1984) suggests an alternative approach to this particular problem in the form of a cyclomatic flow complexity metric. Flow of data is considered in addition to flow of control. Complexity will generally increase with an increase in length of a linear sequence of statements since more data references will almost invariably be made.

A further objection to the cyclomatic complexity metric is its behaviour towards the structuring of software. A number of researchers[4] argue that the cyclomatic complexity can increase when applying generally accepted techniques to improve program structure. Certainly, the metric is insensitive to the use of unstructured techniques such as jumping in and out of loops, since all that is captured is the number of decisions plus 1. Evangelist (1982) reports that the application of only 2 out of 26 of Kernighan and Plauger's (1978) rules of good programming style invariably results in a decrease in cyclomatic complexity.

A development of the unstructured/structured argument is the objection that the metric ignores the context or environment of a decision. All decisions have a uniform weight, regardless of depth of nesting or relationship with other decisions. The complexity of a decision cannot be considered in isolation, but must take into account other decisions within its scope. This has resulted in variants of cyclomatic complexity which allow for nesting depth (Magel 1981; Prather 1984; Piowarski 1982).

It is worth noting that all counting rule variants to the metric are based upon arguments along the lines that it is intuitively obvious that one example is more

---

[3] Ada is a trademark of the US Government Ada Joint Program Office.
[4] See e.g. Baker and Zweben (1980); Oulsnam (1979); Prather (1984); Sinha *et al.* (1986).

complex than another and therefore an adjustment must be made to the counting rules. Such arguments are based upon issues of cognitive complexity or 'perplexity' (Whitty 1985) which is only one view of software complexity. Difficulty of testing is another aspect of software complexity, and one with which McCabe was primarily concerned. These different interpretations of cyclomatic complexity have significant implications upon the validation and application of the metric.

A more fundamental objection to cyclomatic complexity is the inconsistent behaviour when measuring modularized software. As Eq. (12.2) indicates, $v(G)$ is sensitive to the number of subroutines within a program, because McCabe suggests that these should be treated as unconnected components within the control graph. This has the bizarre result of increasing overall complexity as a program is divided into more, presumably simpler, modules. In general, the complexity v of a program P' will be:

$$v(P') = v(P) + i \qquad (12.3)$$

where P is equivalent program to P' but with a single component, and i is the number of modules or subroutines used by P' (i.e. the number of graph components -1).

However, the relationship is further complicated by the observation that graph complexity may be reduced in a situation where modularization eliminates code duplication. Thus,

$$v(P') = v(P) + i - \sum_{j=1}^{j=i}((v_j - 1) * (u_j - 1)) \qquad (12.4)$$

where v_j is the complexity of the jth module or subroutine, and u_j is the number of times the jth module is called.

To summarize, general program complexity increases with the addition of extra modules but decreases with the factoring out of duplicate code. All other aspects of modularity are disregarded. If one were to be prescriptive on the basis of Eq. (12.4), it would be modularized only when a fragment of nonlinear code (i.e. containing decisions) could be factored out. As a model with which to view general software complexity, this appears unacceptable.

Three classes of theoretical objection have been presented. First, there is the issue of the very simplistic approach to decision counting. Ease of program comprehension is unlikely to be completely orthogonal to software complexity. The ease of comprehending a decision is not invariant, and thus a constant weighting of 1 seems inappropriate. Second, the metric appears to be independent of generally accepted program structuring techniques. Since these are intended to reduce complexity, this does not exactly inspire confidence. Third, and most importantly, is the arbitrary impact of modularization upon total program complexity. As a measure of inter-modular complexity, in other words for all non-trivial software, cyclomatic complexity would seem unsatisfactory on theoretical grounds.

12.4 EMPIRICAL VALIDATION OF THE METRIC

Many early validations of the metric were merely based upon intuitive notions of complexity. For example, McCabe states that 'the complexity measure v is designed to conform to our intuitive notion of complexity (McCabe 1976; see Chapter 2 above). Hansen (1978) argues that a good measure of program complexity should satisfy several criteria, including that of relating 'intuitively to the psychological complexity of programs'. He does not suggest that there is a need for any objective validation. Likewise, Myers (1978) treats intuition as sufficient grounds for employing the metric.

This seems a rather curious approach: if intuition is a reliable arbiter of complexity, this eliminates the need for a quantitative measure. On the other hand, if intuition cannot be relied upon, it hardly provides a reasonable basis for validation. Clearly, a more objective approach to validation is required.

The theoretical objections to the metric, i.e. that it ignores other aspects of software such as data and functional complexity, are not necessarily fatal. It is easy to construct certain pathological examples, but this need not invalidate the metric if it is possible to demonstrate that in practice it provides a useful engineering predictor of factors that are associated with complexity. Researchers have usually taken these to include effort involved in testing and maintenance, error incidence, and ability to recall code.

A number of empirical studies have been carried out. These are summarized in Table 12.1. A difficulty that arises in interpretation of many of these studies is that there is no explicit hypothesis being evaluated. Two possible *a posteriori* hypotheses with which to examine the empirical work are as follows:

- *Hypothesis 1* Total program cyclomatic complexity can be used to predict various useful software characteristics (for example development time, incidence of errors and program comprehension).
- *Hypothesis 2* Programs comprising modules with low $v(G)$ (< 10) are easier to test and maintain than those for which this is not the case (McCabe's original hypothesis).

As Table 12.1 indicates, the results of various empirical validation studies do not give a great deal of support to either hypothesis. In general, the results are not very compelling, either at the program level (hypothesis 1) or for the studies that deal with individual modules (hypothesis 2), such as Basili and Perricone (1984; see Chapter 10 above). The major exception is the Henry *et al.* (1981) study of 165 procedures from the UNIX operating system, where the results show a strong correlation between $v(G)$ and module error rates. This result may be slightly artificial, since they appear to have filtered out all error-free modules.

Based upon the observation that large modules tend to contain more errors than small modules, the Basili–Perricone (1984) study uses error density (i.e. errors per thousand LOC) as a size-normalized metric of software error-proneness. Their rather surprising finding was that error density diminishes with increasing cyclomatic complexity. Work by Shen *et al.* (1985) gives support to this result, although there is disagreement as to whether error density is an appropriate means of size

Table 12.1 Empirical validations of cyclomatic complexity

Researchers	LOC	Errors		Programming effort	Bug location	Program recall	Design effort
		Density	Absolute				
Basili and Perricone (1984)	$r^2 = 0.94$	r is $-$ve					
Basili and Selby (1984)				$R = 0.48$	$R = 0.21$		
Bowen (1978)			$r^2 = 0.47$		$r = -0.09$		
Curtis et al. (1979a)	$r^2 = 0.41, 0.81, 0.79$					$r = -0.35^*$	
Curtis et al. (1979b)	$r^2 = 0.81, 0.66$				$r^2 = 0.4, 0.42$		
Davis (1984)						r is $-$ve, $+$ve	
Feuer and Fowlkes (1979)	$r^2 = 0.90^{***}$						
Gaffney (1979a)				$r^2 = 0.60$			
Henry et al. (1981)	$r^2 = 0.84^{****}$		$r^2 = 0.92^{****}$				
Kitchenham (1981)	$r^2 = 0.86, 0.88$		$r^2 = 0.46, 0.49, 0.21^{****}$				
Paige (1980)	$r^2 = 0.90$						
Schneidewind (1979b)	$r^2 = 0.61^{*****}$		$r^2 = 0.32^{*****}$				
Shen et al. (1985)			$r^2 = 0.78^{***}$				
Sheppard et al. (1979a)	$r^2 = 0.79$			$r^2 = 0.38$		$r = 0.35$	
Sunohara et al. (1981)				$r^2 = 0.4, 0.38$			
Wang and Dunsmore (1984)	$r^2 = 0.62$			$r^2 = 0.59$			
Woodfield et al. (1981a)				$r^2 = 0.26, R = 0.39$			
Woodward et al. (1979)	$r^2 = 0.90$						$r^2 = 0.72, 0.7$

r^2 = Pearson moment. R = Rank Spearman.

*   r was 'improved' when modified for potentially 'aberrant' results.

**   correlated with N (i.e. Halstead's token count).

***   a simple decision count (i.e. $v(G) - 1$).

****   indirect error count (i.e. version count, or program change count.

*****   using log–log transformations.

normalization since module size and error density do not appear to be independent. Nevertheless, this strongly underlines the deficiency of a simple intra-modular complexity metric.

The clearest result from the empirical studies is the strong relationship between cyclomatic complexity and LOC. Even in the study of Henry *et al.*, there appears to be a fairly strong association. Ironically, it was the 'inadequacy' of LOC as a module complexity metric that led to McCabe proposing cyclomatic complexity as an alternative. A considerable number of studies indicate that LOC actually out-performs cyclomatic complexity.[5]

The most reasonable inference that can be drawn from the above studies is that there exists a significant class of software for which $v(G)$ is now more than a proxy for LOC. A suggestion of Henry *et al.* (1981) that software can be characterized as either decision- or computation-bound could have a considerable bearing upon interpretation of empirical studies. In cases of decision-bound software such as UNIX, $v(G)$ will closely correspond to LOC. In computation-bound software, with sizeable portions of linear code, this correspondence will be very marginal, and possibly accounts substantially for the erratic results of Table 12.1.

An interesting development of this point has been made by Humphreys (1986), who argues that there exists a trade-off between decision or control flow complexity and data structure complexity. One such example is the use of decision tables to replace multiple IF or CASE statements (a common technique in systems programming). The consequence of this is that the cyclomatic complexity for the decision table solution will be substantially lower than for the alternative solution. Yet, he argues, the two pieces of software appear to have similar complexities. More significantly, they will require a similar amount of testing effort since they have the same number of boundary conditions to contend with. Thus, the claimed association between testing difficulty and $v(G)$ in many cases is distinctly tenuous. The suggestion has been made (Whitty 1987) that this is due to McCabe's ambiguous mapping function of program control flow to a program graph. Either way, it does not bode well for cyclomatic complexity as a predictor of testing effort.

Most of the studies reported above place reliance upon obtaining high correlation coefficients. Use of Pearson's product moment, which is the most widely used correlation coefficient in the studies above, requires the assumption that the data is drawn from a population with a roughly normal distribution. This creates a particular problem when examining module error rates. The impossibility of a negative error count results in a pronounced skew in the error distribution. This skew can be reduced by various transformation techniques, for instance by using the square root or logarithm. Studies such as Bowen (1978) and Henry *et al.* (1981) would be more meaningful if one of these techniques were applied to obtain a more normal distribution so that we could place a higher degree of confidence in the correlation coefficients produced.

---

[5] See Curtis *et al.* (1979a); Kitchenham (1981a); Paige (1980); Wang and Dunsmore (1984); Basili and Hutchens (1983).

There are two alternative empirical approaches; both have considerable difficulties associated with them. The first is large-scale passive observation, where the researcher has little if any influence. The second is more carefully controlled experimentation, which out of practical necessity tends to be very small-scale.[6]

Large-scale passive observation is based upon the notion that the variance introduced into the study from uncontrolled factors such as differences in individual ability, task difficulty and differing environments is compensated by the large sample size involved. Problems include the difficulty of obtaining accurate measurements (Basili *et al.* 1983). Their results showed some improvement when restricted to results validated by various cross-checks. More significant is the problem of variation in individual ability (Schneider, 1981). Brooks (1980) suggests that differences in ability for individuals from similar backgrounds of up to 25 to 1 are such as to make it very difficult to obtain statistically significant results.

The second approach, as typified by (Woodfield *et al.* 1981a), is more carefully controlled since the time scale and number of subjects are relatively small. Here measurements are potentially more accurate; however, variance from external factors is still a major difficulty. Use of within-subject experimental design is a partial solution, although it does not address a number of factors, such as the subject's familiarity with the problem and the comparability of tasks. The small size of tasks being undertaken is another problem area; frequently programs of less than 300 LOC are used.[7] These programs are, by software engineering standards, trivial. In such situations the onus is upon the research to demonstrate that results at a small scale are equally applicable for large systems. Such a finding would be counter to current directions in software engineering.

To summarize, many of the empirical validations of McCabe's metric need to be interpreted with caution. First, the use of correlation coefficients on skewed data causes artificially high correlations. Second, the assumption of causality would seem doubtful given the consistently high association between cyclomatic complexity and LOC. Third, the high variation in programmer ability reduces the statistical significance of correlation coefficients.

However, despite the above reservations, some trends in the results are apparent. The strong association between LOC and cyclomatic complexity gives the impression that the latter may well be no more than a proxy for the former. The ability of $v(G)$ to predict error rates, development time and program recall is quite erratic. Most damning is the out-performing of $v(G)$ by a straightforward LOC metric in over a third of the studies considered.

12.5 CONCLUSIONS

A severe difficulty in evaluating McCabe's metric and associated empirical work is the lack of an explicit model upon which cyclomatic complexity is based. The implicit

---

[6] See e.g. Woodward *et al.* (1979); Curtis *et al.* (1979a,b); Wang and Dunsmore (1984).

[7] See e.g. Davis (1984); Feuer and Fowlkes (1979); Wang and Dunsmore (1984); Woodfield *et al.* (1981a).

model appears to be that the decomposition of a system into suitable components (or modules) is the key issue. The decomposition should be based upon ease of testing individual components. Testing difficulty is entirely determined by the number of basic paths through a program's flowgraph.

Unfortunately, and perhaps not surprisingly, different investigators have interpreted cyclomatic complexity in a variety of ways. For example, some studies treat cyclomatic complexity at a program level by summing individual module complexities (Woodfield *et al.* 1981a) while others consider complexity purely at a module level (Henry *et al.* 1981). Naturally this state of affairs does not facilitate the comparison of results.

An important distinction is made between intra- and inter-modular complexity. Eqs. (12.3 and 12.4) suggest that cyclomatic complexity is rather suspect in the latter area. Thus, the only possible role for cyclomatic complexity is as an *intra*-modular complexity metric. Even this is made to look doubtful in the light of the work of Basili and Perricone. In any case, many researchers (Stevens *et al.* 1974) would argue that the problem of how to modularize a program is better resolved by considerations of 'coupling' and 'cohesion' (i.e. *inter*-modular complexity), which are not adequately captured by the metric.

As noted earlier, most of the empirical work has relied upon obtaining high correlation coefficients to substantiate McCabe's metric. However, a high correlation coefficient between two variables does not necessarily imply causality, as illustrated by the well-known, if slightly apochryphal, example of the spatial distribution of ministers of religion and prostitutes! Setting aside quibbles of experimental methodology (Brooks 1980; Sayward 1984), the fundamental problem remains that, without an explicit underlying model, the empirical 'validation' is meaningless and there is no hypothesis to be refuted.

Even if we disregard all the above problems and accept the correlation coefficients at face value, the results are distinctly erratic. Cyclomatic complexity fails to convince as a general software complexity metric. This impression is strengthened by the close association between $v(G)$ and LOC and the fact that, for a significant number of studies, LOC outperforms $v(G)$.

The majority of modifications to McCabe's original metric remain untested. To what extent do validations of cyclomatic complexity impinge upon these modified metrics, many of which appear to be very minor variants? Prather (1984), in an attempt to provide some unifying framework, suggests a set of axioms that a 'proper' complexity metric must satisfy:

- *Axiom 1* The complexity of the whole must not be less than the sum of the complexities of the parts.
- *Axiom 2* The complexity of a selection must be greater than the sum of all the branches (i.e., the predicate must contribute complexity).
- *Axiom 3* The complexity of an iteration must be greater than the iterated part (for the same reason as axiom 2).

Although an interesting idea, a number of problems remain. First, the axioms are limited to structured programs. Second, the axioms provide very little constraint upon the imaginations of software complexity metrics designers. Third, the axioms, however reasonable, are based purely upon arguments of intuition. This is particularly the case for Prather's suggestion of an upper bound of twice the lower bound for axioms 2 and 3. Finally, the underlying model is incomplete, inasmuch as there are no connections with observable events in the software development process.

This axiomatic approach has been further developed (Fenton *et al*. 1986; Prather 1987) such that any program may be reduced into a hierarchy of irreducibles (prime trees). The benefits are the removal of subjectivity over the issue of counting rules and the ability to draw comparisons between different metrics. Still unresolved are the problems of using intuition when deriving actual complexity values from different irreducibles and the construction of a complete model of the relevant world for a complexity metric. The difficulty is, of course, that the 'real world' is not entirely formal, in the sense that we cannot model it with precise mathematical relationships. The best we can hope for is engineering approximations.

It is arguable that the search for a general complexity metric based upon program properties is a futile task. Given the vast range of programmers, programming environments, programming languages and programming tasks, to unify them into the scope of a single complexity metric is an awesome task. A more fruitful approach might be to derive metrics from the more abstract notations and concepts of software designs. This would have the additional advantage that design metrics are available earlier on in the software development process.

For a software complexity metric to be treated seriously by the software engineering community, considerably more emphasis must be placed on the validation process. It may well be 'intellectually very appealing' (Woodward *et al*. 1979), but this is insufficient. Following from the suggestion that the LOC metric be regarded as a 'baseline' for the evaluation of metrics (Basili and Hutchens 1983), there must exist considerable doubts about the utility of McCabe's cyclomatic complexity metric.

ACKNOWLEDGEMENTS

I would like to thank Professor Darrel Ince of the Open University, Milton Keynes, for the many useful suggestions and kind help he has given during the preparation of this paper. I would also like to record my thanks to the referee who provided constructive criticism and a number of additional insights.

13

MEASURING THE QUALITY OF STRUCTURED DESIGNS

Douglas A. Troy and Stuart H. Zweben

Bell Telephone Laboratories and Ohio State University

ABSTRACT

The purpose of this study is to investigate the possibility of providing some useful measures to aid in the evaluation of software designs. Such measurements should allow some degree of predictability in estimating the quality of a coded software product based upon its design and should allow identification and correction of deficient designs prior to the coding phase, thus providing lower software development costs. The study involves the identification of a set of hypothesized measures of design quality and the collection of these measures from a set of designs for a software system developed in industry. In addition, the number of modifications made to the coded software that resulted from these designs was collected. A data analysis was performed to identify relationships between the measures of design quality and the number of modifications made to the coded programs. The results indicated that module coupling was an important factor in determining the quality of the resulting product. The design metrics accounted for roughly 50–60 per cent of the variability in the modification data, which supports the findings of previous studies. Finally, the weaknesses of the study are identified and proposed improvements are suggested.

13.1 INTRODUCTION AND BACKGROUND

The measurement of the quality of software is an important area of study in the computing field. However, most work in this area has centred on the source

214

program. Models such as McCabe's cyclomatic number (McCabe 1976; see Chapter 2 above) and Halstead's 'software science' measures (Halstead 1977a) have provided quantitative means of assessing the complexity, cost and reliability of coded software. The measurement of the quality of the source code, however, emphasizes only one aspect of the entire life cycle of a software system. This life cycle has been described as a sequence of steps, beginning with requirements specification, progressing through the design, coding and testing phases, and ending in the maintenance phase (Boehm 1976). Measurements of quality should consider each of these phases. In particular, emphasis on the early phases, such as requirements and design, have been shown to provide significant improvements in software quality and a significant decrease in development costs (Boehm 1976; Lattanzi 1979). In fact, studies have shown that a majority of problems in software can be detected before testing begins (Lattanzi 1979; Daly and Mnichowicz 1978).

Lattanzi describes work in analysing the performance of a software development methodology (Lattanzi 1979). Statistics were kept during the development of a large-scale real-time software system in the areas of module design, coding and testing. The statistics included hour distribution data, quantity and types of problems found throughout the development process, and the size of the resulting software. The study found that about half of the errors detected during system integration could have been detected during the earlier phases of the software development.

Daly and Mnichowicz (1978) present further findings from studies of design methodologies. Their study found that 90% of the problems found in the testing phase can be found in the earlier stages of code reading.

Yin and Winchester (1978) have described a study of design quality. The object of this study was a group of software designs consisting of structure charts produced using the structured design methodology (Stevens *et al.* 1974). The authors defined a set of metrics based on the graphical properties of the structure charts. These metrics were used to characterize complexity and coupling and were validated by performing trend and correlation analysis between the metrics and the program errors. The authors do not attempt to predict the number of errors based on a design, but instead suggest that the metrics can be used to locate problem areas in a design.

The results of these studies are very general in nature and do not really identify specific relationships between design metrics and structured design principles. One reason for this is that it is particularly difficult to conduct experiments to test any hypotheses concerning the evaluation of software design methodologies in the environments where they are used. None the less, the above work has shown that it is useful to seek methods to evaluate software designs to facilitate early detection of problems.

This study is an attempt to relate design methodology principles to features of the design documents in order to assess those principles that seem to have the greatest influence on the quality of the resulting product. The study was performed on a medium-size software project developed in industry, and involved the identification and collection of 21 metrics from the design documents of the software. In addition, the number of modifications made during the integration and system test of a unit of software was collected during development and used as a measure of the quality of that unit of code. A data analysis was then performed to identify the effect of each of the metrics on the number of modifications made to the coded software. The intent of the analysis is to identify the metrics that could be used for evaluation of future software designs and to provide a basis for future experiments. After identification of the important metrics, a summary of the study is presented that identifies those methodology principles that most influence quality. In conclusion, improvements for future experiments in this area are suggested.

13.2 DESCRIPTION OF THE DESIGN DOCUMENTS AND MODIFICATION DATA

The software under study has available documented designs along with a historical data bank of recorded modifications made to each program. In the design phase, the system was divided into a set of programs and subroutines. Each program or subroutine was then designed using the structured design methodology of Yourdon and Constantine (1979). Each design was performed prior to the coding of the programs. After coding began, the designs were not modified. Thus, the design documents represent the design of a unit of code prior to coding and code modification.

The design documentation consists of a structure chart for each program and, in some cases, an accompanying description. A structure chart, as shown in Fig. 13.1, is a graphic representation of the modules, or functions, of a design. Each box in the structure chart represents a module. A line from one box to another indicates that

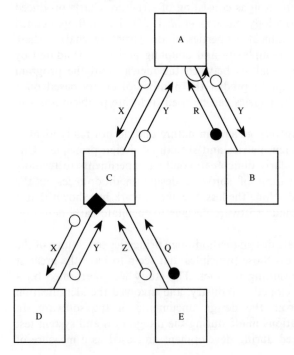

Figure 13.1 Structure chart.

the first module invokes the code contained in the second module. Small labelled arrows illustrate interconnections between modules. A small arrow with an empty tail indicates a data interconnection, while an arrow with a solid tail indicates a control interconnection. A small diamond next to a box indicates a decision. An arrow in the form of an arc which surrounds lines connecting boxes indicates a loop. (For a more detailed discussion of structure charts, see Yourdon and Constantine (1979)). A document accompanying the structure chart elaborated on the function of the design unit. It specified formal parameter data types and the calling sequence for the unit if it was a subroutine. Also, this document lists other effects, or functions, performed by the program that are in addition to the main function of the module. These functions include data validity checking and system error checking.

The historical data bank records any changes made to the code after software was entered into the data bank. Although actual code modifications were recorded, it is difficult to determine the specific part of a design corresponding to each code change. Thus, the error data used for this study were the number of changes made to each unit of code. Consequently, each design and its corresponding code are treated as a unit and no attempt is made to analyse the quality of portions of each design unit. The software was entered into the data bank when the programmer felt that the coded program was ready for integration and testing with the rest of the system.

Two sources of inconsistencies between the designs and the number of program modifications should be noted. First, changes made to the code prior to its entry into the data bank were not recorded and thus are not accounted for in the data bank. The types of changes that were not recorded would include those the programmer found when testing the code before integration. Thus, the errors recorded are expected to be those logic and communication errors the programmer could not detect prior to integration or those relating specifically to integration problems such as inter-module communication flaws. A second source of inconsistency may result if the programmer changed the design of a program as he proceeded with the coding. These design changes would not be reflected in the design documents. The changes could produce errors in the coded programs that require modification. Therefore, there may be some errors that were recorded but were analysed with respect to an inaccurate design document.

13.3 DESCRIPTION OF THE METRICS

The structured design methodology suggests that the quality of a design is based, in large part, on its coupling, cohesiveness, complexity, modularity and size (Yourdon and Constantine 1979). Within these categories, the structured design methodology suggests particular features of a design as indicators of these quality aspects. Using these aspects as guidelines and the goal of objectivity and availability, 21 design metrics were selected for this study. The following is an explanation of the metrics according to the category in which they are assumed to belong. It should be noted that a particular metric may be indicative of more than one of the five design categories, and thus some metrics may appear in more than one category.

13.3.1 Coupling

Coupling is the measure of the strength of association established by the interconnections from one module of a design to another (Stevens *et al.* 1974). The degree of coupling depends on how complicated the connections are and the type of connections. Coupling increases with increasing complexity of the interface between two modules and increases as the type of interconnections varies from data to control. Coupling also increases as extraneous information irrelevant to a module's task is present in the interface. Additionally, when two or more parts of a program interface with the same data, they share a common environment. Common environments increase the level of coupling in the design.

With these indicators of coupling as suggested by structured design, the following design features were chosen as measures of coupling:

$X1$ the maximum number of interconnections per box
$X2$ the average number of interconnections per box
$X3$ the total number of interconnections per box
$X4$ the number of boxes accessing a common interconnection
$X5$ the number of unique common interconnections in a structure chart
$X6$ the number of boxes accessing control interconnections
$X7$ the number of boxes accessing control interconnections other than OK/FAIL, where OK/FAIL indicates successful or unsuccessful completion of processing of a module (since many boxes access OK/FAIL, it was felt that the exclusion of this particular connection may give a more accurate measure of the control coupling in the design)
$X19$ the number of interconnections to the top box
$X20$ the number of data structure interconnections to the top box, obtained from the accompanying design description
$X21$ the number of simple interconnections to the top box, that is, connections not considered data structures.

13.3.2 Cohesion

Cohesion is the measure of the relationships of the elements within a module. The goal here is to strive for modules whose elements (statements or functions) are highly related (Stevens *et al.* 1974). Ideally, a module should perform a single function. The following design features were chosen as measures of cohesion:

$X8$ the number of effects listed in the design document
$X9$ the number of effects other than I/O errors
$X11$ the maximum *fan-in* to any one box in the structure chart, that is, the number of lines emanating upwards from that box
$X12$ the average fan-in in the structure chart
$X16$ the number of possible return values

13.3.3 Complexity

The structured design methodology suggests that simplicity is the primary measurement for evaluating a design (Stevens *et al.* 1974). It is therefore desirable to identify quantities that indicate the relative simplicity or, alternatively, the complexity of a design. Factors influencing the design's complexity might include the scope of control of each module, the relative size of the design, and the number of control constructs in the design. Using these design features as guidelines, the following complexity metrics were collected:

$X10$ the maximum depth of the structure chart
$X13$ the maximum *fan-out* from a box in the structure chart, that is, the number of lines emanating downwards from that box
$X14$ the average fan-out in the structure chart
$X15$ the number of boxes in the design
$X17$ the number of decisions in the structure chart
$X18$ the number of loops in the structure chart

13.3.4 Modularity

Modularity is a measure of the decomposition of a design unit into its subfunctions, or modules. The main goal of modularizing a design is to divide the software into pieces that are functionally cohesive and independently modifiable. The structured design and methodology suggests that a good design is one that is decomposed into independent functions (Stevens *et al.* 1974). A moderate number of boxes in a design or a moderate design depth is assumed to indicate good modularization. On the other hand, a low number of boxes or a low design depth could indicate inadequate design modularization. Also, high fan-out from a module could indicate a lower degree of modularity by increasing the number of dependencies between the modules within that scope of control. These descriptions suggest the following metrics:

$X10$ the maximum design depth of the structure
$X13$ the maximum fan-out from a box in the design
$X14$ the average fan-out in the structure chart
$X15$ the total number of boxes in a structure chart

13.3.5 Size

The size of a unit of software is assumed to be related to its quality. The structured design methodology suggests that the production of large units of software is to be discouraged. A design exhibiting large depth or a large number of modules is assumed to indicate the design of a large unit of software. The following metrics were selected as measures of the size of a design:

$X10$ the maximum design depth of the structure chart
$X15$ the total number of boxes in a structure chart

The categories of metrics are summarized in Table 13.1.

Table 13.1 Categories of metrics

Coupling	Cohesion	Complexity	Modularity	Size
$X1$	$X8$	$X10$	$X10$	$X10$
$X2$	$X9$	$X13$	$X13$	$X15$
$X3$	$X11$	$X14$	$X14$	
$X4$	$X12$	$X15$	$X15$	
$X5$	$X16$	$X17$		
$X6$		$X18$		
$X7$				
$X19$				
$X20$				
$X21$				

As noted, several metrics fall into more than one category of design quality. It is important to note that the value of two of these metrics—design depth and the number of boxes in the design—may indicate aspects of design quality that conflict. A high design depth can indicate high complexity and large size, which is assumed to be indicative of a poor design. On the other hand, a high design depth may indicate a high degree of modularity, which is assumed to be indicative of a good design. A large number of modules, like a high design depth, may imply high complexity and large size. It may also imply high modularity. These conflicts will be kept in mind when evaluating the study results.

13.4 HYPOTHESES TO BE TESTED

The categories of coupling, cohesion, complexity, modularity and size are assumed to be measures of the quality of a software design. Based on these categories and the above metrics, the following hypotheses are proposed for investigation in this experiment.

Coupling hypothesis It is hypothesized that programs with a high coupling will contain more errors than programs not indicating high coupling. It is assumed that high values of the metrics $X1–X7$ and $X19–X21$ indicate high coupling.

Cohesion hypothesis It is hypothesized that programs with low cohesion will contain more errors than programs not indicating low cohesion. It is assumed that high values of the metrics $X8$, $X9$, $X11$, $X12$ and $X16$ indicate low cohesiveness.

Complexity hypothesis It is hypothesized that complex programs will contain more errors than programs of lower complexity. It is assumed that high values of the metrics $X10$, $X13–X15$, $X17$ and $X18$ indicate high complexity.

Modularity hypothesis It is hypothesized that programs with low modularity will contain more errors than programs with higher modularity. It is assumed that low values of the metrics $X10$ and $X13-X15$ indicate low modularity.

Size hypothesis   It is hypothesized that programs of large size will contain more errors than programs of lesser size. It is assumed that high values of the metrics $X10$ and $X15$ indicate large size.

13.5 DESCRIPTION OF THE ANALYSIS

Data were collected from 73 designs and their associated coded programs. An analysis of this data was performed to test the five hypotheses. The goal of the analysis was not to derive specific relationships between the design metrics and the number of program modifications: rather, the goal is to identify those aspects of a design that appear most important and those that do not appear to contribute significantly to quality in terms of errors at integration time. These aspects could then be used to validate the guidelines of structured design, to provide guidelines in evaluating the quality of future software designs, and to provide a basis for future experiments.

The designs under consideration were produced by seven designers. Of special interest, however, is that two designers accounted for 56 of the designs, one designer producing 31 designs and another 25. These two sets of designs were for different sub-systems. One subsystem was a database system and the other was a report generator system. It was felt that the large number of designs resulting from the work of two designers could provide the opportunity to investigate the possibility that the relationship between the number of design modifications and the design metrics could vary with the individual designer or application. In order to carry out this investigation, three separate analyses were performed. Analysis 1 was performed on the complete set of 73 observations. Analysis 2 was performed only on the 31 designs produced by the designer of the database subsystem. Analysis 3 was performed on the 25 designs produced by the designer of the report generator subsystem.

Each analysis consisted of a forward stepwise linear regression (Barr *et al.* 1976) using the program errors as the dependent variable and the selected metrics as the independent variables. In addition to allowing each of the 21 metrics to appear in the model, it was felt that some pruning of this set was appropriate to account for the likelihood of highly intercorrelated variables or variables with very small simple correlation coefficients appearing in the regression model. Hence for each analysis, the stepwise procedure was applied to each of three groups of metrics:

1. All metrics
2. Metrics having simple correlation coefficients with the dependent variable with a significance different from zero at the 0.05 level (it should be noted that, although several metrics exhibited a negative correlation with the number of program modifications, none of these were significant at the 0.05 level)

Table 13.2 Analysis 1

Group	Variables available	Variables selected	r^2
1	$X1-X7$, $X10$, $X11$, $X13$, $X15$, $X17-X21$	$X1-X4$, $X5$, $X7$, $X11$, $X15$, $X17-X21$	0.53
2	$X1$, $X3$, $X4$, $X6$, $X7$, $X9$, $X10$, $X13$	$X1$, $X3$, $X6$, $X7$, $X10$, $X13$	0.24
3	$X1$, $X7$, $X11$, $X17$, $X18$, $X19$	$X1$, $X7$, $X11$, $X18$, $X19$	0.33

3. Metrics with intercorrelations less than 0.50

Since one would not expect each of these groups to give rise to the exact same model, these groupings should provide an additional basis for evaluating the hypotheses.

13.6 RESULTS OF THE ANALYSIS

The results of the analysis are described in detail by Troy (1981). The following is a summary of the results.

Analysis 1

The variables selected by the stepwise regression analysis for each of the three metric groups are shown in Table 13.2. The independent variables (the design metrics) are labelled $X1-X21$ and are defined as described in the previous section. ($X8$, $X9$ and $X16$ were excluded because of missing values in the data; $X12$ and $X14$ were excluded because they were a constant value for all observations.)

Coupling metrics selected were $X1-X7$ and $X19$, with $X3$, $X19$, $X1$ and $X7$ being selected from more than one metric category. The only cohesion metric available for inclusion, $X11$, was in fact selected by two of the models. Similarly, each of the available complexity ($X10$, $X13$, $X15$, $X17$ and $X18$), modularity ($X10$, $X13$ and $X15$) and size ($X10$ and $X15$) metrics were selected, though only $X18$ appeared in more than one model. Each of the above metrics is positively correlated with the dependent variable except for $X17-X19$. From these results, it appears that the coupling hypothesis is well supported. The complexity and size hypotheses are given some support by the presence of more than one metric. The modularity and cohesion hypotheses are more difficult to analyze, since the modularity metrics all have the 'wrong' sign of their correlation coefficients, and there was only one cohesion metric available for inclusion.

Analysis 2

The variables selected by the stepwise regression for each of the three metric groups for analysis 2 are displayed in Table 13.3 ($X12$ and $X14$ were excluded because all observations were a constant.)

Coupling metrics selected by this analysis are $X1$, $X4$, $X5$, $X19$ and $X20$, with none of these belonging to more than one of the metric groups. No

Table 13.3 Analysis 2

Group	Variables available	Variables selected	r^2
1	$X1$–$X11$, $X13$, $X15$–$X21$	$X5$, $X10$, $X13$, $X16$, $X17$, $X19$, $X20$	0.62
2	$X4$, $X10$, $X13$, $X15$	$X4$, $X10$, $X13$, $X15$	0.36
3	$X1$, $X10$, $X17$	$X1$, $X10$, $X17$	0.23

cohesion metrics were selected. The complexity metrics $X10$, $X13$, $X15$ and $X17$ were selected, with $X13$, $X10$ and $X17$ belonging to more than one metric group. The modularity metrics $X10$, $X13$ and $X15$ (all that were available) were chosen, with $X13$ and $X10$ belonging to more than one group. The metrics $X10$ and $X15$ are also measures of size. The above metrics are all positively correlated with the dependent variable except for $X1$, $X2$ and $X18$–$X21$. This analysis, then, seems to lend the most support to the complexity and size hypotheses and some support to the coupling hypothesis. As in analysis 1, the modularity metrics did not have the expected negative correlation coefficients. Similarly, support for the coupling hypothesis is mixed because of the sign of the correlation coefficients for $X1$, $X19$ and $X20$.

Analysis 3

The variables selected by the stepwise regression procedure for analysis 3 are summarized in Table 13.4 ($X8$, $X9$ and $X16$ were excluded because of missing values; $X12$ and $X14$ were excluded because they were a constant value for all observations).

Each of the selected metrics is correlated positively with the number of errors except $X5$ and $X11$. All the above metrics represent coupling measures except for metric $X11$, which is a cohesion metric (the only one available). This result lends support to the coupling hypothesis. It is difficult to argue in favour of the cohesion hypothesis since there was only one metric available and, although it appeared in one of the models, its correlation coefficient was negative. None of the other hypotheses appear supported by this analysis.

Further investigations

The above analysis indicated that complexity seemed to be the most significant category for analysis 2 while coupling appeared most significant in analyses 1 and

Table 13.4 Analysis 3

Group	Variables available	Variables selected	r^2
1	$X1$-7, $X10$, $X11$, $X13$, $X15$, $X17$–$X21$	$X1$, $X2$, $X5$, $X7$, $X11$, $X19$, $X20$	0.62
2	$X2$, $X7$, $X19$, $X20$	$X2$, $X7$, $X19$	0.40
3	$X1$, $X2$, $X7$, $X10$, $X11$	$X2$, $X7$	0.26

3. Additional analyses were performed to attempt to assess more clearly the relative importance of these two categories.

To investigate the possibility that the complexity variables were masked in the results of analyses 1 and 3, the coupling variables were removed from consideration and the stepwise regression procedure was performed on the remaining variables. The results of these analyses showed significantly lower r^2 values and only minor inclusion of additional complexity variables. To assess the relative contribution of the complexity metrics as compared with the coupling metrics in the results of analysis 2, the complexity metrics were removed from consideration and the stepwise regression was applied to this subset of variables. The results revealed only a minor decrease in the r^2 value of the regression model and the inclusion of additional coupling variables as compared with the original analysis. These results appear to indicate that coupling is a consistently significant factor in design quality, while the influence of complexity may be dependent on the application or the designer.

In order to gain some additional insight into the relative influence of the design task and the designer, an additional investigation was performed. A fourth set of designs was identified and was designed with the assistance of the designer of the subsystem in analysis 2. These designs were for a subsystem similar to that of analysis 3. The stepwise regression procedure was performed on the data for this fourth set. The results showed a significant contribution from the coupling variables and none from the complexity variables. This result confirms the relative importance of the coupling aspects and indicates that the importance of complexity aspects may be more dependent on the type of design task than on the individual designer.

13.7 SUMMARY

The results of the analyses indicate that coupling is the most influential of the design principles under consideration on the quality of the resulting product. It appears that reducing the number of interconnections between modules, as well as the number of common interconnections and number of control interconnections, does result in a measurable improvement in the resulting software. Perhaps it is not surprising that coupling metrics were most related to errors, since the errors collected were those detected at integration time. However, those coupling metrics that captured associations between modules *within* a single design unit appeared to be at least as significant as the metrics that captured associations with the 'outside world'.

The complexity and size categories also account for some variability in quality, but to a lesser extent. The features identified are design depth, maximum fan-out, the number of boxes in the design, and the number of decisions shown on the structure chart. The importance of the complexity category seemed to be dependent on the particular type of task under development.

The cohesion and modularity categories were not clearly identified as important principles influencing the quality of the software. The unclear support for cohesion is the result of the actual data points, which forced all but one metric to be eliminated from consideration in two of the analyses. The modularity metrics often had correlation coefficients of the 'wrong' sign. As mentioned, some of these metrics affect complexity and size as well as modularity. While some authors have argued that it is better to err on the side of over-modularizing (Stevens *et al.* 1974), the results of this study would lead one to question this principle.

It is apparent that there are factors other than those identified in this study influencing the quality of the software that results from a design. The largest regression models from each analysis accounted for 53, 62 and 62 per cent of the variability in quality. This result agrees with the work of Lattanzi (1979), which indicated that about half of the errors detected during system integration could be detected in the earlier design phases. Therefore, it may be that one should expect a design document to account for no more than about 50–60 per cent of the variability in the quality of the finished product.

Yin and Winchester (1978) identified the influence of coupling and complexity, as measured from structure charts, on software quality, and our findings support coupling and complexity as the two chief design criteria. We are encouraged from these studies that the value of such methodology principles can in fact be investigated experimentally. In the remainder of the paper we discuss ways in which improvements could be made in future design experiments.

The level of detail and decomposition of the structure charts should be as consistent as possible. Some of our structure charts showed more detail concerning the number of program loops and decisions than others. These problems may reflect on the individual designer, on the problem area for which the design was intended, or both. A detailed control-flow analysis of the source code for the design units could help reveal the extent to which these problems may have been important in this study. Previous work (Yin and Winchester 1978) suggests that large variability in the quality of the finished software is due to the individual designer. However, our own study indicated that the problem area may be an even more significant factor. In addition to controlling the level of detail and decomposition of the structure charts, the completion of all design documentation must be enforced. The absence of the accompanying design description for some design units precluded a complete analysis of all the desired design features, and in particular made the influence of cohesion difficult to evaluate in this study.

It is certainly possible that additional significant quantities exist that are measurable from the design documents and related to coupling, cohesion, etc. For example, this study was only able to provide information about data structure interconnections for the top box in a given design unit. By requiring documentation of these interconnections throughout the structure chart, a more thorough analysis of the effect of this coupling factor can be done. This highlights the need to identify the desired design metrics and to make provisions for their collection prior to beginning development.

The only measure of the quality of the finished software in this study was the *number* of source code modifications. Future collection of error data should provide for identification of the *source* of each modification as well. Modifications due to design errors need to be distinguished from those due to other factors, such as changes in requirements, coding errors or clerical errors.

In addition to the number of modifications to the code, software can be said to have other aspects of quality. Measurements of maintainability and reliability, for example, could be considered as measures of quality. If we are ever to have an acceptable notion of what it means to have a well-developed software product and how we can tell a good one from a bad one, the principles of development (including but not limited to those of design) need to be evaluated on real data. This study represents one such effort in that direction which we believe has shed some light on the promises and problems of this type of research.

14

A VALIDATION OF SOFTWARE METRICS
USING MANY METRICS AND TWO RESOURCES

Dennis Kafura and James T. Canning

Virginia Polytechnic Institute and University of Lowell

ABSTRACT

In this paper are presented the results of a study in which several production software systems are analysed using ten software metrics. The ten metrics include both measures of code details and measures of structure, and combinations of these two. Historical data recording the number of errors and the coding time of each component are used as objective measures of resource expenditure of each component. The metrics are validated by showing that: (1) the metrics singly and in combination are useful indicators of those components which require the most resources; (2) clear patterns between the metrics and the resources expended are visible when both resources are accounted for; (3) measures of structures are as valuable in examining software systems as measures of code details; and (4) the choice of which, or how many, software metrics to employ in practice is suggested by measures of 'yield' and 'coverage'.

14.1 INTRODUCTION

One of the basic objectives of software engineering is to transform the creation of software systems from an artistic, poorly understood and even undisciplined activity into a carefully controlled, methodical and predictable enterprise. To make software an engineerable product, it is important that the designers, implementors and maintainers of software systems be able to express the characteristics of the system

227

in objective and quantitative terms. While some software characteristics are commonly expressed in quantitative terms (e.g., software performance: Lynch and Browne 1981; and software reliability: Musa 1975), those characteristics relating to software quality are typically evaluated only in qualitative terms.

Quantitative measures of quality are collectively referred to as software metrics. One of the key—and, unfortunately, too often neglected—parts of software metric research is the validation of the metric on realistic software systems. The validation, however, is vital because it establishes the relationships between the measures of software products (e.g. a complexity metric) and important resources in the software process (e.g. errors, coding time). One form of a validation analyses the relationship between metric values and historical project data. Such validations provide the compelling evidence needed to gain the acceptance and use of software metrics as a standard industry-wide practice.

Previous validation of software metrics have relied heavily on measures of linear or rank correlations to determine the degree of relationship between software metrics and features of the systems being analysed (see e.g. Halstead 1977a; Basili *et al*. 1983). These validations and, in particular, the use of a linear or rank correlation obscure three critical facts about the nature of software metrics and the manner in which they may be best employed. The attempt to overcome these limitations of previous validations underlies the approach used in this paper.

The first limitation shared by many previous validations is the use of only a single dependent variable. A typical validation, for example, might find the relationship between each member of a set of software metrics, considered as independent variables, and a single dependent variable, such as number of errors. The inherent limitation in these validations is the failure to deal with the many resources expended in constructing a system and the variety of trade-offs that can be made among these resources. For example, consider two programmers who produce equally reliable systems. One programmer may achieve reliability by expending a large amount of time in designing and implementing clear, precise, correct code. This programmer introduces few errors in the code and, hence, few can be discovered. The second programmer achieves reliability by rigorous testing and modification of hastily designed and implemented code. This programmer achieves reliability by removing the many errors that were introduced. Even if both programmers implement exactly the same system, there will be radical discrepencies between the software metric values and error occurrences. Such discrepancies are not attributable, necessarily, to a failure of the metric to measure some realistic property of the software. The failure is in the design of the validation experiment. Furthermore, the existence of these uncounted factors may well explain the low correlations reported in some validations as well as the lack of consistency across different validations.

The second limitation shared by many previous validations is the use of only one independent variable (i.e. one metric). Even when a more general approach using several metrics has been employed, the metrics have been from only one of three major classes of metrics. These three classes are described in the next section. Suffice it to say here that several studies have shown that metrics in these different classes appear to be measuring fundamentally different aspects of software quality (Henry *et al*. 1981; Kafura *et al*. 1984).

The third limitation is that a linear or rank correlation measure suggests a, perhaps misleading, manner in which the metrics should be evaluated and applied. For example, Basili's careful and extensive validation (1983), and our own experience with data taken from the same source (Canning 1985), show inconsistent or, frankly, poor correlations between any metric and the project resource data. Is this to suggest that software metrics are of little or no value? In the same manner, should we be disturbed to find that one component with a high metric value has no errors while another component which has a low metric value has numerous errors? When a linear or rank correlation is used, the answers to these two questions would appear to be yes. However, based on the data in this paper, we will answer these questions in the negative by showing that software metrics do show overall trends and groupings and that, in combination, the metrics can be applied in the manner consistent with the needs of software developers. In retrospect, it was naive to expect that the complex nature of software systems could be captured in a simple linear framework. These comments do not imply that rigorous statistical analysis is unnecessary. Certainly, statistical techniques exist to deal with multiple dependent and independent variables, etc., and we plan to employ such techniques. The data presented in this paper may be viewed as necessary preliminary work to justify these types of more elaborate statistical treatment.

14.2 METRICS AND DATA

The quality of a software product is determined by numerous quality attributes which emerge in increasingly detailed form as the life cycle progresses. Accordingly, numerous quantitative measures must be employed throughout the life cycle—each measure defined to quantify one of the many quality attributes. Three general classes of software metrics can be distinguished: measures based on an automated analysis of the system's design structure, termed 'structure metrics'; measures based only on implementation details, termed 'code metrics'; and measures that are a combination of the other two, termed 'hybrid metrics'. The use of all three types of metrics is important for two reasons. First, as noted in the Introduction, these classes of metrics appear to be measuring different aspects of the system quality. Fundamentally, the quality of a system is too multi-faceted to be measured by any one metric or by metrics in only one of these classes. Second, each class of metrics can be first used at different points in the software life cycle. While code and hybrid metrics may be useful indicators during the testing and maintenance phases, they come too late in the software life cycle to address fundamental design decisions. Structure metrics, on the other hand, can be taken early in the life cycle since they are based only on system features which emerge at the high-level design phase.

There are three code metrics used in this study. The first code metric is a simple size measure, lines of code (LOC). The second code metric is Halstead's software science 'effort' measure (Halstead 1977a). The third code metric is the measure of cyclomatic complexity defined by McCabe (1976; see Chapter 2 above).

Several carefully designed experiments have shown that meaningful relationships exist between these metrics and significant software characteristics (for example Curtis 1979b). Properly used, these metrics can play a useful role during the later phases of the software life cycle (testing, acceptance, maintenance, etc.). However, serious objections have been raised against the experimental design and statistical treatment of a number of the software science experiments (Hamer and Frewin 1982, see Chapter 11 above; Lassez et al. 1981; Shen et al. 1983). Even if these objections can be satisfied, code metrics are available too late in the life cycle to exert a major impact on the life-cycle characteristics and, thus, should not be used alone.

As indicated above, a structure metric is defined in terms of some observed connection between components of the system which have emerged during the (high-level) design phase. A structure measure based on the data relationships among components is the information flow metric mentioned above (Henry 1979). Another structure metric is McClure's metric, which attempts to measure 'invocation complexity' (McClure 1978). A third structure metric, defined by Woodfield (1980), is based on the concept of 'review complexity'. The fourth and final structure metric used in our research is the 'stability' measure defined by Yau and Collofello (1980).

Finally, three hybrid metrics are used. Each of these hybrid measures is a modification of one of the structure metrics. A hybrid metric determines a measure for a component by weighting the structure measure for that component by a code measure. To simplify matters, we have used only lines of code as the weighting term.

For reference, the ten metrics described above will be referred to in subsequent tables and discussion by the following abbreviations:

- LOC (lines of code)
- EFFORT (Halstead's software science effort)
- CYCLO (McCabe's cyclomatic complexity)
- INFO (Henry and Kafura's unweighted information flow complexity)
- INVOKE (McClure's invocation complexity)
- REVIEW (Woodfield's review complexity)
- STABILITY (Yau and Collofello's stability measure)
- INFO–LOC (weighted information flow)
- REV–LOC (weighted review complexity)
- STAB–LOC (weighted stability measure)

Also, recall that the first three metrics are code metrics, the middle four are structure metrics, and the last three are hybrid metrics.

Critical resources necessary for this project were provided by the Software Engineering Laboratory (SEL) headed by Frank McGarry, Jerry Page and Victor Basili. This organization, formed in 1976, is composed of three members: Nasa/Goddard Space Flight Center (GSFC), the University of Maryland (Computer Science Department), and the Computer Science Corporation (Flight Systems Operation). The SEL has defined and implemented an extensive monitoring and data collection process by which the details of all aspects of the software development process and product could be extracted for analysis (NASA 1981).

Through the cooperation of the SEL management, source code and historical development data for three of the larger Fortran projects were made available for this research. The largest project has nine subsystems, while the other two projects possess seven and six subsystems respectively. Each subsystem is a collection of Fortran subroutines, functions and data blocks, known as components. Within a given project, subsystems generally do not share common components. That is, routines from one subsystem rarely call routines from another subsystem. Communication between subsystems is usually achieved through the use of global variables. However, all subsystems share a pool of utility routines written in Fortran and assembly language.

In addition to the three Fortran systems, SEL also provided a developmental database associated with each of the three projects. The database itself contains numerous files and a wide range of information. Selected for this study were the following variables:

- *Component errors*: a discrepancy between a specification and its implementation. The specification might be requirements, design specification, or coding specification.
- *Component coding time*: the time recorded by SEL personnel to implement, read and review the coding of an individual component or subsystem.

In general, the term 'resource' will be used to refer collectively to error and coding time data. The coding time is certainly a resource measure because it represents the direct expenditure of the time of project personnel. Errors are also viewed as a resource measure because some project member(s) must ultimately commit additional time to diagnose and repair these errors.

This resource data is collected by a manual process which, in the case of the effort (coding time) reporting, contains some degree of redundancy to permit consistency checking of the reported times. The components and the resource data used in this paper are a subset of the three projects described earlier. Data failing various consistency checks were eliminated from consideration in order to remove anomalies caused by inaccurate reporting. The details of these consistency checks can be found in part in Basili *et al.* (1983) and in full in Canning (1985).

14.3 RESULTS

The first set of data, presented in Table 14.1, bears on two interrelated questions. The first question is whether significant differences in software metric values are related to corresponding differences in errors and/or effort. The second question is whether the relationships between metrics and resource data become more pronounced when both error and coding time are accounted for. Table 14.1 is based only on the weight information flow hybrid metric (INFO–LOC). Data for the other ten metrics shows essentially the same pattern and is not reported

Table 14.1

Software component types	(a) Controlling for low INFO			(b) Controlling for high INFO		
	Low coding times	High coding time	Row totals	Low coding time	High coding time	Row totals
Low no. of errors*	114	25	139	48	37	85
	71	15	86	28	22	50
	82	18		56	44	
	91	69		73	36	
High no. of errors*	11	11	22	18	67	85
	7	7	14	11	39	50
	50	50		21	79	
	9	31		27	64	
Column totals	125	36	161	66	104	170
	78	22	100	39	61	100

* From top to bottom, a frequency count; the percentage that count is of the total number of observations; the percentage that count is of all things in the same row; and the percentage that count is of all things in the same column.

here. Owing to the asymmetric character of the data, a threshold value for each metric and resource measure was determined using a technique developed by Crawford *et al.* (1985). This technique defines a 'meaningful univariate statistic for asymmetric data'. The two classes defined by the threshold will be referred to as 'high' and 'low'. Part (a) of the table records resource statistics for low INFO–LOC components; part (b) contains the same information for high INFO–LOC components. Similarly, the rows and columns of the tables separate components based on whether they are in the high or low class of errors and the average coding time, respectively. Each main entry in the table contains four simple statistics: from top to bottom, a frequency count, the percentage that count is of the total number of observations, the percentage that count is of all things in the same row, and the percentage that count is of all things in the same column. In addition, individual row and column frequencies and percentages are shown.

For example, Table 14.1(a) presents descriptive statistics of all components that are below average according to the INFO–LOC hybrid metric. The upper left-hand entry of this part of the table records that 114 components were below average in errors and below average in effort. These 114 components represent 71% of the total observations reported in part (a). The total number of observations, 161, is given in the lower right-hand corner of part (a). Furthermore, these 114 components also represent 82% of all those components that were below the average number of errors (row %) and 91% of all those components that were below the average effort. The third column of the table records that 139 components (86%) were below the average number of errors while 22 components (14%) were above this average.

By comparing parts (a) and (b) of the table, the following trends in errors and the coding time can be noted:

- Only 14% of the components with below-average INFO–LOC contained above the average number of errors. However, this was true 50% of the time among components with above-average INFO–LOC.
- Only 22% of the components with below-average INFO–LOC required above average coding time; 61% of the components with above-average INFO–LOC required this greater level of coding time.

Furthermore, the trend evident in these tables is more pronounced if we examine the *combined* coding time and error factors. Let us focus our attention on those components that are high in both errors and coding time. These components will be called 'difficult' components. Also, those components that are low in both errors and coding time will be called 'easy' components. It is important to consider the combination of these factors because, as described in the Introduction, a component with a high metric value may result in few errors because a large amount of time was invested in the coding of this component. Again, by comparing parts (a) and (b) of the table, it can be noted that:

- 71% of the components with low INFO–LOC contained easy components, while this was true for only 28% of the components in the high INFO–LOC class.
- Only 7% of the components with low INFO–LOC were difficult. This was true of 39% of the components with high INFO–LOC.
- The low INFO–LOC class contains only 11 difficult components, whereas the high INFO–LOC class contains 67 difficult components.
- The reverse is true of easy components: the low INFO–LOC class contains 114 easy components, whereas the high INFO–LOC class contains only 48 such components.

The observations made above lead us to conclude that growth in the metric values corresponds to increases in individual error-proneness and coding time requirements, and this trend becomes more sharply defined when the combination of error and coding time is taken into account. This is both a validation of the metrics and a motivation to use multiple resource variables in further validations.

The second set of data to be examined relates to another pair of interrelated questions. In this case the two questions are: Can the most error-prone components be identified by software metrics? and: Is there benefit in using more than one metric? The first question is certainly important. Even if software metrics had no other use, their proven ability to identify the most error-prone components would be of tangible value to software developers. This tangible value is particularly evident if the structure metrics can be used to identify the most error-prone components since this would permit the system to be redesigned so as to avoid components of this type altogether. Furthermore, information on error-prone components would allow the testing or code review processes to be concentrated on these components. The second question is also relevant since it indicates whether any one metric alone can be used or if a battery of metrics should be used in combination.

Table 14.2 Identification of extreme outlier error components

Software metric	1	2	3	4	5	6	7	8	9	10	11	12	13	14	15	16	17	18	19	20	21	22	23	24	25	26	27	28	29	30	31	32	Metric total
LOC	x	x	x		x	x	x	x		x	x	x	x	x				x			x			x	x	x				x			18
EFFORT		x			x							x													x							x	5
CYCLO	x	x		x			x	x				x		x										x	x							x	10
INFO	x	x	x	x	x	x	x	x		x	x	x	x	x				x	x	x	x			x								x	19
INVOKE	x	x	x	x	x	x	x					x					x	x	x	x	x	x		x	x				x				17
REVIEW	x	x												x										x	x	x			x	x			8
STABILITY		x								x	x	x	x	x				x						x	x	x			x		x		12
INFO–LOC	x	x	x	x	x	x	x	x		x	x	x	x	x				x	x	x	x			x	x	x							20
REV–LOC	x	x					x										x	x	x		x	x				x	x		x	x			12
STAB–LOC	x	x		x			x	x	x									x	x	x				x	x	x					x		13

Component totals 8 10 4 5 5 4 7 5 1 4 4 7 4 6 0 0 2 7 5 4 5 2 0 8 8 6 1 0 4 3 2 3

To investigate the above questions, a precise means must be given for defining those components that contain an unusually high number of errors or have coding time requirements markedly in excess of the average. A simple way to define such components is by using the standard deviation as a rule. For any measure, those components that lie more than two standard deviations above the mean are referred to as 'extreme outliers'. Those components that lie more than one standard deviation above the mean are referred to simply as 'outliers'. This classification is used for each of the ten software metrics and also for the resource measures (error and coding time). Thus, for example, a component may be an INFO–LOC 'extreme outlier' if it lies at least two standard deviations above the mean of the INFO–LOC metric; a component may be an error 'outlier' if it lies at least one standard deviation above the mean of the error distribution. We may now restate the two questions of interest as: Are metric (extreme) outliers good indicators of error/coding time (extreme) outliers? and: Are several metrics needed to identify error/coding time (extreme) outliers?

The first step in answering the outlier questions is presented in Table 14.2. Each of the 32 columns in this table represents a component which is an outlier on the error distribution. The components are arbitrarily numbered 1–32. These 32 components are the most error-prone components in the software being analysed. Each row of the table corresponds to one of the ten software metrics. An 'X' appears in a table entry if the error outlier denoted by the column in which the entry appears is also an outlier of the metric corresponding to the row in which the entry appears. For example, column 1 shows that component 1 was an outlier on eight of the metrics. Component 1 was not an outlier on either the EFFORT or the STABILITY metric. Column 2 of the table shows that component 2 was an outlier on all ten of the metrics.

Based on the data in Table 14.2 the following observations can be made:

- 28 of the 32 error outliers are correctly identified by at least one metric.
- No one metric identified more than 20 of the error outliers.

- 25 of the 32 outliers are identified by the combination of INFO, INVOKE and LOC.
- 23 of the error outliers are correctly identified simultaneously by three or more metrics.
- Each class of metrics contains a metric that performs well: the LOC measure in the code metric class (18/32), the INFO (19/32) and INVOKE (17/32) measures in the structure class, and the INFO–LOC measure (20/32) in the hybrid class.

Careful scrutiny will also reveal that the class of structure metrics is a more sensitive indicator than the class of code metrics. This is evidenced by the fact that in 13 cases an error outlier was not detected by any code metric, whereas this occurred in only 6 cases for the three structure metrics INFO, INVOKE and STABILITY. This observation is significant because it supports the need to use metrics from all classes; confirms again that structure and code metrics are measuring different properties of software components; demonstrates that errors may be introduced because of several different forms of 'complexity'; and shows the potential value of employing structure metrics to identify (and, of course, remove) error-prone components at the design stage.

In addition to error outliers, we may also observe the accuracy of the metrics in identifying outliers in coding time or components that are outliers in both errors and coding time. Data to this end is presented in Table 14.3. Part (a) of the table is based on components that are extreme outliers in errors or coding time. Part (b) is based on outliers. The first three columns of each table show the number of times that a metric outlier was also an outlier in errors, coding time, or both. Column 4 shows the total number of error and coding time outliers correctly identified by each metric. These two tables also contain a column, labelled 'non-outliers', which shows how many components were outliers of the software metric but were not outliers of either errors or coding time.

Finally, the last two columns of each table are percentages. The column labelled 'Yield' shows what percentage of the metric outliers were in fact outliers in errors and/or coding time. The yield of a metric is calculated by dividing the 'Total outliers' column by the sum of the 'Total outliers' and 'Non-outliers' columns. A high-yield percentage means that most of the components identified by the metric are outliers in errors and/or coding time. A low-yield percentage would mean that only few error/coding time outliers are properly identified by the metric. The other percentage is labelled 'Coverage'. This column records what fraction of the total outliers was identified by the software metric. The coverage percentage is obtained by dividing the entry in the 'Total outliers' column by the number of outliers given at the top of each table. As we will see, it is not a simple matter to choose which metric is the 'best'.

By examining the coverage percentages in Table 14.3, we may note that:

- By a wide margin LOC identifies the largest fraction of extreme outliers, and, in general, the code metric class does better than the other two classes in identifying these outliers.

Table 14.3 (a)Metric outliers versus resource-extreme outliers*

Software metric	Error outliers	Coding time outliers	Error & time outliers	Total outliers	Non-outliers	Yield (%)	Coverage (%)
LOC	3	20	1	24	35	41	83
EFFORT	2	11	0	13	27	33	45
CYCLO	3	16	0	19	37	34	36
INFO	3	13	1	17	44	28	59
STABILITY	2	3	0	5	36	12	17
REVIEW	2	4	0	6	43	12	21
INVOKE	4	2	1	7	33	18	24
INFO–LOC	4	14	1	19	44	30	66
REV–LOC	2	14	0	16	28	36	55
STAB–LOC	3	4	0	7	26	21	24

(b) Metric outliers versus all resource outliers[†]

Software metric	Error outliers	Coding time outliers	Error & time outliers	Total outliers	Non-outliers	Yield (%)	Coverage (%)
LOC	2	23	16	41	18	69	48
EFFORT	1	16	4	21	19	53	25
CYCLO	2	23	8	33	23	59	39
INFO	2	19	17	38	23	62	45
STABILITY	2	9	10	25	20	51	25
REVIEW	1	6	7	14	35	29	16
INVOKE	2	6	15	23	17	58	27
INFO–LOC	2	22	18	42	21	67	49
REV–LOC	2	17	10	29	15	66	34
STAB–LOC	3	10	10	27	20	53	27

* Total error and coding time outliers: 29.
[†] Total error and coding time outliers: 85.

- The structure and hybrid classes also contain metrics that perform reasonably well. The INFO metric identifies 59% of the extreme outliers, INFO–LOC identifies 66%, and REV–LOC identifies 55%.
- When simple outliers are used (Table 14.3(b)), the LOC, INFO, and INFO–LOC metrics yield the best and approximately the same, coverage (48, 45 and 49% respectively). These three metrics are distinctly better than the remaining metrics (39, 34 and less than 34%). Also, each of these three metrics is from a different metric class.

From the coverage data, we can conclude that the metrics are capable of locating a significant percentage of all of the outliers. In general, the extreme outliers appear to be more closely associated with the code-level metrics. This is certainly reasonable, since most of the outliers in our data are outliers in coding time. Therefore, components that are outliers in metrics related to size, such as LOC, will tend also be outliers in coding time, since it simply takes longer to code a larger component, regardless of other factors. However, when the larger pool of all outliers is considered, structural factors, as reflected in the INFO and INFO–LOC metrics, begin to exert an equal influence.

Counterbalancing the coverage percentage is the yield percentage. While LOC correctly identified 24 (83%) of the extreme outliers, it also identified 35 components which were not extreme outliers in either errors or coding time. These 35 components represent a measure of overhead in using the LOC metric to identify extreme outliers. Thus, only 41% of the outliers of the LOC metric were, in fact, extreme outliers in errors and/or coding time. This percentage, as described above, is called the 'yield' of the metric. An examination of the yields given in Table 14.3 shows that, as a general rule, increasing coverage also corresponds to increasing yield. While this is a desirable trend, it does not mean that the choice among metrics based on considerations of coverage and yield is necessarily simple. The economics of the development environment may dictate that a high yield, though desirable, cannot be afforded because of the greater magnitude of the number of components involved. For example, compare the LOC and REV–LOC measures in Table 14.3(a). The LOC measure is the better of the two in both yield and coverage. However, the LOC measure requires that 59 components be examined, while the REV–LOC metric requires only 44 components, 25% fewer. If sufficient resources are not available to examine the larger set of components properly, a lower yield and a lower coverage metric may be the only possible option. On the other hand, if reliability and/or low coding times across components is desired at any cost, then a high coverage metric would be used regardless of its yield.

We next become concerned with the question of employing many metrics in a concerted fashion. There are a number of ways in which many metrics could be used together to identify components that are resource outliers. The evaluation of one such method is reported in Table 14.4. As in the previous tables, the extreme outliers are the basis of part (a) while part (b) of the table contains information on all outliers.

The scheme evaluated in Table 14.4 operates as follows. Each component is measured by all ten of the software metrics. For each component, we record the number of metrics on which this component is an outlier. These component numbers are determined for all components and are presented in a cumulative fashion in the first column of the table, labelled 'Minimum count'. Column 2 shows the total number of resource outliers simultaneously identified by the given minimum number of metrics. For example, row 1 of part (a) shows that 25 resource outliers were also outliers on *at least* one software metric. Row 5 shows that 17 of the resource outliers were outliers on at least five software metrics. In the extreme case, there is one component that was an outlier on all ten software metrics. Column 3 of parts (a) and (b) show the number of occasions on which a given metric count identified a non-outlier in either the error or coding time data. For example, row 1 of part (a) shows that there are 132 components that were outliers on at least one metric which were not outliers in either errors or coding time. The last two columns of both parts of the table show the yield and coverage percentages, which were defined previously.

Table 14.4

Minimum count	(a) metric count v. extreme resource outliers*				(b) metric count v. all resource outliers†			
	Outliers detected	Non-outliers detected	Yield (%)	Coverage (%)	Outliers detected	Non-outliers detected	Yield (%)	Coverage (%)
1	25	132	16	86	67	90	43	79
2	24	80	23	83	57	47	55	67
3	23	56	29	79	48	31	61	56
4	21	43	33	72	42	22	66	49
5	17	28	38	59	31	14	69	36
6	13	14	48	45	21	6	78	25
7	6	7	46	21	12	1	92	14
8	2	3	40	7	5	0	100	6
9	1	0	100	3	1	0	100	1
10	1	0	100	3	1	0	100	1

* Total error and coding time outliers: 29
† Total error and coding time outliers: 85.

The data in Table 14.4 leads to the following observations:

- Most of the resource outliers are identified by some metric: 86% of the extreme outliers and 79% of all outliers. This is extremely encouraging because it means that we can begin to explain in quantitative terms why components are error-prone or take long to code.
- The yields when considering all outliers are much better than for the extreme outlier case. This is intuitively reasonable. It is much more difficult to pinpoint the most severe outliers than to identify the members of the larger class which are at the upper end of the resource spectrum.
- In the case of extreme resource outliers, it would seem most efficient to use a minimum metric count of 4. Using a higher metric count causes the coverage to decrease more rapidly than the yield increases.
- It is difficult, in general, to decide which is the most efficient metric count. A high coverage would be obtained from a low count at the expense of low yield. Increasing the metric count improves the yield but reduces the coverage. As indicated in analysing Table 14.3, the economics of the development environment may dictate the value to be used.

By comparing Tables 14.3 and 14.4, we can see the difference between using one *metric* and using a *metric count* of 1. The best single metric for the extreme resource outliers is LOC which correctly identified 24 outliers with a yield of 14% and a coverage of 83%. A metric count of 1 does not do appreciably better, identifying 25 outliers with a yield of only 16% and a coverage of 86%. However, when considering all resource outliers a different picture emerges. In this case the best single metric is the INFO–LOC metric, which correctly identified 42 resource outliers (yield of 67%, coverage of 49%) while a metric count of 1 correctly identified 67 outliers (yield of 43%, coverage of 79%). The metric count approach does significantly better than any single metric, but with a lower yield.

Table 14.5 Metric safety

Outlier catgeory	Total components	Non-outliers on any metric	Errors or time outliers	Safety (%)
Extreme outliers	331	174	4	98
All outliers	331	174	18	90

A final observation regarding the use of many metrics concerned what might be called a 'safety' factor. The safety factor is the percentage of components that are not an outlier on *any* metric (i.e. a metric count of 0) and also not a resource outlier. In other words, when all of the metrics agree that the component is 'not difficult' or 'not complex', how often are we safe in taking this advice? As can be seen in Table 14.5 the safety factor is quite high—98 and 90% for the two levels of resource outliers.

It is also interesting to observe that the metrics correctly agree that somewhat more than one-half of the total components should not be resource outliers. This effect is useful because it allows software developers to focus the energies and resources on those components that contain the outliers and 'safely' give less attention to those components which no metric considers an outlier. This may have an influence on management policies, design/code review practices and testing procedures.

14.4 CONCLUSIONS

A variety of specific conclusions have appeared in the previous section. The most global of these observations are the following. First, the nature of software systems and software production can be understood only if the several resources expended in its construction are accounted for and only if a variety of software factors are quantified by corresponding metrics. The interplay between and among the resources and factors is too subtle and fluid to be observed accurately by a single metric, or a single resource. This has implications not only for further validations and applications of software metrics, but also for organizations currently collecting project data. Second, a collection of software metrics can be used to identify those components that contain an unusually high number of errors or require significantly more time to code than the average. Information of this type can be used to target personnel time available for coding and verification. Third, measures of structure are competitive with measures of code details in identifying resource outliers. Since the structure metrics can be taken early in the life-cycle, it would seem that such measures can have a significant impact on the software design and development process. Fourth, the choice of which, or how many, metrics to use is not simple even in the absence of outside factors. Project limitations may impose a choice based on the relationship between yield and coverage.

In ending, we are pursuing the exploration of software metrics based on the concepts in this paper. In particular, it seems advisable to consider in more detail the groups into which the metrics divide software components. Here we have used only two groups. Perhaps other trends can be seen if more groups are used. Also, we have accounted for only two resources. Certainly, other resources should be included, such as design time, review time, testing time, number of compilations, number of test runs, etc. Finally, appropriate statistical techniques, more elaborate than a simple linear or rank correlation, need to be employed to study the many-metrics *v*. many-resources relationship.

15

AN EMPIRICAL AND THEORETICAL ANALYSIS OF AN INFORMATION-FLOW-BASED SYSTEM DESIGN METRIC

D. C. Ince and M. J. Shepperd

Open University and Wolverhampton Polytechnic

ABSTRACT

This chapter examines information flow metrics: a subset of a potentially valuable class of system architecture measures. Theoretical analysis of the underlying model reveals a numbr of anomalies which translate into poor performance, as revealed by a large empirical study. Attention to these theoretical deficiencies results in a marked improvement in performance. There are two themes to this paper. The first theme—a minor one—involves a critique and evaluation of one particular system design metric. The second theme—a major one—entails a critique of the metric derivation process adopted by the vast majority of the researchers in this field.

15.1 INTRODUCTION

An increasing amount of research is currently being carried out into software metrics: numerical measures extracted from program code or system documentation such as a detailed design. Such metrics have the potential to aid software project managers in the decision-making processes that they have to carry out. Ideally, they enable the managers to carry out prediction in a much more organized and accurate way. For example, one aim of research into system design metrics is to extract measures from a system design which enable the manager to predict resource requirements during program maintenance.

The history of product metrics has been a long one. The first metrics were predominantly code-based, with the majority being derived from research carried out by the late Maurice Halstead at Purdue Univeristy in the late 1960s and early 1970s; typical research in this area is described in Laurmaa and Syrjanen (1982) and Love and Bowman (1976). This work was followed by research which could be applied at the detailed design level and which was graph-theoretic in nature; typical research in this area is described in Myers (1978) and McCabe (1976; see Chapter 2 above), the latter being the most cited work in the area.

Recently there has been a major increase in interest in system design metrics. Such metrics have a major advantage over code and detailed design-based metrics in that they can be measured earlier in the software project, at a time when a manager still has considerable scope for stragegic decision-making. Typical research in this area is described in Lohse and Zweben (1984) and Yao and Collofello (1985). Increasingly, more and more attention has focused on system design metrics which are based on measuring the information flow in a system, the classical work in this area being Henry and Kafura (1981a). It is to this metric that we address ourselves. In particular, we examine the basis of this metric, and suggest some changes which seem to lead to a much stronger relationship with empirically measured software quality factors. Based on our work with this metric, we look at the whole metrics derivation process, and make some suggestions about the way in which metrics—irrespective of whether they are based on system designs, detailed designs or program code—should be derived.

There are a number of applications of information flow metrics. First, there is a potential application for prediction. Unfortunately, this has yet to be achieved in practice. There are no widely accepted models of the system design process which underpin system design measurement. Models that are in use are based on simple hypotheses and a small number of dimensions of the system design process (Yin and Winchester 1978; Henry and Kafura 1981a; Benyon-Tinker 1979); indeed, if we wished to be harsh, we would say that the ease of counting some attributes in a system design often overshadows more global considerations. Consequently, there is a dearth of evidence which supports the contention that system design metrics can, *at present*, be used for accurate engineering prediction (Shepperd and Ince 1989).

A second potential use is quality control. Here, the objective would be to use metrics to control the design activities of the software engineers. Currently there is an absence of data which supports the use of system design metrics in such a way. Probably a more serious objection is that, by concentrating on one factor, a quality assurance department may simply cause problems to migrate into factors of the product, or parts of the software project, which are unmeasured (DeMarco 1982).

A third use—and one which we contend is currently feasible—is to use information flow metrics as an aid to designers in order to help them in the decision-making process that they undertake (Shepperd and Ince 1989). Kitchenham and Pickard (1987) is a good review of the statistical basis for this technique.

The remainder of this paper will consider the use of information flow metrics. In particular, the major point which we wish to convey—a point true for all metrics—is that, whatever use of a metric is adopted, it is imperative that the devisors of such metrics take into account, in their formulation, the use for that which they are intended; and that, as a corollary, the users of such metrics employ them within the often narrow limits defined by their inventors. Clearly, any evaluation of a metric is of little utility without a coherent and strong notion of their purpose.

15.2 THE UNDERLYING THEORY OF INFORMATION FLOW METRICS

In 1981 Sallie Henry and Dennis Kafura published what is now regarded as a seminal paper in the area of system design metrics (Henry and Kafura 1981a).[1] This paper, which was based on Henry's doctoral thesis, presented a metric which measured the complexity of a system in terms of the connections of a module with its environment, as measured by the number of information flows that passed through each module. The metric was empirically validated by correlating maintenance change data for UNIX against values of their metric. At first sight, the correlation obtained was impressive.

The Kafura–Henry metric has achieved a great deal of importance. There are three reasons for this. First, the properties upon which the metric was calculated could be extracted from a system design, and hence provides an early predictor. Second, it is a metric which its authors claim can be used for prediction (Henry and Kafura 1984; see Chapter 6 above), but it can also be used as a design feedback mechanism to pinpoint features of concern to the designer such as inadequate modularization. Third, it was virtually the only example of a developed metric which had received some degree of validation on industrial software. It would not be an exaggeration to say that it is regarded as the archetypal system design metric: it is almost invariably cited in current papers on system design measurement.

An example of the calculation of the metric is shown below. Figure 15.1 shows part of the architecture of a word processor. Table 15.1 contains the Kafura–Henry metric values for each module shown in this figure. The calculation is as follows. First, identify the information flows in a system: these can be local direct, local indirect and global. A *local direct flow* is defined to exist if either of two possibilities are true: first, when a module invokes a second module and passes information to it; second, if the invoked module returns a result to the caller. A *local indirect flow* is defined to exist if the invoked module returns information which is subsequently passed to another invoked module. A *global flow* exists if there is a flow of information from one module to another, via a global data structure.

The complexity for each module is calculated on the basis of its fan-in and fan-out. The *fan-in* of a module is defined as the number of local flows that terminate at a module, plus the number of data structures from which information is retrieved.

---

[1] A similar account of the information flow metric to that given in Henry and Kafura (1981a) may be found in Chapter 6 above.

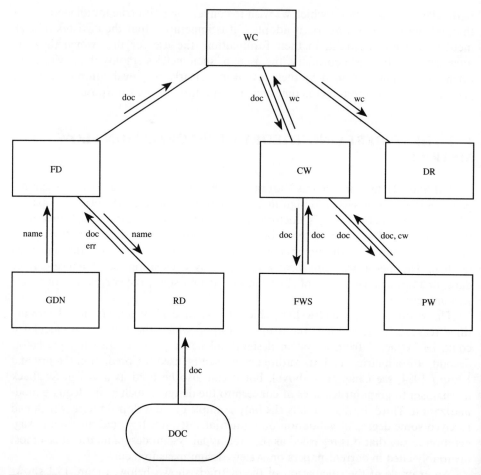

Figure 15.1

Table 15.1[1]

Module	Fan-in	Fan-out	(Fan-in* fan-out)^2	Length	Complexity
WC	2	2	16	30	480
FD	2	3	36	11	396
CW	4	4	256	40	10 240
DR	2	0	0	23	0
GDN	0	2	0	14	0
RD	3	1	9	28	252
FWS	2	2	16	46	736
PW	2	2	16	29	464

[1] [Note that Table 15.1 contains two corrections from the originally published table, namely the fan-in for FWS and the fan-out for PW—M.J.S.]

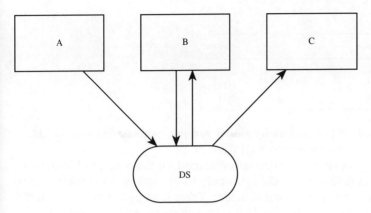

Figure 15.2

The *fan-out* of a module is the number of local flows that emanate from a module, plus the number of data structures that are updated by that module. The complexity of each module is then

$$\text{length}^* \, (\text{fan-in}^*\text{fan-out})^2$$

The original work carried out by Henry and Kafura, which was applied to program code, was followed up by work which reported more detailed statistics (Henry and Kafura 1981a) and which applied the work to design evaluation (Henry and Kafura 1984; see Chapter 6 above). Also, a number of empirical validations have been carried out, for example Kafura and Reddy (1987) and Romback and Basili (1987). Of all the system design metrics that have been devised over the last decade, it is the most published and the most widely cited.

The major problem with the Kafura–Henry metric is that there is no formal definition of a flow. This is a direct consequence of the fact that the metric is based on a poorly articulated and informal model. Probably, the best example of an incidence of this occurs in a quotation from Henry and Kafura (1984):

> Our approach defines the connection between two components to exist if there is a possible flow of information from one to the other.

The problem with such an informal statement is that it gives very little indication of how the information flow metric can be calculated. Anybody looking at the quote above would have a very difficult time deducing the rules used by Kafura and Henry to calculate their metric. Because the authors don't formally describe what is, or is not, a connection, anomalies creep into their metric. The major anomaly is the authors' treatment of global flow. Having defined a global flow, the authors consider only global reads or writes in their metric.

Figure 15.2 and Table 15.2 show examples of this. Figure 15.2 shows part of the architecture of a system. Table 15.2 shows the module complexities; the figures in brackets show the impact if a more consistent treatment of global flow is employed. The effect of the current definition of global flow is to reduce the sensitivity of the metric to global data structure variations. In fact, if you have an architecture

Table 15.2

Module	Fan-in	Fan-out
A	0(0)	2(1)
B	1(1)	1(1)
C	2(0)	0(1)

in which you replaced all parameters by global variable mechanisms you would, in almost all cases, reduce system complexity!

Another problem that stems from the informal model is the concept of local indirect flows. The current definition would seem only to encompass local indirect flow over the scope of two levels of a system structure. There is no good reason why indirect local flows with a greater scope should not contribute to system complexity. For example, Fig. 15.3 shows an indirect local flow which has a scope of three levels. If the informal description of the Henry–Kafura metric was taken literally, this would need to be counted in a complexity equation. Currently, it isn't. However, simply extending the definition of indirect flows to include n levels of a module hierarchy is unsatisfactory, since the outcome is a potential over-counting of flows, particularly if a long chain of flows is involved.

An additional point to make about indirect local flows is shown in Fig. 15.4. The indirect flow that exists between modules B and C cannot be detected unless one has insights into the internal functioning of module A. Such information is unlikely to be available during the system design stage of software development. Even if one obtained the necessary data, a static analysis would be inadequate, as the existence

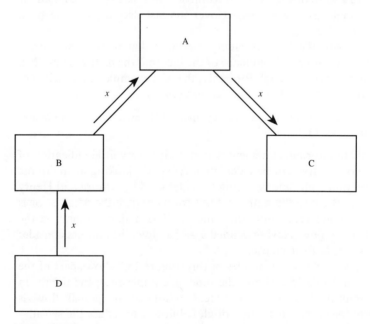

Figure 15.3

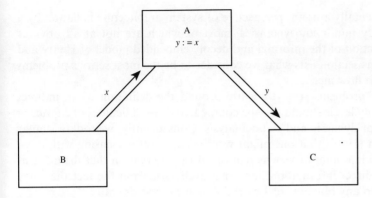

Figure 15.4

of the indirect flow is crucially dependent on the execution order of the code. Dynamic analysis, apart from being a difficult enterprise, generates results that reflect the input chosen to exercise the code. There are no obvious guidelines to steer the measurer as to the choice of input. Therefore, we have grave reservations as to the efficacy of indirect information flows.

Another anomaly that arises from the Henry–Kafura metric is its behaviour with respect to reuse of software components within the same system. Because of the fan-in and fan-out counts, a module that is used many times will receive an abnormally high value of complexity.

A final, and more widely reported, problem is the module length component of the Henry–Kafura model. Apart from the issue of non-availability during design, most researchers (Henry and Kafura 1981a; Kafura and Reddy 1987; Rombach 1987) report that empirical work does not yet support the inclusion of length within a model of architectural complexity. This is corroborated by our own findings reported later in this paper.

15.3. ON MODIFYING THE KAFURA–HENRY METRIC

One of the main reasons for interest in the Henry–Kafura information flow metric was that their underlying idea was in tune with current thinking on software design; that the complexity of the interface between a design component and its environment should be minimized (Alexander 1964; Parnas 1972; Myers 1979). Where an interface is complex, a software engineer is unable to work on a design component in isolation from the rest of the system. There exists far greater potential for a simple maintenance change to ripple through the system and impact other components. A component cannot easily be replaced if, say, a faster algorithm is required, and the scope for software reuse is severely restricted. Plainly, these are undesirable software characteristics, so there is much to be gained through measuring interface complexity which, in the Henry–Kafura model (if length is excluded), is synonymous with information flow complexity.

What is fundamentally a useful perspective of system architecture is flawed by a number of seemingly minor idiosyncrasies, most of which are not at all obvious from a casual inspection of the informal and deeply embedded model of Henry and Kafura. The previous section lists what we consider to be the most serious problems with the information flow metric.

The majority of problems seem to centre around the definition of an indirect flow—over how many levels should they be counted, and the difficulties of capturing all flows by means of dynamic and static analysis. Consequently, we took a similar view to Kitchenham (1988), that one might well be better off dispensing with these flows altogether. Such a point of view is reinforced by observation that the difficulties in modelling indirect information flows may well arise from the fact that they do not correspond to any obvious 'real-world' design process or entity.

Our second modification relates to the anomalous distinction that the original metric makes, between local and global flows. Our model makes no such distinction, so that, whether information flows between modules via a global data structure or by means of parameterized communication, it is treated the same.

This simplification brings a numbr of benefits: architectures that make contrasting uses of parameters and global variables can be more equitably compared; the metric is immune to the presence or absence of particular features in a proposed implementation language; and it is also more sensitive to a wider range of design errors. These errors include the lack of data structure isolation (by not restricting access to a small number of operations as encouraged by the proponents of object-oriented design) and overloaded data structures (which require partitioning).

The modelling of module reuse is our third area of concern, since, as the Henry–Kafura model stands, it would penalize the re-use of any module that imports or exports any information. This would seem to be an extremely undesirable and, rather disturbingly, not unique—*vide* Yin and Winchester (1978)—model of system architecture. Our approach is to count the interface of the reused modules only once, although the module will contribute to the fan-in and fan-out of each calling module.

This is illustrated in Fig. 15.5 and Table 15.3 where the numbers in brackets give the information flows for the unmodified metric. It can be seen that the consequence of this change to the model is to reduce the interface complexity of the re-used module D while leaving that of the calling modules unchanged.

In common with the majority of system design metric researchers, we disregarded module length from our model since such data is unavailable at design time. Although the original model has been subject to a number of other criticisms, we have made no further changes to the Henry–Kafura model. This is because the purpose of the exercise is to establish the importnce of removing demonstrable anomalies from a model upon which a metric is based.

The remaining problems within the Henry–Kafura model are less clear-cut. The multiplication of the fan-in by the fan-out term, although giving rise to the problem of zero complexities, is far less serious than first appears. Modules that do not import any agruments are deterministic, relatively isolated from the rest of the system and, in general, not very complex. Equally, modules that do not generate information flows are, again, only weakly coupled to their system environment. To a large extent, one's conclusions are dependent on one's own perception of the purpose of the metric.

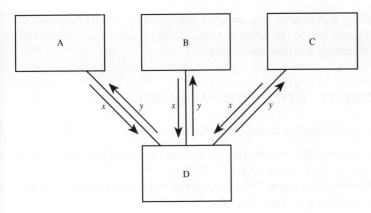

Figure 15.5

If the aim is to measure architectural complexity in terms of information flows, there is no problem. Only if the objective is a more general measure, which also combines a notion of control structure with information flow, do difficulties arise. As a first approximation, we find that the model, and its justification that the multiplication is based upon the number of information paths through a module, is acceptable.

The other moot point is the raising of the equation to the power of 2. Although we find arguments as to whether complexity is a nonlinear function (Henry and Kafura 1981a; Belady 1979) too philosophical to wish to contribute, we believe that a model of system architecture should incorporate some notion of the distribution of flow, and not merely an absolute number. A power law is a very crude method of achieving this aim, and so we have not changed this aspect of the model.

Our revised information flow model does not count duplicate flows, since, like Henry and Kafura, we view flows as a mechanism for the detection of module connections, and connectedness as a binary property. This is appropriate because we are modelling from a software engineering perspective, and the system architecture is a factor that will make the engineer's task more or less difficult. Difficulty can be regarded as the number of parts of a system that an engineer will have to contend with.

Unlike Henry and Kafura's model, ours is uni-dimensional. There are three reasons for this. First, we believe information flow to be the prime contributory factor to system architecture quality. Second, we are unhappy with lines of code as a means of capturing module size. Third, we prefer—initially at least—to restrict our model in

Table 15.3

Module	Fan-in	Fan-out
A	1(1)	1(1)
B	1(1)	1(1)
C	1(1)	1(1)
D	1(3)	1(3)

the interests of simplicity and ease of analysis. The aggregation of many factors is not necessarily an effective technique for dispelling uncertainty from within our models. Certainly, it makes empirical analysis more onerous.

15.4 BACKGROUND TO THE EMPIRICAL STUDY

The hypotheses that we decided to investigate were as follows:

- System architectures with high information flow scores are more difficult to implement than architectures with lower scores.
- The information flow metrics outperforms metrics of system architecture size such as the number of modules and number of flows.
- The information flow metrics significantly outperform the datum metric of ELOC (Basili and Perricone 1984).
- The performance of the information flow measure is improved by the removal of the theoretical anomalies described earlier in this paper.

To investigate the above hypotheses, data was used from 13 software teams, where each team comprised three or four second-year students from the BSc computer science course at Wolverhampton Polytechnic. The students were unaware that an experiment was being conducted. Each team implemented the same problem, thus facilitating comparison between teams. Students were allocated to teams in such a way as to minimize differences in ability. This was achieved by examining past grades in software courses coupled with the judgement of tutors.

The problem was to produce an adventure game shell which could be customized by the players of the game to meet their own requirements. This was carried out in two stages. First, the main data structure was created (essentially, a directed graph representing rooms and connections between rooms) together with associated operations such as *New, Add_room, move_player* etc. and together with a test harness. Second, these operations were incorporated into a full adventure system and a suitable user interface was built.

Development time was measured by modifying the operating system in order to measure connect time. The approach has some limitations, since it does not capture time spent planning, debugging etc., when not at the computer terminal. Unfortunately, given the size of the study, no other alternative was possible. It is hoped that the large number of data points compensates for this problem.

Initially we intended to look at reliability in addition to development effort. Unfortunately, the collection of error data proved troublesome, since it was relatively sparse. The most likely explanation of this is that none of the software was used in a 'live' environment, although we would like to believe that the Wolverhampton Polytechnic students were exceptionally able.

Error report forms were used by students and tutors to report errors, classify error severity from trivial to severe, provide a brief explanation and indicate location. The latter caused some difficulty when a problem manifested itself in several modules, or where the 'solution' was to fix the symptoms rather than the underlying causes. A further problem lay in the difficulty of distinguishing between faults and differing interpretations of the same specification. Although a customer might be uninterested in such a distinction, it was germane to our study where we did not wish to count problems that were a consequence of poor specification, when our concern was with the impact of system architecture on reliability.

The information flow measures were difficult to obtain, partly because a large amount of calculation was required for large-scale software (for that reason a software tool was used), but also because many of Henry and Kafura's definitions are extremely unclear. However, in order to carry out this study, we made a number of assumptions:

- Recursive module calls were treated as normal calls.
- Any variable that was shared by two or more modules was treated as a global data structure.
- Compiler and library modules were ignored.
- Indirect local flows were counted across only one hierarchical level.
- Indirect local flows were ignored, unless the same variable was both imported and exported by the controlling module.
- No attempt was made to make a dynamic analysis of module calls.
- Duplicate flows were ignored.
- Variable parameters were analysed by hand. This is due to the language features of Pascal, dynamic analysis being the only tool available to determine whether they are imported or only exported.

15.5 RESULTS

The first, and not unexpected, observation to make regarding the results from our empirical study are the very marked skews to the distributions of our metric and the unmodified Henry–Kafura metric. Attempts to transform the distribution to a more normal pattern using square roots, logarithms or reciprocals were ineffective. This was significant in that we were unable to apply any of the more usual statistical techniques that assume a normal distribution. The following analysis is based upon ranks and uses the non-parametric Spearman correlation test.

The cross correlations presented in Table 15.4 indicate the strength of association between development effort, the two information flow metrics, the design size metrics (number of modules and number of information flows) and the size of the resultant software measured as executable lines of code (ELOC). The latter was included not as a candidate design metric, but as a form of benchmark (Basili and Hutchens 1983). In Table 15.4 IF0 represents the original Henry–Kafura metric and IF4 our modified version of the metric.

The most striking feature about this table is that our modified information flow is the only metric to have a statistically significant (i.e. to have a less than 5 per cent chance of occurring by chance) relationship with development effort, with a correlation coefficient $r = 0.797$. In comparison, the Henry–Kafura metric has a coefficient $r = 0.434$. This is highly supportive of our hypothesis that the weaknesses in their underlying model are non-trivial.

Table 15.4

	Development	IF4	IF0	Flows	Mods
IF4	0.797				
IF0	0.434	0.399			
Flows	−0.389	−0.508	0.070		
Mods	−0.190	−0.229	0.268	0.848	
XLOC	−0.217	−0.196	0.287	0.669	0.646

The other major results from this study are the very poor performances of the size-based measures, all of which show very weak correlations with development effort. It is noteworthy that all three measures are more strongly correlated with each other than with any of the other factors. Intuitively, it seems reasonable to believe that, over a much larger range (possibly two or three orders of magnitude), size must become an increasingly significant factor in determining development effort. However, this illustrates extremely effectively an earlier point that we made: that one must have a clear understanding of purpose prior to metric evaluation. Our objective is not to identify an effective predictor of development effort. If it were, our model could be considered extremely deficient since it incorporates no notion of size, nor for that matter, of development environment, developer ability and experience and application type.

Instead, our aim is to provide the software engineer with feedback for his or her decision-making during the system design phase. The purpose of the empirical study is to validate the two information flow models with respect to an important software quality factor: ease of implementation. The size metrics act as a form of control and indicate that, when comparing system architectures for the same problem—when size variations will not be that great—information-flow-based metrics are the single most important determinants of development effort.

This suggests that we can have some confidence in our model and metric. There are, though, a number of caveats. First, we have examined only one particular application domain and development environment. Further work is required to demonstrate that these results translate to other situations. The use of students as subjects for analysis has also been criticized, not least by ourselves (Ince and Shepperd 1988). However, early results from a study based on industrial real-time embedded systems corroborate our findings.[2]

A second point that must be underlined is that a uni-dimensional model has limitations. Two problems that we identified were abnormally large modules, in one case almost 50 per cent of the entire system, and abnormally large data structures being used as parameters. Evidently, there is considerable scope for refinement of the model in these two respects.

To summarize our empirical findings, design size measures are shown to be very weakly related to development effort. The original Henry–Kafura metric also exhibits a statistically insignificant association with development effort, owing, we

[2] [See Shepperd (1990b)—M.J.S.]

believe, to some of the anomalies inherent in their model. When these are addressed, this results in a marked strengthening of the relationship, which is found to be statistically significant. These findings support our contention that our modified information flow metric has some utility as a tool for the software designer.

15.6 SUMMARY

This paper has described the utility of system design metrics in software development. It then considered one popular system design metric due to Kafura and Henry. This metric was shown to be theoretically flawed, and we described an empirical validation which confirmed this. By addressing some of the idiosyncrasies of the implicit model adopted by Kafura and Henry, we were able to devise an improved metric. This metric has been confirmed to be of utility by means of an empirical validation.

The informal ideas that are presented by the researchers would appear to be sound. They are also in accordance with current software engineering thought about data abstraction and information hiding, and appear to have some degree of promise. However, in order for us to take full advantage of what seems an intuitively good idea, a much more formal approach to the derivation of a system design metric is needed.

Such a formal model would include definitions for each of its components, thereby eliminating many of the counting problems that have bedevilled our validation. Even more important, it would greatly facilitate the theoretical validation. Ideally, it should be possible to demonstrate three characteristics for a software model. First, the model should be consistent, in the sense that, for any set of circumstances between which the model is able to distinguish, it should produce only one outcome or behaviour. Second, it should be complete, so that there are no set of circumstances for which no behaviour can be derived. Third, it should behave in a manner consistent with current software engineering wisdom. Where this is not the case, the onus is on the author to justify such aspects of the model. This final characteristic is the most nebulous and, yet, possibly, the most revealing.

One technique for assessing models for this characteristic is to identify those strategies the model prescribes to 'improve' the software. From this viewpoint we find that Henry and Kafura make some startling recommendations; for example, that software components should not be re-used, and that global data structures should be used in preference to parameters. We do not believe this was their intention, but is an almost inevitable consequence of a highly informal and deeply embedded model.

It is our contention that this is not a unique occurrence in the field of software metrics, and that our findings of model weaknesses, translating into poor empirical performance, could be reproduced for other metrics. The modelling process must be made more explicit in the derivation of metrics. This allows the creator, or other researchers to explore and refine models, and reject those that are clearly unsatisfactory at an early stage, rather than discover the fact after expensive empirical validation. We consider this to be important, not only because of the cost of empirical studies, but also because we are dubious as to the significance of statistically meaningful results based on theoretically meaningless models.

Our aim in writing this paper was not to attempt a full-scale demolition of the Kafura–Henry metric; we are still fairly confident that, underneath the facade of arbitrariness, there lies a powerful idea. However, the message we would like readers to come away with is; that there are many problems involved in validating a metric which are caused by a lack of formality during the definition of the metric, problems arising from researchers concentrating on those factors of a software product that can be easily counted, nescience of the use to which a metric is to be put, and a flawed perception of the nature of many software engineering processes. An attention to these problems would enable empirical validation to be a less painful task, and would hasten the day when product metrics could be used as a predictive tool on software projects.

What we believe we have shown is that attention to what may be regarded as minor theoretical quibbles can translate into major improvement in performance of a metric. This process is facilitated by the adoption of more formal and explicit models.

ACKNOWLEDGEMENTS

We would like to acknowledge the support of the Esprit 1 project MUSE.

16

AN EMPIRICAL VALIDATION OF SOFTWARE COST ESTIMATION MODELS

Chris F. Kemerer

Carnegie-Mellon University

ABSTRACT

Practitioners have expressed concern over their inability accurately to estimate costs associated with software development. This concern has become even more pressing as costs associated with development continue to increase. As a result, considerable research attention is now directed at gaining a better understanding of the software development process as well as constructing and evaluating software cost estimating tools. This chapter evaluates four of the most popular algorithmic models used to estimate software costs (SLIM, COCOMO, function points and ESTIMACS). Data on 15 large completed business data processing projects were collected and used to test the accuracy of the models' *ex post* effort estimation. One important result was that Albrecht's function points effort estimation model was validated by the independent data provided in this study (Albrecht and Gaffney 1983; see Chapter 8 above). The models not developed in business data processing environments showed significant need for calibration. As models of the software development process, all of the models tested failed to reflect sufficiently the underlying factors affecting productivity. Further research will be required to develop understanding in this area.

16.1 INTRODUCTION

Practitioners have expressed concern over their inability accurately to estimate costs associated with software development. This concern has become even more pressing as costs associated with development continue to increase. As a result, considerable research attention is now directed at gaining a better understanding of the software development process as well as at constructing and evaluating software costs estimating tools.

This paper presents an empirical validation of four algorithmic models from the literature (SLIM, COCOMO, function points, and ESTIMACS) that are proposed as general software development cost estimators. This research has built a database of completed software development projects with the *ex post* estimates obtained from the four models. Of particular interest is the comparison of the results of the four models' use of different measures (metrics) of the outputs underlying their productivity calculations.

Three research questions of interest to practitioners are addressed in this paper:

1. Are these software cost estimating models truly generalizable to environments other than that in which they were developed? If not, can they be easily calibrated to a typical business data processing environment?
2. Are models that do not use source lines of code (SLOC) as an input as accurate as those that do? If so, then this could eliminate the need to attempt to estimate lines of code early in the project.
3. Are the models available in the open literature as accurate as proprietary models? If so, then this could allow practitioners to avoid the costs of purchasing the proprietary models.

Section 16.2 discusses the selection of the four models, followed by brief descriptions of the models. Section 16.3 describes the environment in which the data originated and compares this data set with that of other researchers. Section 16.4 describes the data gathering and data analysis methods, which leads directly into Section 16.5, 'Results'. Finally, Section 16.6 offers some summary conclusions and outlines extensions of this work.

16.2 BACKGROUND TO THE MODELS

16.2.1 Model selection

A review of the literature revealed that the most interesting difference between estimation models is between models that use SLOC as the primary input versus models that do not. SLOC was selected early as a metric by researchers, no doubt due to its quantifiability and seeming objectivity. Since then an entire sub-area of research has developed to determine the best method of counting SLOC (Gaffney *et al.* 1984, C. Jones 1986). In response to this, and to practitioners' complaints about the difficulties in estimating SLOC before a project was well under way, new models have been developed that do not use SLOC as the primary input (Albrecht 1979; Rubin 1983).

The next step was to choose models that were well regarded in the current literature, and to winnow this selection down to a manageable number since each model's

Table 16.1 *Journal of Parametrics* **articles**

	COCOMO	*SLIM*	*PRICE*
Callisen (12/84)	×		
Ferens (12/84)	×	×	×
Masters (3/85)	×	×	×
Pinsky (12/84)	×	×	
Rubin (6/85)	×	×	

idiosyncrasies required the collection of different data. The approach to determining which models were well regarded was twofold. First, Barry Boehm (developer of the COCOMO model, a model eventually selected for this study) has written a widely cited book entitled *Software Engineering Economics* (Boehm 1981), in which he provides an analysis of eight important models. This list was used to generate candidates. The second step was a review of articles in the most recent issues of the *Journal of Parametrics*, a publication of the International Society of Parametric Analysts that devotes a large number of its pages to software estimation articles. This sampling validated whether the models cited in the Boehm study were well represented by their inclusion in other studies.

Boehm examines eight models (including COCOMO in his evaluation. They are: (1) SDC; (2) Wolverton; (3) SLIM; (4) Doty; (5) PRICE (6) IBM-FSD; (7) Boeing; and (8) COCOMO.[1] After examining this list of candidates, a review was undertaken of the most recent issues of the *Journal of Parametrics*, to determine the popularity of these models as demonstrated by their inclusion in other research. The results are presented in Table 16.1 with an '×' signifying that a particular model was discussed or compared in that article.[2]

From this list of candidates, COCOMO and SLIM seem to be the most widely reviewed. The PRICE model is also popular, but was developed primarily for use on aerospace applications and was therefore deemed unsuitable for the business applications that would comprise the database. Therefore, only COCOMO and SLIM were selected for this research.

All of the above analysis centred on SLOC models of one sort or another. This is to be expected, since software estimation research began with these models and is a relatively young field. No similar comparisons for non-SLOC models were found, and in fact, only two models were discovered during the period when this research was being conducted. These two are the function points method, developed by Allan Albrecht at IBM in 1979 (see Albrecht 1979; Albrecht and Gaffney 1983, reproduced as Chapter 8 above), and the ESTIMACS model, developed by Howard Rubin of Hunter College and marketed by Management and Computer Services during the period when these data were being collected (Rubin 1983, 1984). Both of these models were selected, bringing the total number of models compared to four.

---

[1] See Boehm (1981); Putnam (1978); Walston and Felix (1977a); Wolverton (1974).
[2] See Callisen and Colborne (1984); Masters (1985); Pinsky (1984); Rubin (1985); Ferens (1984).

These four exhibit a certain symmetry, perhaps best illustrated in Table 16.2. Therefore, some interesting comparisons can be made not only between measurements methods, but between models that appear in the open literature and those that do not.

16.2.2 Models

Owing to space limitations, the following are necessarily brief descriptions of the four models used in this paper. The interested reader is referred to the references provided for more detailed explanations.

SLIM   The SLIM estimating method was developed in the late 1970s by Larry Putnam of Quantitiative Software Management (see Putnam 1978; Putnam and Fitzsimmons 1979). SLIM depends on an SLOC estimate for the project's general size, then modifies this through the use of the Rayleigh curve model to produce its effort estimates. The user can influence the shape of the curve through two key parameters: the initial slope of the curve (the 'manpower buildup index', or MBI) and a productivity factor (the 'technology constant' or PF). Since these are dimensionless numbers, the SLIM user has two options for choosing their values: the user can calibrate the model by inputting data from completed projects, or he or she can answer a series of 22 questions, from which SLIM will provide a recommended PF and MBI. The second method was chosen for this research owing to the absence of a previously collected calibration database and the feeling that this would more accurately reflect the average user's experience.

COCOMO   The COnstructive COst MOdel (COCOMO) was developed by Barry Boehm of TRW and published in 1981 (Boehm 1981). Based on his analysis of 63 software development projects, Boehm developed an easy-to-understand model that predicts the effort and duration of a project, based on inputs relating to the size of the resulting systems and a number of 'cost drivers' that Boehm believes affect productivity.

A simplified version of the essential COCOMO effort equation for the Basic Model (the Intermediate and Detailed Models are discussed later) is of the form

$$MM = C(\text{KDSI})^k,$$

where

MM = number of man-months[3]
(= 152 working hours),
C = a constant,
KDSI = thousands of 'delivered source instructions'
(DSI)
k = a constant

---

[3] 'Man-months' is used in this paper in its vernacular sense of referring to all the hours worked on a project, whether by men or women.

Table 16.2 Model categories

	Proprietary	*Non-proprietary*
SLOC	SLIM	COCOMO
Non-SLOC	ESTIMACS	Function points

Boehm defines DSI as program instructions created by project personnel that are delivered as part of the final product. They exclude comments and unmodified utility software, and include job control language, format statements and data declarations.

In Boehm's development of COCOMO, he found that the Basic Model predicted effort within a factor of 1.3 only 29 per cent of the time and within a factor of 2 only 60 per cent of the time for his 63-project database. In an effort to improve the model's accuracy, he refined the equation to include the effects of 15 'cost drivers', which are attributes of the end product, the computer used, the personnel staffing and the project environment. He believes that these 15 factors affect the project's productivity and calls this version the Intermediate Model.

The COCOMO Detailed Model is very similar to the Intermediate Model except that the project is divided into four phases: product design, detailed design; coding/unit test; and integration/test. The 15 cost drivers are estimated and applied to each phase separately, rather than to the project as a whole.

Function points   The function points measurement method was developed by Allan Albrecht at IBM and first published in 1979 (see Albrecht 1979; Albrecht and Gaffney 1983, reproduced as Chapter 8 above). Albrecht was interested in the general problem of productivity measurement in systems development and created the function points method as an alternative to estimating SLOC. Albrecht's function points are at a more macro level than SLOC, capturing things like the number of input transaction types and the number of unique reports. He believes that function points offer several significant advantages over SLOC counts. First, it is possible to estimate them early in the life cycle, about the time of the requirements definition document. This can be an important advantage for anyone trying to estimate the level of effort to be required on a software development project. Second, they can be estimated by a relatively non-technical project member. And, finally, they avoid the effects of language and other implementation differences.

There are two steps involved in counting function points: (1) counting the user functions, and (2) adjusting for processing complexity. There are currently five user function categories:[4] external input types, external output types, logical internal file types, external interface file types, and external inquiry types. Albrecht recognized that the effort required to provide a given level of functionality can vary depending on the environment. For example, input transactions are harder to program if a lot of emphasis is placed on system throughput or end-user convenience. In response to this, Albrecht has a list of 14 processing complexity characteristics that are to be rated on a scale from 0 (no influence) to 5 (strong influence). The next step is to

---

[4] Albrecht's (1979) paper has only four, omitting external interface file types.

sum all the processing complexity points assigned. This number is then multiplied by 0.01 and added to 0.65 to obtain a weighting, as follows:

$$PCA = 0.65 + 0.01 \sum_{i=1}^{14} c_i$$

where PCA = processing complexity adjustment $(0.65 \leq PCA \leq 1.35)$, and c_i = complexity factors $(0 \leq c_i \leq 5)$.

This factor is then used in the final equation:

$$FP = FC(PCA)$$

where FP = function points, and FC = previously computed function counts.

The end result is that the function points can vary ± 35 per cent from the original function counts. Once the function points have been computed, they can be used to compare the proposed project with past projects in terms of its size.

ESTIMACS   The ESTIMACS model was developed by Howard Rubin of Hunter College as an outgrowth of a consulting assignment to Equitable Life. It is a proprietary system and, at the time the data were collected, was marketed by Management and Computer Services (MACS). Since it is a proprietary model, details such as the equations used are not available. The model does not require SLOC as an input, relying instead on 'function-point-like' measures. The research here is based on Rubin's paper from the 1983 IEEE conference on software development tools and the documentation provided by MACS (Rubin 1983, 1984). The 25 ESTIMACS input questions are described in these documents.

16.3 DATA

16.3.1 Data source

The source for the project data for this research was a national computer consulting and services firm specializing in the design and development of data processing software (hereafter referred to as the ABC consulting firm). Use of this consulting firm's data conveyed several advantages to this research.

First, because clients are charged by the hours spent on their projects, the consulting firm must maintain strict, auditable timekeeping records. Since a key element of this research is the comparison of estimated effort to actual effort, it was important that the measurement of actual effort be as accurate as possible.

Second, the projects in the database reflect a variety of data processing applications, which should broaden the level of interest in the results, as opposed to, say, a database composed of all insurance or all defence contractor applications. However, within this framework there is a high level of consistency in both the quality of the staff and the methodologies employed, since all the projects were done by the same firm within the time span of a few years.

Third, as professional software developers, ABC is highly interested in software productivity. Since it is their primary business, as opposed to being relegated to a staff function as it might be in another industry, the ABC managers were highly motivated to provide good quality data and cooperate with the research.

16.3.2 Project database

Projects selected possessed two attributes: First, they were medium to large in size, an explicit requirement of the models chosen (see Boehm 1981; QSM 1983). The average project size in this study is just under 200 KSLOC (SLOC stated in thousands), and the smallest project is 39 KSLOC, which was partly written in a fourth-generation language. Second, the project manager must have been available during the summer of 1985 to complete the data collection form. (See Section 16.4 for more details.) This limited the database to fairly recent projects, which had the additional benefit of ensuring consistency in project methodology. The oldest project in the database was started in August 1981, and two-thirds of the projects were started in 1983 or later.

Based on the above criteria, 15 projects qualified for inclusion in the study. The researcher or practitioner interested in large business applications is likely to find this data set to be a useful contribution for two reasons. First, in terms of sheer number of projects, it compares favourably with a number of other published studies.[5] Second, and more important than the number of projects alone, is the content of the database. This database contains large business applications, 12 of which were written entirely in Cobol, the most widely used business data processing language. By contrast, Boehm's 63-project database contains only 7 business applications, of which only 4 were written in Cobol. Albrecht's 1983 database contains 18 Cobol projects, but with an average size of only 66 KSLOC. The average size of Cobol applications in the ABC database is 221 KSLOC.

16.4 METHODOLOGY

16.4.1 Data collection forms

The primary data collection tools were three data collection forms developed for this project. One form was designed to capture background information about the project (e.g., hardware manufacturer and model), as well as the ABC project number and the start and end dates.

After an analysis of each of the model's requirements, two additional consolidated metrics data collection forms were devised. Although each of the models has its own set of data requirements, there is a fair amount of overlap in terms of the areas addressed as they relate to productivity. The questions were organized on the forms into broad categories, such as personnel attributes, rather than by models, in order to help the respondent ensure consistency in his or her answers for all of the models. However, the questions were printed on the form verbatim from the original source

---

[5] See e.g. Behrens (1983); Callisen and Colborne (1984); Golden *et al.* (1981); Ferens (1984).

documents whenever possible to minimize any effects of originality in the wording by the researcher.[6] The net result was a set of two data collection forms, one 'quantitative' (e.g., SLOC, database size) and one 'qualitative' (e.g., complexity ratings). The intent of this procedure was to retain the authenticity of the questions as asked in the original source documents, while providing some overall structure for the respondents.

16.4.2 Data collection procedure

For each of the projects, there was an in-person meeting with the project manager who would be filling out the forms. The one exception to this procedure was a West Coast project manager who was already familiar with the metrics used; data collection for that particular project was done via the mail and the telephone.

There were two main purposes to this labour-intensive approach. The first was to discuss each of the questions to ensure that it was understood and that each of the managers would answer consistently. The second purpose was to impress upon the managers the importance of their participation in this work. Given the amount of data requested (greater than 100 questions per project), this effort was believed necessary. The result was a large increase in the response rate compared with questionaires distributed by the normal channels at ABC.

16.4.3 Data analysis procedures

Once the forms were returned, they were checked for consistency. It was possible to do this owing to the redundancy of many of the questons from the different models. With the exception of the 'function-point-like' questions of the ESTIMACS model, no questions were combined or consolidated.[7] This meant that it was possible to ensure that an answer about, say, project personnel skills for the COCOMO model was consistent with the answer for the similar question for the SLIM model. Next, the project identification information from the 'Project Actuals' form was used to research the ABC accounting records to determine the level of effort expended. Finally, the metrics data were input to each of the four models. For SLIM, COCOMO and function points, this was done by the researcher. MACS staff offered to run a limited number of projects (without having access to the actual results) and to provide the estimates by telephone.

16.4.4 Error analysis

The focus of this paper is on the degree to which the model's estimated effort (MM_{est}) matches the actual effort (MM_{act}). If the models were perfect, then for every project $MM_{est} = MM_{act}$. Clearly, this will rarely, if ever, be the case.

---

[6] The original source documents were, for SLIM. QSM (1984); for COCOMO, Boehm (1981); for function points Albrecht and Gaffney (1983, reproduced as Chapter 8 above); and for ESTIMACS, Rubin (1984).

[7] See the ESTIMACS results section (Section 16.5.5) for discussion of this issue.

There are several possible methods for evaluating the man-month estimates. A simple analysis approach would be to look at the difference between MM_{est} and MM_{act}. The problem with this *absolute error* approach is that the importance of the size of the error varies with project size. For example, on a 10-man-month project, an absolute error of 9 man-months would be likely to cause serious project disruption in terms of staffing, whereas the same error on a 1000-man-month project would be much less of a problem.

In light of this, Boehm (1981) and others have recommended a *percentage error* test, as follows:

$$\text{Percentage error} = \frac{MM_{est} - MM_{act}}{MM_{act}}$$

This test eliminates the problem caused by project size and better reflects the impact of any error.

However, the analysis in this paper concentrates on the models' average performance over the entire set of projects. Errors can be of two types: underestimates, where $MM_{est} < MM_{act}$; and overestimates, where $MM_{est} > MM_{act}$. Both of these errors can have serious impacts on projects. Large underestimates will cause the project to be understaffed, and as the deadline approaches project management will be tempted to add new staff members. This results in a phenomenon known as Brooks' law: 'Adding manpower to a late software project makes it later' (Brooks 1975). Otherwise productive staff are assigned to teaching the new team members, and with this, cost and schedule goals slip even further. Overestimates can also be costly in that staff members, noting the project slack, become less productive (Parkinson's law: 'Work expands to fill the time available for its completion') or add so-called 'gold plating', defined as additional systems features that are not required by the user (Boehm 1981).

In light of the seriousness of both types of errors, overestimates and underestimates, Conte *et al.* (1986) have suggested a *magnitude of relative error*, or *MRE* test, as follows:

$$MRE = \left| \frac{MM_{est} - MM_{act}}{MM_{act}} \right|$$

By means of this test, the two types of errors do not cancel each other out when an average of multiple errors is taken, and therefore is the test used in this analysis.

Still another issue in interpreting the errors concerns bias. A model, because it was developed in an environment, say, less productive than ABC's, may generate errors that are biased towards overestimation. However, this model may be able to be recalibrated to approximate the ABC environment. What is important is that the estimates correlate with the actual results; that is, bigger projects generate bigger estimates than smaller projects.

Albrecht and others have proposed linear regression as a means of measuring this correlation (see Albrecht and Gaffney 1983, Behrens 1983; Conte *et al.* 1986). Since Albrecht's method does not produce a man-month estimate directly, an alternative was needed to validate the function point method. His proposal was to perform a simple linear regression with man-months as the dependent variable and function

Table 16.3 Project background

Project no.	Software	Hardware	Months	MM	KSLOC	SLOC/MM
1	Cobol	IBM 308X	17	287.00	253.60	884
2	Cobol	IBM 43XX	7	82.50	40.50	491
3	Cobol	DEC VAX	15	1107.31	450.00	406
4	Cobol	IBM 308X	18	86.90	214.40	2467
5	Cobol	IBM 43XX	13	336.30	449.90	1338
6	Cobol	DEC 20	5	84.00	50.00	595
7	Bliss	DEC 20	5	23.20	43.00	1853
8	Cobol	IBM 43XX	11	130.30	200.00	1535
9	Cobol	IBM 308X	14	116.00	289.00	2491
10	Cobol, Natural	IBM 308X	5	72.00	39.00	542
11	Cobol	IBM 308X	13	258.70	254.20	983
12	Cobol	IBM 43XX, 308X	31	230.70	128.60	557
13	Cobol	HP 3000, 68	20	157.00	161.40	1028
14	Cobol	IBM 308X	26	246.90	164.80	667
15	Natural	IBM 308X	14	69.90	60.20	861
Mean			14.3	219.25	186.57	1113
Standard deviation			7.5	263.06	136.82	689
Cobol mean					221.37	1120
Cobol standard deviation					131.14	720

points as the independent variable. He also performs regressions with SLOC as the dependent variable to show how function points could be used to generate an SLOC estimate for other models or methods that require it. Regression was used in this research for all of the models by using actual man-months as the dependent variable and the man-months estimated by each model as the independent variable. The advantage of this method is that it can show whether a model's estimates correlate well with experience even when the MRE test does not. A 'perfect' score on the MRE test would be an error per centage of 0, whereas a 'perfect' score on Albrecht's test would be an R^2 of 1.00.[8]

In summary, two tests are used to evaluate the models (as recommended by Theabaut (1983): the MRE test and regression. These tests have the advantage of not only being generally accepted in the literature, but of also having been proposed by some of the models' own developers.

16.5 RESULTS

16.5.1 Project data

Table 16.3 shows the background data on the projects. The 'Months' figures are project durations in calendar months. The man-months ('MM') data refer to the total number of actual hours expended by exempt staff members (i.e. not including secretarial labour) on the project through implementation, divided by 152. This effort

---

[8] In this analysis the more conservative $\bar{R}^2$, R^2 adjusted for degrees of freedom, was used, which results in slighter lower values than R^2.

measure was the only output of the models that was evaluated, although several of them offer other features, such as project planning aids. The 'KSLOC' figures allow Boehm's definition stated earlier (i.e., comments are not counted) with two exceptions.

One project (number 8) had reused code, and this was accounted for in the KSLOC data by counting a modified line as equivalent to a new line. In the KDSI data (used for cocomo), Boehm's conversion formula for modified software was used (Boehm 1981). This resulted in a KDSI count of 167 as opposed to the 200 KSLOC count shown above for project number 8.

The other exception is that Cobol non-procedural statements are not specially weighted. Boehm found this weighting necessary as only 4 of his 63 projects were Cobol, and, as he states, some 'pragmatic' procedure was required to make those projects fit his formula.[9] Since the project data in this research is overwhelmingly Cobol, no such pragmatic weighting was deemed necessary.

16.5.2 SLIM results

SLIM was run using the default parameters provided by the model when the user answers the SLIM set of 22 questions. Table 16.4 shows the actual man-months, the SLIM man-month estimate[10] and the error percentage. Also shown are the SLIM default PF, the default MBI, the calibrated PF and the calibrated MBI. (The calibrated factors were obtained after the fact by using the SLIM 'calibrate' function for use in later analyses.)

SLIM does not do well via the MRE test. The average percentage error is 772 per cent, with the smallest error being 21 per cent. In addition, the errors are all biased; effort is overestimated in all 15 cases. A possible explanation for this is that SLIM was originally developed using data from defence-related projects, including real-time systems. Productivity for these is typically less than that in the business data processing systems developed by ABC (QSM 1983; SPR 1986).

One possibility is that SLIM accurately reflects the project conditions, but is calibrated too high for the ABC environment. To evaluate this, Albrecht's test was applied by means of a regression run with the SLIM estimate as the independent variable and the actual man-months as the dependent variable. The results were that the SLIM estimates correlated well with the actuals, generating an $\bar{R}^2$ of 87.8 per cent, with a coefficient t statistic of 10.11:

$$\text{Actual man-months} = 49.9 + 0.082(\text{SLIM}) \qquad \bar{R}^2:$$

$$(10.11) \qquad\qquad 87.8\%$$

The main input for SLIM is KSLOC, whose regression with actual man-months produced an $\bar{R}^2$ of only 48.5 per cent; so the SLIM model seems to be adding information.

---

[9] See Boehm (1981), p. 479. The unavailability of this data may make the cocomo estimates slightly higher than they would be elsewise.

[10] The SLIM man-month is 168 man-hours. All SLIM man-month estimates were converted to 152 man-hour man-months to aid comparison.

Table 16.4 SLIM **data**

Project no.	Actual MM	SLIM MM estimate	SLIM error (%)	PF	MBI	Calibrated PF	Calibrated MBI
1	287.0	3 857.8	1244.18	12	5	18	2
2	82.5	100.1	21.33	15	4	16	5
3	1107.3	11 982.0	982.08	16	4	19	5
4	86.9	2 017.2	2221.29	13	4	18	1
5	336.3	3 382.0	905.65	15	5	21	4
6	84.0	262.5	212.50	13	4	19	6
7	23.2	106.3	358.19	16	5	20	5
8	130.3	1 224.6	839.83	14	4	20	3
9	116.0	1 454.1	1153.53	15	4	20	2
10	72.0	235.7	227.36	12	4	18	6
11	258.7	1 623.0	527.37	15	5	19	3
12	230.7	513.3	122.50	15	4	12	1
13	157.0	3 119.8	1887.13	11	5	16	1
14	246.9	380.3	54.03	17	4	14	1
15	69.9	643.8	821.03	11	4	15	1
Mean (absolute values)	219.25	2 060.17	771.87	14.0	4.3	17.7	3.1
Standard deviation	263.06	3 014.77	661.33	1.9	0.5	2.6	1.9

16.5.3 COCOMO **results**

The results for the three COCOMO versions (Basic, Intermediate and Detailed Models) appear in Table 16.5. In the table, 'BAS' refers to the Basic Model. 'INT' to the Intermediate Model and 'DET' to the Detailed Model. The 'error %' columns are calculated by dividing the difference between the estimate and the actual man-months by the actual man-months.

All three COCOMO models did poorly according to the MRE percentage error test. The average error for all versions of the model was 601 per cent, with the lowest single error being 83 per cent. As was the case with SLIM, the estimates are biased; effort is overestimated in all 45 cases. Again, this may be due to COCOMO's development on TRW's data. The average KSLOC/MM figure for Boehm's data is much lower than that for the ABC data, probably reflecting the composition of the types of systems developed by TRW and ABC. Again, it is possible that COCOMO is accurately reflecting the project conditions, but is calibrated too high for the ABC environment. In his book, Boehm (1981) acknowledges the probable need for calibration of his model in a new environment.

To evaluate this, Albrecht's regression test was run. The results were as follows:

$$\text{Actual man-months} = 27.7 + 0.156(\text{COCOMO-Basic}) \qquad \bar{R}^2:$$

$$(5.54) \qquad\qquad 68.0\%$$

$$\text{Actual man-months} = 62.1 + 0.123\,(\text{COCOMO-Intermediate}) \qquad 59.9\%$$

$$(4.68)$$

$$\text{Actual man-months} = 66.8 + 0.118\,(\text{COCOMO-Detailed}) \qquad 52.5\%$$

$$(4.06)$$

Table 16.5 COCOMO data

Project no.	Actual MM	COCOMO BAS	COCOMO-BAS error (%)	COCOMO INT	COCOMO-INT error (%)	COCOMO DET	COCOMO-DET error (%)
1	287.00	1095.10	281.57	917.56	219.71	932.96	225.07
2	82.50	189.40	129.58	151.66	83.83	151.19	83.26
3	1107.31	5497.40	396.46	6182.65	458.35	5818.75	425.49
4	86.90	1222.30	1306.56	558.98	543.25	566.50	551.90
5	336.30	1466.00	335.92	1344.20	299.70	1316.04	291.33
6	84.00	393.60	368.57	313.36	273.05	312.24	271.71
7	23.20	328.40	1315.52	234.78	911.98	234.51	910.82
8	130.30	925.30	610.13	1165.70	794.63	1206.17	825.69
9	116.00	3231.00	2685.34	4248.73	3562.70	4577.62	3846.22
10	72.00	181.60	152.22	180.29	150.40	181.36	151.89
11	258.70	1482.20	472.94	1520.04	487.57	1575.68	509.08
12	230.70	691.00	199.52	558.12	141.92	584.37	153.30
13	157.00	891.20	467.64	1073.47	583.74	1124.36	616.15
14	246.90	511.00	106.97	629.22	154.85	663.84	168.87
15	69.90	295.30	322.46	133.94	91.62	130.72	87.01
Mean (absolute values)	219.25	1226.72	610.09	1280.85	583.82	1291.75	607.85
Standard deviation	263.06	1412.58	684.55	1698.43	862.79	1667.24	932.96

Table 16.6 Function points-MM data

Project no.	Actual MM	Function points	Function counts	Albrecth FP MM estimate	Albrecht MM error (%)
1	287.00	1217.10	1010.00	344.30	19.96
2	82.50	507.30	457.00	92.13	11.68
3	1107.31	2306.80	2284.00	731.43	−33.95
4	86.90	788.50	881.00	192.03	120.98
5	336.30	1337.60	1583.00	387.11	15.11
6	84.00	421.30	411.00	61.58	−26.69
7	23.20	99.90	97.00	−52.60	−326.73
8	130.30	993.00	998.00	264.68	103.13
9	116.00	1592.90	1554.00	477.81	311.90
10	72.00	240.00	250.00	−2.83	−103.93
11	258.70	1611.00	1603.00	484.24	87.18
12	230.70	789.00	724.00	192.21	−16.68
13	157.00	690.90	705.00	157.36	0.23
14	246.90	1347.50	1375.00	390.63	58.21
15	69.90	1044.30	976.00	282.91	304.73
Mean (absolute values)	219.25	999.14	993.87	266.87	102.74
Standard deviation	263.06	569.60	577.17	202.36	112.11

Paradoxically, the more advanced versions, COCOMO-Intermediate and COCOMO-Detailed, do not do as well as COCOMO-Basic in this instance. This implies that the cost drivers of the latter two models are not adding any additional explanation of the phenomenon. This is consistent with the results of Kitchenham and Taylor, who evaluated COCOMO on some systems programming and real-time systems projects developed by British Telecom and ICL (Kitchenham and Taylor 1984).

In addition, a regression was run on the primary input to the COCOMO models, delivered source instructions, or KDSI. The result was an $\bar{R}^2$ of 49.4 per cent, which is not as good a fit as any of the COCOMO models. Therefore, COCOMO seems to be adding information.

16.5.4 Function points results

In this section three separate analyses are performed. The first analysis compares the man-month predictions from function points to the actual man-months and is similar to the analysis done for the other models. In addition, two of Albrecht's other models are tested, one for predicting man-months from SLOC, and the other for predicting SLOC from function points.

Function points to man-month results   As shown in Table 16.6, the average MRE is 102.74 per cent, substantially better than either of the two SLOC-based models. This is probably due to the similarity of applications (business data processing) done by ABC and IBM's DP Services group, the source of Albrecht's data. The regression analysis of these estimates and the actual man-months was the following:

Actual (ABC) man-months $= -37 + 0.96$ (function points estimated MM) $\qquad \bar{R}^2$:

$$(4.26) \qquad\qquad\qquad 55.3\%$$

The regression analysis result from the ABC data is as follows:

$$\text{ABC man-months} = -122 + 0.341 \text{ (function points)} \qquad \bar{R}^2:$$

$$(4.28) \qquad\qquad\qquad 55.3\%$$

By way of comparison, in Albrecht's validation paper (Albrecht and Gaffney 1983) he developed the following estimation equation from a data set of 24 projects:

$$\text{IBM man-months} = -88 + 0.355 \text{ (function points)} \qquad \bar{R}^2:$$

$$(12.37) \qquad\qquad\qquad 86.9\%$$

Albrecht's equation developed using IBM data is strikingly similar to the equation using ABC data, differing primarily by the constant term. The results of an F-test comparing the two individual regressions with a single regression on all 39 data points revealed that the null hypothesis that the two models were the same could not be rejected at the 95 per cent confidence level (Weisberg 1980).

A similar regression was performed on the ABC function count data, the main input to function points:

$$\text{ABC man-months} = -111 + 0.333 \text{ (function counts)} \qquad \bar{R}^2:$$

$$(4.16) \qquad\qquad\qquad 53.8\%$$

The difference between using function points, which include 14 factors that modify the function counts, and the function counts themselves, seems slight in this instance.

Source lines of code to man-month results   Albrecht provides another model, showing the relationship for his data between Cobol KSLOC and man-months:

$$\text{IBM man-months} = -19.2 + 2.5 \text{ (Cobol KSLOC)} \qquad \bar{R}^2:$$

$$(6.85) \qquad\qquad\qquad 73.0\%$$

The results are shown in Table 16.7.

The average MRE of 167.3 per cent is not as good as that generated by function points. The equivalent equation for the ABC data is the following:

$$\text{ABC man-months} = -65 + 1.47 \text{ (Cobol KSLOC)} \qquad \bar{R}^2:$$

$$(2.99) \qquad\qquad\qquad 41.9\%$$

The results of an F-test are that we can reject the null hypothesis that the IBM and

Table 16.7 Cobol KSLOC-MM data

Project no.	Actual MM	Albrecht SLOC MM estimate	Albrecht MM error (%)
1	287.00	613.67	113.82
2	82.50	81.90	−0.73
3	1107.31	1103.76	−0.32
4	86.90	515.85	493.61
5	336.30	1103.51	228.13
6	84.00	105.61	25.72
8	130.30	479.91	268.32
9	116.00	702.00	505.18
11	258.70	615.16	137.79
12	230.70	301.74	30.79
13	157.00	383.59	144.33
14	246.90	392.08	58.80
Mean (absolute values)	260.30	533.23	167.29
Standard deviation	280.60	327.25	177.07

ABC models are the same at the 95 per cent confidence level, but not at the 99 per cent level.

Function points to source lines of code results   Another validation that was performed was a check of Albrecht's claim of function points as a predictor of KSLOC. Albrecht provides the following model for estimating Cobol SLOC from function points:

$$\text{IBM Cobol KSLOC} = -6.5 + 0.12 \text{ (function points)} \qquad \bar{R}^2:$$

$$(6.55) \qquad\qquad 71.2\%$$

The results are shown in Table 16.8, and show an average MRE of 38.17 per cent, with a large negative bias. The estimated relationship between the actual KSLOC and the estimates is the following:

$$\text{ABC Cobol KSLOC} = 6 + 1.68 \text{ (function points estimated KSLOC)} \qquad \bar{R}^2:$$

$$(4.69) \qquad\qquad 65.6\%$$

In general, these results seem to validate Albrecht's claims that function points do correlate well with eventual SLOC. The results for the ABC were as follows:

$$\text{ABC Cobol KSLOC} = -5.0 + 0.20 \text{ (function points)} \qquad \bar{R}^2:$$

$$(4.69) \qquad\qquad 65.6\%$$

$$\text{ABC Cobol KSLOC} = -13.2 + 0.207 \text{ (function counts)}$$

$$(5.85) \qquad\qquad 75.1\%$$

Although the IBM and ABC models are apparently fairly similar, the results of an

Table 16.8 Function points: Cobol KSLOC data

Project no.	KSLOC	Albrecth KSLOC estimate	Albrecht error (%)
1	253.60	137.98	−45.59
2	40.50	53.73	32.66
3	450.00	267.33	−40.59
4	214.40	87.10	−59.37
5	449.90	152.28	−66.15
6	50.00	43.52	−12.96
8	200.00	111.38	−44.31
9	289.00	182.59	−36.82
11	254.20	184.74	−27.33
12	128.60	87.16	−32.22
13	161.40	75.52	−53.21
14	164.80	153.46	−6.88
Mean (absolute values)	221.37	128.07	38.17
Standard deviation	131.14	64.65	17.47

F-test are that we can reject the null hypothesis that the models are the same at the 99 per cent level.

The second result is that, for the ABC data, the unmodified function counts have a higher correlation than the modified function points. This suggests that the functionality represented by function counts is related to eventual SLOC, but that the 14 'complexity adjustment' factors are not adding any information for this particular sample.

16.5.5 ESTIMACS results

As explained in Section 16.4, the procedure for testing ESTIMACS was to gather the data (excluding the actual man-months), send them to MACS, and receive the estimate. This procedure was performed on nine of the 15 projects in the database. These nine were simply the first projects for which data were collected. The data for ESTIMACS are presented in Table 16.9.

The ESTIMACS average error is 85 per cent, which includes some over and some underestimates, and is the smallest average error of the four models. This may be due to the similarity of the ESTIMACS application base (originally an insurance firm) and the ABC database, although this cannot be verified owing to the proprietary nature of the ESTIMACS data. The regression data were as follows:

$$\text{Actual man-months} = 31 + 0.723 \, (\text{ESTIMACS}) \qquad \bar{R}^2:$$

$$(1.50) \qquad\qquad\qquad 13.4\%$$

Although the average error was less, the fit with the actual effort is worse than the other models. The t statistic is also less, although still significant at approximately the 92 per cent confidence level.

To check the possibility that the nine-project subset estimated by ESTIMACS was somehow different from the 15-project data set as a whole, each of the models and

Table 16.9 ESTIMACS **data**

Project no.	Actuals MM	ESTIMACS	ESTIMACS error (%)
1	287.00	230.26	−19.77
2	85.20	111.26	34.86
3	1107.31	523.51	−52.72
4	86.90	234.59	169.95
5	336.30	687.63	104.47
8	130.30	389.26	198.74
10	72.00	67.20	−6.67
11	258.70	624.43	141.37
12	230.70	324.78	40.78
Mean (absolute values)	287.97	354.77	85.48
Standard deviation	322.48	219.66	70.36

its inputs were run against only that nine-project data set. The results were the following:

$$\text{Actual man-months} = 54.1 + 0.084\,(\text{SLIM})$$
$$(10.17)$$
$\bar{R}^2$: 92.8%

$$\text{Actual man-months} = 11.4 + 0.195\,(\text{COCOMO–Basic})$$
$$(10.82)$$
93.6%

$$\text{Actual man-months} = 51 + 0.17\,(\text{COCOMO–Intermediate})$$
$$(12.24)$$
94.9%

$$\text{Actual man-months} = 40.3 + 0.181\,(\text{COCOMO–Detailed})$$
$$(11.62)$$
94.4%

$$\text{Actual man-months} = -203 + 0.451\,(\text{function points})$$
$$(4.63)$$
71.8%

$$\text{Actual man-months} = -175 + 0.426\,(\text{function count})$$
$$(4.09)$$
66.2%

$$\text{Actual man-months} = -94 + 1.67\,(\text{KDSI})$$
$$(2.90)$$
44.5%

$$\text{Actual man-months} = -102 + 1.68\,(\text{KSLOC})$$
$$(2.83)$$
43.2%

It does not appear that this nine-project subset was any more difficult to estimate than the full 15-project data set. In fact, SLIM, function points and all three versions of COCOMO did better on the subset. Only KDSI and KSLOC did slightly worse, and these are not inputs to ESTIMACS. If anything, this suggests that the six projects not estimated by ESTIMACS were more difficult to estimate accurately than the original nine.

Another possibility may be related to how the input data for the ESTIMACS analysis were collected. Of the 25 required data items five deserve special mention: (1) number of major business functions; (2) number of unique business inputs; (3) number of unique business outputs; (4) number of logical files; and (5) number of on-line inquiry types. These factors (which ESTIMACS collectively refers to as 'volume') tend to drive most estimates.[11] Upon examining the ESTIMACS documentation, the last four of these questions sound exactly like the 1979 version of Albrecht's function points. For example, here are two direct quotations on the subject of inputs, the first by Albrecht and the second by Rubin:

External Input types   Count each unique user data or user control input type that enters the external boundary of the application being measured, and adds or changes data in a logical internal file type. An external input type should be considered unique if it has a different format, or if the external design requires a processing logic different from other external input types of the same format ... Do not include the input part of the external inquiry types as external input types, because these are counted as external inquiry types. (Albrecht and Gaffney 1983; reproduced as Chapter 8 above)

Number of External Inputs   How many unique logical business inputs will the system process? This is a count of the number of major data types that will enter the system from outside of it. In this way internal data base information is excluded from this total. On-line inquiry only screens are also excluded. Think in terms of major business communication transactions. Inputs counted should be unique in that they require different processing logic from other inputs (Rubin 1984)

These two questions appear to address the same concept, and Albrecht's (1979) paper is cited in Rubin's (1983) paper. Therefore, in conducting this research, the function point definitions were used to answer the matching ESTIMACS questions. According to the MACS staff, however, this may result in overestimating these input quantities by a factor of three[12] or four.[13] How the difference is defined was not available from MACS, so 'correct' use of the model may come only with experience. This begets the question of whether the use of function points for the 'function-point-like' questions affected the model's performance. If the estimates had been uniformly high, then this would seem a likely possibility. However, given that the estimate errors ranged from −52.7 per cent to + 198.7 per cent, this does not seem to be the case.

16.5.6 Sensitivity analysis

As discussed in Section 16.3, this data set of 15 completed software projects is large relative to many other published studies. However, it is still small in terms of what

---

[11] Personal correspondence, P. Madden, July 1985.
[12] Personal correspondence, L. Kleeck, 18 July 1985.
[13] Personal correspondence, P. Madden, 13 August 1985.

researchers might like in order to assure that the results are robust. In particular, readers should note the sensitivity of the regression models to project number 3, which, although almost exactly equal to project number 5 in its KSLOC count, is several times larger in its actual man-months figure. Were this project to be dropped from the data set, almost all of the regression models on the new 14-point data set (particularly COCOMO's would exhibit decreases in their $\bar{R}^2$, the measure of 'goodness of fit'. The sole exceptions to this were the KDSI and KSLOC regressions, which exhibited very slight increases. This last result is likely due to the elimination of one of the two similarly sized projects (450 KSLOC) that had very different productivity rates. This would tend to make the remaining large project somewhat of an 'anchor' for the regression.

A similar analysis was done for the nine-project 'ESTIMACS subset'. The results of the regressions run on the eight-project subset were that the $\bar{R}^2$ for SLIM, COCOMO and ESTIMACS were all in the 38–49 per cent range. The results for function points and function counts decreased to the 54–60 per cent range, and the results for KSLOC and KSI increased to the 56–59 per cent range. Again, this last result is likely due to the elimination of one of the two similarly sized projects (450 KSLOC) that had very different productivity rates. As a test of this, the data were rerun on a seven-project subset without either of the largest projects. The models whose performance improved with the eight-project data set (ESTIMACS, KSLOC, KDSI) all worsened as a result. Therefore, the improvements seemed only related to the creation of project number 5 as a new 'anchor'. Consequently, project number 3 was not dropped, given that there was no *a priori* reason for doing so, plus the new regression models' increased dependence on project number 5, the 'new outlier' if project number 3 were dropped.

Owing to large differences in project productivity, variation such as the difference between projects number 3 and number 5 is not uncommon in project data. As an example, Albrecht's 24-project data set contains the following two projects:

	KSLOC	Man-hours (thousands)
Project no. 1	130	102.4
Project no. 2	318	105.2
24-project mean	61	21.9
24-project standard deviation	62	27.8

The difference between his largest project (number 2) and the next largest (number 1), in terms of KSLOC, is 188, which is a difference of 3.03 standard deviations. The equivalent calculation for the ABC data is 2.93 standard deviations. The difference between Albrecht's largest project and the mean is 257, or 4.15 standard deviations, whereas the equivalent calculation for ABC is 3.38. Therefore, the ABC data has a less severe outlier problem than even Albrecht's data.

The existence of these outliers and large variations in productivity is not a particularly desirable situation from a research perspective. However, given the difficultly and cost in gathering this kind of data, the best available data is relatively small sets that are subject to this type of condition.

16.6 CONCLUSIONS

Having examined each model independently, it seems appropriate to summarize these results. Specifically, it is time to address the questions posed in the Introduction to this paper to see what answers have been provided by this research. Of course, it will be important to bear in mind that these results stem from 15 projects developed by one firm, and overly broad generalizations are not possible. Rather, these results suggest certain hypotheses that may be verifiable with further research.

16.6.1 Implications for practitioners

The first research question to be answered concerned the accuracy of the models outside their original environments and the ease with which they could be recalibrated to fit a new environment. One conclusion is that models developed in different environments do not work very well uncalibrated, as might be expected. Average error rates calculated using the MRE formula ranged from 85 to 772 per cent, with many in the 500–600 per cent range. This variation is most likely due to the degree to which the productivity of the environments in which the models were developed matches the target (ABC) environment. This points out the need for organizations that wish to use algorithmic estimating tools to collect historical data on their projects in order to calibrate the models for local conditions.

After allowing for calibration, the best of the models explain 88 per cent of the behaviour of the actual man-month effort in this data set. The result alone probably justifies consideration of an algorithmic estimating method by a software manager who has sufficient data to calibrate it to his or her environment. In addition, there are benefits to the estimation task simply from the structure the models impose on the estimation process. Providing inputs for model parameters and sizing estimates requires a project team carefully to consider many important aspects of the upcoming project. Of course, as the model developers themselves point out, these models are adjuncts to, not substitutes for, a detailed estimate by task by the project management (Albrecht and Gaffney 1983; reproduced as Chapter 8 above).

The second research question concerned the relative efficacy of SLOC models versus non-SLOC models. In terms of the MRE results, the non-SLOC models (function points and ESTIMACS) did better, although this is likely due to their development in business data processing environments similar to ABC's. In terms of the regression results, both of the SLOC models (COCOMO and SLIM) had higher correlations than either ESTIMACS or function points. However, this data must be considered in light of an important implementation question. The SLOC counts were obtained *ex post* and are therefore likely to be much more accurate than SLOC counts obtained before a project begins. Although SLIM does provide a means for modelling this initial uncertainty (through a beta distribution approach), it is unlikely that a project manager could estimate SLOC counts with the degree of accuracy used in this research. Presumably, the variance between *ex ante* and *ex post* function point counts is less, although verifying this is an open research question.

An additional consideration is that function points and function counts can be used as predictors of KSLOC. In particular, function counts correlated with KSLOC at the level of 75.1 per cent, which is similar to the correlations published by Albrecht (Albrecht and Gaffney 1983), and is likely to be good enough to be of use to the software manager.

The third and final research question concerns the relation between the proprietary and the non-proprietary models. This question was not answered conclusively by this research, as the proprietary SLIM model outperformed (in its $\bar{R}^2$ value) the non-proprietary COCOMO model on this data set, while the non-proprietary function points model outperformed the proprietary ESTIMACS model on this data set.

16.6.2 Directions for future research

This paper has provided several important research results regarding software metrics and models. First, Albrecht's model for estimating man-months of effort from function points has been validated on an independent data set. This is particularly significant in that function points have been proposed by IBM as a general productivity measure and prior to this there was only limited evidence for their utility from non-IBM sources (see Behrens 1983).

One interesting research question raised by this function points result is the degree to which *ex ante* and *ex post* function points counts are similar. As pointed out in the previous section, the higher correlations generated by the SLOC-based models must be tempered by a recognition that, in practice, accurate *ex ante* SLOC estimates may be difficult to achieve. An interesting research question involves the degree to which initial mis-estimates change the results achieved by these models. A more general extension of this is, what impact do the estimates themselves have on projects? A recent paper by Abdel-Hamid and Madnick (1986) discusses this issue from a systems dynamics perspective. The authors make the point that the effort required on a software development project is in part a function of the estimate given at the beginning of the project. From this premise they devise a model (not shown in the cited paper) that presumably includes the estimate as an endogenous variable. They then develop an example to show that an estimate that was more accurate could also be more expensive in terms of creating a bigger project.

Although an interesting example, one problem with it is that the authors draw the unsupported conclusion that the accuracy of software cost estimation models cannot be judged by their performance on historical (completed) projects. Clearly, *ex post* estimates cannot influence the project. Therefore, it seems reasonable to evaluate them by this method. It could be argued that software cost estimation models that do not include their own estimate are deficient, but this is a different conclusion from the one drawn by the authors. However, their idea of the effect of the estimate on a project is an interesting one, and further research should be done in this area.

Finally, although improving estimation techniques within the industry is a worthwhile goal, the ultimate question must concern how the productivity of software developers can be improved. These estimation and productivity questions are related, in that the estimation models contain descriptions of what factors their developers believe affect productivity. How well do these models identify and reflect these factors?

The models researched in this study do not seem to capture productivity factors very well. There are several pieces of evidence to support this conclusion. The first is that the COCOMO-Intermediate and COCOMO-Detailed models (the versions with the productivity factor 'cost drivers') did not perform significantly better than the Basic model and in fact correlated less well with actual man-months. Second, the raw function count data correlated as well as or better than the function point numbers, which reflect the 14 'processing complexity' adjustments. Third, ESTIMACS, with its 20 additional productivity-related questions, did less well than the similar function counts alone. Finally, the model that had the highest correlation, SLIM, has the problem that its questions, designed to elicit productivity-related information, uniformly generated PFs that were too low (the reason why all the default estimates were too large) and MBIs that were too high. This was determined by comparing these values to the values that would have been obtained had the SLIM 'calibrate' feature been used.

A reasonable conclusion from all this is that the models, although an improvement over their raw inputs for estimating project effort, do not model the factors affecting productivity very well. One possible extension of this research is to analyse the data in this study to attempt to determine the causes for the wide swings in accuracy of the estimates across projects. What characteristics make a project amenable to this type of estimation? What factors could be added to the models to enable them to do a better job on all of the projects? On the productivity side, the projects in this data set show a large amount of variance in terms of such traditional metrics as SLOC per man-month. Can these variations be traced to productivity factors controllable by the software manager? What are the effects of modern programming practices, such as the use of fourth-generation languages, or AI techniques? Further research needs to be done to isolate and measure these factors affecting systems professionals' productivity if the profession is to meet the challenges of the future.

ACKNOWLEDGEMENTS

I wish to thank Fred Forman, Charles Kriebel and Mary Shaw for their assistance with this paper. Additional thanks to Douglas Putnam of Quantitative Software Management and Patrick Madden of Management and Computer Services for permission to use their models during this research.

BIBLIOGRAPHY

It should be apparent from the length of this bibliography, that the software engineering metrics literature is extensive. However, there are a number of ways to access these sources. Each paper within this anthology cites references which the interested reader may pursue. In addition, under the headings given below, some primary sources are indicated that are useful starting points for those wishing to delve further into the field.

Annotated bibliographies

See Cook (1982); Waguespack and Badlani (1987); Basili (1990); Ince (1990); Fenton (1991).

Metrics overview

See Perlis *et al.* (1981); Conte *et al.* (1986); Shepperd (1988b); Ince and Shepperd (1988); Rook (1990); for a more theoretical treatment Zuse (1991) and Fenton (1991).

Software engineering background

See Pressman (1992) and Sommerville (1992).

Project management background

See DeMarco (1982); Humphrey (1989); Gilb (1988).

Implementing a metrics programme

See Humphrey (1989) and the classic Grady and Caswell (1987).

Cost estimation

See Jones (1986); Londeix (1987); Boehm (1981).

Abdel-Hamid, T. K. and Madnick, S. E. (1982), 'A model of software project management dynamics', *Proceedings. IEEE. COMPSAC 82*, November pp. 539–54.

—— —— (1986), 'Impact of schedule estimation on software project behaviour', *IEEE Software*, 3(4): 70–5.

ACM (1980), 'Self assessment procedure VII', *CACM*, 23(8).

Adam, M. F., LeGall, G., Moreau, B. and Vallete, B. (1988), 'Towards an observatory aiming at controlling the software quality', *Proceedings. IEE/BCS Conference Software Engineering '88*, pp. 50–4.

Aho, A. V. and Ullman, J. D. (1977), *Principles of Compiler Design*, Addison-Wesley, Reading, Mass., ch. 12.

Akiyama, F. (1971), 'An example of system software debugging', *Proceedings IFIP Congress*, pp. 353–8.

Albrecht, A. J. (1979), 'Measuring application development productivity', *Proceedings IBM Applications Development Symposium, SHARE-GUIDE*, pp. 83–92.

—— (1984) 'AD/M productivity measurement and estimate validation', CIS and A Guideline 313, IBM Corporate Information Systems and Administration, November.

—— and Gaffney, J. R. (1983), 'Software function, source lines of code, and development effort prediction: a software science validation', *IEEE Transactions on Software Engineering*, 9(6): 639–48. Reproduced as Chapter 8 above.

Alexander, C. (1964), *Notes on the Synthesis of Form*, Harvard University Press, Cambridge, Mass.

Allen, A. O. (1978), *Probability, Statistics and Queueing Theory, with Computer Science Applications*, Academic Press, New York.

Allen, F. (1974), 'Interprocedural analysis and the information derived by it', *LNCS*, no. 23, Springer-Verlag, Berlin.

—— and Cooke, J. (1976), 'A program data flow analysis procedure', *CACM*, 19(3).

Anderberg, M. R. (1973), *Cluster Analysis for Applications*, Academic Press, New York.

Aron, J. D. (1969), 'Estimating resources for large programming systems', (unpublished paper), NATO Science Committee, Rome.

Arthur, L. J. (1985), *Measuring Programmer Productivity and Software Quality*, Wiley-Interscience, New York.

Bailey, C. and Dingee, W. (1981), 'A software study using Halstead metrics', *ACM SIGMETRICS Performance Evaluation Review*, 10(Spring): 189–97.

Bailey, J. J. and Basili, V. R. (1981), 'A meta-model for software development resource expenditures', *Proceedings 5th International Conference Software Engineering*, pp. 107–16.

Baker, A. L. and Zweben, S. (1979), 'The use of software science in evaluating modularity concepts', *IEEE Transactions on Software Engineering*, 5(2): 110–20.

—— —— (1980), 'A comparison of measures of control flow complexity', *IEEE Transactions on Software Engineering*, SE-6(6): 506–11.

Balut, N., Halstead, M. H. and Bayer, R. (1974), 'Experimental validation of a structural property of FORTRAN programs', *Proceedings ACM National Conference*, pp. 207–11.

Banker, R. D. and Kemerer, C. F. (1989), 'Scale economies in new software development', *IEEE Transactions on Software Engineering*, 15(10): 1199–1205.

—— Datar, S. M. and Kemerer, C. F. (1991), 'A model to evaluate variables impacting the productivity of software maintenance projects', *Management Science*, 37(1).

Barr, Goodnight, Sall and Helwig, (1976), *A User's Guide to SAS*, SAS Institute, Raleigh, NC.

Basili, V. R. (1979), 'Quantitative software complexity models: a panel summary', *Workshop on Quantitative Software Models for Reliability, Complexity and Cost*, pp. 243–5.

—— (1980), 'Tutorial on models and metrics for software and engineering', IEEE Cat. EHO-167-7, October.

—— (1981), 'Evaluating software development characteristics: an assessment of software measures in the Software Engineering Laboratory', *Proceedings 6th Annual Software Engineering Workshop, NASA/GSFC*.

—— (1985), 'Quantitative evaluation of software engineering methodology, *Proceedings 1st Pan–Pacific Computer Conference* (Melbourne).

—— (1989), 'Software development: a paradigm for the future', *Proceedings COMPSAC, 13th Annual Computer Software and Applications Conference*, pp. 471–85.

—— (1990), 'Recent advances in software measurement', *Proceedings 12th IEEE International Conference on Software Engineering* (Nice), pp. 44-51.

—— and Freburger, K. (1981), 'Programming measurement and estimation in the Software Engineering Laboratory', *J. Systems and Software*, 2: 47–57.

—— and Hutchens, D. H. (1983), 'An empirical study of a syntactic complexity family', *IEEE Transactions on Software Engineering*, 9(6): 664–72.

—— and Katz, E. (1983), 'Metrics of interest in Ada development', *Proceedings IEEE Computer Society Workshop Software Engineering Technology Transfer*, pp. 22–9.

—— and Perricone, B. T. (1984), 'Software errors and complexity: an empirical investigation', *CACM*, 27(1): 42–52. Reproduced as Chapter 10 above.

—— and Phillips, T. (1981), 'Evaluating and comparing the software metrics in the Software Engineering Laboratory', *ACM SIGMETRICS, Performance Evaluation Review*, 10(Spring): 95–106.

—— and Reiter, R. W. (1979a), 'Evaluating automatable measures of software development', *Proceedings of IEEE Workshop on Quantitative Software Models*, pp. 107–16.

—— —— (1979b), 'An investigation of human factors in software development', *IEEE Computer*, 12(12): 21–38.

—— —— (1981), 'A controlled experiment quantitatively comparing software development approaches', *IEEE Transactions on Software Engineering*, 7(5).

—— and Rombach, H. D. (1987), 'Tailoring the software process to project goals and environments', *Proceedings 9th International Software Engineering Conference*, pp. 345–57.

—— —— (1988), 'The TAME project: Towards improvement-oriented software environments', *IEEE Transactions on Software Engineering*, 14(6): 758–73.

—— and Selby, R. W. (1984), 'Data collection and analysis in software research and management', *Proceedings American Statistical Association and Biometric Society Joint Statistics Meetings*, August.

—— —— and Hutchens, D. H. (1986), 'Experimentation in software engineering', *IEEE Transactions on Software Engineering*, 12(7): 733–8.

—— —— —— and Phillips, T. Y. (1983), 'Metric analysis and data validation across Fortran projects', *IEEE Transactions on Software Engineering*, 9(6): 652–63.

—— and Turner, A. J. (1975), 'Iterative enhancements: a practical technique for software development', *IEEE Transactions on Software Engineering*, 1(6): 390–6.

—— and Weiss, D. M. (1981), 'Evaluation of a software requirements document by analysis of change data', *Proceedings 5th International Conference on Software Engineering*, pp. 314–23.

—— —— (1982a), 'A methodology for collecting valid software engineering data', University of Maryland Technical Report, no. TR-1235, December.

—— —— (1982b), 'Evaluating software development by analysis of changes: the data from the Software Engineering Laboratory', University of Maryland Technical Report, no. TR-1236, December.

—— —— (1984), 'A methodology for collecting valid software engineering data', *IEEE Transactions on Software Engineering*, 10(3): 728–38.

—— and Zelkowitz, M. V. (1978), 'Analyzing medium-scale software development', *Proceedings 3rd International Conference on Software Engineering*, pp. 116–23.

—— —— (1979), 'Measuring software development characteristics in local environments', *Computers and Structures*, 10: 39–43.

Bauer, F. (1975), 'Variables considered harmful', *Proceedings International Summer School on Languages, Hierarchies and Interfaces*, LNCS no. 46, Springer-Verlag, Berlin.

Beane, J., Giddings, N. and Silverman, J. (1984), 'Quantifying software designs', *Proceedings 7th International Software Engineering Conference*, pp. 314–22.

Behrens, C. A. (1983), 'Measuring the productivity of computer systems development activities with function points', *IEEE Transactions on Software Engineering*, 9(6): 649–58.

Belady, L. A. (1978), 'Measures and empirical studies', *Proceedings 2nd Software Life Cycle Management Workshop*, pp. 44–6 August.

—— (1979), 'On software complexity', *Proceedings of IEEE Workshop on Quantitative Software Models for Reliability, Complexity and Cost*, pp. 90–4, October.

—— and Evangelisti, C. J. (1979), 'System partitioning and its measure', IBM Research Report No. RC7560.

—— —— (1981), 'System partitioning and its measure', *J. Systems and Software*, 2(1): 23–9.

—— and Lehman, M. M. (1976), 'A model of large system development', *IBM Systems J.*, 15(3): 225–52.

—— —— (1979), 'Characteristics of large systems', in P. Wegner (ed.), *Research Directions in Software Technology*, MIT Press, Cambridge, Mass.

Benington, H. D. (1956), 'Production of large computer programs', *Proceedings ONR Symposium Advanced Programming Methods for Digital Computers*, pp. 115–27, June.

Benyon-Tinker, G. (1979), 'Complexity measures in an evolving large system', *Proceedings ACM Workshop on Quantitative Software Models*, pp. 117–27.

Berge, C. (1973), *Graphs and Hypergraphs*, North-Holland, Amsterdam.

Berland, G. D. (1978), 'Structured design methodologies', *Proceedings of the Design Automation Conference*, no. 15, June.

Beser, N. (1982), 'Foundations and experiments in software science', *ACM SIGMETRICS Performance Evaluation Review*, 11(3): 48–72.

Black, R. K. D., Curnow, R. P., Katz, R. and Gray, M. D. (1977), 'BCS software production data', Boeing Computer Services, Inc.: Final Technical Report, no. RADC-TR-77-116, NTIS AD-A039852, March.

Blum, M. (1967), 'On the size of machines', *Information Control*, 11: 257–65.

Boehm, B. W. (1973), 'Software and its impact: a quantitative assessment', *Datamation*, pp. 48–59, May.

—— (1976), 'Software engineering', *IEEE Transactions on Computers*, C-25(12): 1226–41.

—— (1981), *Software Engineering Economics*, Prentice-Hall, Englewood Cliffs, NJ.

—— (1984), 'Software engineering economics', *IEEE Transactions on Software Engineering*, 10(1): 4–21. Reproduced as Chapter 7 above.

—— Brown, J. R. and Lipow, M. (1976), 'Quantitative evaluation of software quality', *Proceedings 2nd IEEE International Software Engineering Conference*.

—— —— Kaspar, H., Lipow, M., MacLeod, G. J. and Merritt, M. J. (1978), *Characteristics of Software Quality*, North-Holland, Amsterdam.

—— Elwell, J. F., Pyster, A. B., Stuckle, E. D. and Williams, R. D. (1982), 'The TRW software productivity system', *Proceedings IEEE 6th International Conference on Software Engineering*, September.

—— Gray, T. E. and Seewaldt, T. (1984), 'Prototyping vs. specifying: a multi-project experiment', *IEEE Transactions on Software Engineering*, 10(3): 290–303.

Bohrer, R. (1975), 'Halstead's criteria and statistical algorithms', *Proceedings 8th Computer Science/Statistics Interface Symposium*, February.

Bowen, J. B. (1978), 'Are current approaches sufficient for measuring software quality?' *Proceedings Software Quality Assurance Workshop*, pp. 148–55.

—— (1979), 'A survey of standards and proposed metrics for software quality testing', *IEEE Computer*, 12: 37–42.

—— (1984), 'Module size: a standard or heuristic?' *J. Systems and Software*, 4: 327–32.

Bowles, A. J. (1983), 'Effects of design complexity on software maintenance', doctoral thesis, Northwestern University.

Brainerd, W. (1978), 'Fortran 77', *CACM*, 21: 806–20.

Brinch Hansen, P. (1977), *The Architecture of Concurrent Programs*, Prentice-Hall, Englewood Cliffs, NJ.

Britcher, R. N. and Gaffney, J. E. (1982), 'Estimates of software size from state machine designs', *Proceedings NASA–Goddard Software Engineering Workshop*, December.

Brooks, F. P. (1975), *The Mythical Man-month: Essays on Software Engineering*, Addison-Wesley, Reading, Mass.

Brooks, R. (1978), Unpublished algorithm, Department of Information and Computer Science, University of California at Irvine.

Brooks, R. E. (1980), 'Studying programmer behaviour experimentally: the problems of proper methodology, *CACM*, 23(4): 207–13.

Brown, J. R. and Fischer, K. F. (1978), 'A graph-theoretic approach to the verification of program structures', *Proceedings IEEE 3rd International Conference on Software Engineering*, (Atlanta), pp. 136–41, May.

Brown, P. J. (1980), 'Why does software die?' in Life-Cycle Management, *Infotech State of the Art Report*, 8(7).

Bulut, N. and Halstead, M. H. (1974), 'Impurities found in algorithm implementations', *ACM SIGPLAN Notices*, 9(3).

—— —— and Bayer, R. (1974), 'The experimental verification of a structural property of Fortran programs', *Proceedings ACM Annual Conference* (San Diego).

Callisen, H. and Colborne, S. A. (1984), 'A proposed method for estimating software cost from requirements', *J. Parametrics*, 4(4): 23–32.

Cammack, W. B. and Rogers, H. J. (1973), 'Improving the programming process', IBM Technical Report, no. TR 00.2483, October.

Canning, J. T. (1985), 'The application of software metrics to large-scale systems', PhD thesis, Virginia Polytechnic Institute.

Card, D. N. and Agresti, W. W. (1987), 'Resolving the software science anomaly', *J. Systems and Software*, 7: 29–35.

—— —— (1988), 'Measuring software design complexity', *J. Systems and Software*, 8: 185–97.

Carriere, W. M. and Thibodeau, R. (1979), 'Development of a logistics software cost estimating technique for foreign military sales', General Research Corporation Report, no. CR-3-839, June.

Channon, R. N. (1974), 'On a measure of program structure', in Bernard Robinet (ed.), *Programming Symposium Proceedings*, Springer-Verlag, Berlin.

Chapin, N. (1978), 'Data accessibility in structured programming', *Proceedings National Computer Conference '78*, pp. 597–603.

—— (1979), 'A measure of software complexity', *Proceedings National Computer Conference '79*, pp. 995–1002.

Chen, E. T. (1978), 'Programmer complexity and programmer productivity', *IEEE Transactions on Software Engineering*, 4(3): 187–94.

Christensen, K., Fitsos, G. P. and Smith, C. (1981), 'A perspective on software science', *IBM Systems J.*, 20(4): 372–87.

Cobb, G. W. (1978), 'A measurement of structure for unstructured languages', *Proceedings of ACM Sigmetrics/Sigsoft Software Quality Assurance Workshop*.

Cohen, J. and Cohen, P. (1975), *Applied Multiple Regression/Correlation Analysis for the Behavioural Sciences*, John Wiley, New York.

Collofello, J. L. (1983), 'A conceptual foundation for measuring software maintainability', *Proceedings Workshop on Software Maintenance*, pp. 253–4.

—— and Woodfield, S. N. (1983), 'A proposed maintenance environment', *Proceedings Workshop on Software Maintenance*, pp. 118–19.

—— —— and Gibbs, N. E. (1983), 'Software productivity measurement', *Proceedings AFIPS 83*, pp. 757–62.

Comer, D. and Halstead, M. H. (1979), 'A simple experiment in top-down design', *IEEE Transactions on Software Engineering*, 5(2): 105–9.

Conte, S. D., Shen, V. Y. and Dickey, K. (1982), 'On the effect of different counting rules for control flow operators on software science metrics in FORTRAN', *ACM SIGMETRICS Performance Evaluation Review*, 11(2): 118–26.

—— Dunsmore, H. E. and Shen, V. Y. (1986), *Software Engineering Metrics and Models*, Benjamin Cummings, Menlo Park, CA.

Cook, M. L. (1982), 'Software metrics: an introduction and annotated bibliography', *ACM SIGSOFT S.E.N.*, 7(2): 41–60.

Coulter, N. S. (1981), 'Applications of psychology in software science', *Proceedings COMPSAC '81*, pp. 50–1.

—— (1983), 'Software science and cognitive psychology', *IEEE Transactions on Software Engineering*, 9(2): 166–71.

Cowderoy, A. J. C. and Jenkins, J. O. (1988), 'Cost estimation by analogy as a good management practice', *Proceedings IEE/BCS Conference: Software Engineering '88*, pp. 80–4.

Crawford, S., McIntosh, A. and Pregibon, D. (1985), 'An analysis of static metrics and faults in C software', *J. Systems and Software*, 5(1): 37–48.

Cruikshank, R. D. and Gaffney, J. E. (1980), 'Measuring the development process: software design coupling and strength metrics', *Proceedings 5th Annual Software Engineering Workshop*.

Curtis, B. (1979), 'In search of software complexity', *Proceedings of Workshop on Quantitative Software Complexity Models*, pp. 95–106.

—— (1983), 'Software metrics: guest editor's introduction', *IEEE Transactions on Software Engineering*, 9(6): 637–8.

—— Kellner, M. and Over, J. (1992), 'Process modelling', *CACM*, 35(9): 75–90.

—— Sheppard, S., Milliman, P., Borst, M. and Love, T. (1979a), 'Measuring the psychological complexity of software maintenance tasks with the Halstead and McCabe Metrics', *IEEE Transactions on Software Engineering*, 5(2): 96–104.

—— —— —— (1979b), 'Third time charm; stronger prediction of programmer performance by software complexity metrics', *Proceedings 4th IEEE International Conference on Software Engineering*, pp. 356–60. Reproduced as Chapter 9 above.

Dahl, O. J., Dijkstra, E. W. and Hoare, C. A. R. (1972), *Structured Programming*, Academic Press, London.

Daly, E. B. and Mnichowicz, D. A. (1978), 'Management of software development for stored program switching systems', *Telephone Engineering Management*, (May): 120–8.

Davis, J. S. (1984), 'Chunks: a basis for complexity measurement', *Information Processing and Management*, 20(1–2): 119–27.

—— and LeBlanc, R. J. (1988), 'A study of the applicability of complexity measures', *IEEE Transactions on Software Engineering*, 14(9): 1366–72.

Dekerf, J. L. F. (1981), 'APL and Halstead's theory of software metrics', *ACM APL Quote Quad*, (12 Sept.): 89–93.

DeMarco, T. (1982), *Controlling Software Projects: Management, Measurement and Estimation*, Yourdon Press, New York.

Demshki, M., Ligett, D., Linn, B., McCluskey, G. and Miller, R. (1982), 'Wang Institute cost model (WICOMO) tool user's manual', Wang Institute of Graduate Studies, Tyngsboro, Mass., June.

Dijkstra, E. W. (1968a), 'Goto statement considered harmful', *Communications of ACM*, 11(8): 453–7.

—— (1968b), 'The structure of the THE multiprogramming system', *CACM*, 11(5): 341–6.

Dircks, H. F. (1981), 'SOFCOST: Grumman's software cost eliminating model', *IEEE NAECON 1981*, May.

DoD (1982), Reference Manual for the Ada Programming Language, US Department of Defense, draft revised MIL-STD 1815, July.

Doerflinger, C. W. and Basili, V. R. (1983), 'Monitoring software through dynamic variables', *Proceedings IEEE COMPSAC '83*,

Druffel, L. E. (1982), 'Strategy for DoD software initiative', RADC/DACS, Griffiss AFB, New York.

Dubes, R. and Jain, A. K. (1980), 'Clustering methodologies in exploratory data analysis', in M. C. Yovits (ed.), *Advances in Computing*, vol. 19, Academic Press, London.

Duclos, L. C. (1982), 'Simulation model for the life-cycle of a software product: a quality assurance approach', PhD dissertation, University of Southern California.

Dumas, R. L. (1983), 'Final report: software acquisition resource expenditure (SARE) data collection methodology', *MTR 9031*, MITRE Corporation, September.

Dunsmore, H. E. (1984), 'Software metrics: an overview of an evolving methodology', *Information Processing and Management*, 20(1–2): 183–92.

—— (1985), 'The effect of comments, mnemonic names and modularity: some university experiment results', *Proceedings 2nd Symposium on Empirical Foundations of Information and Software Sciences*.

—— and Gannon, J. (1979), 'Data referencing: an empirical investigation', *IEEE Computer*, December.

—— —— (1980), 'An analysis of the effects of programming factors on programming effort', *J. Systems and Software*, 1(2): 141–53.

Duran, B. S. and Odell, P. L. (1974), *Cluster Analysis: A Survey*, Springer-Verlag, New York.

Ejiogu, L. O. (1985), 'Lemcomm softgram: a simple measure of software complexity', *ACM SIGPLAN Notices*, 20(3): 16–31.

Elshoff, J. L. (1976a), 'Measuring commercial programs using Halstead's criteria', *ACM SIGPLAN Notices*, 11(5): 38–46.

—— (1976b), 'An analysis of some commercial PL/1 programs', *IEEE Transactions on Software Engineering*, 2(3): 113–20.

—— (1978a), 'A review of software measurement studies at General Motors Research Laboratories', *Proceedings 2nd IEEE Annual Software Life Cycle Management Workshop*.

—— (1978b), 'An investigation into the effects of the counting method used on software science measurements', *ACM SIGPLAN Notices*, 13(2): 30–45.

—— (1984), 'Characteristic program complexity measures', *Proceedings 7th International Conference on Software Engineering*, pp. 288–93.

Emerson, T. J. (1984), 'A discriminant metric for module cohesion', *Proceedings 7th International Conference on Software Engineering*, pp. 294–303.

Endres, A. (1975), 'An analysis of errors and their causes in system programs', *IEEE Transactions on Software Engineering*, 1(2): 140–9.

Evangelist, W. M. (1982), 'Software complexity metric sensitivity to program structuring rules', *J. Systems and Software*, 3: 231–43.

—— (1983a), 'Relationships among computational, software and intuitional complexity', *ACM SIGPLAN Notices*, 18(12): 57–9.

—— (1983b), 'Software complexity metric sensitivity to program structuring rules', *J. Systems and Software*, 3(3): 231–43.

—— (1984), 'Program complexity and programming style', *Proceedings IEEE International Conference on Data Engineering*, pp. 534–41.

Everitt, B. (1974), *Cluster Analysis*, Heinemann, London.

Fenton, N. E. (1990), 'Software measurement: theory, tools and validation', *Software Engineering J.*, 6(1): 65–78.

—— (1991), *Software Metrics: A Rigorous Approach*, Chapman and Hall, London.

—— and Whitty, R. W. (1986), 'Axiomatic approach to software metrification through program decomposition', *Computer Journal*, 29(4): 330–40.

Ferens, D. V. (1984), 'Software support cost models: quo vadis?' *J. Parametrics*, 4(4): 64–99.

Feuer, A. R. and Fowlkes, E. B. (1979), 'Some results from an empirical study of computer software', *Proceedings of Fourth IEEE International Conference on Software Engineering*, pp. 351–5.

Fitsos, G. (1980), 'Vocabulary effects in software science', *Proceedings COMPSAC 80*, pp. 751–6.

Fitzsimmons, A. (1978), 'Relating the presence of software errors to the theory of software science', *11th Hawaii International Conference on Systems Science*, vol. 1, pp. 40–6.

—— and Love, T. (1978), 'A review and evaluation of software sciences', *ACM Computing Surveys*, 10: 3–18.

Fosdick, L. and Osterweil, L. (1976), 'Data flow analysis in software reliability', *ACM Computer Surveys*, September.

Freiman, F. R. and Park, R. D. (1979), 'PRICE software model. Version 3: An overview', *Proceedings IEEE–PINY Workshop on Quantitative Software Models*, IEEE Cat. TH0067-9, pp. 32–41.

Funami, Y. and Halstead, M. H. (1976), 'A software physics analysis of Akiyama's debugging data', *Proceedings Symposium on Computer Software Engineering*, New York Polytechnic Institute, pp. 133–8.

Gaffney, J. E. (1979a), 'Program control, complexity and productivity', *Proceedings of IEEE Workshop on Quantitative Software Models for Reliability*, pp. 140–2.

—— (1979b), 'A comparison of a complexity-based and Halstead program size estimates', *Proceedings Annual ACM Computer Science Conference*.

—— (1981), 'Software metrics: a key to improved software development management', *Proceedings Computer Science Statistics Conference, 13th Symposium on Interface*, March.

—— Goldberg, R. and Misek-Falkoff, L. (1984), 'SCORE-82 summary', *ACM SIGMETRICS Performance Evaluation Review*, 12(4): 4–12.

Gannon, J. D. (1977), 'An experimental evaluation of data type conventions', *CACM*, 20(8): 584–95.

—— Katz, E. E. and Basili, V. R. (1986), 'Metrics for Ada packages: an initial study', *CACM*, 29(7).

Geritsen, R., Morgan, H. and Zisman, M. (1977), 'On some metrics for databases, or What is a very large database?' *ACM SIGMOD Record*, 50–74. June.

Gibson, V. R. and Senn, J. A. (1989), 'System structure and software maintenance performance', *CACM*, 32(3): 347–58.

Giddings, N. and Colburn, T. (1984), 'An automated software design evaluater', *Proceedings Annual Conference ACM 84*.

Gilb, T. (1977), *Software Metrics*, Winthrop Press, Cambridge, Mass.

—— (1988), *Principles of Software Engineering Management*, Addison-Wesley, Reading, Mass.

Gill, G. K. and Kemerer, C. F. (1991), 'Cyclomatic complexity density and software maintenance productivity', *IEEE Transactions on Software Engineering*, 17(12).

Goldberg, R. and Lorin, H. (1982), *The Economics of Information Processing*, John Wiley, New York.

Golden, J. R., Mueller, J. R. and Anselm, B. (1981), 'Software cost estimating: craft or witchcraft?' *Database*, 12(3): 12–14.

Goodenough, J. B. and Gerhart, S. L. (1975), 'Towards a theory of test data selection', *IEEE Transactions on Software Engineering*, 1(2).

Gordon, R. D. and Halstead, M. H. (1976), 'An experiment comparing Fortran programming times with the Software Physics Hypothesis', *Proceedings AFIPS*, 935–7. Reproduced as Chapter 1 above.

Gould, J. D. (1975), 'Some psychological evidence on how many people debug computer programs', *International J. of Man-Machine Studies*, 7.

Grady, R. B. and Caswell, D. L. (1987), *Software Metrics: Establishing a Company-wide Program*, Prentice-Hall, Englewood Cliffs, NJ.

Gray, R. H. M. *et al.* (1991), 'Design metrics for database systems', *BT Technology J.*, 9(4): 69–79.

Green, T. (1977), 'Conditional program statements and their comprehensibility to professional programmers', *J. of Occupational Psychology*, 50: 93–109.

Habermann, A. N., Fion, L. and Cooprider, L. (1976), 'Modularization and hierarchy in a family of operating systems', *CACM*, 19(5): 266–72.

Hall, N. R. and Preiser, S. (1984), 'Combined network complexity measures, *IBM J. Research and Development*, 28(1): 15–27.

Halstead, M. H. (1972), 'Natural laws controlling structure', *ACM SIGPLAN Notices*, 7(2).

—— (1973a), 'An experimental determination of the "purity" of a trivial algorithm', *ACM SIGMETRICS Performance Evaluation Review*, 2(1).

—— (1973b), 'Language level, a missing concept in information theory', *ACM SIGMETRICS Performance Evaluation Review*, 2(1).

—— (1975), 'Towards a theoretical basis for estimating programming efforts', *Proceedings ACM Annual Conference*.

—— (1977a), *Elements of Software Science*, Elsevier North-Holland, New York.

—— (1977b) 'On lines of code and programmer productivity', letter in *IBM Systems J., 16(4)*.

—— (1978), 'Software science: a progress report', *US Army Computer Systems Command Software Life Cycle Management Workshop*.

—— (1979a), 'Advances in software science', in M. Yovits (ed.), *Advances in Computers*, vol. 18, Academic Press, New York.

—— (1979b), 'Guest editorial on software science', *IEEE Transactions on Software Engineering*, 5(2): 74–5.

—— and Bayer, R. (1973), 'Algorithm dynamics', *Proceedings ACM Annual Conference*.

—— and Schneider, V. (1980), 'Self-assessment procedure VII', *CACM*, 23(8): 475–80.

Hamer, P. G. and Frewin, G. D. (1982), 'M. H. Halstead's software science: a critical examination', *Proceedings 6th International Conference on Software Engineering*, 197–206. Reproduced as Chapter 11 above.

Haney, F. M. (1972), 'Module connection analysis: a tool for scheduling software debugging activities', *Proceedings AFIP Fall Joint Conference*, pp. 173–9.

Hansen, W. J. (1978), 'Measurement of program complexity by the pair (cyclomatic number, operator count)', *ACM SIGPLAN Notices*, 13(3): pp. 29–33.

Harel, E. and McLean, E. R. (1982), 'The effects of using a nonprocedural computer language on programmer productivity', UCLA Information Science Working Paper no. 3-83, November.

Harrison, W. and Magel, K. (1981), 'A complexity measure based on nesting level', *ACM SIGPLAN Notices*, 16(3): 63–74.

—— —— Kluczny, R. and De Kock, A. (1982), 'Applying software complexity metrics to program maintenance', *IEEE Computer* (15 September): 65–79.

Hecht, H. (1978), *Flow Analysis of Computer Programs*, North-Holland, New York.

Henry, S. (1979), 'Information flow metrics for the evaluation of operating systems' structure', PhD thesis, Iowa State University.

—— and Kafura, D. (1981a), 'Software metrics based on information flow', *IEEE Transactions on Software Engineering*, 7(5): 510–18.

—— —— (1981b), 'Software quality metrics based on inter-connectivity', *J. Systems and Software*, 2(2): 121–31.

—— —— (1984), 'The evaluation of software systems' structure using quantitative software metrics', *Software Practice and Experience*, 14(6): 561–73. Reproduced as Chapter 6 above.

—— —— and Harris, K. (1981), 'On the relationship among three software metrics', *ACM SIGMETRICS Performance Evaluation Review*, 10: 81–8.

Herd, J. R., Postak, J. N., Russell, W. E. and Stewart, K. R. (1977), 'Software cost estimation study: study results', *Final Tech. Report. RADC-TR-77-220*, vol. 1 (of 2), Doty Associates, Inc., Rockville, Md.

Houtz, C. and Buschbach, T. (1981), 'Review and analysis of conversion cost-estimating techniques', *Report GSA/FCSC-81/001*, GSA Federal Conversion Support Center, Falls Church, Va.

Humphrey, W. S. (1989), *Managing the Software Process*, SEI Series in Software Engineering, Addison-Wesley, Reading, Mass.

—— Snyder, T. R. and Willis, R. R. (1991), 'Software process improvement at Hughes Aircraft', *IEEE Software* (July): 11–23.

Humphreys, R. A. (1986), 'Control flow as a measure of program complexity', *UK Alvey Programme Software Reliability and Metrics Club Newsletter*, 4: 3–7.

Hutchens, D. H. and Basili, V. R. (1985), 'System structure analysis: clustering with data bindings', *IEEE Transactions on Software Engineering*, 11(8): 749–57. Reproduced as Chapter 5 above.

IFPUG (1992), Function Point Counting Practices Manual: Release 3.3, International Function Point User's Group.

Ince, D. C. (1990), 'Software metrics: an introduction', *Information and Software Technology*, 32(4): 297–303.

—— (1984), 'Module interconnection languages and Prolog', *ACM SIGPLAN Notices*, 19(8): 89–93.

—— and Hekmatpour, S. (1988), 'An approach to automated software design based on product metrics', *Software Engineering J.*, 3(2): 53–6.

—— and Shepperd, M. J. (1988), 'System design metrics: a review and perspective', *Proceedings IEE–BCS Conference Software Engineering '88* (Liverpool), IEE London, pp. 23–7.

—— —— (1989a), 'An empirical and theoretical analysis of an information flow based design metric', *Proceedings European Software Engineering Conference*, pp. 86–99. Reproduced as Chapter 15 above.

—— —— (1989b), 'Quality control of software designs using cluster analysis, *Proceedings EOQC/SQA Conference Management of Quality: Key to the Nineties*, Vienna.

—— —— (1990), 'The use of cluster techniques and system design metrics in software maintenance', *Proceedings IEE/DTI UK IT '90 Conference*, Southampton.

—— —— (1991), 'Software metrics in software engineering and artificial intelligence', *International J. Software Engineering and Knowledge Engineering*, 1(4): 463–76.

—— —— (1992), 'Graphical aids for monitoring quality metrics for project managers', *Proceedings 3rd European Conference on Software Quality Assurance*, Madrid.

Itakura, M. and Takayanagi, A. (1982), 'A model for estimating program size and its evaluation', *Proceedings IEEE 6th International Conference on Software Engineering*, pp. 104–9.

Iyengar, S. S., Parameswaran, N. and Fuller, J. (1982), 'A measure of logical complexity of programs', *Computer Languages*, 7: 147–60.

Jackson, M. A. (1975), *Principles of Program Design*, Academic Press, London.

Janson, P. A. (1977), 'Using type-extension to organise virtual memory mechanisms', IBM Research Report no. RZ858.

Jardin, N. and Sibson, R. (1971), *Mathematical Taxonomy*, John Wiley, New York.

Jensen, R. W. (1983), 'An improved macro-level software development resource estimation model', *Proceedings 5th ISPA Conference*, pp. 88–92, April.

—— (1984), 'A comparison of the Jensen and cocomo schedule and cost estimation models', *Proceedings of the 6th International Society of Parametric Analysis*, pp. 96–106.

—— and Lucas, S. (1983), 'Sensitivity analysis of the Jensen software model', *Proceedings 5th ISPA Conference*, pp. 384–9.

—— and Varian, K. (1985), 'An experimental study of software metrics for real-time software', *IEEE Transactions on Software Engineering*, 11(2): 231–4.

Johnston, D. B. and Lister, A. M. (1981), 'A note on the software science length equation', *Software Practice and Experience*, 11(8).

Jones, C. (1986), *Programmer Productivity*, McGraw-Hill, New York.

—— (1987), 'A short history of function points and feature points', unpublished paper, Software Productivity Research Inc.

—— (1989), 'Software enhancement modelling', *Journal of Software Maintenance*, 1(2): 91–100.

Jones, T. C. (1978), 'Measuring programming quality and productivity', *IBM Systems J.*, 17(1): 39–63.

Kafura, D. (1984), 'The independence of software metrics taken at different life-cycle stages', *Proceedings 9th Annual Software Engineering Workshop*, NASA/GSFC.

—— and Canning, J. T. (1985), 'A validation of software metrics using many metrics and two resources', *Proceedings 8th International Conference Software Engineering*, pp. 378–85. Reproduced as Chapter 14 above.

—— —— and Reddy, G. R. (1984), 'The independence of software metrics taken at different life-cycle stages', *Proceedings 9th Annual Software Engineering Workshop*, pp. 213–22.

—— and Henry, S. (1981), 'Software quality metrics based on interconnectivity', *J. Systems and Software*, 2: 121–31.

—— —— (1982), 'A viewpoint on software quality metrics: criteria, use and integration', *J. Systems and Software*, 4.

—— and Reddy, G. R. (1987), 'The use of software complexity metrics in software maintenance', *IEEE Transactions on Software Engineering*, 13(3): 335–43.

Kasaraju, R. (1974), 'Analysis of structured programs', *J. of Computer Systems Science*, 9: 232–55.

Kearney, J. K., Sedlmeyer, R. L., Thompson, W. B., Gray, M. A. and Adler, M. A. (1986), 'Software complexity measurement', *CACM*, 29(11): 1044–50.

Kemerer, C. F. (1987), 'An empirical validation of software cost estimation models', *CACM*, 30(5): 416–29. Reproduced as Chapter 16 above.

—— (1989), 'An agenda for research in the managerial evaluation of computer-aided software engineering (CASE) tool impacts', *Proceedings 22nd IEEE Annual Hawaii International Conference on System Sciences*, vol. II, pp. 219–28.

—— (1993), 'Reliability of function point measurements: a field experiment', *CACM*, 36(2): 85–97.

Kernighan, B. W. and Plauger, P. (1978), *The Elements of Programming Style*, McGraw-Hill, New York.

Kitchenham, B. A. (1981), 'Measures of programming complexity', *ICL Technical Journal*, 2(3): 298–316.

—— (1982), 'Systems evolution dynamics of VME/B', *ICL Technical J.*, 43–57.

—— (1986), 'Metrics in practice', Pergamon Infotech State of the Art Report on *Software Reliability*, Pergamon Press, Oxford.

—— (1987), 'Towards a constructive quality model. Part I: Software quality modelling, measurement and prediction', *Software Engineering J.*, 2(4): 105–13.

—— (1988), 'An evaluation of software structure metrics', *Proceedings COMPSAC '88*, Chicago.

—— (1992), 'Empirical studies of assumptions that underlie software cost estimation models', *Information and Software Technology*, 32(4): 211–18.

—— and Kitchenham, A. P. (1984), 'The use of measurement to evaluate software production methods', *Proceedings Seminare Approches Quantitatives en Genie Logiciel*.

—— and Linkman, S. J. (1990), 'Design metrics in practice', *Proceedings NDISD '89*, Wolverhampton Polytechnic, pp. 12–39 (also published in *Information and Software Technology*, May 1990).

—— and McDermid, J. A. (1986), 'Software metrics and integrated project support environments', *Software Engineering J.*, 1(1): 58–64.

—— and Pickard, L. (1987), 'Towards a constructive quality model. Part II: Statistical techniques for modelling software quality in the ESPRIT REQUEST project', *Software Engineering J.*, 2(4): 114–26.

—— —— and Linkman, S. J. (1990), 'An evaluation of some design metrics', *Software Engineering J.*, 5(1): 50–8.

—— and Taylor, N. R. (1984), 'Software cost models', *ICL Technical J.*, 4(1): 73–102.

van der Knijff, D. J. J. (1978), 'Software physics and program analysis', *Australian Computer J.*, 10: 82–6.

Knuth, D. (1969), *The Art of Computer Programming*, Addison-Wesley, Reading, Mass.

—— (1974), 'Structured programming with GOTO statements', *Computing Surveys*, 6: 261–301.

Konstam, A. H. and Wood, D. E. (1985), 'Software science applied to APL', *IEEE Transactions on Software Engineering*, 11(10): 994–1000.

Kuhn, W. W. (1982), 'A software lifecycle case study using the PRICE model', *Proceedings IEEE NAECON*.

Kulm, G. (1974), 'Information content: an alternative measure of reading complexity', *American Psychological Association Annual Meeting*, New Orleans.

Kuntzmann-Combelles, A., et al. (eds) (1992), *Handbook of the Application of Metrics in Industry: A Quantitative Approach to Software Management*, AMI ESPRIT project, University of the Southbank, London.

Laranjeira, L. A. (1990), 'Software size estimation of object-oriented systems', *IEEE Transactions on Software Engineering*, 16(5): 510–22.

Lassez, J. L., van der Knijff, D., Shepherd, J. and Lassez, C. (1981), 'A critical examination of software science', *J. Systems and Software*, 2: 105–12.

Lattanzi, L. D. (1979), 'An analysis of the performance of a software development methodology', *IEEE Tutorial: Software Design Strategies*, IEEE, New York.

Laurmaa, T. and Syrjanen, M. (1982), 'APL and Halstead's theory: a measuring tool and some experiments', *ACM SIGMETRICS*, 11(Fall): 32–47.

Lawrence, M. J. (1981), 'Programming methodology organisational environment, and programming productivity', *J. Systems and Software*, 247–70.

—— (1982), 'An examination of evolution dynamics', *Proceedings IEEE 6th International Conference on Software Engineering*, pp. 188–96.

Leach, R. J. (1990), 'Software metrics and software maintenance', *J. Software Maintenance*, 2(2): 133–42.

Ledgard, H. and Marcotty, M. (1975), 'A generalogy of control structures', *CACM*, 18(11): 629–39.

Lehman, M. M. (1980), 'Programs, life cycles, and laws of software evolution', *Proceedings IEEE*, 68: 1060–76.

—— and Belady, L. A. (1976), 'A model of large system development', *IBM Systems J.*, 15(3): 225–52.

Li, H. F. (1987), 'An empirical study of software metrics', *IEEE Transactions on Software Engineering*, 13(6): 697–708.

Lind, R. K. and Vairavan, K. (1989), 'An experimental investigation of software metrics and their relationship to software development effort', *IEEE Transactions on Software Engineering*, 15(5): 649–53.

Linkman, S. and Walker, J. (1991), 'Controlling programmes through measurement', *Information and Software Technology*, 33(1): 93–102.

Lions, J. (1977), 'A commentary on the UNIX operating system', Technical Report, Department of Computer Science, University of New South Wales.

Lipow, M. and Thayer, T. A. (1977), 'Prediction of software failures', *Proceedings IEEE Am. Reliability and Maintainability Symposium*, pp. 489–94.

Liskov, B. A. (1972), 'The design of the Venus operating system', *CACM*, 15(3): 144–9.

Lister, A. M. (1982), 'Software science: the emperor's new clothes?' *Australian Computer J.*, 14(2): 66–71.

Lohse, J. B. and Zweben, S. H. (1984), 'Experimental evaluation of software design principles: an investigation into the effect of modular coupling on system and modifiability', *J. Systems and Software*, 4(4): 301–8.

Londeix, B. (1987), *Cost Estimation for Software Development*, Addison-Wesley, Reading, Mass.

Love, L. T. (1977), 'An experimental investigation of the effect of program structure on program understanding', *ACM SIGPLAN Notices*, 12(3): 105–13.

—— and Bowman, A. B. (1976), 'An independent test of the theory of software physics', *ACM SIGPLAN Notices*, 12(11): 42–9.

Low, G. C. and Jeffery, D. R. (1990a), 'Function points in the estimation and evaluation of the software process', *IEEE Transactions on Software Engineering*, 16(1): 64–71.

—— —— (1990b), 'Calibrating estimation tools for software development', *Software Engineering J.*, 5(4): 215–21.

Luce, R. D. and Raiffa, H. (1957), *Games and Decisions*, John Wiley, New York.

Lynch, W. C. and Browne, J. C. (1981), 'Performance evaluation: a software metrics success story', in A. P. Perlis *et al.* (eds), *Software Metrics*, MIT Press, Cambridge, Mass., pp. 171–83.

Magel, K. (1981), 'Regular expressions in a program complexity metric', *ACM SIGPLAN Notices*, 16(7): 61–5.

Markusz, Z. and Kaposi, A. A. (1985), 'Complexity control in logic-based programming', *Computer J.*, 28(5): 487–95.

Masters, T. F. (1985), 'An overview of software cost estimating at NSA', *J. Parametrics*, 5(1): 72–84.

Maurer, H. A. and Williams, M. R. (1972), *A Collection of Programming Problems and Techniques*, Prentice-Hall, Englewood Cliffs, NJ.

Mayhew, P. J. (1990), 'Controlling the software prototyping process: a change classification approach', *Information and Software Technology*, 31(4): 245–52.

McCabe, T. J. (1976), 'A complexity measure', *IEEE Transactions on Software Eng.*, 2(4): 308–20. Reproduced as Chapter 2 above.

—— (1989), 'Design complexity measurement and testing', *CACM*, 32(12): 1415–25.

McCall, J. A., Richards, P. K. and Walters, G. F. (1977), 'Factors in software quality', Report no. GE-TIS-77CIS02, General Electric, Sunnyvale, Calif.

McClure, C. L. (1978), 'A model for program complexity analysis', *Proceedings 3rd International Conference on Software Engineering*, 149–57.

McGarry, F. E. (1982), 'Measuring software development technology: what have we learned in six years?' *Proceedings NASA–Goddard Software Engineering Workshop*.

Mendenhall, W. and Ramey, M. (1973), *Statistics for Psychology*, Duxbury Press, North Scituate, Mass., pp. 280–315.

Miller, L., (1978), 'Behavioural studies of the programming process', IBM Research Report RC 7367 (no. 31711), November.

Mills, H. D. (1972), 'Mathematical foundations for structured programming', unpublished paper, no. FSC 72-6012, IBM, Gaithersburg, Md.

—— (1976), 'Software development', *IEEE Transactions on Software Engineering*, 2(4): 265–73.

Mohanty, S. N. (1981), 'Software cost estimation: present and future', *Software Practice and Experience*, 11: 103–21.

Munson, J. C. and Khoshgoftaar, T. M. (1990), 'The relative software complexity metric: a validation study', *Proceedings BCS/IEE Software Engineering '90 Conference*, pp. 89–102, Brighton.

Musa, J. D. (1975), 'A theory of software reliability and its application', *IEEE Transactions on Software Engineering*, 1(3): 312–27.

—— (1980), 'The measurement and management of software reliability', *IEEE Proceedings*, 68(9).

Myers, G. J. (1976), *Software Reliability: Principles and Practices*, Wiley-Interscience, New York.

—— (1977), 'An extension to the cyclomatic measure of program complexity', *ACM SIGPLAN Notices*, 12(10): 61–4.

—— (1978), *Composite/Structured Design*, Van Nostrand Reinhold, New York.

—— (1979), *Reliable Software through Composite Design*, Petrocelli, New York.

Myrvold, A. (1990), 'Data analysis for software metrics', *J. System Software*, 12: 271–5.

NASA (1981), 'The Software Engineering Laboratory (SEL) database organization and user's guide', Report no. SEL-81-002, NASA.

—— (1982), *The Software Engineering Laboratory Database organization and user's guide*, Report no. SEL-81-104, NASA.

Navlakha, J. K. (1987), 'A survey of system complexity metrics', *Computer J.*, 30(3): 233–8.

Negrini, R. M. and Sami, M. (1983), 'Some properties derived from structural analysis of program graph models', *IEEE Transactions on Software Engineering*, 9(2): 172–8.

Nelson, E. A. (1966), 'Management handbook for the estimation of computer programming costs', no. AD-A648750, System Development Corporation.

Nolen, R. L. (1971), *Fortran IV Computing and Applications*, Addison-Wesley, Reading, Mass.

Okada, M. and Azuma, M. (1982), 'Software development estimation study: a model from CAD/CAM system development experiences', *Proceedings IEEE COMPSAC '82*, 555–64.

Oldehoeft, R. R. (1979), 'Dynamic software science with applications', *IEEE Transactions on Software Engineering*, 5(5): 497–504.

Ostapko, D. L. (1974a), 'On deriving relations between circuits and input/output by analysing an equivalent program', *ACM SIGPLAN Notices*, 9(6).

—— (1974b), 'An analysis of algorithms implemented in software and hardware', *Proceedings ACM Annual Conference*.

Ottenstein, K. J. (1976a), 'An algorithmic approach to the detection and prevention of plagiarism', *ACM SIGCSE Bulletin*, 8(4): 30–41.

—— (1976b), 'A program to count operators and operands for ANSI Fortran modules', Technical Report no. CSR-TR-196, Purdue University.

—— (1979), 'Quantitative estimates of debugging requirements', *IEEE Transactions on Software Engineering*, 5(5): 504–14.

—— (1981), 'Predicting numbers of errors using software science', *ACM SIGMETRICS Performance Evaluation Review*, 10: 157–64.

Oulsnam, G. (1979), 'Cyclomatic numbers do not measure complexity of unstructured programs', *Information Processing Letters*, 8: 207–11.

Oviedo, E. (1980), 'Control flow, data flow and program complexity', *Proceedings COMPSAC 80*, 146–52. Reproduced as Chapter 3 above.

—— and Ralston, A. (1983), 'An environment to develop and validate program complexity measures', *Proceedings IEEE National Educational Computing Conference*, pp. 115–21.

Paige, M. (1980), 'A metric for software test planning', *Proceedings of COMPSAC 80 Conference*, pp. 499–504.

Parnas, D. L. (1972), 'On the criteria to be used in decomposing systems into modules', *CACM*, 15(2): 1053–8.

—— (1974), 'On a "Buzzword"; hierarchical structure', *Proceedings IFIP Congress*, pp. 336–9.

—— (1976), 'Some hypothesis about the "USES" hierarchy for operating systems', Research Report BS I 76
1, Technische Hochschule Darmstadt, Fachbereich Informatik, Darmstadt, Germany.

—— (1977), 'Use of abstract interfaces in the development of software for embedded computer systems',
NRL Report no. 8047, Naval Research Laboratory, Washington, DC.

Parr, F. N. (1980), 'An alternative to the Rayleigh curve model for software development effort', *IEEE
Transactions on Software Engineering*, 6(3): 291–6.

Perlis, A. P., Sayward, F. and Shaw, M. (eds) (1981), *Software Metrics*, MIT Press, Cambridge, Mass.

Pfleeger, S. L. and McGowan, C. (1990), 'Software metrics in the process maturity framework', *J. Systems
and Software*, 12: 255–61.

Phister, M. Jr. (1981), 'A model of the software development process', *J. Systems and Software*, 2: 237–56.

Pinsky, S. S. (1984), 'The effect of complexity on software trade-off equations', *J. Parametrics*, 4(4): 23–32.

Piowarski, P. (1982), 'A nesting level complexity measure', *ACM SIGPLAN Notices*, 17(9): 40–50.

Pippenger, N. (1978), 'Complexity theory', *Scientific American*, June: 120.

Potier, D., Albin, J., Ferreol, R. and Bilodeau, A. (1982), 'Experiments with computer software complexity
and reliability', *Proceedings 6th IEEE International Conference on Software Engineering*, pp. 94–103.

Prather, R. E. (1984), 'An axiomatic theory of software complexity metrics', *Computer J.*, 27(4): 340–7.

—— (1987), 'On hierarchical software metrics', *Software Engineering J.*, 2(2): 62–5.

—— (1988), 'Comparison and extension of theories of Zipf and Halstead', *Computer J.*, 31(3): 248–52.

Pressman, R. S. (1992), *Software Engineering: A Practitioner's Approach*, 3rd edn, McGraw-Hill, New
York.

Putnam, L. H. (1978), 'A general empirical solution to the macro software sizing and estimating problem',
IEEE Transactions on Software Engineering, 4(4): 345–61.

—— (1980), *Tutorial on Software Cost Estimation and Life-Cycle Control: Getting the Software Numbers*,
IEEE Computer Society Press, New York.

—— (1982), 'The real economics of software development', R. Goldberg and H. Lorin (eds), in *The Economics of Information Processing*, John Wiley, New York.

—— and Fitzsimmons, A. (1979), 'Estimating software costs', *Datamation*, September: 189–98; continued
in October: 171–8 and November: 137–40.

QSM (1983), Reference Notes for the DOD SLIM Software Cost Estimating Course, Quantitative Software
Management, McClean, Va.

—— (1984), SLIM User Manual (IBM Pc Version), draft copy, Quantitative Software Management,
McClean, Va.

Rammoorthy, C. V. and Ho, S. B. (1975), 'Testing large software with automated software evaluation systems', *IEEE Transactions on Software Engineering*, 1(1): 46–58.

Ratcliffe, B. and Rollo, A. L. (1990), 'Adapting function point analysis to Jackson System Development',
Software Engineering Journal, 5(1): 79–84.

Reddy, G. (1984), 'Analysis of a database management system using software metrics', MSc thesis, Virginia
Polytechnic.

Remus, H. and Zilles, S. (1979), 'Prediction and management of program quality', *Proceedings 4th International Software Engineering Conference*, pp. 341–50.

Reynolds, R. G. (1984), 'Metrics to measure the complexity of partial programs', *J. Systems and Software*,
4(1): 75–92.

Ritchie, D. M. and Thompson, K. (1974), 'The UNIX time-sharing system', *CACM*, 17(7): 365–75.

Robillard, P. N., Coupal, D. and Coallier, F. (1991), 'Profiling software through the use of metrics', *Software Pract. and Experience*, 21(5): 507–18.

Robinson, S. and Torsun, I. (1977), 'The automatic measurement of the relative merits of student programs', *ACM SIGPLAN Notices*, 12(4).

Rodriguez, V. and Tsai, W. T. (1987), 'A tool for discriminant analysis and classification of software
metrics', *Information and Software Technology*, 29(3): 137–50.

Rombach, H. D. (1984), 'Software design metrics for maintenance', *Proceedings 9th NASA Workshop on
Software Engineering*.

—— (1985), 'The impact of software structure on maintenance', *Proceedings Conference on Software Maintenance*.

—— (1987), 'A controlled experiment on the impact of software structure on maintainability', *IEEE Transactions on Software Engineering*, 7(5): 510–18.

—— (1989), 'The role of measurement in ISEEs', *Proceedings 2nd European Software Engineering Conference*, pp. 65–85.

—— (1990a), 'Design measurement: some lessons learned', *IEEE Software*, 7(2): 17–25.

—— (1990b), 'MVP: an approach to descriptive process modelling', *Proceedings Software Process Seminar*.

—— and Basili, V. R. (1987), 'A quantitative assessment of software maintenance', *Proceedings Conference on Software Maintenance*, pp. 134–44.

—— —— (1990), 'The benefits of goal-oriented measurement', *Proceedings 7th CSR Annual Conference on Software Reliability and Metrics*.

—— and Ulery, B. T. (1989a), 'Improving software maintenance through measurement', *IEEE Proceedings*, 77(4): 581–95.

—— —— (1989b), 'Establishing a measurement-based maintenance improvement program: lessons learned in the SEL', *Proceedings IEEE Conference on Software Maintenance*, pp. 50–7.

Romeu, J. L. and Gloss-Soler, S. A. (1983), 'Some measurement problems detected in the analysis of software productivity data and their statistical consequences', *Proceedings COMPSAC '83*.

Rook, P. (1990), *Software Reliability Handbook*, Elsevier, London.

Rubin, H. A. (1983), 'Macroestimation of software development parameters: the Estimacs system', *Proceedings SOFTFAIR Conference on Software Development Tools, Techniques and Alternatives*.

—— (1984), *Using Estimacs E*, Management and Computer Services, Valley Forge, Penna.

—— (1985), 'The art and science of software estimation: fifth-generation estimators', *Proceedings 7th Annual IPSA Conference*, pp. 56–72.

Salt, N. (1982), 'Defining software science counting strategies', *ACM SIGPLAN Notices*, 17(3): 58–67.

Samson, W. B., Nevill, D. G. and Dugard, P. I. (1987), 'Predictive software metrics based on a formal specification', *Information and Software Technology*, 29(5): 242–8.

Sayward, F. G. (1984), 'Experimental design methodologies in software science', *Information Processing and Management*, 20(1–2): 223–7.

Schneider, G. M., Sedlmeyer, R. L. and Kearney, J. (1981), 'On the complexity of measuring software complexity', *AFIPS Conference Proceedings*, 50: 317–22.

Schneider, V. (1978), 'Prediction of software effort and project duration: four new formulas', *ACM SIGPLAN Notices*, 13(6): 49–59.

—— (1988), 'Approximations for the Halstead software science error rate and project estimators', *ACM SIGPLAN Notices*, 2(31): 40–7.

Schneidewind, N. F. (1979), 'Software metrics for aiding program development and debugging', *AFIPS Conference Proceedings*, 48: 989–94.

—— and Hoffman, H.-M. (1979), 'An experiment in software error data collection and analysis', *IEEE Transactions on Software Engineering*, 5(3): 276–86.

Selby, R. W. and Basili, V. R. (1988), 'Error localization during maintenance: generating hierarchical system descriptions from source code alone', *Proceedings IEEE Conference on Software Maintenance*.

—— and Marsden, K. M. (1991), 'Metric-driven classification analysis', *Proceedings 3rd European Conference on Software Engineering*, pp. 290–307.

Shaw, W. H., Howatt, J. W., Maness, R. S. and Miller, D. M. (1989), 'A software science model of compile time', *IEEE Transactions on Software Engineering*, 15(5): 543–51.

Shen, V. Y. (1979), 'The relationship between student grades and software science parameters', *Proceedings COMPSAC '79*, pp. 783–7.

—— and Dunsmore, H. E. (1981), 'Analyzing COBOL programs via software science', Purdue University Technical Report CSD TR-348 (rev.), September.

—— Conte, S. D. and Dunsmore, H. E. (1983), 'Software science revisited: a critical analysis of the theory and its empirical support', *IEEE Transactions on Software Engineering*, 9(2): 155–65.

—— Yu, T. J., Thebaut, S. M. and Paulsen, L. R. (1985), 'Identifying error-prone software: an empirical study', *IEEE Transactions on Software Engineering*, 11(4): 317–23.

Sheppard, S. B. and Love, L. T. (1977), 'A preliminary experiment to test influences on human understanding of software', *Proceedings 21st Meeting of the Human Factors Society*.

—— Borst, M. A., Curtis, B. and Love, T. (1978), 'Predicting programmers' ability to modify software', Technical Report no. TR-388100-3, General Electric, Arlington, Va.

—— Curtis, B., Milliman, P., Borst, M. A. and Love, T. (1979a), 'First-year results from a research program on human factors in software engineering', *AFIPS Conference Proceedings*, 48: 1021–7.

—— Borst, M. A., Milliman, P., Love, T. (1979b), 'Modern coding practices and programmer performance', *Computer*, 12(12): 41–9.

Sheperd, J. A. and Lassez, J. L. (1980), 'Opposing views on the use of software science measures for the automatic assessment of student programs', *Australian Computer Science Comms.*, 2(1): 205–15.

Shepperd, M. J. (1988a), 'A critique of cyclomatic complexity as a software metric', *Software Engineering J.*, 3(2): 1–8. Reproduced as Chapter 12 above.

—— (1988b), 'An evaluation of software product metrics', *Information and Software Technology*, 30(3): 177–88.

—— (1989), 'A metrics based tool for software design', *Proceedings 2nd International Conference on Software Engineering for Real Time Systems*.

—— (1990a), 'An empirical study of design measurement', *Software Engineering J.*, 5(1): 3–10.

—— (1990b), 'Early life cycle metrics and software quality models', *Information and Software Technology*, 32(4): 311–16.

—— (1990c), 'The use of metrics for the early detection of software design errors', *Proceedings BCS/IEE Software Engineering 1990*.

—— (1992a), 'Quantitative approaches to process modelling', *IEE Colloq. on Process Planning and Modelling*.

—— (1992b), 'Products, processes and metrics', *Information and Software Technology*, 34(10): 674–80.

—— Ince, D. C. (1989), 'Metrics, outlier analysis and the software design process', *Information and Software Technology*, 31(2): 91–8.

—— —— (1990a) 'The multi-dimensional modelling and measurement of software designs', *Proceedings Annual ACM Computer Science Conference*.

—— —— (1990b) 'Controlling software maintainability', *Proceedings 2nd European Conference on Software Quality Assurance*, Oslo.

—— —— (1991a), 'The algebraic validation of software metrics', *Proceedings 3rd European Software Engineering Conference*.

—— —— (1991b), 'Design metrics and software maintainability: an experimental investigation', *J. Software Maintenance*, 3(4): 215–32.

Shneiderman, B. (1977), 'Measuring computer program quality and comprehension', *International J. Man-Mach. Studies*, 9: 465–78.

Silverman, J., Giddings, N. and Beane, J. (1983a), 'An approach to design-for-maintenance', *Proceedings Software Maintenance Workshop*.

—— —— —— (1983b), 'A component interaction language for evaluating software design quality', Honeywell Technical Report, March.

Sime, M. E., Green, T. R. G. and Guest, D. J. (1977), 'Scope marking in computer conditionals: a psychological evaluation', *International J. Man-Machine Studies*, 9: 107–18.

Sinha, P. K., Jayaprakash, S. and Lakshmanan, K. B. (1986), 'A new look at the control flow complexity of computer programs', in D. Barnes and P. Brown, *Software Engineering 86: Proceedings of BCS-IEE Software Engineering 86 Conference*, Peter Peregrinus, Stevenage.

Smith, C. P. (1979), 'Practical applications of software science', IBM Santa Teresa Laboratory, Technical Report no. 03.067.

—— (1980), 'A software science analysis of programming size', *Proceedings ACM National Computer Conference*, pp. 179–85.

Sommerville, I. (1992), *Software Engineering*, 4th edn, Addison-Wesley, Reading, Mass.

Soong, N. L. (1977), 'A program stability measure', *Proceedings ACM Annual Conference*, pp. 163–73.

SPR (1986), SPQR/20 User Guide, Software Productivity Research, Cambridge, Mass.

Stanat, D. F. and McAllister, D. F. (1977), *Discrete Mathematics in Computer Science*, Prentice-Hall, Englewood Cliffs, NJ.

Stetter, F. (1984), 'A measure of program complexity', *Computer Langs.*, 9(3): 203–10.

Stevens, S. S. (1946), 'On the theory of scales of measurement', *Science*, no. 103: 677–80.

Stevens, W. P., Myers, G. J. and Constantine, L. L. (1974), 'Structured design', *IBM Systems J.*, 13(2): 115–39.

Storm, L. L. and Presier, S. (1979), 'An index of complexity for structured programs', *Proceedings Workshop on Quantitative Software Models*.

Stroud, J. M. (1967), 'The Fine Structure of Psychological Time', *Annals of the New York Academy of Sciences*, 138: 623–31.

Sunohara, T., Takano, A., Vehara, K. and Ohkawa, T. (1981), 'Program complexity measure for software development management', *Proceedings of Fifth IEEE International Conference on Software Engineering*.

Symons, C. R. (1988), 'Function point analysis: difficulties and improvements', *IEEE Transactions on Software Engineering*, 14(1): 2–11.

—— (1991), *Software Sizing and Estimating: Mk II FPA*, John Wiley, Chichester.

SYSCON Corporation (1983), 'Avionics software support cost model', Technical Report, AFWAL-TR-1173, USAF Avionics Laboratory.

Szulewski, P. A., Whitworth, M. H., Buchan, P. and DeWolf, J. B. (1981), 'The measurement of software science parameters in software designs', *ACM SIGMETRICS Performance Evaluation Review*, Spring: 89–94.

Tai, K.-C. (1984), 'A program complexity metric based on data flow information in control graphs', *Proceedings 7th International Conference on Software Engineering*, pp. 239–48.

Tamine, J. (1983), 'On the use of tree-like structures to simplify measures of complexity', *ACM SIGPLAN Notices*, 18(9): 62–9.

Tanik, M. M. (1980), 'A comparison of program complexity prediction models', *ACM SIGSOFT Software Engineering Notes*, 5(4): 10–16.

Tausworthe, R. C. (1981), 'Deep space network software cost estimation model', Technical Report, Jet Propulsion Laboratories, Pasadena, Calif.

—— (1982), 'Staffing implications of software productivity models', *Proceedings 7th Annual Software Engineering Workshop*.

Thadani, A. J. (1984), 'Factors affecting productivity during application development', *IBM Systems Journal*, 23(1): 19–35.

Thayer, T. A. (1976), 'Software reliability study', Technical Report RADC-TR-76-238, Rome Air Development Centre, Griffiss Air Force Base.

Theabaut, S. M. (1983), 'Model evaluation in software metrics research', *Proceedings 15th Symposium on the Interface: Computer Science and Statistics*, pp. 54–73.

Thibodeau, R. (1981), 'An evaluation of software cost estimating models', Report no. T10-2670, General Research Corporation, April.

Topping, J. (1958), *Errors of observation and their treatment*, Chapman and Hall, London.

Troy, D. A. (1981), 'Measuring the quality of structured designs', MSc thesis, Ohio State University.

—— and Zweben, S. H. (1981), 'Measuring the quality of structured designs', *J. Systems and Software*, 2(2): 113–20. Reproduced as Chapter 13 above.

Van Emden, M. H. (1975), *An Analysis of Complexity*, Mathematical Centre Tracts, the Netherlands.

Veldman, D. J. (1967), *Fortran Programming for the Behavioural Sciences*, Holt, Rhinehart and Winston, New York.

Verner, J. M., Tate, G., Jackson, B. and Hayward, R. G. (1989), 'Technology dependence in function point behaviour', *Proceedings 11th International Conference on Software Engineering*, May.

Waguespack, L. J. and Badlani, S. (1987), 'Software complexity assessment: an introduction and annotated bibliography', *ACM SIGSOFT, S.E.N.*, 12(4): 52–71.

Walsh, T. A. (1979), 'A software reliability study using a complexity measure', *Proceedings National Computer Conference*, pp. 761–8.

Walston, C. E. and Felix, C. P. (1977a), 'A method of programming measurement and estimation', *IBM Systems J.*, 16(1): 54–73.

—— —— (1977b), Authors' response in 'Letters' section, *IBM Systems J.*, 16(4).

Wang, A. S. and Dunsmore, H. E. (1984), 'Back-to-front programming effort prediction', *Information Processing and Management*, 29(1–2): 139–49.

Watt, D. A. and Findley, W. (1984), 'Coupling, cohesion and Ada packages', *University Computing*, 6: 38–43.

Weinberg, G. M. and Schulman, E. L. (1974), 'Goals and performance in computer programmings', *Human Factors*, 16(1): 70–7.

Weinwurm, G. F. (ed.), (1970), *On the Management of Computer Programming*, Auerbach, New York.

Weisberg, S. (1980), *Applied Linear Regression*, John Wiley, New York.

Weiser, M. D. (1981), 'Program slicing', *Proceedings 5th International Conference on Software Engineering*.

Weiss, D. M. (1979), 'Evaluating software development by error analysis: the data from the architecture research facility', *J. Systems and Software*, 1(1): 57–70.

—— and Basili, V. R. (1985), 'Evaluating software development by analysis of changes: some data from the Software Engineering Laboratory', *IEEE Transactions on Software Engineering*, 11(2): 157–68.

Weissman, L. A. (1974), 'A methodology for studying the psychological complexity of computer programs', PhD dissertation, University of Toronto.

Weyuker, E. J. (1988), 'Evaluating software complexity measures', *IEEE Transactions on Software Engineering*, 14(9): 1357–65.

Whitty, R. (1987), 'Comments on "Control flow as a measure of program complexity"', *UK Alvey Programme Software Reliability and Metrics Club Newsletter*, 5: 1–2.

—— and Fenton, N. E. (1985), 'The axiomatic approach to systems complexity', in *Designing for System Maturity*, Pergamon Infotech State of the Art Report, Pergamon Press, Oxford.

Whitworth, M. and Szulewski, P., (1980), 'The measurement of control and data flow complexity in software designs', *Proceedings COMPSAC*, pp. 735–43.

Wiener, R. and Sincovec, R. (1984), *Software Engineering with Modula-2 and Ada*, John Wiley, New York.

Wiest, J. D. and Levy, F. K. (1977), *A Management Guide to PERT/CPM*, Prentice Hall, Englewood Cliffs, NJ.

Willis, R. R. (1978), 'DAS: an automated system to support design analysis', *Proceedings 3rd International Conference on Software Engineering*, pp. 109–15.

—— and Jensen, E. P. (1979), 'Computer aided design of software systems', *Proceedings 4th International Conference on Software Engineering*.

Wirth, N. (1976), *Algorithms + Data Structures = Programs*, Prentice-Hall, Englewood Cliffs, NJ.

—— (1977), 'MODULA: a programming language for modular multi-programming', *Software Practice and Experience*, 7: 3–35.

Wolverton, R. W. (1974), 'The cost of developing large-scale software', *IEEE Transactions on Computer*, pp. 615–36, June.

—— (1984), 'Software costing', in C. R. Vicks and C. V. Ramamoorthy (eds.), *Handbook of Software Engineering*, Van Nostrand Reinhold, New York.

Woodfield, S. N. (1980), 'Enhanced effort estimation by extending basic programming models to include modularity factors', PhD thesis, Purdue University.

—— Shen, V. Y. and Dunsmore, H. E. (1981a), 'A study of several metrics for programming effort', *J. Systems and Software*, 2: 97–103.

—— Dunsmore, H. E. and Shen, V. Y. (1981b), 'The effect of modularisation and comments on program comprehension', *Proceedings 5th IEEE International Conference on Software Engineering*, pp. 215–23.

Woodward, M. R., Hennell, M. A. and Hedley, D. A. (1979), 'A measure of control flow complexity in program text', *IEEE Transactions on Software Engineering*, 5(1): 45–50.

Wulf, W. and Shaw, M. (1973), 'Global variables considered harmful', *ACM SIGPLAN Notices*, 8(2).

Yau, S. S. and Collofello, J. S. (1980), 'Some stability measures for software maintenance', *IEEE Transactions on Software Engineering*, 6(6): 545–52.

—— —— (1985), 'Design stability measures for software maintenance', *IEEE Transactions on Software Engineering*, 11(9): 849–56.

—— —— and MacGregor, T. M. (1978), 'Ripple effect analysis of software maintenance', *Proceedings COMPSAC '78*, pp. 60–5. Reproduced as Chapter 4 above.

Yeh, R. T. (1979), 'In memory of Maurice H. Halstead', editorial in commemorative issue in honour of Dr Maurice H. Halstead', *IEEE Transactions on Software Engineering*, 5(2).

Yin, B. H. and Winchester, J. W. (1978), 'The establishment and use of measures to evaluate the quality of software designs', *Proceedings ACM Software Quality Assurance Workshop*, pp. 45–52.

Yourdon, E. (1975), *Techniques of Program Structure and Design*, Prentice-Hall, Englewood Cliffs, NJ.

—— and Constantine, L. (1979), *Structured Design*, Prentice-Hall, Englewood Cliffs, NJ.

Yule, G. U. and Kendal, M. G. (1958), *An Introduction to the Theory of Statistics*, Charles Griffin, London.

Zelkowitz, M. V. (1978), 'Perspective on software engineering', *ACM Computing Surveys*, 10(2): 197–216.

Zislis, P. M. (1975), 'Semantic decomposition of computer programs: an aid to program testing', *ACTA Informatica*, 4: 245–69.

Zolnowski, J. C. and Simmons, D. B. (1981), 'Taking the measure of program complexity', *Proceedings National Computer Conference*, pp. 329–36.

Zuse, H. (1985), 'Mesztheoretische Analyse von statischen Softwarekomplexitaetsmaszen', PhD thesis, Technical University, Berlin.

—— (1988), 'A new set of static software complexity metrics to measure the control flow complexity of programs', IBM Technical Report no. RC 13692.

—— and Bollmann, P. (1989), 'Software metrics: using measurement theory to describe the properties and scales of static complexity metrics', *ACM SIGPLAN Notices*, 24(8): 23–33.

—— (1991), *Software Complexity: Measures and Methods*, de Gruyter, Berlin.

Zweben, S. H. (1974), 'A recent approach to the study of algorithms', *Proceedings ACM Annual Conference*.

—— and Fung, K. (1979), 'Exploring software science relations in COBOL and APL', *Proceedings COMP-SAC '79*, pp. 702–9.

INDEX